SHOPPING CENTER LEASING

SHOPPING CENTER LEASING

International Council of Shopping Centers
New York

The International Council of Shopping Centers (ICSC) is the trade association of the shopping center industry. Serving the shopping center industry since 1957, ICSC is a not-for-profit organization with over 37,000 members in 75 countries worldwide.

ICSC members include shopping center
- owners
- developers
- managers
- marketing specialists
- leasing agents
- retailers
- researchers
- attorneys
- architects
- contractors
- consultants
- investors
- lenders and brokers
- academics
- public officials

ICSC sponsors more than 300 meetings a year and provides a wide array of services and products for shopping center professionals, including publications and research data.

For more information about ICSC, write or call the
International Council of Shopping Centers
1221 Avenue of the Americas
New York, NY 10020-1099
Telephone: 646-728-3800
Fax: 212-589-5555

© 2000 by International Council of Shopping Centers. All rights reserved. No part of this publication may be reproduced, stored in a retrieval system, or transmitted, in any form or by any means, electronic, mechanical, photocopying, recording, or otherwise, without the prior written permission of the publisher.

Chapter 2 Using Market Research to Lease a Center: Exhibits titled "Sample Population Density Map," "Sample Locator Map," "Sample Trade Area By Zip Code," "Sample Competition Key" and "Sample Trade Area Office Worker Survey" courtesy of Donahue Schriber, Newport Beach, California.
Chapter 5 Prospecting for Tenants: Exhibits titled "Trade Area Market Support Factors," "Sample Proposal Form" and "Lease Inquiry Forms" presented at the University of Shopping Centers School of Professional Development, International Council of Shopping Centers (ICSC), New York. Exhibits titled "Intent to Lease Space/Retail" and "Intent to Lease Space/Restaurants" from ICSC Book of Shopping Center Forms, ICSC, New York.
Chapter 10 Lease Management and Administration: Exhibit titled "Tenant Workouts" courtesy of Thomas Dodge, Senior Vice President, Lend Lease.
Chapter 12 Retailing: Exhibits titled "Prospective Tenant Qualification Information," "Pro Forma Operating Statement," and "Pro Forma Statement of Cash Flow" © IREM, Institute of Real Estate Management, Chicago, Illinois.
Chapter 14 Peripheral Land: Exhibits titled "Peripheral Development from the Developer's Perspective," "Peripheral Development from the Anchor's Perspective," "Peripheral Development from the Community Perspective" and "Peripheral Development from the User's Perspective" ©1999 Site Signatures, Inc., New Kensington, Pennsylvania. Exhibits titled "Deal Summary: Land Lease" and "Deal Summary: Land Sale" courtesy of EIR Development Company, North Potomac, Maryland.

This publication is designed to provide accurate and authoritative information in regard to the subject matter covered. It is sold with the understanding that the publisher is not engaged in rendering legal, accounting, or other professional services. If legal advice or other expert assistance is required, the services of a competent professional person should be sought.
—from a Declaration of Principles jointly adopted by a Committee of the American Bar Association and a Committee of Publishers.

Published by
International Council of Shopping Centers
Publications Department
1221 Avenue of the Americas
New York, NY 10020-1099

Cover and text design: H. Roberts Design
Cover photograph: Corona del Mar Plaza, Newport Beach, California (Owner/Developer—The Irvine Company, Newport Beach, California; Architect—Altevers Associates, San Diego, California; Photographer—Anthony Peres Photography, Montrose, California)
ICSC Catalog Number: 185
International Standard Book Number: 1-58268-018-3
Printed in the United States of America

Contents

Acknowledgments ix

About This Book xiii

Introduction xvii
   John E. Phelan

1. **The Leasing Plan** 1
   Keith W. Browning
Development Lease Plan • Redevelopment Lease Plan • Operating Center Plan• Merchandise Mix • Merchandising Plan • Budget Rents • Leasing Summary • The Operating Budget • Allowances and Concessions • Other Budgeted Costs • Timetable • Additional Planning Considerations • Conclusion

2. **Using Market Research to Lease a Center** 19
   Candace K. Rice, CLS/SCMD
Goals for Effective Use of Market Research • Benefits of Effective Market Research • Addressing the Market • Addressing the Center's Competition • Future Trade Area • Know the Retailers • GAFO and Market Share • Market Share in Relation to Customer Retention • Tools for a Leasing Presentation • Additional Market Research and Benchmark Resources

3. **Tenant Mix, Merchandising, and Leasing Strategies** 37
   Charles R. Cope, SCSM/CLS
Tenant Mix • Leasing Strategies • Negotiating Tools and Strategies • (Merchandising Entertainment As Well As Competitive and Comparable Centers *by Michael E. McCarty*) • Alternative Strategies • Conclusion

4. Project Economics 61
John E. Phelan

Valuation Process • Leveraging • Internal Rate of Return • Capitalization Rates • Economics of Development • Market Rent • Breakeven Rents • Rental Feasibility Analysis

5. Prospecting for Tenants 79
Sherry A. Koetting, CLS/SCSM/SCMD

Analyzing the Market • Finding and Identifying the Prospects • Separating the Prospects • Preparing for Negotiations • Making Contact with Tenants • Negotiating the Deal

6. Selling and Negotiating Techniques 99
Rene F. Daniel, CLS

Before the Selling Begins: The Groundwork • Selling Techniques: The Sales Process • Negotiating Techniques: How to Close the Deal • Selling and Negotiating: Final Suggestions • Conclusion

7. The Lease and Its Language 119
Andrew Shedlin, SCSM/CLS

General Lease Provisions • Date of Lease • Parties • The Premises • The Term • Rent • Common Area Maintenance • Real Estate Taxes • Utilities • Insurance • Use • Compliance with Laws • Assignment and Sublease • Rules and Regulations • Merchants' Association • Common Area Configuration and Standards • Repairs and Maintenance • Alterations • Mechanic's Liens • Surrender • Damage and Destruction • Condemnation • Subordination • Landlord's Access • Indemnification • Security for the Tenant's Performance • Quiet Enjoyment • Default • Brokers • Memorandum of Lease • Holding Over • Force Majeure • Financing Modifications and Approvals • Estoppel Certificates • Notices • Attorney Fees • Waiver of Jury Trial • Conclusion

8. Understanding and Negotiating Leases 161
Alan A. Alexander, SCSM/CPM

Leasing Responsibilities • Setting Rents • Impact of Financing • The Lease Document • Rents and Value • Space Measurement • Concessions for Higher Rents • Types of Rent • Natural Breakpoint • Negotiated Breakpoint • Other Percentage Rent Considerations • Additional Monetary Considerations • Negotiating Rents • Alternatives for Negotiating Agreement on Rents • Letter of Intent • Compromise in Negotiations • The Leasing Cycle • Lease Term • Category of Tenant • Build-to-Suit Negotiations • Conclusion

9. Managing the Design and Construction Process — 191
Thomas W. Taylor   Paul J. Mackie

Planning • Organizing • Directing and Controlling • Completion

10. Lease Management and Administration — 205
Karl D. Ehrlich

Overview • Goals of Lease Administration • The Practice of Lease Administration • Obligations of Owner and Tenant • Root Causes of Common Problems • Budget Implications • Conclusion

11. Remerchandising Centers in Redevelopment — 251
Mark N. London, SCSM/SCMD

Planning Is the Core Element • Leasing Is the Key Planning Element • Key Planning Focus Areas for Redevelopment Leasing • A Redevelopment Example • Developing the Core Strategy • Remerchandising Plan Strategies • Evaluation Criteria • Special Remerchandising Situations and Considerations • Executing the Plan • Conclusion

12. Retailing — 273
Shannon Alter, CPM

The Relationship Factor • The Store Visit: What to Look For • The Demographics and Psychographics • The Retailer's Business Strategies • The Key Retailing Processes • Qualifying Prospective Tenants • Recognizing Signs of Trouble • How the Leasing Manager Can Help

13. Specialty Retail Leasing — 295
Frederick J. Delibero, CLS

Specialty Retail Leasing Organizational Structures • Working with Permanent Leasing Representatives • Common Area Space • In-Line Space • Types of Specialty Retail Tenants • Understanding the Property and Market • Marketing Materials • Prospecting for Tenants • License Agreement • Structuring the Economic Deal • Closing the Deal • Administration • Common Expectations • Identifying and Working with Problem Tenants • Incubation • Conclusion

14. Peripheral Land — 319
Richard T. Parker

What Is Peripheral Land? • Peripheral Sales and Leasing Objectives • Balancing Competing Interests • Basic Elements of the Peripheral Land Business • Conclusion

Glossary — 343

List of Resources — 359

Index — 361

Acknowledgments

The International Council of Shopping Centers gratefully acknowledges the following shopping center professionals who contributed the chapters that appear in this book:

Alan A. Alexander, SCSM/CPM
Senior Vice President
Woodmont Management, Inc.
Scottsdale, Arizona

Shannon Alter, CPM
Owner
Retail Management Services
Tustin, California

Keith W. Browning
Senior Vice President
DDR Oliver McMillan
San Diego, California

Charles R. Cope, SCSM/CLS
Consultant
Oakton, Virginia

Rene F. Daniel, CLS
President
The Daniel Group, LLC
Baltimore, Maryland

Frederick J. Delibero, CLS
Senior Manager, Retail Leasing
Copaken, White & Blitt
Leawood, Kansas

Karl D. Ehrlich
Principal
Retail Leasing Solutions
San Mateo, California

Sherry A. Koetting, CLS/SCSM/SCMD
Senior Vice President, Leasing
Coyote Management, L.P.
Addison, Texas

Mark N. London, SCSM/SCMD
President
Mark London & Associates, LLC
Lake Bluff, Illinois

Paul J. Mackie
Vice President, Tenant Coordination
Combined Properties Incorporated
Washington, District of Columbia

Michael E. McCarty
Senior Vice President/
   Community Center Division
Simon Property Group
Indianapolis, Indiana

Richard T. Parker
Principal
EIR Development Company, LLC
North Potomac, Maryland

John E. Phelan
Executive Vice President
New England Development
Newton, Massachusetts

Candace K. Rice, CLS/SCMD
Senior Vice President, Leasing
Donahue Schriber
Newport Beach, California

Andrew Shedlin, SCSM/CLS
President
The Andrew Shedlin
   Companies, Inc.
Highland Park, Illinois

Thomas W. Taylor
Principal
AT Associates, Inc.
Park Ridge, Illinois

In addition, the International Council of Shopping Centers gratefully acknowledges the following individuals and their companies for the time and expertise they offered in reviewing this publication:

Beth Azor
President
Terranova Corp.
Miami, Florida

John Bell, CCIM, CLS
Senior Vice President, Director
   of Leasing
Hiffman Shaffer Associates, Inc.
Chicago, Illinois

Keith W. Browning
Vice President
DER OliverMcMillan
San Diego, California

Albert Corti, CLS
Principal
Corti Gilchrist Partnership, LLC
San Diego, California

Rene F. Daniel, CLS
President
The Daniel Group
Baltimore, Maryland

Amanda Dearborn
Attorney at Law
Morris, Manning & Martin
Altanta, Georgia

Robert M. Fantozzi, P.C.
Director
Goulston & Storr
Boston, Massachusetts

Karen Gentleman
President
Gentleman Associates
Indianapolis, Indiana

Deborah J. Georgetti-Piro
Vice President, Specialty Leasing
General Growth Properties, Inc.
Chicago, Illinois

Sherry A. Koetting, CLS/SCSM/
 SCMD
Senior Vice President, Leasing
Coyote Management, L.P.
Addison, Texas

Elisabeth D. Kozlow
Attorney at Law
Siegfried, Rivera, Lerner,
 De La Torre & Sobel, P.A.
Coral Gables, Florida

David A. Mack
Chief Executive Officer, President
David A. Mack Properties, LLC
Southport, Connecticut

Robert M. McAndrew
Managing Attorney, Real Estate
The Limited, Inc.
Columbus, Ohio

Richard Muhlebach, SCSM/CPM/
 CRE
Senior Managing Director
Kennedy-Wilson Properties
Bellevue, Washington

Rusty Phillips
Director of Peripheral Property
CBL & Associates Properties, Inc.
Chattanooga, Tennessee

Jane R. Robertson, SCMD
Director of Marketing &
 Public Relations
Galleria
Dallas, Texas

Jean Schlemmer
Senior Vice President, Asset
 Management
General Growth Properties, Inc.
Chicago, Illinois

Bruce Tobin
Senior Vice President, Leasing
Simon Property Group
New York, New York

Ronald M. Tucker
Managing Attorney
Simon Property Group
Indianapolis, Indiana

ICSC acknowledges the special contribution of John E. Phelan, who acted as chair of the review process for this publication. Over the course of several months, he participated in reviewing each chapter in the book, along with assessing all individual reviews that were part of the review process. In addition, his introduction serves as an overall summary of the content of this book and the issues central to shopping center leasing.

About This Book

This book covers the following topics that a shopping center professional will want to know about shopping center leasing, including:

- The Leasing Plan
- Using Market Research to Lease a Center
- Tenant Mix, Merchandising, and Leasing Strategies
- Project Economics
- Prospecting for Tenants
- Selling and Negotiating Techniques
- The Lease and Its Language
- Understanding and Negotiating Leases
- Managing the Design and Construction Process
- Lease Management and Administration
- Remerchandising Centers in Redevelopment
- Retailing
- Specialty Retail Leasing, and
- Peripheral Land.

Each chapter has been contributed by a shopping center professional, who explains the principles and practices of each topic—plus some of their own personal insights and applications. Practices may vary from center to center. What is applicable to a strip center may not be appropriate for a regional mall. The viewpoints are those of the various authors and are not policies or recommendations of the International Council of Shopping Centers (ICSC).

Shopping Center Leasing contains forms, illustrative examples and common-sense information and advice. Please keep in mind the following points when reading the text:

- Numbers, which are often impacted by the geographical location of a center, the current economy and other factors, are only used to illustrate examples. Where dollar amounts or other figures are used, they are used for illustration only and are not meant to suggest industry standards or guidelines.
- When developing policies and practices, each individual shopping center manager should consult the owner and shopping center counsel, among others.
- Similarly, forms, lease clauses and other documents are samples only and can be adapted for use for the reader's own shopping center. They are not to be construed as being endorsed or recommended by the contributor or ICSC. Readers are again advised to consult legal counsel to devise appropriate documents for their centers.

Before formulating and implementing policy and documents, checking with legal counsel is always advised.

For guidance on how to obtain additional information tailored to meet more specific needs, here are additional resources you may want to consult:

- The Glossary toward the end of the book offers an explanation of terms used throughout the book.
- The book's index will help you locate information throughout the various chapters. For example, Common Area Maintenance (CAM) and other terms may be discussed in more than one chapter.
- The Resources at the end of the book list some additional resources to consult on leasing topics.
- The ICSC Albert Sussman Library is available to respond to requests for specific information and additional resources.

Shopping centers are dynamic, changing institutions. ICSC's programs and services, such as its Centerbuild Conference devoted to shopping center design and architecture, will keep you up-to-date on changes in the industry.

For more information on ICSC contact:

International Council of Shopping Centers, New York, NY, USA
ICSCNET: www.icsc.org

The viewpoints contained in this book are those of the contributors and are not policies or recommendations of the International Council of Shopping Centers. Where dollar amounts or other figures are used, they are used for illustration only and are not meant to suggest industry standards or guidelines.

Introduction

Over the past few decades shopping center development has exploded, literally blanketing the landscape with an array of goods and services previously unavailable. Beginning as a loose collection of stores sharing some common facilities, shopping centers have evolved into highly sophisticated destinations offering an expansive mix of retailers appealing to a very broad market. Shopping centers themselves are not an end product but rather a conduit for the distribution of retail products. This characteristic allows shopping centers to transform themselves periodically to satisfy the ever-changing desires and tastes of the consumer market.

As the concept evolved, great improvements have occurred in the architecture, planning, marketing, and management of shopping centers. Leasing, which has always played a major role in shopping center development, has also evolved and today is a highly sophisticated function encompassing a broad range of disciplines.

In the early years of the shopping center industry, the leasing function was almost singularly focused on deal production. Leasing agents typically had little input relative to the configuration of the development, the pro forma rent levels, or the legal aspects of the lease itself. Often the leasing task was considered complete when a lease was requested and the leasing agent turned the transaction over to the legal department as well as to tenant coordinators for execution and construction. Today the leasing process does not end with a lease request and the leasing professional inevitably plays a key role in the execution of the lease and the delivery of the space.

The level of sophistication required is also far broader than in years past. The leasing professional must not only understand and master sales techniques and negotiation, but must also be well versed in the legal components of the lease. Other crucial elements in the deal process include the requirements of construction and a deal's impact on the overall economics of the shopping center investment. With competition among centers keen, the leasing professional must also appreciate the nuances of marketing and management. A successful leasing agent must comprehend the results of market research as well as articulate the market position of the center.

A relatively short time ago, indoctrination into a leasing career consisted of a cursory education on the basics of the shopping center, a quick review of merchandising and then total immersion into on-the-job training. This kind of expedited training served the industry well in its enterprising infancy when the collective knowledge of the business was just forming. In the early 1990s, however, proliferation of institutional investment in shopping centers along with retail instability amplified investor scrutiny of the development, management and leasing process. Consequently, professionals seeking to excel in this new environment now need an expanded skill set encompassing finance, law, research, construction, and marketing.

The shopping center industry formerly possessed no mechanism to satisfy the increasing demands for the professional education and training of the leasing representative. The International Council of Shopping Center's Advanced Leasing Institute was created to help fill this void. Additional seminars and a professional designation have been added to further enhance the careers of leasing professionals.

This publication endeavors to present an overall picture of the knowledge base necessary for a successful career in the leasing of shopping centers. Many of the concepts presented in the 14 chapters that follow may be unfamiliar to even the most seasoned leasing agents. Our experiences in this business are different and much can be gained from the sharing of knowledge. Hopefully, the reader will be challenged to gain a far deeper understanding of the leasing discipline and its application in the development and management of shopping centers today.

As chair of the review process for this publication, I would like to take this opportunity to thank each contributor for the energy expended to complete each and every chapter. Without their efforts the industry would not be as prepared to confront a highly competitive future.

—John E. Phelan

1 | The Leasing Plan

Keith W. Browning

Development Lease Plan

As a part of the development process, the lease plan—and the subsequent lease-up—is what fulfills the pro forma income requirements. With this in mind, setting an attainable plan in motion is all-important.

Lease plan evaluation should start early, since required physical changes become costlier as the project becomes interdependent. At some point changes become unjustifiable due to cost. At the same time, any proposed change must be cost-effective. All changes should be evaluated based on the return that can be expected and then implemented. Evaluation of this return is somewhat subjective in that it may include sales projections forecasting percentage rent, and it will need to be converted to an objective analysis.

Evaluation of the lease plan must continue throughout the development and lease-up. Many different aspects of the physical layout of the lease plan will need to be reviewed. These include total leasable square footage on gross leasable area (GLA), depth of space, impediments to sight lines, and customer flow. Physical layout may also include design elements, should they impede leasability. Even the most thorough evaluation and well-thought-out plan will need to be modified, allowing management and the leasing team to react to changing conditions.

SIZE

An evaluation of the size of the project needs to be done as early in the planning process as possible. The size may be more a function of the

GLA necessary to get a return on investment (ROI) of the development cost, rather than simply creating a center of proper scale that will meet the needs of its market. A basic market function, supply and demand, should be applied. If a project is oversized, getting income for excess space will be difficult, and if the project is substantially overbuilt, that excess space may not be leasable. One solution for an oversized project may be to expand the tenant categories into nonretail uses such as offices, or to expand the type of users; for example, adding big box tenants. Premarketing the property to a select group of target retailers may help determine if the project is the right size. With input from these prospective occupants as to size required and interest in the project, management will have time to evaluate options that later would not be possible. These options often include expanding the merchandise mix or phasing the project as actual lease-up occurs.

DEPTH OF SPACE

As the project review moves toward configuration, consider what can be done if the leasable spaces are either too deep or too shallow. One way to determine this is through the premarketing of the project while it is still in predevelopment. If any adjustments can make the building configuration tenant-friendly, revenues will be enhanced and the return improved for dollars invested. If the spaces are found to be too deep or too shallow, and no adjustments can be made due to site, project, or other constraints, alternative solutions should be considered.

Depth can be altered without changing the building. If the space is too deep, for example, consider turning the rear of the space toward the outside. Shortening the interior space will maximize the income for the square footage leased and allow the leasing professional to secure another tenant best suited for the space left. The space turned to the outside could be better utilized as restaurant, office, nonretail, or service uses. The best tenant or use of such a converted area can be determined only by evaluating each circumstance and the project in which it occurs.

In some cases, the space may prove too shallow. When this occurs, it means that management is giving too much frontage to a tenant in an effort to provide the required area.

An alternative configuration might give the tenant a rectangular area for sales and locate the stock area to either side. This configuration preserves a very valuable part of the center, the frontage, while also creating small, "in line" spaces with significant exposure that typically command higher rent. If management and leasing simply cut a space by the square footage required, the resulting small space might not be easily leasable because of limited exposure. A small space with significant frontage is sometimes an alternative to a corner, which in most cases is the most valuable square footage in the center.

SIGHT LINES

The next area of review involves sight lines. Anything that blocks the view of a space may decrease the value of that space. Tenants prefer as much unobstructed visibility as possible, thereby increasing the store's exposure to customers as they flow through the project. Obstructions often occur because of required amenities such as escalators, elevators, structural support, and the like. The design, layout, and location of such obstructions should be reviewed to minimize their effect. Obstructions to sight lines are often caused by improvements that were intended to enhance the property. If an enhancement reduces visibility, however, and subsequently the value or rent, it should be reconsidered, redesigned, or relocated. Still, sometimes sight line obstruction has a positive effect. Most people have an instinctual drive to explore. With enough inducement such as good design or the fulfillment of expectations, leasing professionals can feed on this instinct. If standing in one place produces a full view of a space, that permits a decision either to view another space in sight or remain at the original site. If someone cannot view all selections but has a reasonable expectation that the effort to move will be rewarded, the person may choose to go explore. The shopper makes similar choices. To get to that point, however, the leasing professional must first secure the tenant, and this requires that the tenant buy into the layout and believe the customer will come around the corner or explore behind the obstruction.

CUSTOMER FLOW

Applying the term *inertia* adds to insight as to what is or may be necessary for desired customer flow through a shopping center. To get customers to continue moving without consciously considering whether they should do so takes constant reinforcement. Once they stop, they are subject to the rule of inertia, which states that a body at rest will tend to stay at rest. Keep this in mind when evaluating the lease plan. Consider what can be done to keep customers moving without stopping, including giving them constant inducement to continue. If the path is not obvious, they may choose not to continue. If they continue to see more of the same, they have no incentive to go on. If they do not have their expectations fulfilled, it becomes an effort to continue. When reviewing the plan, consider what can be done to get customers moving, and then to keep them moving throughout the center.

Redevelopment Lease Plan

The redevelopment process is very similar to the development process, in that it is necessary to review the plan for the size of the project, depth and configuration, sight lines, and customer flow. The reason the project is being redeveloped, and what can be done to ensure that it achieves its near-term goals, also must be considered. In addition, this process is an opportunity to position the project to fulfill long-term objectives, which should include delaying any need to redevelop the project yet again.

Once the objectives are understood, an evaluation of the project must be done. A wealth of information is available by researching existing tenants and "experiencing" the physical plant by doing a "walk-through." Regardless of the status of any project prior to redevelopment, much can be gained by an evaluation of the project as it exists. The tenants that occupy the center should be reviewed not only by looking at existing sales volume; they should also be researched for sales history. Trends either up or down can be extremely beneficial and could provide an indication as to what has worked and what might again. It is a good idea to review the list of past tenants. If certain uses have failed before, there should be a compelling reason before they are tried again. Just looking at a project at one moment in time will not result in the high-quality insight necessary to develop a successful plan.

A WALK-THROUGH

Experiencing the physical plant itself is often even more beneficial than evaluating plans. Walking through a project with a list of considerations is the best way to understand clearly what does and does not need changing. Site lines should be evaluated. Are the storefronts visible, and what, if anything, could be done to increase their impact? Dead zones are areas in a center that, for various reasons, lack traffic. This could be caused by a setback condition, the location of an entry, lack of vertical transportation, traffic obstacles, or a weak anchor. Flow is very important. Can the leasing professional—or a customer—walk easily through the center? Is the layout understandable so that customers know where they are at all times in relationship to their entry point—and, more importantly, where they parked? These are a few of the items that need to be considered.

REVIEW OF FIXED CONDITIONS
An extensive on-site review is usually the best way to reveal required modifications. Once the specific needed changes are discovered and solutions found, a cost-effective review has to be conducted. However, the cost of doing the work should not be paramount at this stage. Considering expense too early often means that required modifications will not be considered at all.

Any redevelopment project requires a thorough evaluation of fixed conditions. These may include a tight site, poor ingress or egress, sloping conditions, and existing leases, to name a few. The one affecting the leasing plan most is the existing leases. Still, most things can be changed. It is only a question of how much it costs and if any costs incurred will be justified by the return. This is the case with existing tenants that have leases running through the redevelopment period.

Consider the existing tenants when evaluating a project and what gains can be expected if the space is redeveloped. If redevelopment includes a desire to reposition a project, any given tenant may become an encumbrance to that process. Management may not have to accept the tenant as part of the project, but it is necessary to evaluate and provide for financial ramifications. The best advice is to start early, conducting discussions with tenants even before the work begins. This step reduces the sense of urgency and allows time to make changes should resolution not occur. Depending on the size of a center, the impact of any tenants found to be inappropriate, along with location, size, and cost factors, can be determined only once actual resolution is negotiated.

A redevelopment plan should provide for the possibility that the tenants stay. If management cannot remove a tenant from the mix, its impact on the project will be determined by the store's percentage of the total square footage. Each tenant's impact is diminished as the size of the project, and therefore the store count, increases.

When trying to change a center's point of view, it is important to consider the impact and evaluate the need to remove an inappropriate tenant based on its actual effect versus perception. If a tenant that has been deemed "wrong" stays, it will be necessary to develop an explanation of why that tenant is still present in the center, how long it will stay, and what leasing intends to do with the space once it expires. Do not be tempted to gloss over these factors; otherwise the leasing plan will be much less credible.

As management and leasing continues to evaluate the fixed conditions, this process should be applied to each factor. What cannot be changed on a cost-effective basis will need to be tolerated. Explain why a condition is not being changed, and what is being done to mitigate the effect of that. During the planning period leading up to the redevelopment, do not overlook any aspect of the total center.

Operating Center Plan

An operating shopping center requires planning and regular evaluation as well. Periodically, evaluate all aspects of the center and develop a plan to solve any deficiencies. A center must move in the direction that best serves changing demographics, while protecting its market share against competition. Since leases run an average of eight to ten years, it is important to consider a future time frame. With this average in mind, change can occur only in 10 to 15 percent of a fully leased center on an annual basis. This percentage of leasable space may increase during the ninth or tenth anniversary of the original development, when the leases of many original tenants coincidentally expire. During these large turnover years, it is imperative to use the substantial percentage of the GLA available to make changes necessary to position a center in the direction of this forward-looking plan. If a comprehensive plan is not developed, the opportunity for decline, and eventually failure, will increase.

Demographics are seldom constant. Leasing based only on what exists today, in most cases, predisposes the project to being behind when change comes. Use all available demographic data to understand trends by reviewing an extended period of 10 to 15 years. The longer the time covered by this information, the better the forecast will be regarding future trends. Reviews of existing trends should take note of significant changes, including new growth, which may provide insight about an energy shift. Then it is desirable to forecast five to ten years out and lease to that future point. As suggested earlier, only the percentage of space that is vacant, added to the terminations for that year, allows for change in the tenant mix to occur. This understood, as much as 90 percent cannot be used to effect change; therefore, the relatively small amount that is available must be taken advantage of to move the shopping center forward.

In planning for the future, do not overlook the successes that can be found in a center. Evaluate each tenant and its category. Look for tenants that perform above the center's average or add to the center in ways that are not as quantifiable, and consider them to be priorities in your plan. Try not to assume that an outstanding performer will not even consider a move that upsizes or relocates it, just because it has a substantial term remaining. A tenant whose sales per square foot are high or that has developed a prototype requiring more space may consider a move to a lesser location to be certain of the future and be able to display a full array of products. These expansions and relocations require a constant monitoring of sales performance. They also require ongoing communication with existing tenants, in that the timing of a proposed move or expansion will determine the outcome.

Even when such a move requires consideration on behalf of the landlord for unamortized leasehold, it may be justifiable based on contributing factors:

- The possible rental uplift for the existing location
- The fact that a relocated tenant is providing a more contemporary presentation
- The opportunity to increase the area available to meet changing demographic requirements.

An operating center requires a plan, and this plan must look further into the future than a development, redevelopment, or expansion because of the small percentage of space typically available during the same period. The landlord must be diligent in pursuing the fulfillment of a plan. This plan should be designed to expand successes, eliminate poor performers, and introduce tenants that fill the requirements of the market as determined by demographic trends.

Merchandise Mix

Demographics are in a constant state of change. The merchandise mix of a center must be based on trends, and it should include retailers and services that fill the needs that these trends forecast. Many times projects have been developed that simply duplicate another successful center's merchandise mix. While such thinking is good in principle, the realities of leasing suggest otherwise. To copy another center, however successful, means a project will be three to five years out of step by the time the leasing effort is complete. This is because leases average ten years in duration, so the center being replicated is not current in terms of demographics. The lease-up occurs over a 12-to-18-month period, with another three to four months added for tenant buildout. Add this year and a half or more to the age of the other center, and the result is that more than 50 percent of the space might consist of declining retailers or ones that are simply wrong for the market and its changing demographics.

A successful shopping center provides the merchandise and services demanded by its primary and secondary trade areas. A center must position itself to identify with its customers and the ambience created by the tenants it includes. Many retailers are basic to a given type of center; customers expect them, and their absence may disappoint potential shoppers. Establishing a mix of stores that does not duplicate those in competing centers is desirable; however, the stronger the competition, the more difficult it will be to exclude all of the tenants operating there. Nevertheless, while a good mix of merchandise and vendors generally produces success, the leasing team will need to make a decision to be unique by excluding all or most tenants that are operating in a competing center. Alternatively, leasing can also choose to include the outstanding retailers operating in the market regardless of where they are. Assembling the best of the competition, both national and local, as well as a group of contemporary retail stores that are new to the market and, most importantly, are able to meet the market's consumer needs, will allow the center to compete. The tenants chosen for the center form what is called merchandise mix.

Merchandise mix is what defines a center, and every center needs to develop a point of view by including tenants that contribute to its desired statement. The smaller the center, the more important every tenant becomes in helping to define a property. Regardless of size, however, each tenant selected should contribute to the center's point of view. Following are some examples of this process.

All goods and services under one roof: A regional mall concept that was successful in the early development of malls. This is a concept that works well in middle markets where competition is minimal. Not all goods and services can actually be included in any project, of course; this is more of an approach that embraces all categories of traditional center tenants. The idea is to be the destination that will fulfill the most needs, thus encouraging customers to shop there first, as they will assume the products or services they need will be available due to the diverse mix.

Price point: This center typically has an anchor that will set the standard. Price factors affected by varying tenants can give an obvious indication of one end or the other of the price continuum. Many times, it is less clear. What is clear, however, is that leasing to stores that are significantly different in price point might put the tenant and ultimately the project at risk. The center should plan its focus and secure the best available retailers that fulfill that plan.

Entertainment retailing: This has become common; however, it continues to evolve as a concept. The entertainment center could include a multiplex theater, restaurants, and an ice-skating rink or skating park. It could also embrace uses that relate to the pure entertainment retailer, such as outfitters and apparel for skating or movie memorabilia as a tie-in to the theaters. This concept could also fit as a component substituting for a traditional anchor.

Project profiles such as fashion and service are too numerous to cover here. The important consideration is that every project needs an understandable and promotable point of view or focus. The plan for a project must discover a need and then fill it. Any project leased without a specific, carefully thought out niche will compete for customers who have shopping habits that will need to be changed, and there will be no compelling reason for this change. The merchandise mix determines a center's point of view. To establish a center's identity a large percentage of the leasable area will need to be dedicated to a very focused group of retailers. The balance of the space and storefronts should have some tie, albeit lose, to the primary uses. The significant test is whether or not a customer will visit a given store when visiting the center for its primary group.

Merchandising Plan

Once the merchandise mix is established, tenants are placed on the actual lease plan. There are generally three approaches to the placement of tenants:

- Grouping similar tenants together
- Spreading related uses throughout
- Using destination tenants that are primary to the project's focus to draw customers past stores to allow for impulse shopping.

The placement of primary tenants in remote locations or deep into the project is best understood with the comparison to a grocery store. Items that you would need to get during most visits are bread, milk, and eggs. These are placed in the back of the store layout and often in opposite corners. This placement requires the shopper to pass candy, other snack items, and additional nonessentials. In the case of a two-level shopping center with access limited to the first level and management developing a fashion center, this means putting all pure fashion tenants on the second level. This accomplishes two things: It causes customers to flow past stores they might not otherwise be exposed to, and it may help solve a weakness in the project's basic design.

The placement of tenants in such a way as to cause customers to flow throughout the center is the reasoning behind separating like uses. In order for comparison-shopping to be successful, customers must move from area to area to see like merchandise available from various vendors. The opposite is to group like uses and price points together in neighborhoods. This allows the customer to experience all offerings quickly and conveniently. Given the limited time of shoppers—research indicates a decline in the amount of time shoppers spend in a center—gathering or clustering of like stores may be a better approach. Another theory is that centers have become less compelling and are viewed more as something that has to be endured. This problem is being resolved in many of today's innovative and better-focused centers.

The selection of a style or approach to merchandising is best done on a center-specific basis. The best way to merchandise a project may be a function of design, but more likely it is what the market that it serves requires.

Budget Rents

Once the lease plan has been cut up and merchandise mix established, the allocation of the pro forma rent on a space-by-space basis should take place. The first step in this process is assignment of use to every space, since different categories of retailers pay different rents. This is typically tied to margins generated and sales volume attainable by the various tenant types. Research usually precedes this step by using in-house sales history as well as pre-leasing discussions with prospective retailers. Try to discover what they project in volume, should they decide to become a tenant in the center being developed. Do not assume historical performance over project rent, as the projected volume by the tenant is what determines the rent it will be able to support. This is determined by each on a project-by-project, as well as market-specific, basis. Allow for limits on the rent based on what a tenant has paid in other centers in your portfolio. This is due in large part to a concern for setting precedents.

Leasing Summary

Develop a leasing summary that includes a listing of every space by assigned number and square footage. Layer on the specific tenant category or anticipated occupant and project the rent developed as outlined in this chapter. Determine if the pro forma rental is attainable. If it falls short, reevaluate either the merchandise mix or the specific tenants. If, despite changes in these, the result is still short of projected revenue, then a change in scope, cost, or the center type may need to be considered.

The leasing summary itself not only will be a plan but can and should be used as a touchstone as lease-up occurs. This summary or spreadsheet can be comprehensive in scope or contain only basic income. The dynamics need to be determined based on what it is to be used for, and it can be expanded if necessary. Once the per-space rent is assigned, it should become fixed; an actual rent entry will then provide a running variance. The format for this tracking tool is as varied as there are numbers of companies. Many times different people or project types within the same company may have their own format. The important point is that such a summary needs to be developed and used for any development or redevelopment project.

In operating properties, the leasing summary will serve as the budget. It is just as important that a space-by-space tracking tool be developed and used. In operating centers, this could—and should—include the lease term or termination. By referring to this budget for a given space, management and leasing can quickly evaluate reconfiguration opportunities that could be considered. Allowances for adjustments in term should coincide with those of adjacent tenant spaces. Taking the long view means that improved flexibility often can be gained without serious economic impact.

The Operating Budget

The operating budget or summary should include all activity anticipated during the time covered. By including this activity, the leasing team is able to identify changes in cash flow and cost that may be encountered over a given period. These may include, but are not limited to, allowances, concessions, downtime, and cost to reconfigure. It can also be used to schedule uplifts or other changes in rental income as well as commissions and other rents such as common area maintenance (CAM), taxes, trash, and the like.

An operating budget should be part of a longer view. As discussed, a plan should cover a minimum of five years and needs to use forecasts gleaned from the demographics of the market that it serves. A project leased without a forward-thinking plan will not meet changing customer expectations. Assuming changes are occurring in the market, leasing cannot simply renew all tenants. It is necessary to make adjustments in the mix, and whenever a change is made, provisions have to be made for its effects on cash flow.

This impact on cash flow takes into consideration the downtime between when the existing tenant exits and the new tenant produces income. A projection of this downtime must be realistic and if possible should consider the actual buildout period for the tenant that is replacing the one not being renewed. Take into account whether hazardous materials will need to be abated, reconfiguration work is required, or any other conditions exist that will require extra time. Establishing this total downtime is imperative if a good-quality budget is going to be developed, and this will allow accurate space delivery scheduling.

Allowances and Concessions

The budget should also forecast allowances and concessions. To be able to estimate required allowances accurately points to the need to determine specific tenants as part of the plan. Listing these target tenants makes it possible to research past requirements and include a more accurate assessment of the actual required cash that is needed. In addition, take note of when payment of these dollars will be made, since some tenants require in-progress payments, some will wait until work is complete, and a few will demand substantial cash before work begins. Disregarding the timing of these payouts will diminish the quality of the cash flow projections.

A plan should forecast all costs, including the payout forecast for allowances. Rental concessions are another factor affecting cash flow, and they are occasionally in lieu of cash allowances. Both allowances and rental concessions might be part of the same transaction, as some combination of cash and free rent could be required. Before any type of tenant inducement is negotiated, it is important to understand which is most beneficial for the particular project. In many cases cash allowances can be capitalized, allowing them to be amortized, which could be advantageous from a tax standpoint. In some cases partners or other stockholders may participate in cash flow but may not be required to fund cash allowances. If this is the case and a center represents a minority owner, it can mean asking that owner to fund 100 percent of required cash while being able to receive only a percentage of the rent the inducement secured. The best suggestion is to do the necessary homework prior to negotiations and develop accurate budgets that contain reliable forecasts.

Other Budgeted Costs

Another way to help the tenant offset the cost of building their store and to help justify the leasehold investment is called a "recapture out of percentage rent." This means either allowing the tenant to forgo payment of all percentage rent due or allowing payment of only a portion of the total overage due until an agreed upon amount is recaptured. Many times such a recapture is limited to a number of years. If the tenant, through generation of sales, does not produce enough overage rent to gain full benefit during a specific period, it forgoes the balance and pays all rents due. Giving a tenant the ability to recapture out of percentage rent has an additional benefit to the landlord in that percentage rent is discounted for valuation purposes. Forgoing some or all of this discountable income is used to pay for today's investment in future dollars.

Other costs often include reconfiguration expense. If it is determined that there is an enhancement to the center, through the upgrading of either the tenancy or the cash flow, that will require re-demising (dividing up) the space again, then an estimate of these costs should be scheduled. This estimate needs to include all work required prior to space turnover. The work may be as simple as moving a wall. More often, however, one change will require other adjustments that can be determined only after investigation. Examples of some of the work that might need evaluation include additional electrical service, heating and air-conditioning, and other services. Depending on the particular conditions, any one of these could be so costly that the change is not cost-effective.

To spend time structuring a real estate deal that is not justifiable when the cost is evaluated is an avoidable waste of time. It could get even worse if leasing were to commit to a new tenant and terminate the existing tenant, only to lose the deal once costs are evaluated. A good budget and plan will lessen the likelihood of unbudgeted expenditures to deliver the space. A thorough investigation can also reveal issues that could be extremely prohibitive, such as sprinkler zones, bearing walls, or structural elements. The best advice is, do not assume anything; if it is impossible to verify conditions or the costs to modify the space, it might be better to reconsider the modification.

Timetable

Milestones charted showing all aspects of the lease-up process are important for both new developments and redevelopments. These charted milestones include commitments, the signing of leases, plan submittal and approval, the start of construction, and the opening of the project and the new or renovated stores. Tracking the plan and construction may not seem leasing related, but considering that the leasing objective is to get tenants operating and paying rent, monitoring all steps toward this goal is prudent.

Be realistic. Tenants may commit early to a center, but they tend to delay signing the lease. If pre-leasing needs to occur, cover the need to have early signed documents when the deal is being negotiated, and support this with your schedule. Developing this timetable requires evaluation of staff dedicated to each milestone. Looking at a strong pre-leasing effort requires increased staff early in the process. If it is impossible to commit the number of people needed, adjustments to the schedule must be considered. Do not rely on the minimum time from extending a lease for signature to getting it signed; instead, review the time actually required in the past. If a review of past performance determines that the timetable is unrealistic, then either staff levels or the schedule itself must be reevaluated.

Many aspects in the schedule are interdependent. Some retailers require approved plans before signing a lease, and in many cases they require the approved construction documents to be an attachment to the lease. Taking this into consideration, evaluation of the plan approval process and the time required needs to be part of the projected lease-signing milestone. These tenant-specific issues point to the importance of a detailed plan that includes not only tenant type and categories, but also the precise tenant. The more detail that is layered onto the plan, the better the plan will be, and the better able it will be to predict the outcome.

With a comprehensive plan in hand, the leasing agent has the responsibility to cover required, project-specific issues with the tenant as early in the negotiations as possible. Ignoring any extraordinary items in the initial contacts stage does not help to meet the plan requirements and instead could waste allocable hours that could be better spent on deals that can meet project milestones.

Additional Planning Considerations

It is unlikely that any list of planning considerations can include all project idiosyncrasies. A few of the additional items that need to be evaluated prior to actual leasing are restrictive covenants, reciprocal easement agreements (REAs), and operating covenants.

Restrictive covenants include specific prohibitions placed on a project as a condition of approval by a city or other governmental body. Such a covenant could also be an agreement with an anchor or other occupant of the development. A retailer or adjacent landowner might require certain exclusions as a condition of sale, to protect its sales or retained property value. Management should be informed about such exclusions. Say, for example, that a partnership or other development arrangement was structured with an existing anchor. As a part of this agreement, management might be prohibited from introducing direct competition and might be required to lease only to retailers that operate within certain parameters. A clear understanding of restrictive covenants is required, as a violation could cause very serious consequences.

The REA may also include prohibitions on uses that require excessive parking. It is easy to understand how these requirements can have a negative impact on the ability to maximize sales if adequate parking is not available. Other restrictions may not be so apparent. The REA can include operating covenants. It is important to have a clear understanding of these, as most tenants will require this information and an inadvertent misrepresentation could be quite costly. The best advice is to be well informed as to the specific understandings in these documents, just as with other agreements. Do all research before beginning your leasing; any well-formulated plan requires extensive investigation.

Conclusion

As with any planning process, there are many steps. These steps may not always require a specific order, but each step must be taken. The time and effort given to each step will directly affect the quality of the resulting plan. The planning process begins with a clear understanding of the desired result and the requirements.

Only after developing a plan can management determine if there is a reasonable opportunity to accomplish the goal. In addition, more potential might be discovered than originally thought. In today's business environment, the prospect of spending limited capital on a project that fails to generate an appropriate return must be avoided. With competition as strong as it is today and the prospects for failure abounding, the development of a plan resulting from in-depth investigation has never been more important.

Keith W. Browning is Senior Vice President at DDR Oliver McMillan, San Diego, California.

2 Using Market Research to Lease a Center

Candace K. Rice, CLS/SCMD

Market research is the process of collecting, analyzing, and synthesizing information for the purpose of making knowledgeable business decisions. As it pertains to leasing shopping centers, market research includes understanding demographic shifts within a center's trade area (and from inflow/tertiary markets), analyzing a center's customer profile as well as shopping and purchasing habits, and knowing whom prospective tenants target with their merchandise or services. A retailer's market potential is, in part, assessed by the degree of overlap among these three factors: the total market population, the strength of the shopping center to draw from the total population, and the retailer's ability to convert traffic coming into the center.

Goals for Effective Use of Market Research

The effective use of market research depends on six overall goals that include the ability to:

- Focus core prospecting on retailers that fit the center
- Avoid the "easy deal"
- Improve the weakest elements of the center
- Develop an approach to grow sales and achieve success for tenants and the center

- Position the center for maximum, ongoing growth
- Act on the market research.

Focus your time commitments on prospecting for tenants that make the most sense for the center and the retailers. In the long run, leasing to tenants that will fill a void, as well as provide the quality of service and product that the customer expects, helps ensure successful sales for not only that tenant but also other retailers. In the perfect model, sales will grow and rents will follow. Remember, you are seeking to offer a shopping environment that consumers want to patronize and be ambassadors for, in order to help the owner evolve and change as needed. This is the ideal story that you want to be able to tell over and over, to new prospects as well as to existing tenants.

Avoid the pitfalls that inevitably result from simply getting the deal done for the sake of getting the deal done. Market research is necessary and useful even when the short-term objective is just to lease space and increase occupancy. It is especially important in difficult situations to be honest, knowledgeable, objective, and sincere about the opportunities presented to the retailer. A key goal for using market research in this instance is to present to the client all of the possible opportunities, as well as caveats, in exploring the deal. Here, the leasing staff should be knowledgeable about actual case studies, performances, and outcomes of similar situations, particularly if the staff members can research the client's company or a related type of retail. When they have information on market trends and are knowledgeable about the types and price points of retailers that are successful in the market, that may steer them into areas they had not originally considered for prospecting. The more they know, the more ideas, as well as productive questions, they will have.

Improve the weakest elements of the shopping centers. Customers not only notice what is lacking in a center, but also are aware when there is too much of something. The result is lost opportunities for the center owner, the existing tenants, and the consumers—and real losses for the owner and tenants. Using market research helps keep management and leasing efforts focused on what is in the best interest of the property—for both mid- and long-term success.

Develop an approach to growing sales while creating success stories for the tenants, the prospective retailers, and the property. Assess the center's category voids. This is especially important in smaller markets that retailers previously avoided because of population constraints. Retailers need a growth vehicle. They may be creating new prototypes that not only make the numbers work effectively, but also deliver the products and services that customers want. This helps a community retain demand and spending potential while reducing the degree of leakage to outside markets.

Position the center to maximize its growth on a continuing and consistent basis which is in line with changing market demands and lifestyle shifts. Evaluating the different generations in terms of such shifts makes you better able to anticipate who the customers are likely to be in, say, five years. Expressed in generations, present age groups represent the following generalized groups: "echo bust" (approximate ages through age 5, with parents doing the actual buying); "generation Y" (approximate ages 5 to 22); "echo boomers" (approximate ages 21 to 32); "generation X" (approximate ages 23 to 34); "tweeners" (approximate ages 31 to 36); "baby boomers" (approximate ages 35 to 53); "war and depression eras" (approximate ages 54 to 64); and "mature adults" (approximate ages 65 and older). Each group represents its own distinct patterns of buying.

Allow the users of market research to effectively attain their objectives. In more tangible terms, market research helps leasing people minimize their risk of filling a good space with a wrong tenant and vice versa, thus protecting the landlord's investment.

Benefits of Effective Market Research

The information obtained through effective market research offers the leasing professional the tools necessary to assist in determining the best prospects and the best mix of merchandise for the center. The benefits of market research to the leasing professional include the ability to be confident, conversant and resourceful. In effect, leasing professionals use market research to act as educators and facilitators to their clients.

Through market research, the leasing professional will become comfortable and confident in the ability to obtain the information that is needed, synthesize it, appropriate it, and understand its importance for both the center's strategic direction and the client's goals.

The leasing professional will become conversant because of the information gained from the market research. Actual knowledge is power. The biggest, but most preventable, mistake you can make is simply to assume that you know more about a particular market, center, consumer or competitor than your client does. Conversely, do not assume your retailer contact is necessarily knowledgeable about how the criteria for selecting new locations are derived. It is common to see such criteria in dealmaker types of publications as "needs 40,000 households within ten miles with average incomes above $50,000." This is not the complete picture, however, and should not be considered unalterable; in most cases, such criteria are guidelines. With the continued fragmentation of the marketplace, avoid making general assumptions or offer mass appeal.

The leasing professional will become resourceful. Part of market research includes conducting your own study of a center's historical performance. With the advent of new traffic and people counters, more flexible sales management databases, and integrated marketing techniques, real-time information is more readily available. The center management office, the finance department, and the market research can sometimes provide resources for maximizing the support necessary to assess sales or traffic trends according to the following:

- Merchandise category
- Geographic area of a property
- Customer profiles.

The Internet is a powerful and cost-effective source for remaining current on consumer demographics, social trends, purchasing habits, and growth patterns, to name a few areas. The Internet offers hundreds of sites with free, published data and other relevant information.

An effective resource for market information are the existing tenants at the center, clients that have chain stores, and anchor tenants. Supermarket chains and department stores are the most research-savvy, and they usually have extensive internal research departments. These are typically site location or area research departments that are responsible for analyzing a store's potential sales volume, given certain knowledge and assumptions about its market, including the effects of the transfer of sales from existing stores and formats in a market. National and regional chains have comprehensive customer databases, including credit card and point of sale (POS) databases that contain customer addresses, demographics, and expenditures. When possible, tap into your center's anchor or department store data for additional input.

Addressing the Market

Understand the general demographic trends of your market, and if you have a portfolio, note the similarities and differences across your properties in terms of market size, density, growth trends, race and ethnic composition, age and income breakdowns, and other characteristics that have been linked to a household's use of discretionary income, such as employment, household composition, and education.

A technology called GIS (Geographic Information Systems) is available either from management or from outside sources. The goal of the GIS is to collect and link a variety of information—demographics, lifestyle, spending habits—on consumers who reside within a center's trading area and to use data and maps to create a visual representation of the dynamics of a market. Shopping center owners and specialty retailers are bringing this technology in-house to allow the user to analyze market demographics by a defined geographic level (such as trade area, zip code, and block group). The five exhibits that accompany this chapter include a sample population density map, a sample location map, a sample trade area by zip code, a sample competition key, and a sample area survey. These exhibits illustrate how this type of data allows the user to analyze current conditions as well as what-if scenarios, using customer sales data, psychographic profiles, and updated census and economic data. Leasing professionals can use these tools to assess areas of growth opportunities, as well as weaknesses and potential vulnerabilities.

It is essential to focus on both the present and the future. Most demographic databases provide estimates and projections five years out. Remember how long it takes to complete a deal, open a store, and see it establish itself as a strong and profitable tenant. What will this market look like in five years or in ten years? Discuss predicted trends with local government officials, who may more accurately feel the pulse of what is going on in the community. In addition, make contact and develop relationships with local residential developers. This is especially true for ethnic markets and areas with households that are being turned over to a younger generation, growing fringe cities, and locales that are more sensitive or vulnerable to changes in the economy, including seasonal and tourism-oriented designations, as well as those that depend on a few primary industries for employment opportunities. Many properties also have an inflow of strong daytime demand because of nearby office complexes.

When assessing any market research or report, know where the information came from, and be careful of making assumptions using percentages. For instance, aggregate discretionary income, potential expenditures, and market share are based on calculations of raw numbers. Therefore, if a market is expected to suffer a decline in total population but you report to a retailer that there is an increase in demand for its product or service because the share of its targeted customer is expected to increase, you may be misleading your prospect—and the center.

Addressing the Center's Competition

Assess what major changes have occurred in competing centers, including shifts in ownership or management, redevelopment and expansion possibilities, tenant mix and sales, traffic trends, new openings, and store closings. In a few sentences, describe the positioning and image of these competitors whether they are targeting specific consumer groups in the market, and how well differentiated they are from your center and others. Note locations, driving distances, and retail magnets when it comes to other retail hubs, eating places, and entertainment. Determine if there are any smaller-niched or larger-use voids in the market. Call or visit the city's local chamber or planning agency and ask if there have been proposals for retail development, and if so, then by whom, when, and the project's status. Do not assume that just because a company turned down a site, space, or deal a year ago, the opportunity no longer exists; companies frequently review and often change their growth plans and criteria. Nothing remains static.

Future Trade Area

As everyone in the business understands, there is an ongoing revolution in trends and psychographic changes. No one can develop a shopping center precinct, whether it be a village, community center, regional mall, or specialty entertainment center, without understanding the area's population growth in terms of age groups, income and education levels, the price of housing, and future planned residential development. All of this data is critical to address when creating the overall merchandise mix for a shopping center. Positioning a property, and the image of the property, with a department store lineup is how one draws customers and therefore supports the future success of a development. For instance, with the strength of the younger shopper ages 12 to 25 (second only to the "baby boomer" in power of shopping), a shopping environment leased to attract the age group of 35 to 45 will be nowhere near as successful as a shopping center whose merchandise mix supports the younger generations.

It is imperative that the developer and all the prospective tenants understand the existing market and the inflow markets. While understanding there will be dramatic shifts through the preliminary term of the tenant's leases, a developer nonetheless cannot depend on a tenant's understanding when and how this shift will occur. Remember, some of the tenants have 500 to 2,000 stores nationwide and cannot keep on top of all local shifts. Therefore, it is often up to the leasing representative and the developer to continually educate existing and prospective tenants alike on the customer base and how it changes. Take, for example, Los Angeles, where there are more than 100 language dialects at one local high school and an ethnicity base that is more than 50 percent non-Caucasian. Creating a successful retail environment in a population of more than 25 million with these dynamics is very challenging. Most importantly, this should be understood throughout the process of the development and the leasing strategies.

Know the Retailers

Because both retailers and developers are learning to serve increasingly fragmented markets, chances are that their business strategies will reflect this. This is why it is important to research both the history and growth strategies of your retailers. Grappling with uncertainty in business planning requires a look at what has already happened to determine the factors that will create the future. The place to look is in the demographics. Coupled with this is the importance of analyzing consumer values, attitudes, behaviors, and lifestyles in order to understand what will come next.

Knowing your retailers includes understanding how each company emerged, how its concept or product evolved, who its targeted customers are, and what companies and other brands or product lines it competes against. Research the existing tenants in the center and identify which tenants this retailer will complement, supplement, or replace. Research the property's rent roll and lease expirations and know which tenants will be renewing or leaving, and why. National and regional retailers typically identify their targeted shopper by using point of sale (POS) and credit card databases. Your initial contact should facilitate a sound understanding of the retailer's overall business and strategies. Ask if it is testing any new prototypes, expanding its existing product line to include more variety or breadth of merchandise, broadening its products or services, or making plans to merge or acquire other companies. These types of conversations are important to define key trends within the company's product line. The more you know, the more successful your approach will be in forthcoming negotiations.

Be aware of where retailers are opening or closing stores, and try to isolate both external and implicit patterns to understand these factors. The role for market research fluctuates depending on whether you are working with a national, regional, or local prospect for specialty leasing. Do not assume that the larger the company, the more sophisticated its information systems or requirements for assessing new locations will be. It can be quite the contrary. Smaller, local entrepreneurs that are considering expanding have a lot at stake, and their research toolbox for business venture planning can range from nonexistent to an extensive working knowledge of the marketplace and its financial opportunities.

GAFO and Market Share

GAFO is an acronym that stands for the following retail expenditure categories provided every five years by the U.S. Census of Retail Trade.

- General merchandise (department stores, variety, miscellaneous)
- Apparel (all clothing and shoe categories)

- Furnishings (home furniture, appliances, electronics, and entertainment)
- Other retail stores (sporting goods, cards and gifts, jewelry, books, hobby, toys, cameras and photographic supplies, luggage, miscellaneous)
- Miscellaneous retail stores.

GAFO does not include eating and drinking establishments; however, this information is available from the Census of Retail Trade and can be added to reports. The key is to be consistent with the base numbers, to ensure year-to-year comparisons.

Generally, GAFO applies to between 12.5 and 14.5 percent of aggregate household income for a given state, city, or metropolitan area (which can be estimated from U.S. Census demographics for the most recent year available). Determine the benchmark percentage that you will use. To determine a trade area's total GAFO potential (total retail sales), multiply this benchmark percentage (that remains the same every time you calculate market share for a particular market area) by your center's trade area aggregate income. The total market share for your shopping center is its sales (in comparative GAFO categories) divided into the trade area's total potential.

Market Share in Relation to Customer Retention

Increases (fluctuations) in aggregate income (and retail sales potential) for a trade area is primarily a function of a trade area's population growth and economic conditions. Having a leasing strategy that focuses on the needs of the customer, and offering a complementary merchandise mix, helps protect and foster customer retention. This approach will help propagate shopping frequency and cross-shopping opportunities between retailers that may increase a center's market share, which is particularly important in a highly competitive market, or where the market is vulnerable to economic downturns or stagnant growth patterns.

Tools for a Leasing Presentation

At one time, providing demographic radius studies and a one-dimensional map with your center plotted in the middle was regarded as using research. While this method of presenting a general picture of a market's characteristics continues to be a popular initial request, beware of the implications of an interpretive approach. Radius demographics overlook the simple geographic barriers that can create or impede opportunities. They do not take into account a property's trade area characteristics, customer profile, and inflow traffic, which can be substantial due to daytime or weekend draws, including the effects of merchandising, tourism, and seasonal influences. It is easy to understand why retailers use this technique to flush out prospective new sites, as they can efficiently compare and contrast locations across multiple markets or within the same area.

Market research, coupled with the development of a sales team strategy that uses the expertise of your available resources, will increase leasing professionals' success rates in terms of identifying good tenant leads and solidifying deals. This includes utilizing the core competencies of the leasing professionals, research contacts, the property management staff, and marketing techniques. Such an approach is critical for developing retailer retention strategies that use research to communicate productivity and performance issues, changes in customer shopping habits, and foresight into the retailers' needs. Establishing this type of discipline puts in place ready-made tools for prospective new tenants. These research tools are often used as the primary sources for feeling the pulse of what is taking place in the marketplace and often include the following according to primary research and secondary research sources.

Primary research involves research for questions that remain unanswered such as:

- Market research focus groups, intercept surveys, telephone market surveys, and shopper profiles
- The use of lifestyle segmentation systems
- Marketing plans
- Chamber and community development departments that offer data on housing starts, economic trends, and new commercial growth.

Secondary research sources include research that consists of complete information such as:

- Traffic counts both in and around the perimeter of the property
- People counts

- Trade area maps and demographics
- Income, population density, ethnic, and competitive maps.

Refer to the five exhibits accompanying this chapter. Each highlights a different aspect of center demographies.

Leverage all retailer and portfolio databases through the analysis of data collected from sales, traffic, advertising, and promotional programs. Research the availability and content of tenant surveys, merchant programs, testimonials, and community public relations articles to establish a sound base of credibility for the property.

Always keep an eye on the larger picture. This includes staying abreast of key consumer and business trends so you can work and talk more effectively. For example, a marketing publication reported that retail sales of candles and candle accessories reached $2.1 billion in 1999, making these one of the largest and fastest-growing products in the U.S. giftware industry. Purchasers of candles tend to be women (although many men are also buying candles, for themselves as well as for gifts) between 24 and 54 years old with household incomes greater than $25,000. The big picture also includes keeping track of key economic indicators, immigration and emigration trends, and global patterns in the financial and commercial sectors that may affect retailer growth decisions, particularly for broader markets, as well as consumer sentiment and shopping habits.

Sometimes, using creative research techniques can be effective in collecting quick information and sending an intriguing message to your client. Some examples include starting a questionnaire for a store or product, and allowing existing tenants and consumers to comment on what they want and how to tell their story, or directly talking to customers in your center and obtaining testimonial or sound-bite comments and suggestions.

Additional Market Research and Benchmark Resources

Demographic and GIS sources make available expenditure potential reports, which analyze consumers' average total expenditures of products and services. These reports also use a relative index to compare such data to national norms. This information should be used in conjunction with actual productivity data and other retail sales databases to evaluate the propensity or strength of specific retail categories in a marketplace.

The most popular and prominent types of consumer information collected from surveys include customer demographics, shopping frequency, types of stores visited, cross-shopping patterns, expenditures, requests about stores, products, and services, and competitor usage. Information of this type is typically available through the research or marketing department at the corporate level and/or at the center management level. Be cautious when using research data or customer information that is more than two or three years old. A study reported in *American Demographics* magazine indicates that the average period of time it takes consumer attitudes to change had accelerated to 9 to 12 months by the year 2000, compared with 2 to 3 years in 1980.

Sharing proprietary customer information with existing and prospective retailers is an extremely effective, yet often overlooked, opportunity to build credibility for both the center and leasing team, to create a respectable forum for a productive dialogue on how the center is being perceived and used, and to point out areas that the center and/or retailers can leverage for increased productivity. For example, most consumer research studies provide an analysis of key shopping habits and behavior for each of the major demographic segments: age, income, and ethnicity. Drawing out key areas of interest such as expenditures, frequency of visits, or cross-shopping habits can identify quantitative opportunities that retailers can measure and objectively evaluate.

While more formalized research collected both internally and externally form the core of market research, leasing professionals are also encouraged to use more informal and creative research techniques such as simple observation; for instance, the types of shoppers who enter various stores and how shoppers use the center overall.

Coming back full circle to an approach to market research, shopping center market research includes understanding demographic shifts within a center's trade area and analyzing a center's customer profile as well as shopping and purchasing habits. However, successful market research is research that is applied, realized, and utilized to the best possible benefit of the center, its tenants, and prospective retail tenants.

Candace K. Rice, CLS/SCMD, is Senior Vice President, Leasing at Donahue Schriber, Newport Beach, California.

USING MARKET RESEARCH TO LEASE A CENTER ■ 31

Exhibit A
Sample Population Density Map
Center #1

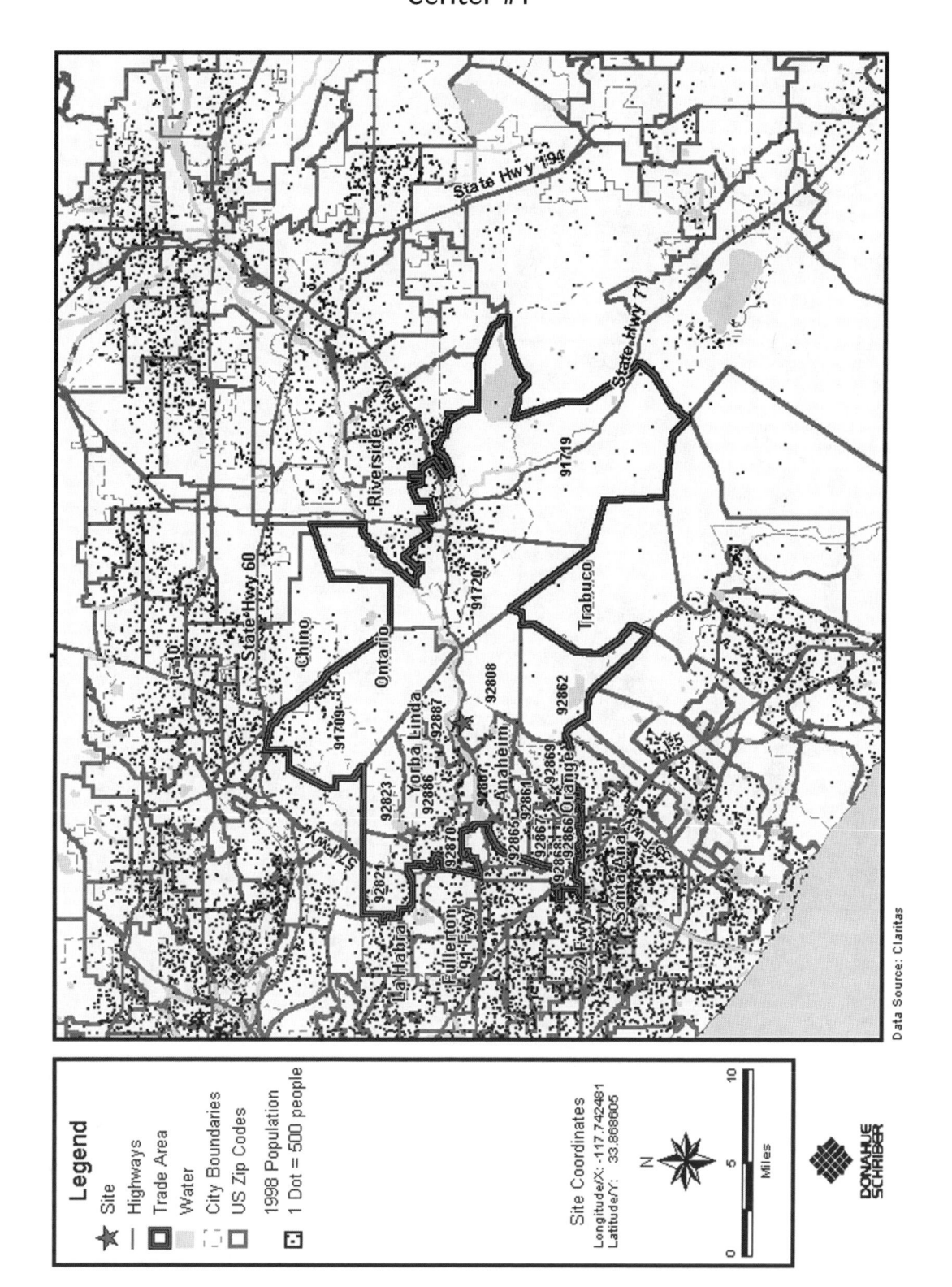

32 ■ *SHOPPING CENTER LEASING*

**Exhibit B
Sample Locator Map
Center #1**

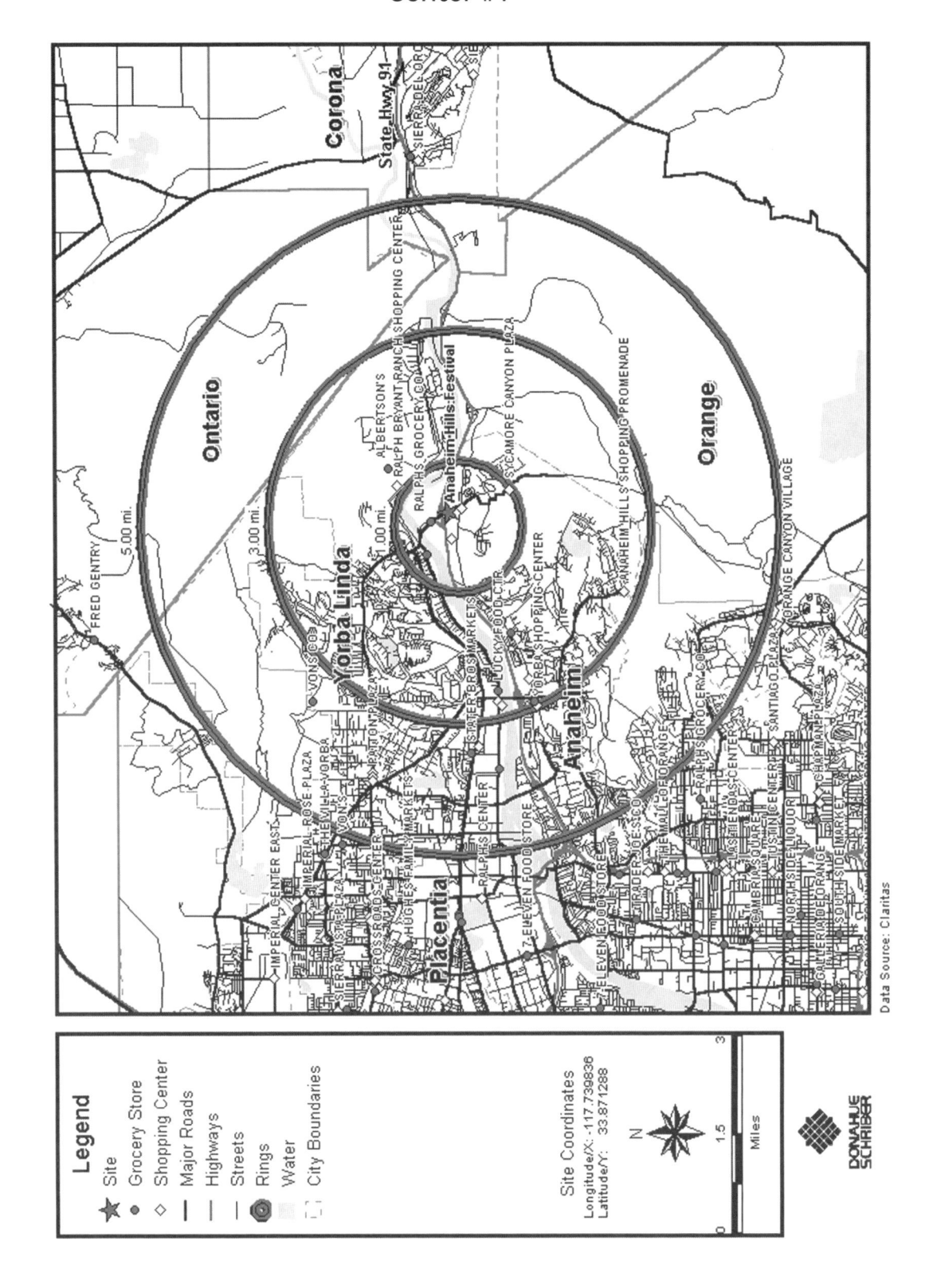

USING MARKET RESEARCH TO LEASE A CENTER ■ 33

Exhibit C
Sample Trade Area By Zip Code
Center #1

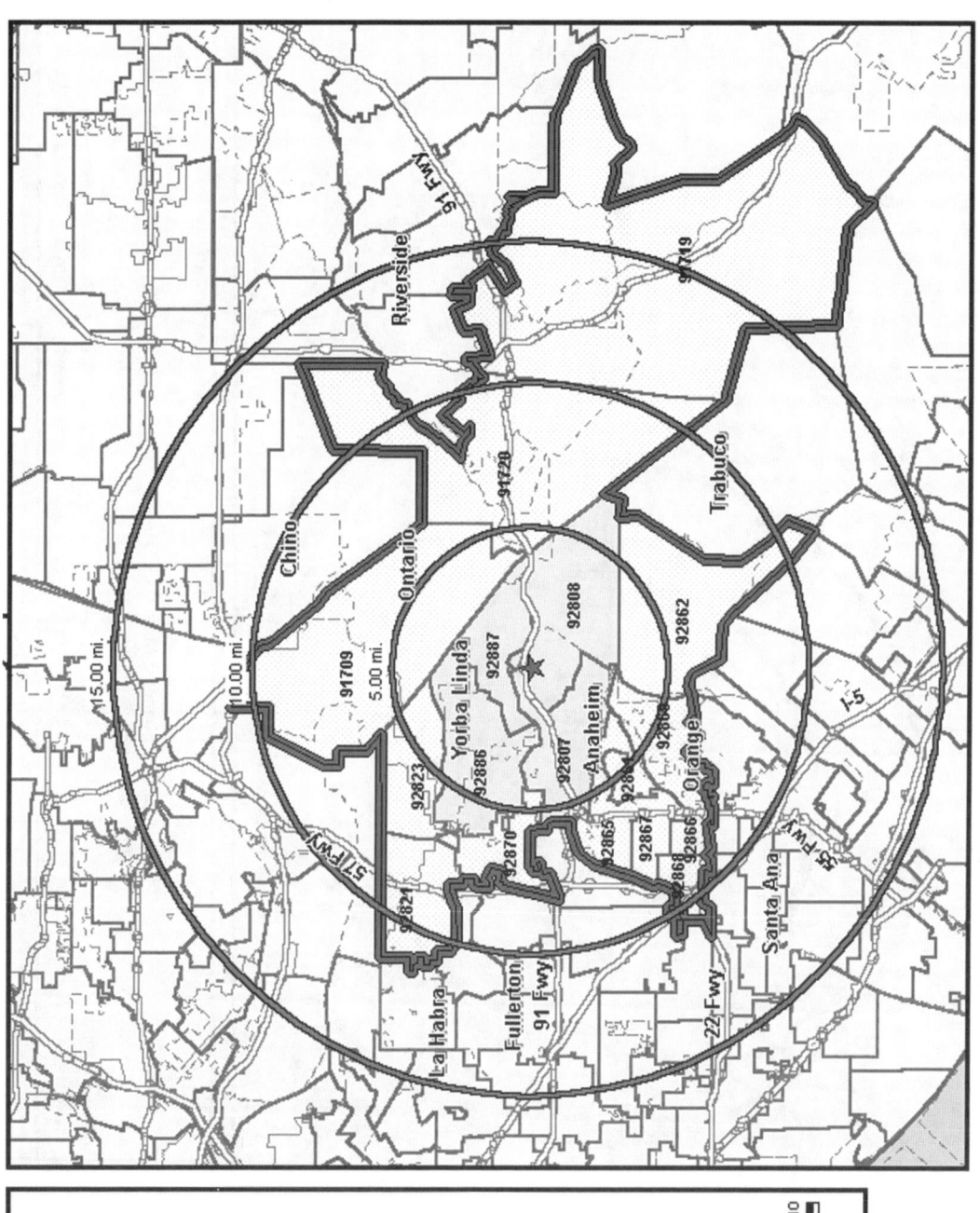

34 ■ *SHOPPING CENTER LEASING*

Exhibit D
Sample Competition Key
Center #2

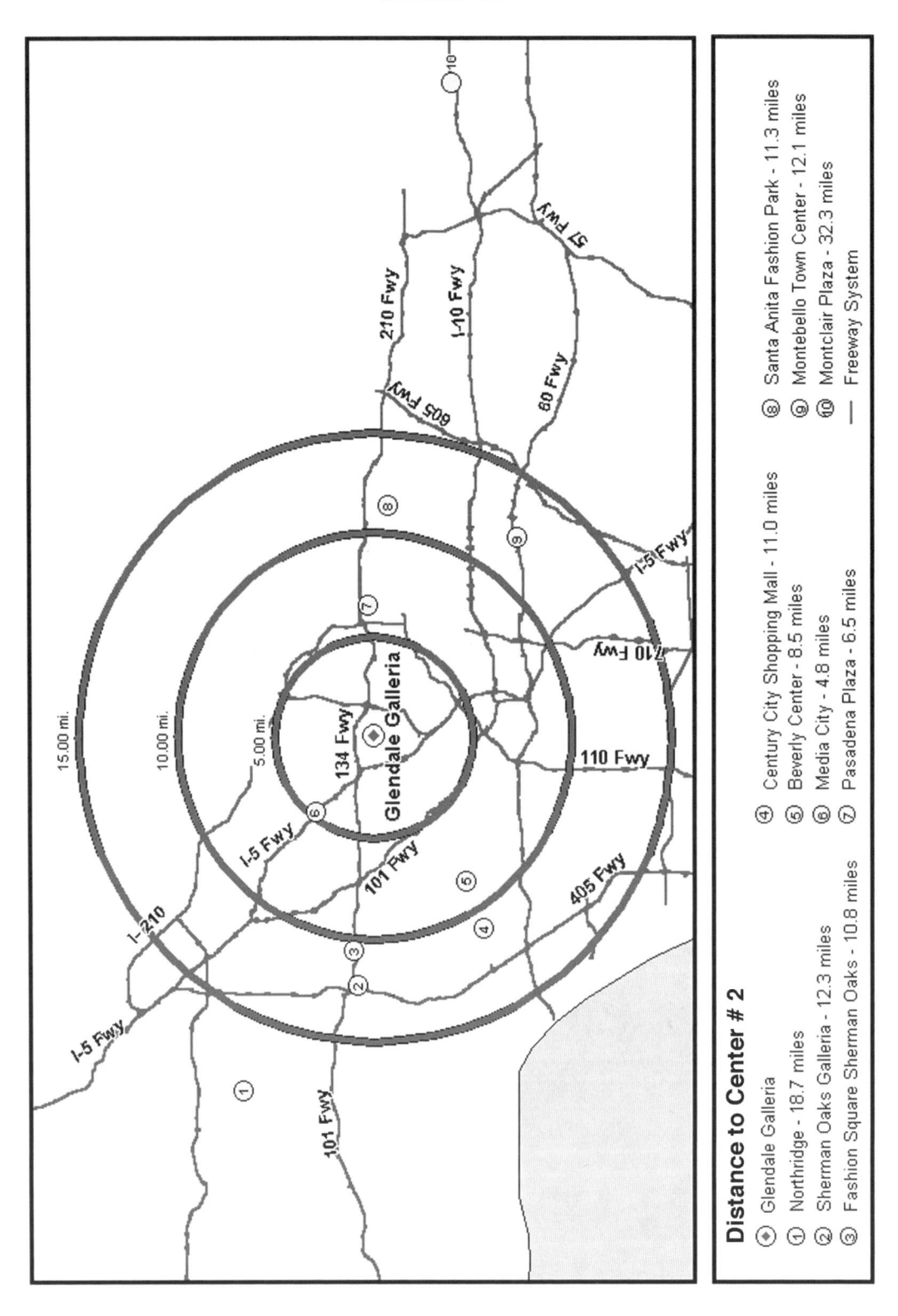

Distance to Center # 2

- ◆ Glendale Galleria
- ① Northridge - 18.7 miles
- ② Sherman Oaks Galleria - 12.3 miles
- ③ Fashion Square Sherman Oaks - 10.8 miles
- ④ Century City Shopping Mall - 11.0 miles
- ⑤ Beverly Center - 8.5 miles
- ⑥ Media City - 4.8 miles
- ⑦ Pasadena Plaza - 6.5 miles
- ⑧ Santa Anita Fashion Park - 11.3 miles
- ⑨ Montebello Town Center - 12.1 miles
- ⑩ Montclair Plaza - 32.3 miles
- — Freeway System

USING MARKET RESEARCH TO LEASE A CENTER   ■   35

**Exhibit E
Sample Trade Area Office Worker Survey
Center #2**

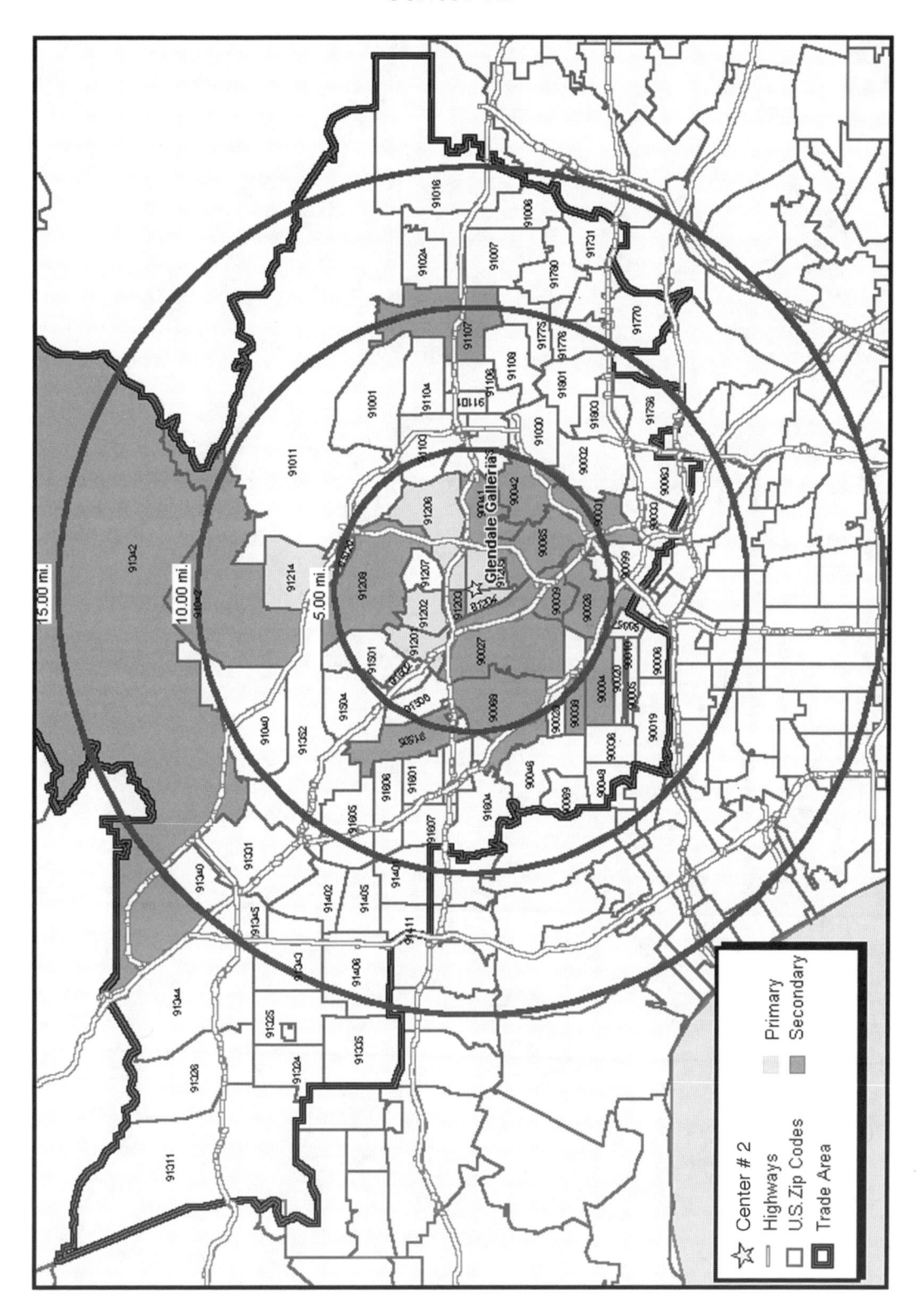

3 | Tenant Mix, Merchandising, and Leasing Strategies

Charles R. Cope, SCSM/CLS

The leasing of space in a shopping center is one of the most critical elements to a center's success. Leases determine the income and productivity of a center. Successful leasing requires knowing who the players are, analyzing the center's trade area, prospecting for tenants, determining rents and negotiating the lease deal. Just as the success of a center involves profitable leasing, the success of center management is often based on effective, profitable leasing. When a project is fully leased or exceeds the leasing goals, management succeeds. When there are too many vacancies or the economic side falls short, management falls short of the goal.

Experience on a leasing team is often the best way to learn all the elements that go into making a leasing deal possible, whether negotiating, merchandising, or motivating staff out in the field. The goal of this chapter is to connect what you learn from reading directly to your leasing experiences and to enhance your success in leasing efforts.

Long before the lease is signed, the business of leasing begins. Leasing is a process that begins with understanding the tenant mix of a center and then utilizing several leasing strategies with the goal of merchandising a center with a unique mix of tenants who define the center, attract shoppers from the center's primary trade area, and register profit for the tenants and the center. This chapter examines some of the factors that contribute to an effective tenant mix, merchandising, and profitable leasing strategies.

Adapted from *Shopping Center Management*. © 1999 by International Council of Shopping Centers, New York, NY.

Tenant Mix

Tenant mix is the combination of store types and price levels of retail and service businesses in a shopping center. Whether a center has ten stores or two hundred, an effective mix strengthens the center by creating a synergy calculated to appeal to a range of center customers, increase traffic at the center and—through placement and price—encourage customers to make multiple purchases or cross-shop at different types of retailers. A center mix typically includes different percentages of the following types of retailers:

- Specialty shops
- High-end stores
- Women's ready-to-wear
- Menswear
- Shoe stores
- Specialty restaurants
- Fast food
- Gifts
- Accessories
- Cards and stationery
- Jewelry
- Music, records, videos
- Entertainment
- Services.

EVALUATE THE TENANT MIX

While it is essential for shopping center managers to understand the different classes, categories and classifications of retailers, it is also necessary to acknowledge that what applies today may not necessarily apply tomorrow. Therefore, at times it may be necessary to break out of the mold and explore other tenant mix possibilities for a center. There is no exact formula for a right or wrong tenant mix. In a small center, a grocery store, a dry cleaner, a Chinese restaurant, and a hobby shop may represent four key tenant categories that bring success. In a mall, fashion, services, entertainment and food, intermingled with department stores, are analyzed and balanced to create the right strategic mix. Are the price points aligned with a center's demographics? What is the competition doing?

MARKET ANALYSIS

A *market analysis* examines trends in the trade area and identifies the characteristics that will offer a center an advantage over its competition, attract more customers to the center, and extend the length of the customer visit in the center.

CENTER ANALYSIS

A *center analysis* can be accomplished through a simple, more direct evaluation called a *penetration study*. A penetration study examines the gross leasable area (GLA) of each merchandising category and the total volume of each category as a percentage. A productivity higher than the norm suggests the addition of another store to that group. While this evaluation is not foolproof, it does offer an indication of where to improve a center's merchandising. Two very different examples follow. The jewelry category is an example for malls. In instances where this category may comprise 3 percent of the GLA and produce 6 percent of the sales, the result indicates a workable mix. However, in an instance where women's wear occupies 32 percent of the GLA and registers 22 percent of sales, this may suggest replacing an expiring women's wear store with another category use. In other words, the category is not carrying its weight with the center's customer base.

Other analysis and marketing tools that provide invaluable direction for merchandising include focus groups consisting of customers who regularly shop at the center or telephone surveys of those who do not regularly visit the center. Another excellent source of merchandising knowledge is the existing merchants in a center. They are anxious to share their ideas and perceived customer needs with management. The best way to obtain this information is through casual conversation during a mall walk with the center's merchants. Finally, monitor the busiest, most heavily staffed and completely merchandised departments in the center's anchor stores. For example, if they have a very successful line of apparel as a department, explore with that apparel company the possibility of an in-line store.

OWNERSHIP EXPECTATIONS

Many shopping center professionals say that the single most important factor in tenant mix is ownership expectations. An understanding of the owner's goals and objectives will enable the shopping center manager to make more informed decisions in all aspects of management, especially leasing. This is accomplished by:

- Meeting with ownership on a scheduled basis
- Ascertaining the economic value of the lease.

Meet at least annually with ownership to learn and acknowledge their expectations for tenant mix and leasing. Incorporate this step into the process of preparing the annual shopping center business plan.

Ascertain the economic value of the leases and how key provisions are negotiated. When the value of a center is determined, a capitalization rate is applied to the income derived from the leases. Expiring leases—where a prospective buyer can realize a positive impact on income through releasing—impact the value of the center. Understand the significance of various clauses in the lease, including the relocation clause, percentage rents, breakpoints, and landlord kick-outs or termination clauses. Know the economic issues that contribute to the overall value of your shopping center.

Leasing Strategies

The process of leasing, including building a tenant mix, prospecting, developing strategies and negotiating, represents the work of a team of people, not just one person. This team often includes the:

- Shopping center manager
- Marketing manager
- Accounting staff
- Document coordinator
- Leasing attorney
- Tenant coordinator
- Leasing team member.

Since the jobs of each of these people or departments are connected, the following section describes the responsibilities of each team member in light of some of the leasing strategies and negotiating tools frequently utilized.

TEAM MEMBERS AND LEASING STRATEGIES

Various companies will take differing views regarding a manager's involvement, but it is critical for the process that the *shopping center manager* become an integral part of the leasing team. Likewise, it is critical that the manager become familiar with all aspects of leasing and contribute to the team's efforts, becoming as valuable to the team as possible.

The center's *marketing manager* is usually included in various aspects of the process, taking on different tasks. They are pivotal to the shopper survey and focus group process. Marketing frequently maintains good contact with the merchants and is in an excellent position to engage them in a discussion of new retailing ideas under consideration at the center. At present, many retailers are looking hard at required participation in marketing and media funds. Involve the marketing manager early in the negotiations to demonstrate to current and prospective retailers the effectiveness of the center's overall marketing plan. Inclusion of the marketing manager on the leasing team brings new concepts and ideas to the team's efforts. It is also a natural extension of marketing managers' functions to visit other centers, collecting directories and highlighting the stores that they perceive as convincing additions to their center's mix. Finally, marketing professionals maintain strong networking ties with one another and share information about new concepts in practice at centers around the country.

The *accounting staff* is a very important part of the team, setting up a center's budget, pro forma, and other financial goals. While the manager establishes the objectives for the financial goals, the accounting staff assists by reviewing with the manager critical provisions of the lease and other documents, including lease termination dates, renewal options, rent bumps, and other key provisions. Once the financial objectives are established, the accounting team also assists the manager in matching the economics of a proposed deal with the established objectives. For example, the net present value (NPV) for the to-be-leased space is matched so that the manager can see the total value of the deal and make better, more informed economic decisions. (Exhibit D is a sample form for a "Net Present Value Analysis of Proposed Lease.")

The accounting staff also assists in one increasingly critical aspect of prospecting and lease development—evaluating the financial strengths of proposed tenants. The manager collects an annual report, the previous year's financial statement, federal tax returns and credit references from the proposed tenant. If the proposed tenant has other existing store locations, the manager contacts the landlord at another location. That person often proves to be the best reference, offering more information than whether the proposed tenant pays its rent on time. The accounting staff takes all information supplied by the manager and document coordinator and completes a form that categorizes financial areas, states an approval of the deal, and describes any reservations concerning the deal.

If staffing permits, designate a *document coordinator*. This can be the shopping center manager, leasing team person, assistant manager or support staff. This team member tracks all documentation from initial contact letters through executed leases, commencement date verification, amendments and finally, if required, termination documents. Working with both tenant and landlord attorneys, the document coordinator closes the gap in the length of time required to execute a lease. In many organizations, documents often delay the delivery of space, construction, openings and ultimately the rent commencement. The rationale for a document coordinator is compelling. For example, say a center completes ten deals a year. If each store is opened just one month earlier, a significant contribution is made to the center's bottom line. Weekly meetings with agendas written by the document coordinator keep staff accountable for meeting established schedules for a center's leasing timetable goals. The document coordinator may also be assigned to handle other contracts, such as roofing and housekeeping, as well as any contracted security services.

The *leasing attorney* is the person who clearly understands the manager's shopping center business goals and objectives. Similar temperaments between the leasing attorney and center manager are helpful, since they work together on pivotal leasing issues. The job of the leasing attorney is to advise the center manager on many issues. The leasing team then makes the best possible decision for the center in light of that advice. However, the attorney must also protect the center from bad legal decisions and guide the leasing team around legal pitfalls. As with the document coordinator, it is also important for the leasing attorney to deliver a prompt turnaround on all documents. Keep track of the time it takes from turnover to execution and discuss ways to shorten that time.

Another key member of the leasing team is the *tenant coordinator*.

This team member is especially important for new projects, or when the center enters a releasing or expansion phase. This team member can be an operations director or another staff person who focuses on tenant criteria. The tenant coordinator assists in negotiating the construction exhibit of the lease, reviewing and making suggestions, granting approval of the plans, and helping the tenant obtain permits. The tenant coordinator assists in enforcing construction rules and regulations that are established and reviewing the construction for conformance to the approved set of drawings. Upon completion, the coordinator produces a checklist for all to review and correct, as well as billing for construction chargebacks, which may include the following:

- Plan review
- Sprinkler shutdown
- Floor materials
- Temporary electricity
- Construction trash
- Other items.

Depending on the property management, a center may also have on-site leasing assistance or leasing through the home office, hire a broker to assist or initiate the leasing work internally by staff. For those centers with a leasing person, make sure the leasing person is aware of all of the team members and their respective tasks. The primary objective of the *leasing team member* is to seek out and assess interest of potential new merchants on behalf of the center.

PROSPECTING STRATEGIES

The leasing team member should be thoroughly acquainted with the budget/pro forma and the merchandise mix plan. The leasing team member should utilize a combination of established contacts and cold calls in those areas with merchandising similar to the center's plan. Shopping center managers, leasing team members, and marketing managers should keep detailed files on all of their key leasing prospects. These prospects are the potential tenants to address when the center is planning to remerchandise vacancies, expirations or the recapturing of space. On an ongoing basis, the leasing person maintains good relationships with colleagues in the industry to remain current with new trends and information on what is going on in other companies. For example, the leasing person should know when a retailing company opens a new division and ascertain if that new concept represents a potential new retailer for the center. Likewise, remaining current will highlight information concerning the financial health of retailers presently occupying space within the leasing person's center.

The following steps assist in building credibility when prospecting:

- Get to know the owners of the stores the center is seeking
- Develop a list of prospective tenant stores ranging from best to worst
- Obtain referrals from merchants about their competitors
- Ask questions about the prospects' businesses to build a familiarity with issues they are facing, and what works or does not work.

After prospecting and cold-calling, the leasing team member assembles all necessary background information collected on prospects and presents to the leasing team those prospects who meet the center's criteria.

Negotiating Tools and Strategies

It is often acknowledged that a good negotiator needs to know both sides' positions and goals as well as they do. Always operate under the assumption that the center's negotiating opponents have educated themselves about shopping center issues. It is imperative in negotiations to know your business inside and out as well as have a strong familiarity with your opponent's businesses. Take advantage of opportunities to read industry magazines and articles that indicate trends that retailers are following.

NEGOTIATING WITH EXISTING TENANTS

In some cases an existing merchant is performing so well that its sales are good, it pays rent on time, and it diligently follows your center's rules and regulations. It services its customers well and is well staffed and stocked with desirable merchandise. When its lease expires, in such instances, center management will probably want to renew the tenant in its present location or perhaps offer it a more advantageous location that better suits its needs. To determine the renewal proposal, look to see what similar spaces have been renting for, then compare effective rent (a combination of minimum rent and percentage rent) to see if it holds market. In most instances, a center should be able to achieve at least 80 percent of the effective rent if the merchants are paying percentage rent. In many cases it is better to accept slightly below market rents from an existing merchant, acknowledging that the center will incur downtime, potential leasing fees, higher attorney fees, possible construction allowances and other costs with a replacement merchant.

Other key renewal factors include the extent of required remodeling and whether a center can use a new or existing lease or use an amendment to adjust term, rents, and any other key factors in the lease document. Do the common area maintenance (CAM) and insurance sections need updating? How about the environmental clause? Seek advice from the leasing attorney and review the existing documents in order to make an informed decision.

NEGOTIATING WITH NEW MERCHANTS
Perhaps the most significant factor in lease negotiations is the perceived strength of the shopping center and the retailer. If a center is fortunate enough to be considered a "dominant" shopping center, it will gain certain advantages: for example, using its own lease form, achieving top market rents, keeping pro rata CAM charges and real estate taxes and maintaining its full marketing plan, as well as having much to say in store design and other critical areas. Should the retailer be in a stronger perceived position, a center may need to use the retailer's form, pay tenant allowances, settle for gross rents, and have other terms dictated to it.

Throughout the negotiating process these and many more issues will be decided. This brings the discussion back to the "team" for help in negotiating the lease. It is best to have the center's insurance broker assist with the complicated provisions that seem insignificant now, but are significant to any property that has been involved in a casualty, fire, flood, or building failure. Be particularly careful with loss limits and rights to terminate or suspend rents in the event of a casualty.

Seek specialized advice on all construction issues. For example, electric loads are to be calculated to determine if there is enough power to serve the requested needs of the tenant. If power is lack-

Merchandising Entertainment As Well As Competitive And Comparable Centers

by Michael E. McCarty

MERCHANDISING ENTERTAINMENT

Merchandising is creating an overall experience for the shopper. This experience can go far beyond the procuring of goods and services, in which shoppers take with them something they have purchased.

Entertainment has added an entirely new segment to the shopping center industry. Years ago, the first blush of entertainment, in the form of restaurants, meant that portions of the center were converted to food courts. This not only provided an opportunity to feed people, but also created an atmosphere that was comfortable and convenient for people to congregate, relax, and hopefully spend money.

Now, in addition to the responsibility of leasing a food court, a leasing representative needs to go further in determining the level of restaurants needed in the project. These restaurants also set a tone for the type of customer to which they cater. There are different customers for a buffet-type operation, a steakhouse, a white-tablecloth operation, and one of the theme-type restaurants that provide much more entertainment than food. Thus, in creating a merchandising mix for a project, it is necessary to consider the type of restaurant operations and the number of restaurants desired for the project.

Entertainment, though, is more than just restaurants. Entertainment now means movie theaters—ranging from one or two screens to a multiplex with many screens. Incorporating movie theaters into the project is a very important process and needs to be very well thought out. In addition to restaurants and movie theaters, the idea of entertainment even carries over to regular retail. Three categories of retailers now overlap with the entertainment focus: books, music, and sporting goods. By incorporating books, music, or sporting goods into their mix, developers can lengthen the customer's stay in the development. In many cases these types of retailers provide additional activities in which the customer can participate while in the store; for example, coffee bars, listening booths, or wall climbing.

This notion of entertainment in retail has blended considerably over the last several years; for example, many restaurants offer clothing while many retailers are selling coffee. This again leads to the bottom-line notion that merchandising means creating a total experience for the customer, in hopes it is such a comfortable experience that the customer will come again and spend more.

MERCHANDISING COMPETITIVE AND COMPARABLE CENTERS

Once developers determine the type of anchor merchandise they would like to have in their developments, how do they select the balance of merchandise for the rest of the center?

In many cases it is not necessary to continually reinvent a wheel. If a development has a particular anchor mix, that center should identify other properties with the same anchor mix. Canvass those projects to determine what level of merchandising or names of retailers are doing business within the property. Investigate whether those stores are successful in that environment.

In developing a brand-new project, determine which particular discount department store is an appropriate anchor. Proceed to identify the same anchor in other locations within the center's marketplace, compile a demographic profile of those marketplaces (even in a three- or a five-mile ring), and compare these demographics to those of the project. If key indicators are comparable to those in existing locations, the site might make sense as planned.

Avoid underestimating the value of being out in the market and seeing what works and what does not work with competitive or comparable projects. Retailers often indicate that they are comfortable with a certain type of development or type of position, store size, frontage, and so forth. It may be possible to replicate that same type of environment that has been successful for a particular retailer, thus increasing the chance of making a deal with an already successful tenant.

MERCHANDISING TIPS

Merchandising is where science and art converge in any shopping center. The science of merchandising is in the demographic review and the understanding of customers within the trade area. The art is in offering the right retailer in each of these particular environments. Understand the marketplace for each particular product. If fortunate enough to be dealing with a site that is not yet developed, then whatever stores are chosen to be the anchors of the development will begin to set the tone for the balance of the merchandising in the center. This decision is therefore critical. Having market research on board early will help lead the developer in the proper direction to address the largest possible market it can in order to create the best potential for the development's success.

In dealing with an existing product, the re-leasing of anchor stores is critical. If an opportunity presents itself when an anchor has left the center, it is important to revisit the demographic makeup of the market. The replacement anchor needs to raise the expectations of the marketplace, thus encouraging additional leasing in the balance of the center to reflect the customers that will now be brought into the center.

Finally, there are no set rules as to what demographic profile is used, or which retailer is selected. It is not a question of wanting to deal only with one retailer or one demographic profile. It is an understanding of what profile exists, doing the best possible to address that by finding retailers that provide those goods and services needed by that demographic profile. Aligning these needs with the right retailers creates the best opportunity for success within the project. As retailers open their stores, the developer's success will follow their own. A developer cannot be successful while its retailers are misaligned and unsuccessful. The developer is successful—and percentage rent follows—only in those instances in which the retailers are properly aligned and successful in their business. This is merchandising.

Michael E. McCarty is Senior Vice President/Community Center Division at Simon Property Group, Indianapolis, Indiana.

ing, costly improvements to the infrastructure will certainly have an impact on the calculated returns.

It is imperative when negotiating the lease to state clearly as much as possible. Who removes existing abandoned heating, ventilation and air-conditioning (HVAC) equipment on the roof? If the landlord is to handle demolition, does the new tenant want the center to leave anything behind? Are utilities to be brought to a location designated by the tenant or just near to the demised premises? When can certain types of disruptive work take place and when is such work prohibited? It is far easier to negotiate these issues up front rather than in the heat of the moment, when the lease or construction is under pressure.

Some basic forms can serve as automatic reminders for some of these issues from the beginning. An effective way to start with local and some regional merchants is the lease application (see Exhibit A). This form provides the leasing team member with an excellent review of the prospective business. The form states the type of business, how it operates, who is involved in ownership, and lists several business references, credit references and preliminary financial data. Much can be learned about a potential merchant just by how the questions are answered.

The center does not need all this information for national companies, but even with the nationals you should ask for comparative center sales, recent financial statements, or an annual report. After the manager or leasing team member has met with and scrutinized the prospective tenant and discussed the basic terms of the lease, document these discussions with a lease term sheet (see Exhibit B). This form allows both parties to have in writing the key points needed to structure a lease document. While most of these issues are economic, it is helpful to expand the term sheet to include key provisions of the deal that were important to each party in choosing to go forward.

The next form to advance to is the lease approval form (see Exhibit C). This document serves multiple uses. First, it is used to document approvals through the center's real estate committee and for preparation of the lease itself. Second, it can be used to approve and issue a new lease, or to amend or renew an existing lease. This is an internal document that flows through accounting, management, and corporate as necessary, with each signing all approvals as necessary. Once complete, the lease approval form is then used to prepare the lease document. If any major terms are adjusted during negotiations, a box on the upper right-hand corner is checked and the lease approval form can be recirculated to gain written approval of those changes. It is a good idea to attach a copy of the first form circulated and highlight any changes needing approvals.

Alternative Strategies

The leasing of carts, retail merchandising units (RMUs), and vacant storefronts has become a major emphasis in enclosed centers. In the early stages of this trend, it was handled by the marketing staff. It has now grown into a specialized field with full-time, highly competent leasing experts who often generate in excess of $1 million in rents and extra charges for their properties. There are several very good companies that specialize in this type of leasing. They provide the equipment, the plan, the management, and the merchants. These experts will address a financial income-sharing agreement with a center.

A common practice is to "incubate" retailers from carts to regular in-line stores; however, most operators of carts are better suited to a smaller, less intense type of operation. They can respond quickly to trends. There will be trade-offs. These operations are often management-intensive; for instance, making sure they open in time to display their goods in a professional manner. Often there are concerns about return policies. The center can assist in this matter by establishing return policies in the license agreement. Another excellent area to negotiate is a "quick" termination, effective either immediately or in one to three days. This will ensure compliance with many of leasing's critical issues.

Some centers also require these merchants to provide a substantial security deposit. Should a default occur, it is often difficult to track them down and collect past-due rents. When merchandising, keep in mind the center's regular, in-line, full-time merchants. Try not to place competitive merchandise in the center, especially in front of a store carrying the same goods.

Planned or unplanned vacancies will occur. Barricades look imposing and can make a vacancy appear obvious. Some good solutions include the use of temporary merchants such as Christmas shops, Halloween shops, flower and cart merchants, and temporary displays. These temporary solutions are effective in filling any vacant storefront. In the case of temporary merchants, remember to keep termination options short so that space can be turned over quickly to a permanent merchant. Alternatively, most existing stores are glad to use their staff to merchandise these vacant storefront windows for additional mall exposure. In these cases, set high standards for appearance and regularly change the displays to avoid a stale look.

Conclusion

Leasing is one of the most important aspects in the overall success of a shopping center, determining income and productivity for a center. Leasing programs must be carefully planned and organized. Study the tenant mix, the physical plant, the market, and the competition. Keep detailed records of all leases and consider creative alternative uses for spaces which standard tenants may not lease. Employ prospecting techniques that will result in the best mix for the center. Negotiate so that the tenant and the leasing team are both satisfied with the lease.

Leasing creates value and uniqueness and allows the manager and leasing team members to experiment with new concepts. Leasing allows the manager to respond to customer needs, and it is one factor which sets a manager apart from other managers. As a shopping center manager, learn from your experiences, learn to utilize successful ideas from other properties or professionals and learn to be fair in all leasing negotiations.

Charles R. Cope, SCSM/CLS, is a consultant in Oakton, Virginia.

Exhibit A:

Sample Lease Application

I. **GENERAL**
   Legal Business Name: _____
   Doing Business As: _____
   Present (Most Recent) Location of Business: _____
   _____
   Reason for This Move: _____
   Phone:(___) _____
   How Long at Current Location: _____
   ( ) Own ( ) Lease _____
   Mailing Address: _____
   Landlord or Mortgage Holder: _____
   Address: _____
   Name of Contact: _____ Phone:(___) _____
   (If more than one location, please attach additional list of Landlord references.)

II. **FORM OF BUSINESS**
   Unincorporated (Complete Part III (A) and attach Certificate of Assumed Name)
   ( ) Proprietorship ( ) General Partnership ( ) Limited Partnership
   ( ) Joint Venture, Association ( ) Other _____
   Incorporated (Complete Part III (B) or III (C)
   ( ) Corporation
   ( ) Other: _____
   Federal Employer I.D. Number (or Social Security # if an Individual):
   _____ Date Business Started: ___/___/___
   Type of Business: ( ) Oil & Gas ( ) Real Estate ( ) Manufacturing
   ( ) Insurance ( ) Finance ( ) Construction ( ) Communication
   ( ) Legal/Accounting ( ) Other: _____
   ( ) Retail (Attach Merchandising Plan including Estimated Value of Inventory
      and Fixtures.)

   Hazardous Materials to be Stored in the Space: Yes / No Attach List or MSDS
   (Material Safety Date Sheet).

   Insurance:
   Carrier: _____ Agent: _____
   Address: _____
   City/State: _____ Zip: _____
   Phone:(___) _____ Provide valid certificate for current occupancy
   or quotation for this occupancy.

Note: This is a sample only and is not to be construed as being endorsed or recommended by the author or the International Council of Shopping Centers. Readers are advised to consult legal counsel to devise appropriate documents for their centers.

III. OWNERSHIP

(A) Complete this section if entity is an unincorporated Partnership, Joint Venture, Association or Proprietorship. Please identify General Partners and/or Principals as appropriate.

Principal(s)/Partner(s) Name: _____ Title: _____
Home Address: _____
City/State: _____ Zip: _____
Home Phone:(___) _____ Social Security Number: _____
Personal Banking Information:
Bank: _____ Bank Officer: _____
Address: _____
City/State: _____ Zip: _____ Phone:(___) _____

Principal(s)/Partner(s) Name: _____ Title: _____
Home Address: _____
City/State: _____ Zip: _____
Home Phone:(___) _____ Social Security Number: _____
Personal Banking Information:
Bank: _____ Bank Officer: _____
Address: _____
City/State: _____ Zip: _____ Phone:(___) _____

Principal(s)/Partner(s) Name: _____ Title: _____
Home Address: _____
City/State: _____ Zip: _____
Home Phone:(___) _____ Social Security Number: _____
Personal Banking Information:
Bank: _____ Bank Officer: _____
Address: _____
City/State: _____ Zip: _____ Phone:(___) _____

(B) Complete this section if entity is not a publicly traded corporation. Please list the Principal(s) and Officer(s) as well as the ownership interest.

Name: _____ Title: _____
Address: _____
City/State: _____ Zip: _____ Phone:(___) _____
Percentage Owned: _____ Social Security Number: _____

Name: _____ Title: _____
Address: _____
City/State: _____ Zip: _____ Phone:(___) _____
Percentage Owned: _____ Social Security Number: _____

Name: _____ Title: _____
Address: _____
City/State: _____ Zip: _____ Phone:(___) _____
Percentage Owned: _____ Social Security Number: _____

(C) Complete this section if entity is a publicly traded corporation. List all third-party ratings assigned to this entity (i.e., D&B, Moody, S&P). _____

Provide most recent annual report.
Provide most recent SEC filing.

(D) For (B) and (C) above complete the following:
State of Incorporation: _____ Charter Number: _____
State(s) Where Qualified to Do Business: _____
Registered Agent for Service: _____

IV. BUSINESS CREDIT REFERENCES
Supplier: _____ Account Number: _____
Goods/Services Purchased: _____ Monthly Value: _____
Bank: _____Bank Officer: _____
Address: _____
City/State: _____ Zip: _____ Phone:(___) _____

Supplier: _____ Account Number: _____
Goods/Services Purchased: _____ Monthly Value: _____
Bank: _____Bank Officer: _____
Address: _____
City/State: _____ Zip: _____ Phone:(___) _____

Supplier: _____ Account Number: _____
Goods/Services Purchased: _____ Monthly Value: _____
Bank: _____Bank Officer: _____
Address: _____
City/State: _____ Zip: _____ Phone:(___) _____

Supplier: _____ Account Number: _____
Goods/Services Purchased: _____ Monthly Value: _____
Bank: _____Bank Officer: _____
Address: _____
City/State: _____ Zip: _____ Phone:(___) _____

V. BUSINESS BANKING INFORMATION
Bank: _____
Address: _____
City/State: _____ Zip: _____ Phone:(___) _____
Bank Officer: _____
Type of Account(s): _____ Account Number: _____
Date Account Opened: _____

Bank: _____
Address: _____
City/State: _____ Zip: _____ Phone:(___) _____
Bank Officer: _____
Type of Account(s): _____ Account Number: _____
Date Account Opened: _____

VI. <u>FINANCIAL INFORMATION</u>
   A. During the last 10 years, has the entity making this application or any subsidiary, predecessor, officer or principal (provide full details if the answer is "yes" to any of the following):
      Filed bankruptcy? Yes/No _____
      Been named as a defendant in any legal proceedings? Yes/No _____
      Had a judgment or lien filed against it? Yes/No _____
         Have they been satisfied? Yes/No _____
   B. Upon completion of this application and prior to its return, please review carefully. In addition, please provide copies of the latest fiscal year and year-to-date financial statements (balance sheet, income statement and statement of cash flows) that you have available for the prospective Tenant under consideration. If unaudited, the financial statements should be certified as true and correct by the Owner or an authorized Partner, Principal or Officer of the business. Your cooperation will expedite the processing of your application.

DECLARATION

Under penalty of perjury, I, the undersigned, declare that this credit application is true and correct to the best of my knowledge, and I am authorized to submit this application. I recognize that _____ will rely on the information provided herein in determining the credit status of this application and that any substantial discrepancies which may come to _____'s attention before or after execution of a lease may result in _____ finding the lease to be in default and may exercise any of the remedies prescribed in the lease.

Further, I authorize any person or entity to release or furnish information to _____ as may be requested in connection with their review and evaluation of this application. I UNDERSTAND THAT ADDITIONAL INFORMATION MAY BE REQUIRED WHICH COULD INCLUDE, BUT IS NOT LIMITED TO, BALANCE SHEETS AND INCOME STATEMENTS, PRO FORMAS, TAX RETURNS AND BUSINESS PLANS. I further agree that all financial statements, tax returns, reports and other materials furnished or obtained in connection herewith shall become the property of _____.

Entity: _____
Print Name: _____
Title: _____

By: (Signed) _____
Date: _____

ID: Driver's License # _____
                  (State)   (Number)

Exhibit B:

Sample Lease Term

SUMMARY OF TERMS AND CONDITIONS

LEGAL NAME: _____
BUSINESS NAME: _____
LEGAL ADDRESS: _____

TELEPHONE: _____ FACSIMILE: _____
PROPOSED USE:

SPACE: _____ SQUARE FEET: _____
FRONT: _____

	MINIMUM RENT:
	LEASE TERM:
	LEASE COMMENCEMENT RENT:
	LEASE TERMINATION:
PERCENTAGE RENT:	
PRO RATA CHARGES:	Tenant shall be responsible for its pro rata share of COMMON AREA MAINTENANCE, REAL ESTATE TAXES and INSURANCE COSTS. Based upon current billing, these are estimated for calendar year _____ to be as follows: Common Area Maintenance: _____ Real Estate Taxes: _____ Insurance: _____
OTHER CHARGES:	Tenant shall also be responsible for the following Other Charges which based upon current billing are estimated for calendar year _____ to be as follows: HVAC Energy: _____ Electric: _____ Water: _____ Marketing Fund: _____ Special Assessment: _____

Note: This is a sample only and is not to be construed as being endorsed or recommended by the author or the International Council of Shopping Centers. Readers are advised to consult legal counsel to devise appropriate documents for their centers.

ONE-TIME CHARGES: Tenant shall be responsible for its pro rata share of the following one-time charges:
Sprinkler: _____
HVAC Equipment: _____
Initial Marketing Charge: _____
Landlord's Standard Floor Finish: _____
Temporary Barricade Enclosure: _____
Coming Soon Logo: _____
Plan Review Fees: _____

PRE-OPENING CHARGES: Includes LOD package, temporary signage, temporary electric, water, asbestos abatement inspection report, etc.
Typical Retail Tenants: _____
Food Tenants: _____

SECURITY DEPOSIT: To Be Determined

GUARANTOR: To Be Determined

DESIGN CRITERIA: It should be understood that Landlord will implement a comprehensive control of store design in order to achieve a unified quality tone throughout the project.

NOT BINDING: The business terms and conditions as outlined above are being submitted solely for review. Neither party will be legally bound by these terms and conditions until a mutually acceptable lease has been fully executed by both parties. Once executed, the terms and conditions of the lease between Landlord and Tenant shall supercede the terms and conditions of this Summary.

AVAILABILITY OF SPACE: This proposal is conditioned upon the availability of the above referenced space, and approval by the Real Estate Committee.

FINANCIAL: Tenant lease application, corporate or personal finance statement (whichever is applicable), balance sheet, income statement, tax returns and business plan must be returned with signed Summary of Terms and Conditions before a lease will be drafted.

OTHER: *(INSERT RADIUS, RELOCATION, OTHER NEGOTIATED TERMS TO BE INSERTED IN DRAFT OF LEASE)*

THIS PROPOSAL WILL BE WITHDRAWN IF NOT ACTED UPON BY:
PREPARED BY: _____ DATE: _____
ACCEPTED BY: _____ DATE: _____

Exhibit C:

Sample Lease Approval Form

Property:		Date:	
Submitted by:			
❏ New Lease　　❏ Renewal　　❏ Amendment			
Tenant			
Legal Name:		DBA:	
Contact Name:		State of Incorporation:	
Address:			
Telephone Number:			
Guarantor:		State of Incorporation:	
❏ Full Guarantee　　❏ Guarantee Limited to:			
Tenant Notice Address:			

Lease Provisions

Space No:				
Renewal/Relocation Existing Deal:	Space No.:	Sq. Ft.:	Min. Rent:	Effective Rent:
Use:				

Term	Years:	Months:	Opening Date:	Expiration Date:

Minimum Annual Rent
　Budget:

Years:	Dollars/Sq.Ft.	Dollars/Yr.	% Rent	❏ Natural ❏ Unnatural Breakpoint

Department Store Increase:
Security Deposit:
Tenant Allowance
Budget:

Cash to Tenant:	$	/sq.ft.	$		
Abated Rent:	$	/sq.ft.	$		
Abated Extra Charges:	$	/sq.ft.	$		
Recapture:	$	/sq.ft.	$		
Landlord's Work:	$	/sq.ft.	$		
Brokerage Commission:	$	/sq.ft.	$	% ❏ INHOUSE	❏ Outside

Broker

Total Cost:	$	/sq.ft.	$

Ancillary Charges

CAM	❏ Full pro-rata	$	sq.ft.	❏ Other		
Taxes	❏ Full pro-rata	$	sq.ft.	❏ Other		
Utilities	HVAC	$	sq.ft.	Electric	$	/sq.ft.
Marketing Fund	$	/sq.ft.	Media Fund　$		/sq.ft.	
Escalations			Initial Marketing Charge $	Special Assessments:		

Construction Chargebacks:

Special Lease Provisions:

Note: This is a sample only and is not to be construed as being endorsed or recommended by the author or the International Council of Shopping Centers. Readers are advised to consult legal counsel to devise appropriate documents for their centers.

Approvals:

Property Manager	Date
Leasing Representative	Date
Asset Manager	Date
Director of Leasing	Date
Director of Shopping Centers	Date
President (If Needed)	Date

Lease Reconciliation Approval

Asset Manager/Final Approval   Date

Attachments	
❐	Credit Analysis
❐	NPV
❐	Press Release

Exhibit D:

Sample Net Present Value (NPV) Analysis of Proposed Lease

PROPERTY:	DISCOUNT RATE:	10%
TENANT:	MONTHLY OR ANNUAL:	Annually

SUMMARY OF DEALPOINTS:	LEASING GUIDELINE	THIS PROPOSAL	APPRAISAL ASSUMPTIONS
TENANCY SIZE IN SQ. FT.			
LEASE TERM IN YEARS			
LEASE COMMENCEMENT DATE			
BASE RENTAL IN $/SQ. FT./YEAR:	Year 1		
	Year 2		
	Year 3		
	Year 4		
	Year 5		
FREE RENTAL IN MONTHS			
RECOVERABLE EXPENSES IN $/SQ. FT./YEAR 1			
RECOVERABLE EXPENSE INFLATOR			
EXPENSE STOP IN $/SQ. FT./YEAR			
TENANT CAPITAL ALLOWANCE IN $/SQ. FT.			
LEASE COMMISSION IN $/SQ. FT.			

DOLLAR AND PERCENT VARIANCE

NPV OF RENTAL INCOME

NPV OF CASH FLOW

CASH FLOW ANALYSIS PER LEASING GUIDELINE:

PERIOD	BASE RENTAL	FREE RENT	EXPENSE RECOVERY	CAPITAL	CASH FLOW
0					
1					
2					
3					
4					
5					
6					
7					
8					
9					
10					
11					
12					
13					
14					
15					

Comments

CASH FLOW ANALYSIS PER THIS PROPOSAL:

PERIOD	BASE RENTAL	FREE RENT	EXPENSE RECOVERY	CAPITAL	CASH FLOW
0					
1					
2					
3					
4					
5					
6					
7					
8					
9					
10					
11					
12					
13					
14					
15					

Comments:

Note: This is a sample only and is not to be construed as being endorsed or recommended by the author or the International Council of Shopping Centers. Readers are advised to consult legal counsel to devise appropriate documents for their centers.

4 Project Economics

John E. Phelan

During the infancy of the shopping center industry, the role of leasing was singularly focused on making deals. The role of the leasing representative was not only to fill space and generate rental income, but also to establish a tenant mix appropriate for the market and attempt to maximize the sales productivity of the center. As the shopping center concept evolved, the arts of selling space and defining a merchandise mix merged with the science of financial analysis and investment evaluation. The solid growth in income, predictable cash flows, and franchise characteristics of this type of property attracted huge inflow of capital from institutional investors and permanently changed the ownership structures of shopping centers. These institutions were not content to monitor their investments passively, but rather assumed an active role in asset management and, consequently, leasing decisions. More recently, leasing professionals have not been able simply to commit to a deal with a retailer and then seek approval from their corporate managers; instead, they have additionally been required to obtain consent from institutional partners.

The institutions' active engagement concerning property decisions have established the role of asset managers assigned to interact with shopping center professionals. These asset managers typically have a financial background and hence a deeper understanding of project economics than a leasing specialist. One of the foremost challenges facing leasing professionals is to gain a better understanding of the financial impact of their leasing decisions and to develop at least a working knowledge of the language of the financial institutions. As any true professional understands, the focus of the shopping center business is one founded upon long-term value enhancement. Although the impact of leasing decisions may have an immediate effect relative to the financial performance of the asset, the ultimate importance of leasing rests in the ability to position a center properly with a merchandise mix that will create value over the long term. Both the long-term enhancements and the short-term financial results often need to be balanced when reviewing a leasing deal. The goal of the leasing professional must be to defend leasing decisions regarding merchandise mix and tenant selection, with quantifiable results that the asset manager can understand. Consequently, part of the education process in training leasing professionals must be to instill a thorough understanding of the financial dynamics of property valuation and to relate everyday leasing decisions to the performance of the property as a whole.

Valuation Process

To initiate this learning process, it is important to discuss first how shopping center properties are valued.

INCOME PROJECTION

Real estate investors are primarily interested in purchasing the rights to a stream of future cash flows projected to be generated from rental income. The price an investor is willing to pay for a property is derived by analyzing the amount and timing of these anticipated cash flows. Of course, the degree of confidence applied to the future cash flows and the investor's tolerance for bearing risk are additional factors in the valuation analysis. Therefore, the investment value of real estate can be expressed as the present value of an anticipated income stream adjusted for differences in perceived risks relative to alternative investments. A more thorough discussion of risk adjustments and the mechanics of discounting for present value is presented later in this chapter. The first step in assessing the value of a shopping center is to complete a detailed projection of income over the long term.

An income projection will typically encompass the assumed length of the investment, which is referred to as the holding period. For a large-scale investment in commercial real estate, this holding period is usually ten years, but an additional year is projected to derive a selling price at the end of the investment horizon. A detailed example of an income projection can be found at the end of the chapter in Exhibit A: Regional Shopping Center Ten-Year Income Projection. When producing an income projection, certain assumptions must be made relative to sales performance, tenant retention, market rents, expanse growth, expense recoveries, and capital investments. Typically, an appraiser will use relatively conservative, realistic assumptions for growth that largely mirror the anticipated rate of inflation. Therefore, the most prudent course of action is to utilize the same growth rates for sales, market rents, and expenses. Often, especially in new developments, sales will grow a point or two faster than expenses in the first two or three years of a project, but after the center achieves maturity, the sales growth rate will decline to that of expenses.

After compiling all of the existing lease information, including assumptions regarding lease up of current vacancy, tenant retention, and re-leasing, you can obtain a projection of total income over the holding period. This should more accurately be referred to as total potential income, because it is typical to include a contingency factor or vacancy/loss reserve. The amount for contingencies depends on a number of factors, including historical performance, the number of current vacancies and lease expirations, and the creditworthiness of the tenant base. Usually, in a mature, stable center, the amount of loss reserve will range from 1.5 to 2.5 percent of total potential income. To arrive at net operating income (NOI), deduct expenses from the adjusted income. In this context, expenses include all common area expenses, real estate taxes, utilities, general and administrative expenses, and the management fee. Some expenses are often deemed capital expenses, including tenant allowances, leasing fees, and the legal costs associated with leasing transactions. These expenses do not affect the NOI of the property but are amortized on a straight-line basis over the term of the associated lease. Capital expenses result in a reduction of cash flow in the year incurred, but they do not affect the calculation of NOI or of funds from operations (FFO).

Net operating income is the most important determinant of value in a shopping center. A property's ability to manage debt is directly tied to net operating income, and it is NOI that is capped to arrive at an estimation of value. A more thorough explanation of capitalization rates follows later in this chapter. After establishing a realistic projection of income over the holding period, an analyst will have an array of operating incomes extending for 11 years. There are two components of value in an income-producing property. One consists of periodic returns to the investor in the form of income, and the other comprises the proceeds from an assumed sale of the property, commonly referred to as the residual. In estimating the investment value of a shopping center, these income streams—both the periodic income and the residual—are discounted to arrive at a present value.

DISCOUNT RATE
The discount rate is the rate of return on investment that a developer or purchaser finds attractive given the risks associated with the property. A discount rate is based on the assumption that investors must seek compensation for bearing risk, sacrificing liquidity, and forgoing the current use of capital. The presence of inflation in the general economy reduces purchasing power and must be factored into the discount rate. Consequently, the discount rate may be simply defined as a summation of the compensation rates for all these aforementioned factors. A significant portion of this compensation is readily priced in the form of U.S. Treasury instrument yields. Given the zero risk of default inherent in a U.S. Treasury issue, every other investment is compared to this risk-free, or safe, rate of return. The risk-free rate includes both an inflation premium and compensation to the investor for loss of the use of capital. Because real estate investments are typically long term and analyzed under the assumption of a ten-year holding period, the safe rate is correlated to like-maturity Treasury issues; thus, a shopping center's discount rate would be compared to a ten-year Treasury note. The difference between the two rates is referred to as the risk premium. A risk premium compensates the investor for inherent market risks, specific business risks, portfolio management costs, and loss of liquidity. This component is often referred to as the marginal cost of capital. The shopping center industry must compete with all other industries in the now global capital markets. If investments in other industries comparable to shopping centers are perceived as less risky, returns for retail real estate (in other words, discount rates) must increase to continue to attract capital; hence, values of shopping centers will correspondingly decrease.

Factors that influence perceptions of risk include competition, future prospects for retailing, and the liquidity of the investment. To illustrate the components of a discount rate, assume that a shopping center is valued using a discount rate of 11.5 percent. If the prevailing ten-year Treasury note yields 5.5 percent, that safe rate might imply a 3.5 percent inflation premium and a 2 percent real return. Subtracting the Treasury rate from the nominal discount rate leaves a 6 percent risk premium as the hurdle rate, available for other investments with the same degree of risk. A portion of this risk premium is attributed to the inherent risks of real estate and shopping centers as an investment class. The balance of the risk premium is property specific and often under the control of management. Because property value has an inverse relationship to the discount rate, professional property management can indeed affect the value of a center. Superior locations, strong anchors, solid sales performance, and a well-focused merchandise mix tend to enhance quality and reduce investment risk.

NET PRESENT VALUE

Once an income projection is established and a discount rate determined, the preliminary estimate of value is simply a mathematical exercise. The formula used for this purpose is expressed as follows:

$$PV = CF_1/(1+i) + CF_2/(1+i)^2 + CF_3/(1+i)^3 + CF_n/(1+i)^n$$

where CF is the net operating income, i is the discount rate, and n corresponds to the year. The following table illustrates the mechanics of this formula:

Year	NOI (in millions)	Discount Factor	PV (in millions)
1	$9,138.9	1.115	$8,196.3
2	$9,273.9	1.243	$7,459.6
3	$9,727.7	1.386	$7,017.6
4	$10,381.1	1.546	$6,716.5
5	$10,793.2	1.723	$6,262.9
6	$11,304.7	1.922	$5,883.1
7	$11,898.4	2.143	$5,553.5
8	$12,208.4	2.389	$5,110.5
9	$12,663.7	2.664	$4,754.3
10	$13,198.6	2.970	$4,444.1
			$61,398.3

The column labeled "Discount Factor" is derived from the denominator of the present value formula $[(1+i)^n]$. In this case, an 11.5 percent discount rate was determined to be appropriate for the underlying property. Present value of each income event is therefore the respective NOI divided by the corresponding discount factor, and total value is the summation of each year's discounted or present value income.

Recall, however, that there are two components of value for an income-producing property: annual income and the residual upon sale. The income projection establishes the annual returns to the property, but it also provides the basis for an estimation of the projected sales proceeds. Remember that although the holding period is assumed to be ten years, the income projection should include an eleventh year. For the purposes of evaluation, an assumption is made that the property will be sold at the close of the tenth year. When speculating about the terminal value, a capitalization rate is applied to the eleventh-year income to derive the price. The simple mathematical formula for capitalization rate is given below:

Cap Rate = Net Operating Income / Value

To solve for value, the inverse of the formula is used:

Value = Net Operating Income / Cap Rate

Using the eleventh-year NOI from Exhibit A ($13,767,900) and assuming a residual cap rate of 7.5 percent, one could realistically assume that the subject property would command a selling price of approximately $183,572,000 at the end of the investment. Normally a reduction is assumed for selling costs, in the range of 1.5 to 2.5 percent of the sales price. Allocating 1.5 percent of the sale ($2,753,000) to selling costs yields a net price of $180,819,000. Because the sale is expected to occur at the end of the tenth year, this figure must be discounted to present value. Using the table above, the discount factor corresponding to the tenth year is 2.97. Therefore, the present value of the residual would be approximately $60,881,820. Adding the residual to the present value of the income stream ($61,398,300) results in a property value of $122,280,120.

SENSITIVITY ANALYSIS

Calculating net present value provides a solid reference point for determining a property's value. Before rendering a final determination of value, a series of benchmarks is typically conducted to test the preliminary value estimate. Assume that the example property contains 300,000 square feet of gross leasable area (GLA) and is producing $400 per square foot in sales. Market rents for the center amount to $42 per square foot, with common area maintenance (CAM) and real estate taxes adding another $16 per square foot.

Because market rents are the most important assumptions in a property valuation, it is imperative that reasonable, sustainable figures are used when projecting income. Therefore, a burden ratio is calculated to validate initial estimations of market rent. In this case, $58 per square foot in total occupancy charges represents a 14.5 percent market occupancy cost to the tenants. In a strong center performing at $400 per square foot, this would be a tolerable figure and would serve to reinforce the market rent assumptions. From Exhibit A, it is found that current rental achievement from minimum and percentage rent is $9,792,000, or $32.64 per square foot for the 300,000 square feet of mall stores. A ratio of current rent ($32.64/sf) divided by market rent ($42) yields a result of 77.7 percent. Consequently, a portion of future income growth is achieved by rolling rents to market rather than relying on market rent growth. Because this is less risky than expectations of market growth, a low ratio is usually more desirable. A ratio greater than 100 percent connotes that the property is not meeting sales expectations and may have difficulty sustaining even current rents over the long term.

Another sensitivity test focuses on the growth of net operating income over the holding period. In this test, only the initial and final year of the projection are utilized. The appraiser determines what compound rate of growth is required for income to reach the expected level at the end of the projection. The result is compared to expectations of inflation and may engender a more detailed explanation of income growth. A similar test is conducted relative to the expected appreciation of the property—in this case, the rate of appreciation that is necessary to realize the anticipated terminal value. When compared to inflation, a large difference might raise another red flag, provoking a further inspection of the base assumptions.

As previously noted, property value is derived from returns comprising income and residual value. Because income is received periodically over the life of the investment and the residual is based solely on a single event far in the future, returns from income tend to be less risky. Another sensitivity test compares the percentage contribution from each component of value. Recall that the initial estimate of value resulted in a figure of $122,280,120. The previous table shows that $61,398,300 of present value is the result of net operating income over the life of the investment. Therefore, the remaining $60,881,820 is the assumed present value of the residual. Dividing each component by the total property value shows the respective contributions. In this example, 50.2 percent of total value is composed of income generated ($61,398,300/$122,280,120). Consequently, 49.8 percent of present value is based on the terminal value. Because expectations for the terminal value are inherently riskier, the appraiser will be wary if too much of the value is composed of residual proceeds. In such a case, one would be bound to reexamine the discount rate and increase it to compensate for this additional risk. A value much greater than 50 percent for the terminal value would indeed raise concerns. In a prudent investment analysis, the residual value should range from 40 to 50 percent of total property value.

Leveraging

With the overall valuation process completed, a value estimate for the property has been substantiated. Typically, equity investors in real estate will place debt on the property in an effort to leverage, or increase, their return. A mortgagee will exchange a lower rate of return on invested funds for the first claims to income of the property. The mortgagee will also expect a cushion ensuring that mortgage payments will continue even if income declines. Therefore, a lender will provide that initial income comply with an acceptable ratio, called the debt service coverage ratio. This ratio is calculated by dividing net operating income by the annual debt service payments. In the example, the property is subject to a $75,000,000 loan, which is amortized over 30 years at 7.5 percent interest. The debt service payment of $6,920,300 is then divided into the first year NOI of $9,138,900 for a debt service coverage ratio of 1.32. Simply, this means that the property generates $1.32 in income for every $1.00 in debt obligations.

With this level of safety, a lender is willing to take a lesser return (7.5%) than the property as a whole and thus shifts much of the risk to the equity position. Consequently, the equity investor will receive a higher rate of return if the property performs as projected. The subject property would require an equity investment of $47,250,000 and would yield a return on investment of 14.1 percent.

Internal Rate of Return

The term *internal rate of return* (IRR) is often used interchangeably with discount rate. In fact, the IRR is simply a subset of the discount rate. Discount rates and present value have been shown to exhibit an inverse relationship. As the discount rate decreases, the corresponding present value increases and eventually creates value in excess of the initial capital investment. At one point, there is a rate at which the present value of projected cash flows exactly equals the initial investment. The formula for this rate is:

$$0 = {}_{1}\Sigma^{n}[CF_n/(1+i)^n] - PV$$

where "n" is the years in the holding period, CF is the corresponding net operating income, and PV is the property value or development cost. In this equation, you are solving for "i," the IRR, and employ a trial-and-error method using successive increments in the rate. As a practical matter, if a project produces an IRR that equals or exceeds the investor's minimum acceptable rate of return, or hurdle rate, that project would warrant further investigation. Projects falling short of that hurdle rate would require a reexamination of the assumptions or a repricing.

The example property has a simple capital structure consisting of a debt holder and an equity investor. In this center, the mortgagee's internal rate of return would be 7.5 percent on a $75,000,000 investment while the equity owner would receive an IRR of 14.1 percent on a $47,250,000 investment. Remember that the property's overall IRR or discount rate was 11.5 percent. An owner's substantially higher IRR arises from a willingness to shoulder a disproportionate share of the property risk.

Capitalization Rates

The relationship between net operating income and property value is typically expressed as a percentage called the capitalization rate (often referred to as cap rate). Mathematically, the formula is very simple:

$$\text{Cap Rate} = \text{NOI} / \text{Value}$$

Capitalization rates are often defined as the going-in yield, meaning the initial rate of return assuming a cash purchase. These rates are determined by the overall investment market and will change with the cost of capital or the investor's perceptions of risk. When properties are traded in the market, cap rates are often quoted as common denominators for comparison purposes. Arraying cap rates with property transactions can lead to a better understanding of market perceptions of value.

As previously noted, the capitalization rate formula is also used in determining a terminal value of the investment. A knowledge of current market cap rates is essential when making projections of the residual or exit cap rate. To hedge against error in this exercise, an analyst may add perhaps 50 basis points to existing market cap rates in estimating an exit cap. Residual cap rates tend to mirror initial cap rates in periods of industry and national economic stability. Just past cyclical bottoms in the market, there may be times when cap rate compression is anticipated and exit caps will actually be lower than initial caps. Markets with this characteristic can present substantial opportunity for investors willing to bear the additional risk.

Economics of Development

Investment decisions regarding new developments present a greater set of challenges relative to the valuation of existing property. Obviously, without historical income data or even executed leases, there is more inherent risk in the income projection of a new development. Additional risks include zoning issues, project timing, and the construction budget. Many developments may also incur financing risks, especially if long-term debt is not secured in advance. Developers assume these risks and have a reasonable expectation of significant returns as a consequence.

Exhibit B (Development Project Valuation Analysis) details a valuation analysis similar to that of an existing property, but it clearly shows the significantly better returns that the developer enjoys in a successful project. In this example, development costs are projected to be $120,000,000, and the project is expected to generate $12,500,000 in NOI when stabilized. In a prudent development analysis, the initial NOI after completion might be projected at only 80 percent of stabilized due to lease up and tenant construction. The subject project reaches full stabilization in the third year, and thereafter income is grown at 3 percent. When estimating a residual cap rate, remember that the property will have matured and should trade at rates comparable to those of established centers of similar quality. The result of the analysis is an anticipated internal rate of return of 13.4 percent, which is considerably higher than that in the example of the existing property. Again, the reason for this disparity is the increased risks associated with a new development.

Using traditional debt leveraging, the developer can further increase returns. In the sample project, assume that permanent financing will be arranged that covers 75 percent of development costs and will carry an 8.0 percent interest rate. Consequently, the developer will be required to invest $30,000,000 in the project and will receive a leveraged IRR of 23.8 percent. The debt service coverage ratio is projected to be 1.38 in the initial year after completion and will rise to 1.74 when the property stabilizes in year three. These are conservative ratios and perhaps indicate a potential to place more debt on the property when operating stability is reached.

Hence, the completed value of a successful development project should be substantially greater than its construction costs. Essentially, this increase is the creation of value attributed to the vision of the developer, and it is referred to as the developer's premium. To illustrate the concept of the developer's premium, refer to the project example. The pro forma details a stabilized NOI of $12,500,000 against development costs of $120,000,000. The going-in yield, or initial cap rate, for the project would be 10.42 percent. This rate is obviously high due to the risks associated with leasing and development costs. But when the project is completed and reaches operating stability, these risks are no longer present. The cap rate on the project then would contract to reflect reduced risks, and the property's value would rise accordingly. If other properties of a similar quality were trading at a 7.5 percent cap rate, it is reasonable to assume that the subject center would command a cap rate of perhaps 8.25 percent. Even after completion, a new development will not completely eliminate the disparity in cap rates, because all leases will be new and conceivably at market rent rates.

Still, an 8.25 percent cap rate stipulates a completed value of $151,500,000. If the development were to sell at that price, the developer would receive in excess of $60,000,000 for the original investment. The buyer of the center could execute the purchase with an assumption of the existing debt and still expect approximately a 12 percent return on investment. Another option to the developer might be to continue to hold the property and attempt to refinance and recover most of the original investment, thus freeing capital for further development activities. This has often been referred to as mortgaging out of the investment.

Market Rent

Leasing assumes a very crucial role in the project economics of a development. Establishing realistic targets for market rents in each space is an essential exercise that must be undertaken for every property or proposed development. In existing properties with a sales history, this process is often easier and more accurate than in new developments. All rents should be viewed as a reasonable, sustainable percentage of sales that affords the tenant an opportunity to generate an attractive return. For the purposes of this exercise, the term *rent* should be defined as occupancy costs, including minimum rent, common area maintenance charges, real estate taxes, and any tenant contributions to marketing the property.

In a regional center, total occupancy costs as defined above typically range from 10 percent to 15 percent of the center's sales productivity. One might argue that the stated range is relatively wide, and why would the leasing agent not simply choose the highest percentage in the range to maximize rents? The center's performance is what drives demand and therefore the rental burdens that tenants are willing to assume. In more productive centers, performing at perhaps $400 per square foot, tenants feel far more comfortable with their sales projections and will pay for that added predictability. Also, in higher-volume centers, leasehold improvements and other fixed expenses that are not a function of sales are generally less of a percentage; even variable costs such as labor can be more efficiently utilized than in less productive centers. Consequently, not only does the more productive center enjoy higher nominal rents, but also it can command a higher percentage of total occupancy costs. This fact certainly reinforces the ultimate leasing objective of driving sales to their highest levels. The simple example that follows illustrates the rather dramatic effect that sales productivity can have on minimum rents:

Shopping Center	X	Y
Sales Productivity	$300	$400
Occupancy Costs/Sales	12%	14%
Gross Market Rent	$36	$56
CAM, Taxes, Marketing	$12	$16
Net Market Rent	$24	$40

In the table, lower demand and higher fixed costs as a percentage of sales drive market occupancy costs down. Assuming ancillary charges of 4 percent of sales in both centers, a retailer negotiating a lease for property X would likely accept a 12 percent total occupancy cost. Net rent to the landlord is this instance would be $24 per square foot. Given the efficiency of higher-volume stores, the retailer would agree not only to a higher nominal rent in property Y but also to a higher-percentage occupancy cost. This would yield a far higher net return to the developer, largely explaining the premium placed on high-volume properties.

When determining market rents for the pro forma, a space-by-space analysis is the only judicious approach. Each space in a center has unique characteristics that affect its appeal to tenants, and those characteristics have a great impact on the corresponding market rent. Elements that need to be considered include:

- Size of space
- Proximity to anchors
- Proximity to entrances and traffic flow
- Linear footage of storefront
- Configuration of premises
- Proposed use of premises.

When considering market rents for a center, a general idea of the desired tenant mix is necessary. Often the fashion focus or price point orientation of the center will greatly affect market rents. Also, the average store size or uniformity in size ranges will affect the level of achievable market rents. Therefore, the only fiscally prudent method of estimating potential rent levels is the performance of a space-specific analysis.

Breakeven Rents

Market rents are often inaccurately labeled as the level necessary to produce a desired return on the investment or to cover development costs. The inaccuracy in this thinking stems from attributing the level of market rents to the unit costs of the project. In practice, sales potential, and consequently the balance of supply and demand, is the only determinant of market rent. This is not to say that a rent sensitivity analysis is useless in determining project feasibility. During the conceptual phase of a development, a breakeven rent level must be established and later compared to a market rent estimate based on an independently researched sales potential. In an acquisition analysis, an identical exercise is undertaken to validate the offering price. In an established project, obviously, historical sales data supplant estimated sales potential.

The formulas for determining breakeven rents are as follows:

Development Cost × (1 − Loan/Value Ratio) = Equity Capital
Equity Capital × Hurdle Rate = Equity Cash Flow
Equity Cash Flow + Debt Service = Net Operating Income
Net Operating Income / (1 − Vacancy Reserve) = Required Gross Income
Required Gross Income / Gross Leasable Area = Breakeven Rent per Square Foot

Please note that the above series of formulas incorporate the only most basic assumptions of a feasibility analysis. Net recoveries of property expenses are assumed to be zero, percentage rent is overlooked as a factor, and the impact of tax considerations is disregarded. Nevertheless, the exercise produces a solid estimate of the amount of minimum rent needed to produce a viable development project or substantiate a property acquisition.

Rental Feasibility Analysis

Once the breakeven rent level is established, a comparison to market rent estimates is made. If market rents are projected to be higher than the breakeven level, there will be a greater level of comfort in the project overall. In the reverse case, when breakeven rents exceed anticipated market rent, the cost of the project or capital structure may need to be reevaluated. Possibly the inherent risks of the project will be reevaluated, causing an adjustment in the anticipated internal rate of return.

The following example illustrates the use of the breakeven rent formulas in a rental feasibility analysis. The assumptions used in this example are as follows:

- 15% return (IRR) to the equity partner
- 9% debt service constant
- 5% reserve for vacancy and credit loss
- 70% loan to value ratio.

Perhaps most important, it is assumed that an independent study based on a space-by-space analysis of the actual lease plan has determined a market rent level of $35 per square foot. This figure represents a weighted average of the rent targets for each space in the property and is supported solely by realistic sales projections.

Breakeven Rent Analysis		
Development Cost	$100,000,000	
Permanent Financing		$70,000,000
Equity Capital		$30,000,000
Equity Cash Flow	15.0%	$4,500,000
Debt Service	9.0%	$6,300,000
Required Net Operating Income		$10,800,000
Vacancy Reserve	5.0%	
Required Gross Income		$11,368,421
[NOI / (1 - Vacancy Reserve)]		
Gross Leasable Area	350,000	
Breakeven Rent		$32.48
Market Rent		$35.00

The example establishes that a base minimum rent of approximately $32.48 per square foot is necessary at a stabilized occupancy level for the project to achieve the developer's hurdle rate for equity while continuing to service the property's debt. A separate estimate of market rent for the project concludes that a $35-per-square-foot level is reasonable and will be supported by sales. The positive spread in market to breakeven rents in this example provides a strong contingency against inherent leasing and development risks. If the development is completed on budget and the leasing pro forma is achieved at a $35-per-square-foot market, the developer will enjoy returns far higher than initially anticipated. The developer's position will also be compounded by the leveraged position behind the 70 percent financing.

The parallel procedures of determining breakeven rent and market rent form the basis of the leasing pro forma. Incorporation of a tenant allowance budget into the pro forma completes the financial blueprint of the property relative to the leasing effort. Each proposed leasing transaction will now be measured against this blueprint to determine how the deal affects the property from a financial perspective.

Every leasing strategy must balance the often conflicting goals of improving tenant mix and achieving financial results. The level of financial sophistication in the business today requires that leasing professionals understand how value is created and maintained in the shopping center. Leasing professionals must also comprehend the financial impact that their decisions have on the investment performance of the asset.

John E. Phelan is Executive Vice President at New England Development, Newton, Massachusetts.

Exhibit A
Regional Shopping Center
Ten-Year Income Projection

	1	2	3	4	5	6	7	8	9	10	11
Minimum Rent	$8,937.5	$9,012.2	$9,455.7	$10,137.5	$10,555.3	$11,023.5	$11,760.5	$12,014.3	$12,457.9	$12,978.0	$13,655.3
Percentage Rent	$854.5	$925.2	$967.7	$985.9	$1,009.7	$1,089.7	$988.8	$1,067.8	$1,112.3	$1,165.7	$1,098.7
Recoveries	$4,062.4	$4,265.5	$4,478.8	$4,702.7	$4,937.9	$5,184.8	$5,444.0	$5,716.2	$6,002.0	$6,302.1	$6,617.2
Other Income	$450.0	$472.5	$496.1	$520.9	$547.3	$574.3	$603.0	$633.2	$664.9	$698.1	$733.0
Total Potential Income	$14,304.4	$14,675.4	$15,398.3	$16,347.0	$17,049.9	$17,872.3	$18,796.3	$19,431.5	$20,237.1	$21,143.9	$22,104.2
Vacancy/Loss Reserve	$214.6	$220.1	$231.0	$245.2	$255.7	$268.1	$281.9	$291.5	$303.6	$317.2	$331.6
Common Area	$2,681.3	$2,815.4	$2,956.1	$3,103.9	$3,259.1	$3,422.1	$3,593.2	$3,772.9	$3,961.5	$4,159.6	$4,367.6
Real Estate Taxes	$1,365.0	$1,433.3	$1,504.9	$1,580.2	$1,659.2	$1,742.1	$1,829.2	$1,920.7	$2,016.7	$2,117.6	$2,223.4
General & Administrative	$415.0	$435.8	$457.5	$480.4	$504.4	$529.7	$556.1	$583.9	$613.1	$643.8	$676.0
Management Fee	$489.6	$496.9	$521.2	$556.2	$578.3	$605.7	$637.5	$654.1	$678.5	$707.2	$737.7
Total Expenses	$4,950.9	$5,181.4	$5,439.7	$5,720.7	$6,001.0	$6,299.6	$6,616.0	$6,931.6	$7,269.8	$7,628.2	$8,004.7
Net Operating Income	$9,138.9	$9,273.9	$9,727.7	$10,381.1	$10,793.2	$11,304.7	$11,898.4	$12,208.4	$12,663.7	$13,198.6	$13,767.9
Debt Service	$6,920.3	$6,920.3	$6,920.3	$6,920.3	$6,920.3	$6,920.3	$6,920.3	$6,920.3	$6,920.3	$6,920.3	$6,920.3
Tenant Allowances	$300.0	$225.0	$275.0	$325.0	$350.0	$500.0	$275.0	$325.0	$300.0	$300.0	$300.0
Capital Improvements	$150.0	$157.5	$165.4	$173.6	$182.3	$191.4	$201.0	$211.1	$221.6	$232.7	$244.3
Total	$7,370.3	$7,302.8	$7,360.7	$7,418.9	$7,452.6	$7,611.7	$7,396.3	$7,456.4	$7,441.9	$7,453.0	$7,464.6
Cash Flow	$1,768.6	$1,971.1	$2,367.0	$2,962.2	$3,340.6	$3,692.9	$4,502.1	$4,752.1	$5,221.8	$5,745.6	$6,303.3
Debt Service Coverage	1.32	1.34	1.41	1.50	1.56	1.63	1.72	1.76	1.83	1.91	1.99

78 ■ SHOPPING CENTER LEASING

Exhibit B
Development Project Valuation Analysis

	1	2	3	4	5	6	7	8	9	10	11
Developments Costs	($120,000.0)										
Income Pro Forma		$10,000.0	$11,250.0	$12,500.0	$12,875.0	$13,261.3	$13,659.1	$14,068.9	$14,490.9	$14,925.7	$15,373.4	$15,834.6
Residual at 8.5%											$186,289.72	
Selling Costs at 1.5%											$2,794.35	
Total	($120,000.0)	$10,000.0	$11,250.0	$12,500.0	$12,875.0	$13,261.3	$13,659.1	$14,068.9	$14,490.9	$14,925.7	$198,868.8	
Internal Rate of Return	13.4%											
Leveraged Returns												
Debt Service at 8.0%	($90,000.0)	$7,200.0	$7,200.0	$7,200.0	$7,200.0	$7,200.0	$7,200.0	$7,200.0	$7,200.0	$7,200.0	$97,200.0	
Developer's Position	($30,000.0)	$2,800.0	$4,050.0	$5,300.0	$5,675.0	$6,061.3	$6,459.1	$6,868.9	$7,290.9	$7,725.7	$101,668.8	
Developer IRR	23.8%											

5 | Prospecting for Tenants

Sherry A. Koetting, CLS/SCSM/SCMD

A shopping center is a group of retail and other commercial establishments that is planned, developed, owned, and managed as a single property. The center's size and orientation are generally determined by the market characteristics of the trade area that the center serves (*Research Quarterly,* International Council of Shopping Centers "Shopping Center Definitions"). As defined by the Random House Dictionary, a shopping center is "a group of stores within a single architectural plan, supplying most of the basic shopping needs." This sounds simple, but the task of designing, building, and leasing a shopping center to meet the needs of its market is not a simple one. This chapter covers the essential factors involved in successfully marketing and leasing a project, including:

- Analyzing the market
- Finding and identifying the prospects
- Preparing for negotiations
- Making contact with tenants
- Negotiating the deal.

Prospecting for tenants is not just filling space. Each lease that is signed needs to fill a consumer merchandise requirement and fulfill the long-term results of the owner. Each owner and project has very different goals and objectives and requires different approaches. By taking the five steps outlined in this chapter, the leasing representative will have some of the tools and information needed to successfully lease a project and create maximum value for the owner.

Analyzing the Market

The first step in working on any type of retail project is to have a thorough understanding of the market area it serves. A leasing representative must have a thorough understanding of market research data before beginning the leasing process. (Refer to Chapter 2 on "Using Market Research to Lease a Center" for a more thorough discussion on using market research.) Key information about the primary and secondary markets includes the following basic demographics:

- Average age and distribution for each age group. Numbers and percentage of age distribution are of major importance in obtaining retailers who sell directly to a particular age category, such as children's apparel or maternity.
- Average household income and projected changes by income categories. This is a key indicator of disposable income, and most retailers market to a specific income level.
- Occupation breakdowns by percentage in each field, compared to regional and national averages. Who are the major employers, and does this affect customers' buying habits? Is there dominance by a single company or a single industry?
- Ethnic and racial composition of the market and projected changes.
- Regional and cultural differences for the market area that affect shopping habits.
- Home ownership as compared to rental housing. Cost of housing is an indicator of relative affluence and availability of disposable income. Number of owners versus renters is an important consideration for many retailers, especially those dealing in housewares, home furnishings, home improvements, and the like.
- Psychological profile of the area. Is the population base older, more affluent, and more interested in quality than in trends? Or is the population base largely composed of younger people who are starting out and focusing on basic needs?

Once the leasing professional has a thorough understanding of the market characteristics, these should be compared to those of the competition. Identifying a project's strengths and weaknesses will greatly enhance the success of all leasing efforts. When comparing your center to the competition, analyze the following information:

- What are the demographics for the primary and secondary market, such as average age, household income, and total population base, of the competition?
- What are the psychographics of the competition's markets: white collar versus blue collar, young versus retirement age, higher education, and so on?
- Location: Does the competition have better or less desirable access and visibility?
- Tenant mix: Does the competition have a hold on a certain mix you are trying to achieve? Is the competition high end, and can the market support only one high-end center? Does the competition control another niche, such as grocery anchored, power center, or outlet? How will this affect your leasing efforts?
- What is the size and gross leasable area (GLA) of the competition?

For every project, it is necessary to identify the strengths that will make it successful. If you do not have the elements needed for the retailers to be successful, you will be losing a considerable amount of time contacting prospective tenants who are not right for the property. (See Exhibit A: Trade Area Market Support Factors at the end of the chapter.)

Understanding and evaluating your center and site plan are also basic to the leasing effort. A leasing representative should know the following information:

- Traffic patterns for the major streets surrounding the property and how they affect ingress and egress for the center. Is it difficult or easy to enter and exit the center?
- Where are the major parking fields, and what is the parking ratio versus code? Parking considerations are a key business point for leasing to certain categories of retailers.
- Are pad sites available? Where are they? What is the size of each? What kind of access to utilities is there?
- What are the sight lines to the property from freeways and major arteries? For a strip center, visibility from the street is a critical factor. Are there any visibility issues related to center walkways, corridors, setbacks, amenities, and so on?

- How do you rank the entrances to the property? What types of retailers would be most likely to lease these types of locations?
- What are the traffic counts for major streets surrounding your site? What are the people counts or car counts for existing centers?
- Are there any proposed improvements to your site or the area surrounding your project? What are the positive and negative effects of these improvements?

Once the leasing professional and the leasing team has determined its market and your site, it is necessary to develop a merchandising plan for the project. A detailed plan should include a space-by-space leasing schedule with expiration dates (in the case of existing centers), pro forma base rents, percentage rent factors, extra charges, projected merchandise categories for the planned tenant mix, and any capital costs for tenant allowances or space renovations. A leasing representative should thoroughly understand this leasing/merchandising plan.

Additional information to consider includes understanding how the center has been laid out to optimize the leasing. Be prepared to answer questions regarding the visibility of the space, size, frontage, location in the center relative to department stores and amenities, traffic patterns, access for deliveries, access to utilities, and so on. For example, does your center have a central plant or rooftop heating, ventilating, and air-conditioning (HVAC) units? A professional will know the answers.

Finding and Identifying the Prospects

Now you have a keen understanding of all of the data outlined above, but where do you go from here? Prospective retailers for your projects are all around you. The task before you is to develop a system for identifying retailers, keeping track of information gathered, and devising an organized plan for contacting prospective tenants and moving forward to negotiations.

CANVASS THE COMPETITION
The logical place to begin a search is to identify retailers already doing business in your center's market. Visit all of the retail sites and develop a list of these tenants. As you tour the competition, talk to

sales clerks and store managers to gather facts about sales levels, merchandise mix, price points, current locations, and expansion plans. Ask the retailers you talk to about other concepts they might recommend. People in the business are normally the ones who will be most informed about their own industry. Be sure to collect directories, retailer's brochures, and advertising materials for the centers and the retailers. Do not limit yourself only to centers perceived as being successful; visit those projects that may be in a down cycle. If you find tenants doing business in a less desirable location, they may be looking for a new site.

After site visits and touring the competition, develop a competitive environment analysis. On one page, include the name, location, owner and manager of any centers within your center's market. Indicate the distance or direction from your center. Include the year the center opened, its anchors, and the gross square footage of each.

When prospecting for existing tenants in the center's market, gather as much information as possible to determine if each particular tenant is the right fit for your project. The following checklist will be a helpful tool in the evaluation:

1. MERCHANDISE
- Labels (branded/unbranded)
- Fabrics (natural fiber, polyester)
- Depth of category: narrow or deep
- Age of merchandise, in season or out of season
- Determine the target customer
- What do they carry that their competition does not?
- Price points.

2. DISPLAY
- Do the windows tell a story that is carried throughout the store?
- How are displays facing the window used?
- Are displays accessorized to produce multiple sales?
- Where are sale items found?
- How do they display size and price?
- Signs: professional, unobtrusive?
- Use of display materials
- Any negative signs (for instance, "No Eating Allowed")

3. STORE DESIGN
- Windows
- Lease line
- Relation of wrap desk to customers
- How many dressing rooms, and type (individual or gymnasium)
- Ceiling treatment (2 × 4 vs. 2 × 2 grid)
- Lighting (use of spots, fluorescent)
- Traffic pattern through store
- Colors (warm or cold)
- Music
- Size of store.

4. HOUSEKEEPING
- Condition of surfaces that wear out (carpet, wrap desk, lights) with the age of the store
- Exterior sign
- Clutter behind wrap desk
- Dust in the windows
- Holes in merchandise categories.

5. PERSONNEL
- Enough floor coverage
- Knowledgeable about merchandise
- Relate well with customers
- Proper training to close the sale.

BROKERAGE COMMUNITY

The brokerage community is another valuable source for new and expanding retailers. Determine what the center's company policy is regarding payment of brokerage fees. Depending on the type of center, these fees may be paid by the landlord, the tenant, or both. Networking with the brokerage community can result in tenants that are new to the market opening in your project first. There are several national firms that represent retailers. In addition, networks have been set up across the country by independent brokerage firms to work in conjunction with one another to expand retailers nationwide.

TRADE SHOWS AND PUBLICATIONS

New retail concepts are being developed daily and can be identified at a variety of trade shows:

Specialty tenant or temporary tenant conventions: Retailers with new concepts to be tested attend and display their merchandise at shopping center industry specialty tenant conventions in an effort to test the products before committing to in-line long-term leases.

Wholesale trade shows by various industries, such as the apparel, toy, gift, electronic, and restaurant associations, offer vendors an opportunity to display merchandise that they sell directly to the retailers or in their own retail outlets. These shows sometimes provide retail leads as well as valuable information on new concepts and emerging merchandise trends. Every merchandise category has its own trade show where vendors and retailers meet. Many of these industries publish trade magazines or newsletters and can offer valuable leads to new retail concepts.

Franchise shows: This type of trade show includes displays and representatives from companies offering franchise concepts to the public for investment and operating opportunities.

Flea markets, state fairs, and open air markets often provide local manufacturers with outlets for their products. You never know when you will spot an emerging trend at this type of market.

Local trade shows featuring a certain category of merchandise such as home improvement or lawn and garden will identify local retailers in these respective areas. Talking to manufacturer's representatives at such shows may lead to possible retailers for your center.

Fixture manufacturers and retail design shows: The trades in this industry present shows attended by architects and retail store designers to get ideas and purchase products for new locations. Such vendors often provide information on retailers who are expanding.

International Council of Shopping Center events: ICSC hosts regional and national deal-making sessions. Usually held in conjunction with "idea exchange" programs, these sessions bring together local retailers attending for educational reasons as well as local, regional, and national tenants looking to expand.

ADVERTISING AND PUBLICITY

Leasing representatives sometimes overlook the power of the local and/or national media when looking for prospects. Place a focus on advertising the new project or the landlord's total portfolio. Press releases with information on the development or on new retailers opening in a center may prompt a retailer to call.

ON-PROPERTY ADVERTISING

Advertising for tenants can be as simple as placing a "for lease" sign on the property or in the center. Networking existing tenants is often overlooked as a source of good leads. Talk with existing center merchants. They may recommend other retailers. If your center publishes a newsletter, include requests for recommendations.

When interested retailers contact the office, pertinent information should be taken with the assurance to the prospective tenant that a leasing representative will follow-up on the inquiry. Each leasing representative and center manager should utilize a leasing inquiry form to record interest from potential tenants at the mall. The form should be used for screening as well as follow-up purposes. Include as much information as you deem necessary to reasonably track leasing opportunities.

Each center manager should also maintain a system for monitoring leasing discussions. A diary format is recommended, with handwritten notes by each person holding discussions or negotiations with a prospective tenant.

If a discussion or negotiation results in a signed lease, this form should be included in the lease file for future reference. Even if it does not lead to a lease, the form can be kept for future reference and follow-up. Examples of forms and follow-up letters are included as exhibits to this chapter. (See Exhibit B, C, D, E, and F.)

CATALOGS

Catalogs have become so numerous and category specific that you can now find catalogs of catalogs. Do not overlook the retailer who is currently doing business only by catalog. It may be testing a line of merchandise before committing to permanent retail outlets. In addition, certain retailers may have a nationwide catalog distribution but retail stores only in some parts of the country. Catalogs will normally include a list of any retail sites.

THE INTERNET

The Internet is changing the retail business in a variety of ways. A tenant may be operating by catalog, Internet, and retail site, or it may be only on the Internet to test a product line. If you are searching for a certain category of retailer, check to see if there are any possible start-up retailers on the Internet. Check general business sites on a regular basis and search for retail news articles.

THE MEDIA: PRINT AND BROADCAST

With the expansion of basic broadcast media to include specialized stations in both radio and television, there is naturally an expanded list of retail concepts advertising and being featured in these media. Consumer publications are also becoming more and more fragmented, again featuring a wealth of information on merchandise trends and retail concepts. And, of course, do not forget to canvass the home shopping channels for retailers or merchandise that may not be offered in your area.

Separating the Prospects

Now that you have gathered a long list of potential prospects, how do you organize all of this information in a meaningful manner? First, divide all retailer prospects into the industry standard categories listed below and note whether each is a local, regional, or national retailer:

1. GAFO (General merchandise, Apparel, Furniture/home furnishings, and Other types of similar merchandise) categories:
   - Women's ready-to-wear
   - Women's accessories and specialties
   - Men's apparel
   - Children's apparel
   - Family apparel
   - Women's shoes
   - Men's shoes
   - Family/miscellaneous shoes
   - Apparel and accessories (miscellaneous)
   - Home furniture and furnishings
   - Home entertainment and electronics
   - Stationery, cards, gifts, novelties
   - Books
   - Sporting goods/bicycles
   - Jewelry
   - Other GAFO (miscellaneous)

2. Non-GAFO categories:
- Fast food
- Restaurants
- Food services (miscellaneous)
- Specialty food stores
- Supermarkets
- Drugstores
- Personal services
- Automotive
- Home improvement
- Entertainment
- Other non-GAFO (miscellaneous)

Further subdivide each category by specialties within each respective area. Some examples include: Women's ready-to-wear includes junior, career, misses, better, bridge, special sizes, popular price, off-price/promotional, and couture. The jewelry category includes credit, guild, costume, and custom. Your list is now organized in a manner that allows you to quickly identify prospects to fill the needs of your merchandise plan.

Preparing for Negotiations

Negotiations between the landlord's representative and prospective tenant will vary in content and style depending on the project and each respective situation. There are basic tools and information, however, that every leasing representative needs.

- Lease plan is a detailed leasing plan or merchandise plan with pro forma rents and other economic factors
- Printed lease plan with spaces, dimensions, common areas, and ingress and egress indicated
- Site plan, detailing major roadways, anchors, the center, pad sites, ring roads, and so on
- Leasing brochure detailing the information pertinent to this center, including renderings for new projects and photographs for existing ones
- Demographic package, with details of the customer profile for the project
- Construction criteria, including a package of information that the project architect develops for a retailer to follow in the preparation of plans and construction of the store; it also details the landlord's and tenant's work

- Lease form is a standard lease form to be used at the center, developing a list of all lease points that need to be covered up front in the deal negotiation
- Extra charges include a list of such things as common area maintenance (CAM), real estate taxes, insurance, marketing, trash, and utilities
- Presentation package typically includes maps of the trade area, pictures of the property, renderings of new construction or proposed renovations, sales projections, and other information pertinent to the success of the center.

Following are nine other important details to keep in mind when leasing a new or existing project:

NEW PROJECT	EXISTING PROJECT
(1) Preliminary demographic profile of trade area	Actual demographic profile for the primary and secondary market areas, supported by shopper intercept surveys
(2) Aerial map of proposed site	Aerial photograph of center
(3) Proposed lease and site plan	Actual lease and site plan, with tenant list
(4) Merchandise and/or proposed tenant mix	Existing tenant list and merchandise mix, with any proposed changes such as upgrading in price points of mix
(5) Artist renderings of proposed center	Photographs of center; renderings of any proposed renovations
(6) Targeted sales projections and targeted market share	Preparation to discuss actual sales for the center, trends by category, and captured market share
(7) Proposed extra charges	Actual charges for pass-throughs. Trends for utility charges
(8) Construction criteria manual	Construction criteria manual with sample photographs of existing retailers
(9) Proposed opening occupancy levels	Actual occupancy and leasing objective(s) for the coming year

Making Contact with Tenants

Lists and more lists are a basic tool for a leasing representative. Begin with a list of the key tenants for a center showing which retailers take longer to build out a store and open. For example, anchor tenants require considerable lead time (12 to 18 months), and restaurants may take 4 to 6 months to build. If a certain retailer is key to the needs of your center, then this deal should be on your list of tenants to contact first. Next, take your categories and identify a specific list of retailers to contact that fit the remaining needs of your project.

Tenants may be contacted in a variety of ways. The most common methods are cold calls, direct mail, telephone, and now e-mail. Depending on your own personal style, you may feel comfortable with the direct approach of telephoning, or you may want to contact by mail or e-mail first and then follow up by telephoning. Initial contact may also be made at regional and national International Council of Shopping Centers (ICSC) deal-making events. Above all, be prepared in your initial contact with the tenant. Know as much as you can about the prospective retailer and what you hope to accomplish. Know everything you can gather regarding the specific retailer, merchandise category, and retailing in general. To be considered a professional, a leasing representative needs to be able to talk to a tenant in that person's language.

Negotiating the Deal

You have made contact and explained the project, and the tenant is ready for a proposal letter. The proposal letter should always include the following:

- Proposed location in the project, size, and dimensions
- Minimum base rent
- Percentage rent
- Proposed use clause with any restrictions
- Delivery of possession
- Time allowed for construction
- Extra charges
- Construction allowance or landlord's work versus an as-is deal
- Legal entity
- Contact person with address, phone, fax, and e-mail information.

Three samples of a proposal letter and intent to lease are included as exhibits at the end of this chapter (see Exhibits B, C, D). Although it can take considerable research and information gathering to get this prospect to the negotiation table, you will be prepared to move forward with the negotiations by sending the proposal letter.

Negotiating economics of the deal itself, including negotiating techniques, is discussed in Chapter 4 on Project Economics and in Chapter 6 on Selling and Negotiating Techniques. Refer to the previous and the following chapters for a full discussion.

The final step in the leasing process is to submit the deal to the landlord or appropriate committee. The leasing process began by identifying a tenant that should fill a merchandise need for the center. This prospective retailer was contacted and all of the strengths of the center were explained. The tenant and leasing agent then negotiated economics for a specific location, after which both parties were prepared to negotiate a lease for the center.

To move the negotiations to the document stage, a leasing agent needs to prepare the following information for presentation:

- Financial statement for the tenant
- History of the retailer
- Photographs of existing locations
- Sales in other locations
- Outline of deal economics
- Lease request form or commitment letter
- Agreed-on use clause language
- Other deal points required by your company.

When the final presentation is finished, forward the deal for approval.

The process of prospecting for tenants involves different dynamics depending on the type of project, but the basic steps are the same: Know your market, your competition, and your center; canvass the retailer arena for prospective tenants; thoroughly prepare for negotiations; contact the desired merchants; and negotiate the deal. The end result should be a win-win situation, with the retailer and developer producing a successful project.

Sherry A. Koetting, CLS/SCSM/SCMD, is Senior Vice President, Leasing at Coyote Management, L.P., Addison, Texas.

Exhibit A: TRADE AREA MARKET SUPPORT FACTORS

POPULATION
- 1990 CENSUS*
- 1996 ESTIMATE
- 2001 PROJECTION
- ANNUAL CHANGE 1990–1996
- ANNUAL CHANGE 1996–2001

HOUSEHOLDS
- 1990 CENSUS
- 1996 ESTIMATE
- 2001 PROJECTION
- ANNUAL CHANGE 1990-1996
- ANNUAL CHANGE 1996-2001

AVERAGE HOUSEHOLD INCOME (PERCENTAGES)
- 1990 CENSUS (1989 actual)
- 1996 ESTIMATE
- 2001 PROJECTION
- ANNUAL CHANGE 1990–1996
- ANNUAL CHANGE 1996–2001

1996 HOUSEHOLD INCOME DISTRIBUTION
- $100,000 +
- $75,000 − $99,999
- $50,000 − $74,999
- $35,000 − $49,999
- $25,000 − $34,999
- $15,000 − $24,999
- <$15,000

SHOPPERS GOODS EXPENDITURE POTENTIAL ($MILLIONS)
- 1990 CENSUS
- 1996 ESTIMATE
- 2001 PROJECTION
- ANNUAL CHANGE 1990–1996
- ANNUAL CHANGE 1996–2001

CONSTANT 1996 DOLLARS
- 1990 CENSUS
- 2001 PROJECTION
- ANNUAL CHANGE 1990–1996
- ANNUAL CHANGE 1996–2001

---

*Dates can be updated after the 2000 Census for forthcoming years.

Exhibit B: SAMPLE PROPOSAL FORM

LEASE PROPOSAL

TRADE NAME: CONTACT:
LEGAL ADDRESS: PHONE:

PROPOSED USE:

SPACE: SQUARE FEET: FRONTAGE:

TERMS:

BASE RENT: **$ psf YEARS 1–3**   PERCENTAGE RENT FACTOR: %
                    $ psf YEARS 4–7   LEASE TERM: **Years**
                    $ psf YEARS 8–10   LEASE COMMENCEMENT:

EXTRA CHARGES: (per square foot) (1999 estimates, subject to change)
CAM: $
INSURANCE: $
TAXES: $
PROMOTION SERVICES: $
WATER/SEWAGE: **Based on usage.**
ELECTRIC: **Based on usage.**
TRASH: **Based on usage.**
TENANT HVAC:
OTHER:

This proposal will be withdrawn if not acted upon by

The business terms and conditions, as outlined above, are being submitted solely for review. Neither party will be legally bound by these terms and conditions until a mutually acceptable lease has been fully executed by both parties. This proposal is subject to approval of tenant's financial statement and credit report and upon final approval of the owner. Neither party may claim any legal rights against the other by reason of actions taken in reliance upon this non-binding lease proposal, including, without limitation, any partial performance of the transactions contemplated herein.

Prepared by: Date:

Accepted by: _____   Date: _____

MALL NAME
ADDRESS
PHONE

Exhibit C: SAMPLE RETAIL LEASE

INTENT TO LEASE SPACE: RETAIL

Date._____
We propose to lease from you Store No._____ of approximately_____ square feet, having approximately_____ feet of frontage in the _____ indicated on the adjacent store location plan. The following terms and conditions apply:
Shopping Canter

1. **Trade name** _____
2. **Business use** Sale of _____
3. **Rent** _____ per sq. ft. Minimum rent to increase _____% per year for term of lease.
4. **Percentage rent** Tenant to pay_____% on total annual sales volume in
5. **Breakpoint** excess of $_____.
6. **Lease term** _____ years.
7. **Rent commencement** _____
8. **Common area maintenance** Tenant to pay pro rata share.
9. **Taxes** Tenant to pay pro rata share.
10. **Sprinkler charge** Tenant to pay_____¢ per sq. ft. or $_____per annum, whichever is greater.
11. **Utilities** Tenant to pay for own utilities.
12. **Insurance** Tenant to pay pro rata share.
13. **Marketing fund** Tenant to pay_____¢ per sq. ft. or $_____per annum, whichever is greater. As an initial marketing fund assessment, Tenant to pay a sum equal to the greater of_____¢ per sq. ft. or $_____.
14. **Deposit** Tenant to pay a minimum of $_____upon execution of this intent.
15. **Additional rent** Tenant's rent shall increase by_____% upon opening of each additional department store.
16. **Inflation adjustment** For each full year that the Opening Date shall be delayed beyond_____, Tenant's minimum rent, additional rent and construction reimbursements shall increase by_____percent (_____%).
17. **Construction** Landlord to provide the following work at tenant's expense. Tenant to employ an architect to prepare plans for landlord's approval.

Landlord's Work at Tenant's Expense
Construction standards to meet or exceed applicable codes.
1. **Floor Slab**—Landlord to provide a standard concrete floor slab at Tenant's cost of $_____per sq. ft. of footprint.
2. **Walls**—Landlord, at Tenant's expense of $_____per sq. ft., will provide stud framing to divide leased premises from adjacent tenants. Stud framed walls adjacent to service corridors shall be surfaced on service corridor side by Landlord. Exterior walls shall be of noncombustible construction and finish to be designated by Landlord.
3. **Roof**—Landlord to provide insulated roof with a "U" value of_____. Additional insulation (_____"U" value) to benefit Tenant may be installed by Landlord, at Tenant's expense of_____¢ per sq. ft.
4. **HVAC**—Landlord to furnish and install rooftop unit(s) at Tenant's expense.
5. **Electrical**—Landlord to bring electric service to leased premises at Tenant's expense of $_____ per sq. ft

6. **Plumbing**—Landlord to provide water and sanitary sewer service to leased premises at Tenant's expense of_____¢ per sq. ft. Location to be determined by Landlord.
7. **Sprinklers**—Landlord to install a standard automatic wet sprinkler system throughout the leased premises. The design criteria will be an average of_____square feet of coverage per sprinkler head. If Tenant requires a greater density or nonstandard design, Tenant will bear the additional costs.
8. **Miscellaneous Items**—As required, Landlord to provide the following at Tenant's expense:
   (a) Exterior door, vertical neutral pier, mail directory—$_____.
   (b) Design reviews, temporary electric service, trash removal service, energy economiser system—$_____ per square foot.
   (c) Any work necessary for Tenant to obtain appropriate licenses to conduct business in the premises.

Tenant Signature _____

Tenant Name _____

Title _____

Date _____

Leasing Representative _____

> It is understood and agreed that this letter of intent shall not be legally binding on either Landlord or Tenant until it's terms and conditions have been incorporated into a lease agreement and it has been executed by both landlord and tenant.

Exhibit D: SAMPLE RESTAURANT LEASE

INTENT TO LEASE SPACE: RESTAURANTS

Date._____

We propose to lease from you Store No._____ of approximately_____ square feet, having approximately_____ feet of frontage in the_____ indicated on the adjacent store location plan. The following terms and conditions apply: Shopping Canter

1. Trade name	_____
2. Business use	_____
3. Rent	_____ per sq. ft. Minimum rent to increase_____% per year for term of lease.
4. Percentage rent	Tenant to pay_____% on total annual sales volume in excess of $_____. For each additional $_____ in excess of $_____, Tenant to pay an additional_____%.
5. Lease term	_____ years.
6. Rent commencement	_____.
7. Common area maintenance	Tenant to pay pro rata share.
8. Restaurant area maintenance	Tenant to pay pro rata share based on annual sales volume.
9. Taxes	Tenant to pay pro rata share.
10. Sprinkler charge	Tenant to pay_____¢ per sq. ft. or $_____ per annum, whichever is greater.
11. Utilities	Tenant to pay for own utilities.
12. Insurance	Tenant to pay pro rata share.
13. Mall marketing fund	Tenant to pay_____¢ per sq. ft. or $_____ per annum, whichever is greater. As an initial marketing fund assessment, Tenant to pay $_____.
14. Restaurant area marketing fund	Tenant to pay_____% of sales by volume per annum.
15. Deposit	Tenant to pay a minimum of $_____ upon execution of this intent.
16. Additional rent	Tenant's rent shall increase by_____% upon opening of each additional department store.
17. Inflation adjustment	For each full year that the Opening Date shall be delayed beyond_____, Tenant's minimum rent, additional rent and construction reimbursements shall increase by_____ percent (_____%).
18. Construction	Landlord to provide the following work at tenant's expense. Tenant to employ an architect to prepare plans for landlord's approval.

Landlord's Work at Tenant's Expense

Construction standards to meet or exceed applicable codes.

1. Floor Slab—Landlord to provide a standard concrete floor slab at Tenant's cost of $_____ per sq. ft. of footprint.

2. Walls—Landlord, at Tenant's expense of $_____ per sq. ft., will provide stud framing to divide leased premises from adjacent tenants. Stud framed walls adjacent to service corridors shall be surfaced on service corridor side by Landlord. Exterior walls shall be of noncombustible construction and finish to be designated by Landlord.

3. Roof—Landlord to provide insulated roof with a "U" value of_____. Additional insulation (_____ "U" value) to benefit Tenant may be installed by Landlord, at Tenant's expense of_____¢ per sq. ft.

4. HVAC—Landlord to furnish and install rooftop unit(s) at Tenant's expense.

5. Electrical—Landlord to bring electric service to leased premises at Tenant's expense of $_____ per sq. ft.

6. Plumbing—Landlord to provide water and sanitary sewer service to leased premises at Tenant's expense of_____¢ per sq. ft. Location to be determined by Landlord.

7. Sprinklers—Landlord to install a standard automatic wet sprinkler system throughout the leased premises. The design criteria will be an average of_____square feet of coverage per sprinkler head. If Tenant requires a greater density or nonstandard design, Tenant will bear the additional costs.

8. Restaurant Area—Tenant to pay capital contribution of $_____ per sq. ft. for Landlord's cost in supplying and installing furniture and accessories.

9. Restaurant Storefront—In lieu of Tenant's constructing storefront, Landlord shall construct and Tenant shall reimburse Landlord at the rate of $_____ per lineal foot of storefront.

10. Miscellaneous Items—As required, Landlord to provide the following at Tenant's expense:
  (a) Exterior door, vertical neutral pier, mall directory—$_____.
  (b) Design reviews, temporary electric service, trash removal service, energy economiser system—$_____ per square foot.
  (c) Any work necessary for Tenant to obtain appropriate licenses to conduct business in the premises.

Tenant Signature _____

Tenant Name _____

Title _____

Date _____

Leasing Representative _____

> It is understood and agreed that this letter of intent shall not be legally binding on either Landlord or Tenant until it's terms and conditions have been incorporated into a lease agreement and it has been executed by both landlord and tenant.

Exhibit E: SAMPLE FORMAT FOR LEASE INQUIRY

LEASE INQUIRY FORM

INSTRUCTIONS:
1. This form is to be completed for all walk-in, letter, or telephone inquiries.
2. The prospective tenants should be informed that the Leasing Representative or Center Manager will respond to their inquiry.
3. One copy of this form should be kept in a Leasing Log and one copy forwarded to the appropriate person for action.

LEASING INQUIRY

DATE: _____
SHOPPING CENTER: _____
CONTACT: _____
　　　　　　Name

　　　　　　_____
　　　　　　Company

　　　　　　_____
　　　　　　Street Address

　　　　　　_____
　　　　　　City, State and Zip Code
　　　　　　(_____)_____
　　　　　　Telephone Number

Name of store(s) and location of store(s) / Business experience: (If prospective tenant has no stores, write NONE.).
_____
_____

Type of Merchandise / Stores: _____

Square Feet Desired: _____

Other Comments:_____
_____
_____

LEASING / MANAGEMENT FOLLOW-UP

Action Taken:
Sent Follow-up Letter: _____ Phoned for Follow-up: _____
Letter Sent By: _____ Phoned By: _____
Action Taken:
#1_____Leasing Inquiry Letter and Form Date sent _____
#2_____Leasing Inquiry Letter only   Date sent _____
#3_____Management Phoned   Date   Conversation and Recommended Action
　　　　　　　　　　　　　　_____   _____
　　　　　　　　　　　　　　_____   _____

Exhibit F: LEASING INQUIRY FORM

ABC SHOPPING CENTER
LEASE INQUIRY

1. Name: _____

Address: _____
         Street Address

Phone ( ) _____

2. Store Name: _____

3. Description of store, including merchandise mix, brand names, customers, etc.
   _____
   _____
   _____

4. Other existing location(s) of your business:
   _____
   _____

5. Sales volume of other locations and/or projected annual sales of proposed store:
   _____
   _____

6. Space Requirements: Minimum Square Feet: _____
                      Maximum Square Feet: _____

7. Attach personal financial statements and/or the most recent annual report/financial statements of your company.

8. Attach brochures, photographs, and other information about your stores that may assist us in evaluating your store.

9. Attach a résumé of the owners of the proposed store which describes retail qualifications.

10. Are you interested in our other shopping centers?
    _____ A
    _____ B
    _____ C

11. RETURN TO:
                    Leasing Representative
                          Address
                    City, State Zip Code

6 | Selling and Negotiating Techniques

Rene F. Daniel, CLS

In trying to establish the methodology for successful selling and negotiating in shopping center leasing, the correct approach is always relative to the desired goal. Whether you represent a particular property or a retail tenancy, there are time-tested techniques that should be of great value to the leasing specialist. This chapter develops a distinct methodology to follow in the pursuit of successful sales results.

Before the Selling Begins: The Groundwork

The art of sales has been widely discussed, and although specific methods differ, most of these discussions agree on starting with the basics—where to begin. Regardless of whether the property or the retailer is being represented, certain groundwork must be laid before the start of selling. Clearly, anyone interested in selling must understand whatever product is to be sold, as well as the target to whom it will ultimately be marketed.

When it comes to shopping center leasing, a good way to begin is to look at the overall situation in order to understanding the deal. There are three components that make up a potential sale: the project, the prospects, and the elements of the deal.

DEFINING THE PROJECT

The property itself exists not only in and of itself but also in relation to the size and number of stores it has and, more important, its position in the overall market.

The market should be investigated through the use of outside demographic and psychographic studies, which are available from companies long established in providing this type of basic information to the industry. If you are interested in finding out where these services are available, one source of information can be found in the *ICSC Products & Services Directory,* published annually by ICSC. Most of the reports are available on computer and can be made as specific as needed for an individual project and its immediate market—for example, in defining typical market age, sex, income, education, and occupation. Other specific information can be obtained about the people who, it is hoped, will make the project their shopping center of choice. This outside information begins to define how and why the center is, or will be, in existence in the first place.

The market must also be investigated through an inside study, which should be conducted by the salesperson. This study consists of an intensive examination of the composition of the market to provide a less specific and more internal basis of comparison. Begin by taking a ride around the market in the daytime hours, to look not only at the type of housing that makes up the market, but at how well kept the neighborhood and larger area are in general. Are the homes in good repair, or have the older ones become a bit run-down?

Depending on what you observe, you may get clues as to whether the potential market is one that needs the center in the first place. For example, do many driveways have late-model, expensive sport utility vehicles, or are older and cheaper vehicles the norm for the area? The type and style of automobile, especially any designated as the second or family car (which may be those seen in the daytime), helps to define how the market perceives itself. In another example, what are the people walking around in the market wearing? If the clothing looks stylish and expensive, you are beginning to understand something about what the potential needs of the market are and how the property should be trying to fulfill those needs. In addition, visit the local supermarket to see what is on the shelves of the gourmet section. If there is a large ethnic food selection, you may get a clue as to who is currently shopping in the broader market and for what types of products.

The inside study should be repeated in the evening hours to further define how the people dress, live, and play in the market. The evening visit to the neighborhood will reveal the type and size of primary cars being driven in the market, whether there are large or small family groups gathered in the market area, and how people might dress to buy groceries. Extensive observation of the potential market area will begin to define an in-depth feeling for it, and for the likely success of the property being considered.

With the market defined, the next step is the definition of the center itself. The International Council of Shopping Centers (ICSC) identifies eight types of centers: neighborhood center, community center, regional center, superregional center, fashion/specialty center, power center, theme/festival center, and outlet center. These definitions are understood in most cases to be fairly precise, but this is just the beginning of the exercise in definition.

It is also necessary to determine what type of merchandise should be sold, and how. For example, it is possible to sell fashion merchandise in either a small, expensive boutique setting or a large, open store presentation. The price points of the merchandise will also help to define the project and its potential. Assuming that the center will be selling expensive merchandise, will it be conservative or follow the latest fashions in presentation?

Will footwear be branded, or non-branded and sold in a self-service presentation? The market definitions above may help to answer these types of questions.

In addition, is the center to have some unique feature that will make it a stopping place for the market? This might include something as subtle as having a post office in the center or as obvious as offering a public library facility. The definition of the center will help determine whom the property will appeal to, and which tenants can be expected to want to locate there.

The final element of understanding the project is the financial definition of the property. This includes not only the obvious elements such as the rental pro forma, the allowance budget (if any), and the ancillary charges that make up the deal, but also those less obvious expenses related to the operation of a store within the center. The latter might include the cost of the buildout of the space (for example, is this in an area where construction help is easily accessible, or is a great deal of other construction going on at the same time?), the amount of available labor to work in the store, the energy costs to operate it, and various other potential financial obstacles.

When the financial analysis is completed, the next step in laying the groundwork, before actually going out and selling the property, is the definition of the prospects.

DEFINING THE PROSPECTS

The definition of the prospects begins with a discussion of who, what, and where is the type of retailer that is being sought as a potential tenant.

Who would make a good tenant in this center relates to three elements: size, type, and experience. An investigation into the desired size means an understanding of what space each retail user is accustomed to operating in. As an example, one restaurant might need space for a lounge area, while another might need to dedicate space for a cafeteria line—the sorts of things that make a user's needs very easy to define.

The type of prospective tenant will be determined in no small way by the findings of the earlier investigation into the definition of the project. There are a number of different types of retailers within each category; for instance, within the category of footwear, there are self-service stores, men's shoe stores, ladies' shoe stores, family and children's shoe stores, leisure and casual shoe stores, designer shoe stores, and on and on. The type that best suits the property complements either the existing tenants or the anticipated mix of tenants that will make up the property.

Finally, the element of experience will help determine who is a good prospect. It is usually desirable to be able to observe firsthand what you are getting in a tenant, and this is where the tenant's experience comes in. The merchant who is able to operate successfully in other properties has a potential edge in proving to be a viable tenant, worth considering for inclusion in any new or expanding project. Experience in operating stores successfully can make up for any number of other shortcomings.

What type of operator you want in the center can be defined in a number of ways. Is the prospect a self-service business requiring little, if any, product knowledge on the part of the sales staff, or a very intensive service business that requires well-trained and experienced sales help? Does it involve products that are always in demand, or ones that have only seasonal appeal? Is it expensive specialty merchandise, or the everyday disposable kind? For example, the retailer might be an expensive, high-fashion tenant that sells clothing on the cutting edge of style or, conversely, an expensive, conservative-fashion tenant with merchandise that will always sell to its customers. It is apparent that the what question may require more than a passing knowledge of the merchandise to be sold in the store, and it is the leasing person's obligation to research this sufficiently to establish the viability of each prospect.

In order to analyze whether a potential tenant will work in the property, it is also necessary to determine what each prospect perceives itself to be. There is also a major difference between a merchant who needs the benefit of a high-visibility location (such as a jeweler) and one who is confident that customers will seek out the store regardless of where it is located in the property (such as an optometrist).

The final question in definition of the prospect is where the prospect should be located. In order to understand the prospect's needs and desires, it is a good idea to look at where the retailer is currently operating. If the project, as defined earlier, is a regional property and the prospect operates only in power centers, is this indeed a potentially successful candidate for inclusion in the tenant mix? Although some might argue that anyone can make a living if the traffic in the center is right, this has not always proved to be the case. The prospect's location in other centers will help determine how the prospect sees itself, as well as how the consumer sees the prospect, and in many cases it gives some direction as to where the prospect expects to be located in any additional stores.

Perhaps the most important question asked to this point relates to where, because this leads to the idea of canvassing for potential prospects in other properties. In any effort with regard to leasing, the most fertile area for potential tenants is found by examining other properties. Whether or not the other centers visited are part of the primary market for the new or existing center, canvassing for tenants is invaluable. Walking through another retail property is the best way to discover the concepts that are currently in use by others; it not only may provide a plethora of new ideas to emulate, but also may indicate what you should try to avoid in merchandising.

Most retailers that operate multiple units of stores endeavor to create a look or ambiance that is repeated and consistent in all their units. This may be entirely appropriate for your property—or may indeed be exactly wrong for the situation being considered. The efforts that the leasing professional makes in researching other centers should result in a wealth of knowledge about the market and the potential prospects, which can now be analyzed. The last piece of the puzzle to complete the groundwork phase of the selling is understanding the elements of the deal.

DEFINING THE ELEMENTS OF THE DEAL

The elements of the deal include the basic financial considerations, business parameters, and merchandising parameters.

The financial parameters include some basic elements such as base rental per square foot, percentage rent, common area maintenance, real estate taxes, insurance, utilities, merchants association, promotional fund, advertising contribution, and garbage service, among other things. A comprehensive understanding of these matters is essential before the sales effort commences, because many prospective tenants do not fully comprehend these elements or what goes into defining them. For example, although the concept of percentage rental may appear to be a simple formula, it is the responsibility of the leasing professional to explain how it is derived and how and when it is due and collectible under the terms of the lease. It is imperative that the leasing agent be able to explain how the extra charges are determined and how they are applied to each space and tenant.

Many leases provide for a proration with regard to all extra charges, and the various formulas to determine these pro rata charges need to be fully understood before they are presented to any prospects. The agent must also understand the elements of any construction allowance in order to answer any question the prospect may have. The cost to build out retail space is on the rise, and this is a major part of the financial considerations related to the completion of a real estate negotiation.

The business parameters include numerous concepts such as use clauses, inducement consideration, competitive considerations, length of term, assignment provisions, among others. No prospect will have all the answers to the relevant questions, and it therefore becomes the responsibility of the leasing professional to explain them. There are real business reasons, for example, why a use clause should be specific and not just a simple statement of what the tenant might want to sell at any time in the future. The language of the use clause is the basis for many other details of a lease and always has implications dealing with assignment and competition. The issues of a lease's term may relate not only to a positive commitment to operate a business, but also to the period during which the prospect may be able to write off the expense of construction. The assignment language will ultimately determine whether the landlord can expect to keep the same tenant for the full term, or if that tenant has the right to sell his or her business at will.

In essence, almost all the parts of the lease that do not specifically refer to financial consideration become part of the business parameters of the deal. No lease will be signed without both parties being satisfied that the business terms are acceptable, and will be throughout the term of the lease.

The merchandising parameters of the deal are the final and sometimes most difficult parts of the lease. Each and every tenant has to operate under a specific set of criteria that will ultimately determine whether the project is successful. How the lease interprets the elements of display and product quality definitely affects the consumers' acceptance of the center, and how much control the landlord has over these elements significantly affects the landlord's ability to create a great retail project. Many retail tenants may be unwilling to cooperate with management unless that cooperation is dictated by the lease itself.

Now that the details of the groundwork to be completed before the sale is to begin have been discussed, it is time to discuss the actual selling process and how it might be successfully accomplished.

Selling Techniques: The Sales Process

In order to understand the basic techniques of successful selling, it is important to look at the various situations that make up the actual presentation of the deal to the prospect. The following sections discuss how this process works, first from the perspective of the leasing professional representing the property, and then from the perspective of the retailer looking to lease space at the property.

SELLING TO RETAILERS
In order to better understand how to sell to various types of retailers, it must be understood that situations vary depending on whether the

sale is being made to a national or regional chain of stores, to a local retailer, or to a first-time retail operator.

SELLING TO NATIONAL OR CHAIN RETAIL TENANTS

A sales presentation to a sophisticated chain of retail stores should speak to the concerns and interests of the prospect. In order to sell to the leasing representative, whether an in-house employee or a consultant, you should use the terminology that the prospect is most comfortable with. In this situation, rent should be quoted by the square foot. Consider the following example:

Assume that a fashion retailer is considering leasing a space of 2,000 square feet that is to be in the main traffic area of a regional shopping center. The landlord's representative would like to achieve a rental of $25 per square foot for the space, or a total of $50,000 per year. The leasing agent should first prepare a detailed plan showing the potential location on the plan and should be prepared to explain to the prospect why this location works well for the intended use.

The agent must be aware of the total sales not only of the center, but also the sales of similar fashion retailers currently operating in the property. If the average volume of similar fashion retailers at this property is in the range of $350–$375 per square foot, and the average size of the stores in that category is in the 3,500-square-foot range, the retail prospect will begin by analyzing how much sales potential can be predicted. If it is assumed that volume will be on the high side of the sales in the category because the prospect's store size is much less than the average size of the competing stores, the following formula will probably be used:

$$\frac{\$25 \text{ per square foot (rental rate)}}{\$375 \text{ per square foot (average volume per square foot)}} = 6.7\% \text{ rental factor (rental/sales)}$$

The 6.7 percent relationship between rental rate and projected sales is well within the industry standards for center tenants, and it will probably be acceptable as the basis for a reasonable potential deal.

In the above example, the landlord's agent should already be prepared to discuss how the average volume of the stores in the center relate to the average volume of the stores in the chain being considered. The agent should also be sure to point out a volume of $375 per square foot would result in sales at the prospective store of $750,000 per year. One can easily see that if the retail prospect operates stores that average near or below that $750,000 number, the rental quote is on target, and the tenant will probably negotiate a deal at close to the desired rental level. In order to complete this negotiation, there will be much additional discussion with regard to percentage rental, extra charges, and construction costs, but the basic parameters of a business deal seem to be on track for both parties.

The point of this example is to outline some of the selling skills required to negotiate with national or regional retailers. When making a presentation to an experienced real estate representative, it is imperative that different possible scenarios be contemplated to prepare adequately for the negotiation, that the salesperson understand the various components of sales at the center, and that the salesperson is ready to answer any and all questions relating to the center as a potential site for the retailer.

A basic understanding of how sales and volume relate in different retail categories can be gleaned by studying various publications that detail much of this information. An alternative approach is to study how similar tenants perform in other properties that the landlord owns, to give the agent some more details of sales performance in an effort to make a deal with a national or regional retail leasing representative.

SELLING TO LOCAL RETAILERS

A sales presentation to a local retailer is made at a different level from that of the preceding section. The local retailer probably has a consultant working in its interest, but the negotiation will probably be directly between the local retailer and the agent. The concerns of this prospect relate much more to the total cost of operating than just to the rental elements. For a merchant who is trying to negotiate a real estate deal, the most successful way to quote rental is by the month, not by the square foot.

The rental quote to the local retailer should be made so that this prospect can relate that number to monthly sales. Therefore, although the landlord's agent should prepare much of the same information used in the example above, it should be in a format more appropriate to the local tenant. Consider the following example:

Assume that the leasing agent wants the owner of a dress shop in a downtown retail setting to expand to a suburban strip center, and that there is only one available space of 2,000 square feet in the property. The agent has established that a fair market rental for the space would be approximately $15 per square foot. Assume further that the center has a children's shop performing at $225 per square foot, a unisex boutique performing at $275 per square foot, and a ladies' sportswear operator performing at $250 per square foot.

In order to present this deal properly, the agent has added to the $30,000 annual rental all extra charges, which total an additional $6,000 per year, for a grand total of $36,000 rental per year for the 2,000-square-foot space. This would be presented to the retailer as a rental rate of $3,000 per month. The retailer would be able to analyze this against a stated projection of sales for this store of approximately $45,000 per month, which according to the previous rental/sales formula above equates again to a 6.7 percent rental factor. It should also be noted that the projection of sales volume equates to a performance of $270 per square foot, which also seems to be within the comparative range of volumes for similar stores in the center. The landlord's agent is still presenting the same facts as in other negotiations, but in a way that is more appropriate to the local retailer's understanding and that should prove to be more effective in selling to that retailer.

The local retailer wants to know the total rental package and may not be interested in details during the early stages of the negotiation. The leasing agent should be prepared to discuss such details at a later date, however, probably with the tenant's lawyer or accountant.

SELLING TO FIRST-TIME RETAIL OPERATORS

This is probably the most difficult sale to make, because it involves teaching the prospective tenant how to relate potential sales to actual rental charges. In many instances, this must include a discussion of rent by the week, or even by the day. The person who has little or no retail experience must be helped in arriving first at the proper size of the store, then at the proper location for the store, and finally at the proper lease rental rate for the store.

An easy way to begin the discussion is to walk the prospect through either the proposed center or another, similar center and ask which store might be similar in size to what the prospect has in mind. Explaining how the previously described details of retail turnover, inventory, pricing, and markup relate to this first-time retailer's expectations should help determine if there is a potential for success in the property being considered. This sale may be the most difficult, yet it is an extremely rewarding experience for the leasing agent as a new retail concept becomes a reality.

SELLING TO A LANDLORD'S AGENTS

Although most tenants or their representatives are eager to be in high-volume centers, they are usually in competition with other retailers for the precious few available spaces left. In trying to sell individual stores to potential tenants, the greatest emphasis should be placed on the uniqueness of the store, and the consequent value that the particular retailer represents as part of any retail project. Landlords are always interested in having the most dominant property in a market and can generally be persuaded to work with successful tenants that possess positive track records of sales performance.

As is true of any negotiation, the laws of supply and demand rule the outcome. Many approaches exist to sell the concept; however, when working with a professional leasing agent, the most direct approach is the best. In today's economic environment almost all potential real estate deals must be approved by the tenant's operations department, and it would help the negotiation if that approval were in hand at the time of the negotiation. If the tenant representative has some preapproved volume assigned to the potential location, it will save a great deal of time in getting to a mutually acceptable rental package.

Many landlords will work with a tenant if they perceive that the tenant has a legitimate interest in the property, and the strongest indicator of that interest is the establishment of a pre-negotiation sales volume estimate. In many instances, the volume estimates and the rental quote may be out of alignment, but the people working on the deal are often able to step the rent to a level that both parties can agree upon.

Negotiating Techniques: How to Close the Deal

The landlord's agent must legitimize the rent request to the prospect and thereby, through negotiation, achieve a rental number that is budgeted by the owner. It is essential the agent understand that the negotiation has numerous variables, but that the end product—a signed lease—will always depend on timing.

TIME THE NEGOTIATIONS

The rule of thumb is that the less time it takes, the more likely it is that the deal will close. It is in the best interest of both parties that all approvals and necessary negotiation take place in a timely manner, with a concentrated effort by each to ensure completion. One of the best ways for the landlord's agent to ensure a quick response to the offer is to put a time limit on the offer. Never allow a tenant to evaluate an offer for an extended period, because this will merely distract the tenant from making a decision one way or the other.

DISCUSS THE ENTIRE LEASE

It is always a good idea to discuss the entire lease at one time before going forward and closing the deal. Making sure there are no surprise clauses helps gain the confidence of the retailer's leasing agent and assures the agent that no last-minute problems will arise. The landlord's agent should be familiar enough with the lease document to know which clauses cause the most objections; those should be addressed before any sale is contemplated.

DETERMINE THE OPENING DATE

An excellent negotiating technique is to let the prospect know what date the space will be ready, and to add that if the tenant will work in a timely manner with regard to when the store will open, the landlord will make it worthwhile by providing some additional inducement, such as free rent for some period of time. Many negotiations break down when opening conversations go on without the two parties understanding what the other is really trying to accomplish. For example, if the tenant has seasonal considerations with regard to opening, the landlord's agent should plan ahead to make sure that everything can be accomplished to accommodate those needs. No tenant wants to miss a holiday season, and it is up to the landlord's agent to make sure there is enough time to build out and open to avoid this problem.

ADDRESS THE NEEDS OF BOTH PARTIES

Almost all negotiating situations rely on some standard language to define the terms, but each situation also involves an effort to address the specific needs of both parties. No two tenants or landlords have the same problems, so it becomes the responsibility of each party in the negotiation to find out what is most important to the other. If a tenant seems incredibly stubborn about the elements of the real estate tax proration, for example, it can be assumed that there was a problem in some prior location the tenant was involved with; if the landlord will not alter a position regarding a relocation provision, most likely it relates to a previous situation that was difficult to resolve. In negotiating, it is necessary to listen to the other party to hear any hints about major elements that may affect that party's ability to make the deal work.

REVIEW THE LEASE COMMENTS
In the actual negotiation of the lease, it is essential to review all comments about all sections at the same time. The lease document contains numerous clauses that limit the rights of both parties. The negotiator should understand all concerns before responding to any one element of the lease. A response to any one objection may preclude a similar or contrary response later in the document. The definition of a negotiation is the give and take required to assure both parties that they have gotten what they really need so that the deal is as fair as it can be. Being certain that every section of the document has been reviewed for comment will result in a fair assessment of the total lease deal.

UNDERSTAND BUSINESS AND LEGAL TERMS
A key to successful negotiation technique is to understand what is a "business term" and what is a "legal term." Many leases do not go forward because the parties to the negotiation do not understand who is responsible for what portions of the lease document. If both real estate representatives have explained their positions before the lease is ever sent out, there should be no questions as to what is a business parameter of the proposed deal. Although some tenants feel, for example, that a radius clause is an onerous restriction on the ability of the tenant to open new units that may be near the center, most landlords feel it is the only way to protect the long-term interests of their property. This is clearly something that should be a part of the real estate negotiation, not left to the attorneys.

Another important business term that is often overlooked has to do with the actual time it takes for the space to be prepared, and what happens if the preparation does not occur on a timely basis. This is a business consideration that really has a major impact on both parties and, as such, should be discussed at a time when the rest of the terms are agreed upon.

It makes no sense to leave business terms to the attorneys. This will only delay the time it takes for each attorney to get in touch with the appropriate businessperson to discuss what went on in the negotiation. More and more attorneys want to be involved in the business negotiation, but a competent leasing professional should strive to make sure that this trend is put to a halt.

KEEP AN OPEN MIND

In negotiating for a shopping center location, one should never say never. Even if no one has ever asked for a particular protection or a particular clause before, it is good to be open-minded in trying to understand the position and why this is so important to the party asking for it. In negotiation, it serves neither party to simply say no before fully comprehending what has led to the request in the first place. If a tenant asks for some kind of competitive protection, for example, a landlord may be willing to provide that protection for a specific portion of the term of the lease. If a landlord insists on the right to relocate a tenant, perhaps the tenant should consider it if that tenant has the right to approve the new location and if the relocation is without expense to the tenant. No center stays the same, and what looks like a great location in the present may evolve into something else in the future. Being firm in a negotiation is important, but having made up one's mind beforehand will not help to close the deal.

ALLOW FOR CREATIVITY

The single most important element in successful negotiation is creativity. In most cases, the major stumbling blocks become insurmountable if either or both parties fail to use their innate creativity to resolve differences. Some practical thinking will go a long way to making a success out of a negative situation.

- If the rent is too high, why not sell the prospect on leasing less space—in other words, a smaller store?
- If the tenant will not consider any percentage rental at all, why not accept an annual increase in the base minimum rental?
- If the landlord insists on a contribution to the merchant's association, why not suggest that the contribution come out of the base rental internally?
- If the required tenant improvements are too expensive to be affordable, why not suggest a phase-in of all the changes that

need to be made so that the tenant has some working capital to accomplish those improvements?
- If the tenant feels that the time to build out the space is not enough, why not allow the tenant to pay only extra charges until the space is ready to open?
- If the landlord insists on a personal guarantee, why not have the guarantee cover only a portion of the entire lease term?
- If the space is just too small for the tenant to operate the store, why not suggest a storage mezzanine?
- If the tenant insists on the right to a cancellation provision, why not make the provision relative to sales performance, or, for that matter, why not make the right to cancel a mutual right?
- If there is no construction allowance budget to help the tenant build out the space, why not allow the tenant some free rental period in lieu of a contribution by the landlord?

There are numerous ways to continue to simplify the negotiation process. The major approach that continues to produce positive results is for each party to understand the process that the other must go through to gain final approval.

APPROVAL FOR THE LANDLORD'S AGENT
The decision to approve a real estate deal does not generally lie in the hands of just one person. The owner (landlord) invariably has a financial partner to satisfy as well. Most financing arrangements include some form of approval by the lender, as simple as acceptance by telephone or as extensive as a review of the actual lease documentation. Modern real estate ownership is not generally in the hands of individuals, but instead tends to include major real estate investment trusts, pension funds, partnerships of many varieties, and various other forms of corporate ownership.

The landlord's representative not only may have to report to an immediate superior, but also may have to justify the deal to an asset manager, a banker, an attorney, a property manager, a project manager, or some form of management group. This trend has made the approval process even more difficult and complicated to work through. The lease itself has become a much more detailed and lengthy document and, as such, requires more effort to fully comprehend and effectively utilize. Most landlord's agents are personally responsible for the lease being signed, and so they must review this paperwork with numerous people, both inside and outside the organization, for it to be in an acceptable execution format.

After the construction comments, legal comments, and business comments have been gathered, and after each has been responded to in a way acceptable to the prospective tenants as well as to the ownership group, it then becomes imperative to close the deal as soon as possible by getting both parties to sign the papers. Final physical execution of the approved lease is also no longer a simple process, again due to the varying forms of ownership of real estate.

APPROVAL FOR THE RETAIL LEASING REPRESENTATIVE

The process involved in approval by a retail operation has also become more complex. Although the leasing representative's input is still the focal point for the consideration of any deal, the approval is no longer in one person's hands. Most retailers make these decisions as part of a committee process, including input from not only the real estate department but also the operations department, store management group, merchants or buyers, financial advisers, principals, attorneys, and anyone else who has profit responsibility for the success or failure of the store.

Approval of the real estate deal depends on how effectively the leasing representative is able to present all of its variables to the people who are part of the approval process. Because approval hinges on the creation of a sales estimate for the premises that covers not only the rental requirements of the deal but also the extra charges, cost of construction, and any other ancillary operating costs, the leasing representative must establish a reliable number for sales. Knowing everything from the basic demography to the finite details of the components of the common area maintenance charges enables the real estate person to answer any questions. If the operations people, for instance, want to know how well the competition is doing in the center, it is up to the real estate representative to have specific information on hand. No one is prepared for all potential questions, but spending a lot of time preparing the details of the proposal for everyone to review serves to shorten the process.

The final lease execution also depends on having everyone else sign off before the person who actually executes the leases adds his or her signature. Knowing that the construction issues, for example, have all been satisfied may sound like the responsibility of the construction department, but in reality it is the leasing representative who must see to it that those details have actually been incorporated into the lease document. Too often the attorney is held responsible for getting something signed, when it should really be the final duty of the person in charge of having made the deal to get it executed.

Selling and Negotiating: Final Suggestions

For success in the process of the sale, observe the following final suggestions.

SUGGESTION #1
Always be prepared to discuss the rental in any of the ways it might be asked about. Although it is significant to be aware of the rental rate per square foot, for example, it is also very important to be able to discuss that rental in terms of total annual dollars, monthly dollars, and perhaps even the equivalent weekly amount. This requires preparing the numbers in many ways so that there will be a potential explanation at hand for any eventual kind of question, with regard to rental justification.

SUGGESTION #2
Understand all the proration formulas for the collection of any and all extra charges related to the deal. Knowing the various percentages and being able to justify how they have been arrived at will make explaining them to a prospect or a committee an easier task. Too often these extra charges make or break the deal, and if the representative is cognizant of how they are arrived at, as well as how reasonable they are, it will make the sales and negotiation job easier.

SUGGESTION #3
Never overplan for the situation. If a party to the presentation is convinced that only one way will work to create a successful negotiation, that negotiation probably is doomed from the start. It is not logical to assume that every tenant prospect wants to know the very same information, or for that matter that the only thing the landlord's representative wants is for one to pay enormous rent. Each situation has nuances that create a different scenario, and flexibility in thinking is essential to success.

SUGGESTION #4

Prepare a detailed written proposal format that addresses all the variables that might be appropriate for any prospective tenant. It is not difficult to edit out from a written form any superfluous details that have no meaning in any one specific set of circumstances, but having all the information ready to disseminate will help make the sale take less time to consummate. The formal synopsis of a deal in a proposal will ensure that both parties have agreed to the same terms and conditions.

SUGGESTION #5

The key to ensuring that the deal will be completed is follow-up. In spite of all prior efforts, all details of preparation and presentation, and all the other work that has been done, if there is no effort to see that things keep moving along through continual follow-up, the results will not be satisfactory. Each party to the negotiation has responsibilities beyond this particular deal, and therefore may lose sight of the progress of the papers that make this a completed lease. Follow-up by all those concerned is the only way to ensure success.

SUGGESTION #6

Understand at all times that nothing stands still. The market is always in flux, and alternative opportunities can occur without notice. The basics of why and how any deal is going forward depend on keeping aware of the market and the retail scenario on a day-to-day basis. For example, anchor stores can announce plans that affect each marketplace; in many ways, the players making up the market are always changing. Both parties to the negotiation should constantly monitor the circumstances and situations in the marketplace that may, in some way, affect the specific deal that is being worked on.

Conclusion

Successful sales result from positive selling and negotiating techniques. The basic element of the entire process is the groundwork that is necessary for each of the two parties not only to understand the potential deal, but also to investigate and pursue its interest in the deal. Definition of the market, the project, the prospect, and the varied elements of the deal constitute a basic foundation from which to go forward with the sale.

Regardless of whether the sale is made to an individual or a committee, correct technique differs with each situation. The method that produces positive results is most often determined by the type of tenant—national, regional, local chain, or independent—being given a presentation.

The negotiation itself can follow various formats, but certain elements hold true regardless. A full and complete understanding and description of the details of the proposed deal should be accomplished through the art of detailed negotiation of each element making up the final terms and conditions. Although there are different approaches to negotiation, success is most dependent on both parties' ability to be creative.

Finally, there is no excuse for not closing a deal that has been approved and deemed acceptable by both parties to the negotiation. Hard work and effort will pay off by resulting in an executed document that satisfies the needs of both of the parties to it. Every part of the negotiation should be treated as if it might threaten the completion of the deal. With this in mind, planning for the signing by thoroughly preparing for the negotiation will make the deal a reality.

Rene F. Daniel, CLS, is President at The Daniel Group, LLC, Baltimore, Maryland.

7 The Lease and Its Language

Andrew Shedlin, SCSM/CLS

Legal and commercial matters are bound together in documents called leases. The lease states clearly the agreements between the landlord and the tenant. Leases also distinguish between ownership and simple possession of property. During the term of the lease, possession is with the tenant; at the end of the term, possession reverts to the landlord. The tenant's leasehold interest confers possession.

A lease is a contract by which rent is exchanged for possession and services such as payment of taxes, insurance, utilities, and maintenance. In shopping center leases, landlords seek to pass through to tenants many of the costs of services. Overlaying the relationship of landlord and tenant is the role of the landlord's lender, which is concerned with provisions in leases that may interrupt cash flow or impair the property.

The choice of whose lease form to use depends on the leverage of the parties—the type, size, and desirability of the shopping center as opposed to the creditworthiness and importance of the tenant. With bigger tenants now leasing larger spaces, it is no longer uncommon for the lease negotiation to begin with a tenant's form. Regardless of whose form is used, the completed document should ultimately represent a balancing of the interests of the parties involved, taking into account the reality of which party needs the other more. The completed lease represents a point at which the legitimate interests of the landlord and the tenant are balanced.

Because there is no clear demarcation between "business points" and "legal points," it is important for all shopping center professionals to have a basic understanding of all of the terms of the lease. What follows is an attempt to review and explain the significant provisions in a typical shopping center lease so that the shopping center professional will understand their importance as well as their interrelationship with the other lease provisions.

General Lease Provisions

The essential lease provisions must include the following:

- The date
- An identification of the parties, namely, the landlord and tenant
- The premises
- The term
- The consideration or rent.

Other provisions deal with various costs associated with the shopping center such as maintenance, taxes, utilities, and insurance, and the tenant's share of those costs. Additionally, the shopping center lease contains provisions by which landlords impose control over the tenant's transfer rights, compliance with laws, and specific rules imposed by landlords. The lease also typically requires tenants to join an association and/or contribute to the marketing of the property.

In addition, the tenant is given certain rights and is provided with certain services. These may include protecting the tenant from unreasonable competition and ensuring that the shopping center is adequately occupied by complementary tenants.

The lease also deals with other, related matters, such as the physical aspects of the shopping center, including the shopping center property as a whole and the specific premises. The lease recites the rights and obligations of the parties to maintain the property and to prevent liens. It also sets forth the rights and obligations of the parties as they relate to damage and condemnation, as well as assurances that the landlord has adequate security for the performance of the tenant's obligations. This may include the landlord's right to enter the property as well as encumber (mortgage) the property. The lease also provides for appropriate rights and remedies in the event one of the parties defaults in its obligations.

Date of Lease

The date helps identify the lease, but it also may signify the commencement date of the term or the date on which the obligations of the parties begin. Typically in a shopping center lease, the nonmonetary obligations of the parties begins as of the date of the lease, whereas the obligation to pay rent and additional charges commences following a finite number of days during which the tenant can construct the premises. However, if the tenant opens for business on an earlier date, its monetary obligations will start on the actual date of opening.

Parties

Shopping center leases can be among and between individuals, co-owners, partnerships, corporations, or a combination of these. A lease to a married person that is signed by that person's spouse deters fraudulent spousal transfers if the business fails. Sole proprietorships usually prompt a landlord to request a security deposit or guaranty. Regardless of the identity of the individual or entity signing the lease, the landlord should verify the credit history and carefully examine the tenant's current financial statement. Any such statements should be certified by a certified public accountant.

All co-owners should sign a lease, to ensure its enforceability. When there is more than one tenant, all tenants are jointly and severally obligated. A corporation's Certificate of Incorporation should be reviewed to ascertain that the corporation itself and the individual signing on behalf of the corporation both have the authority to bind the corporation. It must also be authorized to do business in the state in which the shopping center is located. A lease to a partnership raises questions about the purposes for which the partnership was formed, the term of the partnership, and the authority and required number of signatory partners.

Each of the parties to the lease will seek to limit its potential liability to the other. For the landlord this is called exculpation. The landlord's liability and the tenant's ability to enforce a judgment against the landlord will typically be limited to the landlord's equity interest in the shopping center. Because the landlord frequently obtains very substantial mortgage financing on the property, the landlord's actual equity interest may be minimal or, under the circumstances, even nonexistent. This provision of the lease is usually the one that the landlord will be most hesitant to modify.

Similarly, the prudent tenant will seek to limit its liability by forming a single-purpose (shell) corporation whose sole asset may be its interest in the lease. The individual tenant may also limit its liability to a finite period of time (for instance, "the first two years of the lease term") or a specific dollar amount (for instance, "50,000" or "an amount equal to one year's rent and additional rent"). Similarly, the tenant may offer a security deposit in the form of cash or a letter of credit that the landlord may draw upon in the event of the tenant's default. The desire of the tenant to limit its liability has become one of the most heavily negotiated and contentious issues in a lease negotiation.

The Premises

The tenant in a shopping center lease occupies less than all of what the landlord owns and is dependent upon other parts of the development that it shares with others known as common areas. The shopping center premises are described in the body of the lease and depicted on a plan of the shopping center that is included as a lease exhibit. Sometimes a legal description of the shopping center is also attached as an exhibit. The description of the premises usually excludes the exterior walls and the roof, thereby limiting the tenant's rights to attach signs and equipment.

Tenants will often seek to limit the landlord's right to install or maintain columns, pipes, ducts, and the like within the premises, or at least to require a limitation on them since they may limit the tenant's ability to conduct its business. At a minimum, the tenant should demand that none of these penetrations be present in the selling area or that they be severely limited. The landlord may agree that these penetrations will be limited to a bare minimum and that the landlord will cause as little interference as possible during their installations and maintenance.

The size of the premises is typically measured from the outside of the exterior walls and the common areas or corridors to the centerline of party walls or common partitions. No deduction is made for interior penetration unless it is substantial. The size of the premises is important in calculating not only the tenant's rent but also its proportional share of common charges. Often a tenant will request that its architect have the right to remeasure or reconfirm the landlord's calculations so as to verify their accuracy. From time to time the tenant may request the ability to use basement space (if any) or create a mezzanine space. The parties frequently weigh space that is above or below the premises on a different basis in the calculation of rent and additional rent.

The common areas of the shopping center may be nearly as significant to a tenant as the premises itself. This may include not only the tenant's actual position within the shopping center but also the parking areas, relationship to other stores (particularly anchor stores), and maintenance of unimpeded access to and visibility of the premises. The tenant may want to designate an unobstructed view of the premises and may therefore prohibit the landlord from building in a predetermined area. The tenant may also seek to restrict the landlord from placing or projecting any other tenant's storefront leaseline in front of, or farther into, the common areas than the tenant's. If the landlord wants to preserve its ability to further develop the shopping center, it must clearly exclude future development areas from such restrictions.

A particular traffic pattern may already exist, and the tenant may wish to ensure that this will be neither impaired nor eliminated. Remedies for this breach may include a reduction in rent or even lease termination. The site plan may designate the locations of specific tenants, including key tenants that may be inducements for the tenant to enter into the lease. The site plan may also show locations of pylon signs and outparcels.

Because the landlord owns a larger parcel than the tenant's premises, it will seek to retain the greatest degree of flexibility in making changes to the shopping center. This may include adding or subtracting spaces, or even moving buildings or common areas. This is essential if the landlord wants to expand or reconfigure the shopping center to add key tenants or account for changes in the marketplace.

RELOCATION CLAUSE

The landlord's desire for flexibility may cause it to want to move the tenant to another location at some point. This is known as relocation, and it is another lease provision that is often heavily contested by the tenant. The tenant may insist on remaining in its existing location, or it may consent to a relocation but only with the following stipulations:

- It be within a previously approved and designated area
- It costs the tenant nothing
- The substitute premises are approximately the same size and shape as the existing premises
- The replacement premises are built to the same standard as tenant's existing or then-current standard
- There is no period of time when the tenant is not open for business.

The tenant sometimes demands that relocation will be consented to only in connection with the addition of a new anchor tenant utilizing the tenant's premises or when major expansion/reconfiguration of the shopping center requires the premises, not merely as a means for the landlord to replace the tenant with another tenant of similar size or perceived by the landlord to be a more desirable use or tenancy. Also, the tenant may restrict the relocation from occurring except during certain times of year such as peak selling seasons.

STORAGE SPACE

Although not common in shopping center leases, it is sometimes helpful for a tenant to lease storage space not contiguous to the premises. When this is done, it should be coterminous with the lease.

OPTIONS

Another provision sometimes found in leases is an option for the tenant to expand. This can be in the form of a right of first negotiation (the landlord must first negotiate with the tenant for a fixed period of time before it offers space to another tenant); a right of first offer (the landlord must offer vacant space to the tenant before offering it for lease to anyone else); or a right of first refusal (the landlord must give the tenant an option to lease space on the terms it has negotiated with another prospective tenant). Each of these provisions is more favorable to the tenant than to the landlord in that it confers rights but not obligations upon tenants, and obligations but not rights upon landlords. Options restrict the landlord's use of the property and therefore its value.

The Term

The term of the lease must have a commencement, a duration, and an end. The term may begin on an exact date or when a specified event occurs, such as the completion of construction. The term may begin when a lease is executed, which may be the beginning of the tenant's obligations such as preparation of plans; when possession is delivered, which begins obligations such as insurance and indemnity; or, most commonly, when a certain number of days pass during which the tenant may complete its improvements.

The tenant will want to have its time to complete its work (and begin paying rent) run not simply from delivery of possession (with the landlord's work, if any, completed), but from the date on which the landlord will have approved tenant's plans, as well as when the tenant will have received a building permit from the governmental authority that issues them and the landlord has returned a fully executed lease. If the tenant does not condition its construction period on the satisfaction of each party as to possession, plan approval, and permits, it may find that its obligation to pay rent and other charges will commence on a date that does not give it adequate time to prepare the premises for the conduct of its business. Conversely, the landlord will seek to establish specific timetables for when the tenant must submit plans, revise them in accordance with shopping center criteria, and submit the landlord-approved plans to the governmental authorities having jurisdiction.

Issues may arise if the landlord has difficulty in delivering possession because a previous tenant remains in possession, or if the landlord has not completed its construction of the premises. Possession should usually be established by a formal written notice from the landlord to the tenant specifying the date on which possession will be delivered.

DELAYED OCCUPANCY

Both the landlord and the tenant may have reasons to delay the opening of the premises. The landlord may want to ensure the simultaneous opening of all or a number of stores at a shopping center's grand opening. On the other hand, the tenant may want to condition the opening of its store on the concurrent opening of a certain number or percentage of anchor stores or a finite percentage of smaller tenants (also known as satellite tenants). The tenant may decline to open until one or both of the anchor and satellite contingencies are satisfied (also known as co-tenancy), or it may agree to open notwithstanding but instead pay a reduced minimum rent or only a straight percentage of its sales until the co-tenancy is satisfied.

Another reason a tenant may wish to delay the initial opening of its store is if the opening would occur too close to a holiday season and the costs associated with opening would not be justified by the revenues to be derived or there is inadequate time to properly train the tenant's store personnel. These nonopening periods are referred to as black-out or dark periods.

EARLY OCCUPANCY

In instances in which a landlord has an incentive for a tenant to open at the earliest possible time (such as to meet certain occupancy thresholds to enable the landlord to obtain financing or to satisfy co-tenancy requirements of other tenants), the parties may agree to defer rent or other occupancy payments for a period of time after the tenant has opened for business. This is referred to as an abatement period, and it causes the tenant to be bound by the nonmonetary provisions of the lease, with the monetary provisions applying after the landlord has satisfied its co-tenancy obligations.

This monetary deferral or abatement technique may include minimum rent and a tenant's obligations to record its gross sales and pay percentage rent. It may also defer the tenant's obligation to share costs in common with other tenants (for example, real estate taxes and common area maintenance charges). Additionally, in instances in which the landlord is contributing to the costs of the buildout of the tenant's improvements, the landlord may wish to abate rent (and other of the tenant's monetary obligations) for a period of time equivalent to the abated amount. In the case of a construction allowance abatement, it is typically granted only for minimum rent, so that the landlord has continuity in the receipt of funds to pay real estate taxes and to maintain the shopping center.

EXTENDED OCCUPANCY

The seasonality of a tenant's business and the disproportionate amount of business most tenants generate during the last one-third of each calendar year makes it desirable for the tenant to extend its lease so that it will expire early in the calendar year following the last Christmas selling season. This extension is not necessarily disadvantageous to the landlord, because it fosters continuity and a lack of construction disruption during the busy holiday season, sidesteps the issue of the dark period for the replacement tenant, increases the possibility of receiving percentage rent from holiday sales, and potentially gives the landlord greater flexibility in simultaneously being able to vary space sizes to account for the changing size requirements of adjacent tenants. Of course, the downside of concurrent lease expirations (say, on January 31 of any calendar year) is that if the shopping center is not performing well, the landlord will find itself with a significant amount of empty space all at one time.

EARLY TERMINATION
Many leases are structured in such a way that although the tenant may have the right to possession and its tenancy for a period of time, it may enjoy the right only in segments or finite incremental periods. This may take the form of early termination based upon the failure of the tenant to achieve a specified sales volume during a specific period of time (for example, "at any time during the first three years of the Term" or "during the fifth calendar year") and may be written in favor of either the landlord or the tenant, or both. This provision is sometimes called a kickout or right of early termination. The landlord's justification for the inclusion of such a provision may be stated as its desire to keep its shopping center filled with tenants that are "current" or "hot" and can perform at certain sales levels with attendant customer acceptance. The tenant's rationale for the provision is its desire to minimize its risk in not continuing to sustain losses in an unprofitable enterprise.

It is not uncommon for the lease to provide that when one party exercises its right to terminate the lease because of insufficient gross sales, it must do so with adequate notice to the other party, as well as with a reimbursement to that party for the unamortized investment in the leasehold improvements made by the party whose rights to possession are being terminated. The amortization period is typically over the term of the lease without account for the kickout (for example, a ten-year lease with a five-year kickout will utilize a ten-year amortization schedule). The advantage of a kickout is that it is measurable and often predictable, because the tenant will regularly record and report its gross sales to the landlord, and both parties should be able to anticipate the tenant's inability to achieve the required sales level.

OPTION TO EXTEND OR RENEW

The option to extend or renew is the landlord's offer to prolong the term of the lease. Although it must be exercised within a period of time prescribed in the lease with precise language, it is usually exercised more subjectively and typically is written in favor of the tenant (but the provision may be drafted so that the tenant may not exercise the option unless it has met certain criteria such as a minimum amount of gross sales, or has not transferred its interest in the lease, or has not been in default during the term). The terms *extension* and *renewal* are used synonymously, even though a renewal technically requires a new agreement whereas an extension continues the same lease.

Options are usually exercised by written notice given by a specific date. Because a tenant's failure to exercise such an option in a timely manner will typically deprive it of a valuable right, sometimes the landlord will have to prove actual damage in order for it to be successful in terminating a lease as a result of the tenant's failure to exercise its right in a timely way. Legal cases in various states are nearly evenly divided on the subject of strict enforceability of deadlines for exercise of renewal options.

The terms of the renewal should be stated as specifically as the terms of the lease itself. Although many terms may remain the same, most frequently the rent will be different. It may be stated as one of the following:

- A specific amount
- A cost-of-living adjustment (which should be clearly defined)
- A "grossing up" of the minimum and percentage rent payable by the tenant during a specific period such as the final year of the term
- A "market rent," which the parties are advised to define clearly so as to avoid confusion, ambiguity, and possibly eventual litigation.

Setting the renewal rental at rates "to be mutually agreed upon" is nothing more than an agreement to agree and may be unenforceable.

Rent

Base rent is typically paid in monthly installments in advance, without prior demand and without abatement, deduction, or setoff. It is also prorated and adjusted to account for fractional months. The term *minimum rent,* or *base rent,* implies that it is not all that the tenant is required to pay. This is distinguishable from a gross lease, in which the tenant pays a gross amount of fixed rent, from which the landlord must pay all of the incidentals of ownership such as maintenance, insurance, and real estate taxes. However, such gross leases are quite rare, being typically found only in short-term agreements (such as temporary holiday leases) in which the landlord is confident that it can anticipate all associated costs.

In addition to gross leases, there are also net leases (in which the tenant pays taxes, utilities, and assessments), net-net leases (a net lease, plus the tenant pays for repairs and maintenance), and triple net leases (a net-net lease, plus the tenant pays for some capital improvements). Most shopping center leases are triple net leases.

Minimum rent is typically paid together with certain other amounts such as pass-throughs or escalations. Pass-throughs include real estate taxes, utilities, and operating expenses ("common area expenses"); escalations include cost-of-living adjustments and percentage rent. In addition, the tenant is frequently asked to reimburse the landlord for repairs and attorneys' fees. These amounts in addition to the minimum rent are usually referred to as additional rent, which assures the landlord of expedited remedies available for the nonpayment of rent. Finally, the lease typically requires the tenant to pay any rent tax, which can be a very significant amount in some states, such as Florida.

A provision for late payment, if not drafted as liquidated damages, may be construed as a penalty that courts may not enforce, or as interest that may violate usury laws. A onetime charge is most frequently used; however, it is often coupled with the tenant's obligation to pay interest on past due amounts. This encourages the tenant to pay on time. Often the lease is drafted so as to excuse an infrequent late payment but to prevent repeated lateness by requiring more stringent obligations such as automatic bank transfers after two late payments. Certain tenants have historically profited from the so-called float on money paid at the end of the month rather than at the beginning. Clearly the landlord has obligations to its lender, employees, contractors, the taxing authorities and others, and should receive the rent and additional rent in advance and not in arrears.

RENT ABATEMENT
In some markets the landlord may have to attract tenants with free rent or rent abatement. Free rent is also used during the period of time when the tenant will be constructing improvements. Care should be taken to specify whether the abatement is of minimum rent or if it is intended to include additional rent as well. Usually the abatement during construction is of all rent, while abatement other than during construction may oblige the tenant to pay the pass-throughs or escalations because these are important to the landlord's lender.

Frequently landlords seek to protect themselves against inflation and unanticipated costs by escalating the minimum rent by fixed amounts and at fixed intervals. This is known as stepped-up rent. The increases may be stated in dollar amounts or in percentage increases. The parties often opt for the certainty of these increases rather than the uncertainty of cost-of-living adjustments. However, when a cost-of-living adjustment is used, it is important to clarify the rent that is the subject of the escalation; to identify the index to be used, together with a reference point and a formula for calculation; and to define upper and lower limits for the calculation (for instance, "not to exceed 3 percent cumulatively"). The fairest adjustments take place after the first calendar year of the tenant's occupancy.

PERCENTAGE RENT
Percentage rent is intended to measure the amount of rent a tenant is obliged to pay as a percentage of the sales that the tenant generates in the premises. The greater the sales, the greater the tenant's ability to pay. Percentage rent is commonly paid as a percentage of gross sales over a base, or breakpoint. The natural breakpoint is calculated by dividing the annual minimum rent by the percentage rent factor. Percentage rent breakpoints can also be artificially calculated; a higher artificial breakpoint favors the tenant and a lower one favors the landlord.

Care should be taken in drafting the lease language so that percentage rent is payable when the percentage exceeds the minimum rent rather than all rent; otherwise the breakpoint becomes an artificially high number that includes not only the minimum rent but all pass-throughs as well. Care must also be taken that when the minimum rent is increased, the breakpoint will increase as well; otherwise an artificially low breakpoint will work to the tenant's detriment.

Percentage rent has several components:

- A definition of gross sales, which the landlord will seek to state broadly and the tenant narrowly
- A statement of exclusions from gross sales, which the landlord will try to make restrictive and the tenant generous
- A percentage
- A computation and payment period
- A method of tenant record keeping
- A method of verification.

From time to time, landlords seek to gross up rent in subsequent years based on either all or a portion of the aggregate of the minimum rent and percentage rent paid by the tenant in the previous year. Tenants usually seek to resist this increase by claiming that past performance is no guarantee of future success. If the minimum rent is increased in this manner, the tenant will want to proportionately increase the breakpoint.

For example purposes, consider the following explanation as it relates to gross-up rent. The landlord will want to include all revenues from sales, services, or rentals made by or through the tenant, whether for cash, credit, exchange, or other value; whether or not collected or collectible in, from, on, or through the premises, including telephone, electronic, mail order, computer, video, and Internet or other similar present or future technological means; whether or not filled at, or delivered at, the premises, as well as sales made off the premises but delivered to or filled at the premises.

Issues often arise over the treatment of trade-ins. If a portion of the sales price is paid in trade, should all of the trade be included in sales? If it is, should it not be excluded when it is subsequently sold so that the tenant does not pay twice? The answer seems to be yes.

Other interesting questions arise in the case of a licensee's or subtenant's sales or subrent (regarding which should be included in the reporting of the tenant's gross sales), and a tenant's use of coupons (regarding whether the full or reduced amount of the sale should be included).

Deductions and Exclusions Deductions are the amount by which gross sales are reduced (for example, sales taxes collected for the taxing authorities). Unless these are subtracted, the tenant will be paying percentage rent on amounts it is merely collecting and passing on. Exclusions are amounts that never should be included in gross sales because they have never been part of the sale in the first place (for example, returns to shippers).

The tenant's goal is to limit its percentage rent to sales on which it has truly made a profit. The following is a list of common exclusions:

- Exchanges of merchandise between a tenant's stores, when it is an accommodation for multistore tenants—not when it seeks to divert sales from a higher-percentage store to a lower-percentage store
- Returns to suppliers and manufacturers
- Cash or credit refunds to customers
- Sales of trade fixtures, machinery, and equipment after a tenant's use
- Amounts collected and paid by a tenant to any governmental agency for any sales or excise tax
- Sales to employees at a discount (often landlords seek to state that the discount must be meaningful, such as 30 percent, and limited to the tenant's employees working in the premises)
- Interest, finance charges, carrying charges, and charges paid to credit card companies
- Credits or payments in settlement of losses
- Fire sales, bulk sales, or closeouts
- Receipts incidental to a tenant's main line of business such as pay telephones, vending machines, or lottery tickets
- Amounts received for alterations or for delivery charges or installations
- Service charges
- Mail order catalog sales
- Internet sales not originating/filled at the premises
- Gift certificates, until they are redeemed
- Losses or bad debts for credit sales and the unpaid balance of layaway plans

Obviously, the list of exclusions from gross sales can be extremely lengthy and can result in substantial amounts being subtracted from the tenant's reported sales, thereby depriving the landlord of anticipated revenues. Conversely, the tenant should not be obliged to pay the landlord rent on profits it does not actually receive. Often a cap, or limitation, is placed on any individual exclusion. An interesting compromise might be to cap the aggregate amount of all exclusions, for example, at 6 percent.

Taken one step further, some landlords and tenants have utilized a concept whereby the tenant does not have to itemize the exclusions but can merely report to the landlord a fixed percentage of its sales. This concept can save the landlord and the tenant both time and money in preparing the report of sales and verifying the accuracy of the exclusions. With Internet sales beginning to become a meaningful factor, an interesting question arises if the tenant seeks to exclude from gross sales in the premises a return to the premises of an item that was purchased over the Internet. The prudent landlord should be increasingly aware of this possibility and should resist such an exclusion.

The Percentage This is a negotiated number that will vary based on factors including store size, intended use, and anticipated profit margins. Often, the percentage is low for high-volume, low-margin goods in stores occupying large square footage such as grocery stores, and high for low-volume, high-margin goods in stores occupying small spaces such as jewelry stores.

Computation and Payment Periods Although many leases provide for the tenant to pay percentage rent every month, based on the gross sales for that month, the most equitable provision will oblige the tenant to pay monthly only after the annual breakpoint has been exceeded. This is because the seasonality of most businesses will result in differing amounts of gross sales in separate months—Easter, back-to-school, and Christmas are usually higher-volume periods. Without an annual reconciliation, an overpayment can result. An interesting and often used compromise is for percentage rent to be calculated and paid quarterly, with an annual adjustment. If the landlord has to wait until the end of the year it may be difficult to collect percentage rent, because the tenant may not have the funds on hand. Therefore, either quarterly payments with annual adjustments or monthly payments after the annual breakpoint has been exceeded constitute the most equitable approaches.

Other issues can arise when the first computation period is less than the full year. If the term commences on September 1 and the year and breakpoint are merely prorated—as in one-third of the months and one-third of the breakpoint—the tenant will likely be penalized, because it will generate perhaps one-half of its annual sales during that busy holiday season. The prudent tenant will seek to average the gross sales for that short period with its gross sales for the first full lease year so as to avoid disproportionality and distortions resulting in overpayment.

Record Keeping The lease will typically specify where, how, and by what means a sale is to be recorded. It will also oblige the tenant to certify the accuracy of its report of gross sales. Such certification may be either by a certified public accountant (which a landlord wants so as to add a level of independent professional verification, and a tenant usually wants to avoid because it adds a level of cost) or, more commonly, by an authorized officer of the tenant. The lease will specify where the records are to be kept as well as specifically what records are to be maintained. The tenant will want records kept at its home office rather than at the premises. Most common records include cash register summary tapes, separate bank account statements, a sales journal, a general ledger, and copies of all tax returns. The tenant will want to oblige the landlord to keep these reports and records confidential.

Verification The verification provision should contain the following elements:

- An obligation for the tenant to retain relevant books and records
- A time within which verification must be undertaken (the tenant will want to limit the number and the disruption during busy seasons)
- The number of audits the landlord may conduct during the term
- The scope of verification
- The party that bears the cost of verification if an error is found
- The size of the errors that give rise to liability for the cost of ver-

ification (the error should be found in percentage rent due, not in the gross sales, unless there is habitual underreporting)
- The consequences of underpayment or overpayment.

The landlord may want the right to terminate the lease if the tenant's gross sales do not reach a specified level, to ensure that the particular tenant is performing up to minimum standards. Conversely, the tenant may request the right to terminate if its level of gross sales do not enable it to achieve a minimum profitability level. This provision is the kickout. In uncertain economic times, this safety valve is important for both the landlord and the tenant. A complicating factor relates to the lost investment in construction costs or free rent or construction allowance made or given by the parties. The common compromise is for the party that exercises its right to terminate to reimburse the other party for its unamortized investment, usually on a straight-line basis over the term. (See also the glossary for an explanation of a kickout.)

Common Area Maintenance

Satellite tenants in large shopping centers often pay a disproportionate share of the expenses, because anchor tenants are excused from some or all of those expenses and the areas of their premises are deducted from the area of the shopping center when expenses are allocated. The method by which the tenant's share is calculated is vitally important in determining what amounts the tenant is obliged to pay. Obviously, the higher the tenant's percentage of those costs, the greater amount the tenant will be required to pay.

Many landlord lease forms define the tenant's share as containing a numerator of the square footage of the premises and a denominator of the "leased and occupied" square footage of the shopping center after deducting the square footage of the "major" stores. The definition of a major store can be as low as the landlord's imagination (for example, at 10,000 square feet) or as high as infinity (for example, at 200,000 square feet). Most satellite tenants recognize that either the landlord or the tenant, or both, must subsidize the true major tenant, or else the small tenant will have either no shopping center built or no meaningful foot traffic.

However, the prudent tenant will request a deduction from

expenses of the payments made by the major stores. It will also demand a formula based on the "leasable" square footage of the shopping center, as well as a definition of the term *major* that considers only true anchor tenants. The careful tenant will also want to ascertain that multiple stores of single owners in the same shopping center are not aggregated as one major space. The usual compromise in the calculation of the satellite tenant's share is for the parties to agree that the amount of "leased and occupied" space will never be less than a certain percentage of the "leaseable" space of the shopping center.

The tenant also may control common area maintenance costs by requesting the landlord exclude certain expenses. The most common of these exclusions are:

- Capital items
- Costs, to the extent to which the landlord is reimbursed by insurance proceeds
- Costs incurred with respect to any other tenants' improvements
- Depreciation or amortization other than over the useful life of the item being depreciated
- Marketing costs, leasing commissions, or legal fees in connection with leases
- Costs incurred by the landlord for other tenants
- The landlord's general corporate overhead and administrative expenses
- Management fees in excess of what is customary
- Costs arising from the presence of hazardous materials
- In-house legal and accounting fees.

With common area maintenance (CAM) costs routinely escalating, many tenants seek to limit annual increases based on a formula usually tied to a cost-of-living index. In an effort to reduce both the administrative costs of calculating CAM costs and the tenant's share of those costs, many landlords are fixing initial CAM costs and annual increases. The benefit to both the landlord and the tenant is readily apparent as it relates to the elimination of many potential disputes between the parties. In calculating the fixed CAM and the increases, the parties will need to carefully examine the amounts. Additionally, the landlord will want to exclude from these fixed increases items over which it has no control, such as the costs of snow removal, insurance, and security.

As CAM costs have increased, tenants have paid great attention to these costs. The CAM audit is the tenant's protection of the CAM rights it has negotiated. Because of the obvious inconvenience of multiple tenants reviewing and analyzing the landlord's books and records, many landlords resist a tenant's audit request. A useful compromise may be for the landlord to agree to furnish a summary of CAM costs broken down by category.

CAM costs are usually paid in advance, based on the landlord's reasonably calculated estimates of costs.

Real Estate Taxes

Real estate taxes (RET) are yet another element of occupancy costs that the prudent tenant will seek to control. The landlord, on the other hand, will want to pass through all of the RET to the satellite tenants.

Just as the calculation of the tenant's share of CAM is of critical importance, the same can be said for the tenant's share of RET. Typically the calculations of RET and CAM are the same.

Taxes refer to charges imposed on all owners of real estate in the area of the taxing authority, and they are usually based on the assessed value of the property. Assessments often refer to charges on the property that are specifically benefited by the expenses to which the assessment relates.

The tenant should request a share of any refunds that a landlord receives, as well as a share of the interest that a landlord receives on an overpayment. Tenants should also ask to exclude late payment charges and penalties. Other taxes typically excluded are inheritance taxes, transfer taxes, and net income taxes, as well as (to the extent possible and calculable) any increases in taxes as a result of the sale of the shopping center occurring within a specified time period. The tenant should also request that the RET should be paid in installments if the law allows. Finally, the tenant usually requests verification of the amount of RET by obtaining a copy of the paid tax bill.

RET are usually paid in advance, together with the tenant's monthly payments of minimum rent and CAM. Tenants will sometimes request the right to contest with the taxing authorities any RET that it considers to be excessive. The landlord will almost never permit a satellite tenant to contest RET, because the tenant's interests relative to those of the landlord and the shopping center are small. In respect to tenants occupying larger spaces in the shopping center, the landlord should exercise great caution in permitting these tenants to contest taxes. At times, the mere contest can result in RET being increased by the tax assessor. The tenant should request the right to recover the costs of its RET contest.

From time to time a lease will provide for the tenant to pay only its share of the RET over a "base year." Obviously it is imperative to define the base year. While the tenant wants it to be as late as possible, the landlord wants the earliest possible date. Usually the base year is the year in which the term commences. The tenant should be careful that the base year is indeed the year in which the shopping center is fully assessed, or else the increases may prove to be very large.

Utilities

Tenants depend on the landlord for the connection and provision of gas, electricity, water, and sewer. Usually tenants contract directly with telephone utilities.

Utilities in shopping centers are usually separately metered. If that is the case, there should be little about which the tenant and landlord will disagree. Disputes may arise in instances in which multiple tenants share utilities and the landlord seeks to allocate costs among those tenants. The prudent tenant will insist on a formula in which the landlord prorates based on not only size but also use. Certain tenants, such as restaurants and jewelry stores, require greater amounts of utilities than other tenants of comparable size.

Another area of potential dispute arises when the landlord furnishes any utility service from equipment that the landlord installed and maintains. The tenant will want to make certain that the landlord will not charge more for that utility than the tenant would have paid had the tenant obtained the service directly from the utility company.

Insurance

The subject of insurance is extremely complex, and its details and nuances are well beyond the scope of this chapter. However, the leasing professional should be aware of the following basics as they apply to aspects of the lease.

The property owner bears the risks of damage to its property and liabilities for injury to people on the property. When the owner is the landlord, it shares those risks and liabilities with its tenants. The insurance provisions in the shopping center lease are interrelated to provisions regarding damage and destruction, waiver and release, indemnification, alterations, repairs and maintenance, and surrender. The goal of both the landlord and the tenant should be to obtain the best coverage for the most risks at the least cost.

Property insurance covers the direct losses from damage to or destruction of the insured property, such as fixtures, leasehold improvements, equipment, and buildings, as well as resulting reductions in the income produced from them. The losses covered by a property policy are payable to the insured. Its goal is to return the insured to its position before the loss.

Liability insurance protects the insured from the claims of third parties for an injury or damage to their property as a result of the insured's conduct, usually negligence.

The property and liability insurance contracts are contracts of indemnity. They are intended to preserve the position the insured would have had if the loss had not occurred.

Many shopping center leases require one of the parties to buy relatively inexpensive rent insurance that ensures the payment of rent if the premises are rendered untenantable by a covered loss. Three different coverages are offered:

- Business interruption insurance, which a tenant purchases if the lease does not provide for an abatement of rent after a casualty
- Rental income insurance, which the landlord purchases if its lease abates rent after a casualty
- Rental value insurance, which both a landlord and tenant purchase to insure against the loss of value of the occupied premises.

In determining the amount of coverage, the parties must consider the greatest period of time for which the tenant will be obliged to pay rent or the landlord will be deprived of rent.

When an insured property loss occurs, the insurance company pays the insured for the loss according to the property policy, and the payment is generally made without regard to fault by the insured. If a third party is at fault, the insured has a claim against that third party. The insurer then is the only proper claimant against the party causing the loss. The insurer is said to be subrogated to the rights that its insured has against the person who causes the loss, and it may assert a claim against that person. Insurers will agree to allow waivers of their rights of subrogation given before a loss. In the lease the waiver will extend to risks included in the property policy to the extent of its limits. The waiver should be mutual.

The landlord typically requests the tenant to furnish evidence of the tenant's insurance. Usually this is in the form of a certificate. Many leases oblige the tenant to use an insurance company that has a minimum rating by one of the principal rating agencies. Leases will also require the insurance company to be qualified or licensed to do business in the state in which the property is located. Because most tenants want to retain flexibility in choosing their own insurance carrier, they will usually resist the ratings demand. Tenants will also seek to have the landlord accept insurance as part of the tenant's blanket coverage, a policy covering the premises as well as other of the tenant's locations. Coverage under a blanket policy will result in lower premiums payable for individual locations.

Another cost-saving device used by the most creditworthy tenants is self-insurance. By self-insuring, the tenant provides its own insurance rather than the insurance prescribed by the lease. Commonly requested risks for self-insurance include worker's compensation, rent insurance, and environmental hazards. Environmental hazards are almost another topic, too important to be limited to a mere mention in this chapter; however, the shopping center professional should know when to seek experts or legal counsel in this area.

Use

The use provision not only prescribes what a tenant can do with its premises, but also affects the tenant's ability to change an unsuccessful business, assign the lease or sublease the premises, discontinue operations, and be protected from competition. A broad use is most advantageous to tenants and may facilitate the tenant's exit strategy, whereas a narrow use may impede it.

Shopping center leases usually state the use of the premises affirmatively. This is typically accomplished restrictively by the use of words such as "solely," "only," and "for no other purpose."

The use provision is a device to ensure compatible uses, fair allocation of shopping center resources such as utilities and parking, and protection of one tenant from another's competing use. From time to time landlords may require tenants to attach an inventory list or a menu stating the specific items to be sold. Although mentioning specific prices may be illegal, quality may be specified (for example, "high quality").

EXCLUSIVES

In the highly competitive world of retail, many tenants now demand that the landlord limit the number or square footage of other tenants in the shopping center who have the right to make the same or substantially similar use of their premises. This is known as an exclusive. The justification for the tenant requesting such protection is that there is a finite amount of merchandise being consumed in any category; if there is no limitation on the number or square footage of tenants permitted to sell such merchandise, then the tenant cannot generate enough sales to maintain profitability. Obviously the landlord of a shopping center will not want to restrict its ability to fill each of the spaces in its shopping center with tenants of its choice. Indeed, in difficult economic times the landlord may have no alternative but to try to lease space to any rent-paying tenant in order to meet its debt service and real estate tax obligations.

Before considering whether to grant an exclusive, the landlord must carefully review the permitted uses in existing leases in order to be certain it has not already allowed—or, alternatively, not prohibited—the proposed exclusive use.

Common exclusives will prohibit the landlord from entering into leases, or permitting the assignment or subleasing, of any or a specified amount of space in any premises other than that of the tenant. This restriction may be for all or a portion of the following:

- The lease term (for instance, "during the first three years")
- The premises (for instance, "no more than 100 square feet" or "not in the front one-half of the premises")
- A percentage of sales (for instance, "not more than 25 percent of its gross sales").

Since the landlord believes that the granting of exclusive uses limits its flexibility in future leasing or development of the shopping center, the landlord may seek to limit the tenant's right to only the shopping center as presently constructed, thereby preserving its rights to future development. Another limitation is to grant the exclusive only so long as the tenant is achieving certain minimum sales levels; if the tenant cannot succeed with protection against competition, then it is not worthy of having protection at all.

The prudent landlord will also seek to exclude or except from the exclusive any major store or anchor. The tenant may recognize the reasons for this, but it may request that the landlord not permit the major to be totally of a competing use. Obviously a huge competitor is more deleterious to the tenant than a small one. Another variation on the anchor exception may be for the tenant to have relief if the anchor installs a separate customer entrance or a separate sign identifying or giving access to the space within its store devoted to the competing use.

Anchor leases usually do not have restrictive use provisions and may indeed contain a use clause that permits "any lawful purpose." Such an unlimited use is probably too permissive and may be reduced to "a department store" or "a grocery store."

When an agreeable provision has been prepared, often the landlord will state that the exclusive is "personal" to the tenant and will not benefit assignees or subtenants. The logic behind this request is that the landlord has confidence in the tenant's ability to succeed in the premises but may not have similar faith in the tenant's transferees. Since the exclusive is such a valuable right, the tenant will likely resist this "personal" argument because it diminishes the tenant's ability to transfer its interest in the lease.

The tenant will want to make certain that the exclusive affects not only the shopping center as shown on the plan, but also any outparcels or any adjacent property that the landlord owns or controls.

The properly drafted exclusive also includes the remedies available to the tenant: for example, legal remedies such as specified damages, an abatement or reduction of rent, lease termination, reimbursement of the tenant's unamortized construction costs, or reimbursement of the tenant's lost profits. It may also include the equitable remedy of injunctive relief. In the case of an injunction, the tenant will be faced with a number of substantial hurdles such as the posting of a bond and proof of irreparable harm (for instance, was the landlord's property so unique that the tenant would be irreparably damaged without it).

Many people wrongly believe that exclusives granted in shopping centers are anticompetitive and in violation of federal trade practice laws. In fact, when restrictions against competing uses are incidental to an otherwise lawful agreement and are reasonable in scope, they are perfectly legal.

Shopping center leases contain an express covenant obliging the tenant to operate under a specific trade name and no other. Landlords favor this limitation because it compels the tenant to use a name that is likely to be well known in the market or regionally (even nationally), and the landlord derives the benefit of the tenant's broader advertising and name recognition. Secondarily, by obliging the tenant to operate under a specific name, the landlord often thwarts the tenant's ability to assign or sublease, because the transferee will likely prefer to operate under its own name.

Obviously, the tenant wants to be able to change its name as market conditions dictate. Perhaps the tenant has other divisions that are operating more successfully, and it may want the ability to change its name to that of one of those divisions.

CO-TENANCY

The shopping center tenant enters into a lease in expectation of the drawing power of the shopping center, including not only the major stores but the synergy of the other satellite stores as well. To protect itself against the possibility that the tenant may be the only one operating in the shopping center, the tenant asks for co-tenancy protection. This provision may relate to the tenant's initial opening obligation, its obligation to operate continuously, or both. Under such a provision, a tenant's operation in the shopping center (and/or its obligation to pay rent and additional rent) is conditioned upon the presence of other tenants.

The most common co-tenancy requirements make the tenant's obligations conditional upon some or all of the anchors "and" (as distinguished from "or") upon some percentage of the other tenants (by number or by square footage) actually open for business (as opposed to "obligated" to be open for business, which is preferable to the landlord). Usually the tenant's remedies for the landlord's breach of this provision are similar to the remedies for a breach of a tenant's exclusive use provision.

Issues can sometimes arise over whether the co-tenancy requirement is satisfied if a portion of an anchor is open and operating, or whether a mere temporary closure for renovation or remodeling is a trigger event, or whether the landlord can substitute one anchor for another. These are issues that the parties should address, particularly if a specific anchor tenant is a major draw for the shopping center.

Sometimes the landlord agrees to a co-tenancy provision, but conditions the tenant's relief on a proof of damages sustained by the tenant. Usually this is in the form of a sales test, wherein the tenant must demonstrate that its gross sales have been negatively affected. Tenants try to resist sales tests.

Shopping center leases also specify that tenants are obliged to remain open during prescribed business hours. This is called continuous operation. Tenants often seek to condition their agreement to operate on other tenants being similarly open (as distinguished from "obligated to be open") during the same hours.

To a shopping center landlord, the tenant's continuous operation of its business is of vital importance—not only because it generates activity, but because it produces gross sales from which percentage rent is paid. It may also be significant in helping the landlord meet its co-tenancy obligations. The shopping center is not so desirable a destination for customers if not all of the tenants are open for business. The typical shopping center lease prescribes a penalty, typically additional minimum rent, for a tenant's failure to operate continuously. The landlord can justify this on the theory that if a tenant is not open and operating, it cannot generate gross sales and the landlord will be deprived of percentage rent revenue.

Sometimes a tenant may actually need to close for a specified time to perform repairs or conduct inventory. Usually landlords permit this if the landlord is given notice and if the time period is both prescribed and limited.

In the case of larger-format stores, it is not uncommon for a tenant such as a multiscreen cinema or a supermarket to abandon an outmoded facility for a replacement store in the immediate area. The landlord will want to protect against being forced to sit with a large, unattractive vacancy on which the former tenant may be willing to continue paying rent in order to prevent a competing tenant from opening in the premises. Indeed, the landlord of the substitute property may even be willing to subsidize the tenant's rental obligation.

RADIUS RESTRICTION

The mirror image of the tenant's exclusive use protection is the radius restriction. The radius restriction is the shopping center landlord's effort to assure itself that the tenant will devote its energy to the operation of its business at the shopping center, generate the greatest possible sales from the premises, and not be induced by competing landlords. The radius restriction prohibits a tenant from conducting the same or substantially similar business within a specified distance from the shopping center. The landlord also typically seeks to restrict the tenant's shareholders, directors, partners, managers, and guarantors as well.

Tenants generally want to exclude their existing stores as well as stores added as part of an acquisition. The tenant also usually wants to except stores operating under a different trade name or as outlet stores, in different types of shopping centers (e.g., entertainment facilities), or stores acquired by or from a competitor.

So long as the radius restriction is deemed to be reasonable, it will not be considered to be a restraint of trade.

Compliance with Laws

The obligation to comply with laws arises at the outset, during the term, and as relates to the use of the premises. Usually the tenant requests the landlord to represent that the premises is in compliance with all laws as of the commencement of the term. Although the shopping center lease requires the tenant to comply with covenants affecting the premises during the term, the prudent tenant will seek to limit this almost unlimited obligation, which can, theoretically, even make the tenant responsible for capital improvements. The tenant seeks to qualify its duty to be limited to those matters specifically relating to the tenant's use of the premises. For example, a requirement that the premises be covered by a sprinkler system becomes the tenant's obligation only if it is the result of the tenant's specific use—as in the case of a restaurant—rather than a requirement for generally all retail stores in the shopping center.

The responsibility for removal of hazardous materials is a new issue between shopping center landlords and tenants. Because the cost of such removal is often high, it is important for the parties to apportion those risks. The usual compromise is for the tenant to assume responsibility for all hazardous materials it has brought upon or into the premises, and for the landlord to remove or bear the cost of anything already existing in the premises or introduced by the landlord. The parties generally request indemnification in that regard.

The Americans With Disabilities Act (ADA) of 1990 is intended to provide a comprehensive mandate for the elimination of discrimination against individuals with disabilities. Part of the ADA relates to the removal of architectural barriers in places of public accommodations such as shopping centers. The shopping center lease allocates who should bear responsibility for compliance with those costs. Usually the tenant is solely responsible within its premises and proportionately responsible with other tenants for the landlord's ADA compliance costs.

Assignment and Sublease

The assignment and sublease provisions are vitally important to both the landlord and the tenant. The landlord believes it has a greater and longer commitment to the shopping center than the tenant and should therefore control the premises. The tenant belives it has authority over the premises during the term, and so any use or user that complies with the lease should be permitted.

An assignment is a disposition of all of the assignor's rights in the lease and its interest in the premises. An assignment does not release the tenant; rather, its liability continues.

A sublease is the creation of a lease within a lease, in which the tenant transfers less than all of its rights in all or a part of the premises. The relationship between tenant and subtenant is the same as the relationship between the landlord and the tenant. The sublease depends on the continued existence of the lease. The landlord has no relationship with the subtenant.

The general rule of transfer (both assignments and subleases) is that they are permitted unless they are prohibited. Most shopping center leases prohibit transfers without the landlord's prior consent, which it may withhold for any reason or no reason. Sometimes the tenant requests that the landlord agree not to unreasonably withhold its consent to a transfer. Precedent in state courts determines the standards of reasonableness, and those decisions vary substantially from state to state. Some courts will imply reasonableness even if the lease gives the landlord sole discretion.

Shopping center landlords commonly prohibit transfers that result in a subdivision of the premises, because they change the premises and may make subsequent leasing of it more difficult.

Landlords often seek to adjust the rental rate upon a lease transfer. This adjustment is usually done in the form of grossing up the effective rent being paid by the transferor, on the theory that the landlord should not be forced to accept less total rent from a transferee, which may be an inferior operator.

The careful landlord will define assignment and subletting broadly so that it includes a transfer by operation of law as in bankruptcy, a change of voting control, or a transfer of greater than 50 percent of the stock or beneficial ownership of the tenant. It also prohibits transfers if the tenant is in default.

The shopping center lease typically sets forth the information to be submitted by the tenant in order for the landlord to consider the tenant's request for a lease transfer. This information normally includes name, address, copy of transfer document, business history, references, and financial information.

Contentious matters can arise when the transfer is for a rental amount greater than set forth in the lease. The landlord's position is typically that it owns the property and the tenant is in the retail business, not the real estate business. Therefore, if a profit is to be made the profit belongs to the landlord. The tenant commonly counters that it bears the risk if the premises are less valuable and so, conversely, the tenant should be entitled to an increase in value. The tenant is also likely to claim that the landlord is not making any less than it expected as a result of the transfer. Other factors to consider before calculating profit are the cost of the original leasehold improvements and the profit on the value of the business itself.

Another way in which landlords seek to prohibit lease transfers is by a provision that enables the landlord to terminate the lease and recapture the premises in the event the tenant requests an assignment or subletting. Obviously the landlord will exercise its recapture rights only if it has a better use or a more desirable tenant ready to take the space, or if the landlord is confident it can secure a substitute tenant at a higher rent or in a stronger financial position. The prudent tenant will request the ability to withdraw its request for lease transfer under those circumstances. The tenant may, however, permit the landlord to recapture but request lost profits and the unamortized value of its leasehold improvements.

Rules and Regulations

Most shopping center leases contain rules and regulations either as a part of the lease or as an exhibit to it. The rules and regulations usually deal with housekeeping matters, which a tenant must be certain are consistent with its operations. These rules may relate to the premises as well as the common areas, including the parking areas. The tenant should make certain that these rules are enforced uniformly as to all satellite tenants.

Merchants' Association

The merchants' association is an unincorporated association or not-for-profit corporation formed to advance the interests of the tenants of the shopping center. An association is helpful for activities such as grand openings, holiday promotions, and center-wide sales. Most shopping center leases require the tenant to join the association, pay dues, and participate and obey the association rules. The prudent tenant seeks to limit the dues it pays (and any increases in those dues) and condition the tenant's membership by requiring that all or virtually all other tenants have to be members and have to pay at the same rate (as opposed to being "obligated to be members" and "paying dues at substantially the same rate"). The tenant also wants to make certain that the landlord is contributing to the merchants' association as well.

Unlike merchants' associations, which are usually controlled by tenants, promotional funds and media funds are typically created, controlled, and managed by landlords to advertise their shopping center.

Common Area Configuration and Standards

Common areas are those parts of the shopping center that the landlord controls and that are intended for the common benefit or use by tenants, their customers, visitors, and invitees. Common areas are areas from which the tenant will derive a benefit. As important as the definition of the common areas is the allocation of the costs of maintenance of the common areas.

Often the common areas are illustrated on a site plan attached to the lease. In doing so, the landlord must take particular care that the attachment of the site plan is not deemed a representation that the shopping center will always be configured as it is on the plan. The landlord always wants the right to expand, contract, or otherwise change the layout of the shopping center.

The tenant may want the following assurances from the landlord:

- It will not erect barriers that may divert traffic or impede access to the premises, including kiosks, structures, and planters.
- It will maintain an agreed ratio of car parking spaces to leaseable area of the shopping center.
- It will maintain a proximate employee parking area at no charge to the tenant.
- It will not impose parking fees unless obliged to do so by governmental authorities.

The landlord usually agrees only to maintain parking ratios as required by code, and that the changes the landlord may make to the common areas will not materially interfere with access to or visibility of the premises.

Landlords often add an administrative fee (usually 15 percent) to the aggregate costs of maintaining the common areas. They also sometimes seek to impose a management fee to compensate the landlord for its allocable share of home office expenses.

The tenant should insist on a certain standard of services and cleanliness in the common areas, just as the landlord requires of the tenant in the premises. This common area standard is often expressed in terms such as "a first-class shopping center" or "consistent with other comparable shopping centers."

Repairs and Maintenance

The tenant is typically obliged to maintain the premises. Reasonable wear and tear are usually excepted from the condition in which the premises are to be returned to the landlord. The landlord will not want to make any repair that is subject to the damage provisions discussed later. The landlord will agree to repair the areas outside the premises that are damaged by its agents or employees. The landlord will not want to incur any obligation for repair until it has been given notice. In addition, the landlord will not want to assume any of the tenant's consequential damages, such as for loss of business; rather, the landlord will argue for business interruption insurance. A landlord's repair obligations are usually limited to the foundations, exterior walls, and any structural elements. The landlord will usually except from its obligations any damage that is caused by any act, negligence, or omission of the tenant, its employees, agents, contractors, or customers. The landlord is also usually obliged to repair the utilities outside the premises unless damage thereto is caused by the tenant, its employees, agents, contractors, or customers.

Alterations

At the time it enters into a lease, a tenant must consider the alterations it is contemplating. The landlord is concerned that the tenant not be allowed to make alterations that are to be considered structural. The tenant is likely to want to make alterations that are merely decorative, such as painting, carpeting, fixturization, and the like, without the necessity (and cost) of obtaining the landlord's consent.

Often landlords request the right to approve alterations that affect the systems of the shopping center or the premises (such as electrical, mechanical, or plumbing), the storefront, and the signage of the premises, because these alterations are clearly visible to the public and should blend with the landlord's design standards for the shopping center. Additionally, the landlord invariably demands the right to approve alterations costing more than a prescribed dollar amount (for example, $10,000).

The landlord also wants the right to approve the tenant's contractor. This is often used to protect the tenant against its use of a contractor who previously failed to perform satisfactorily. The tenant should resist having the landlord actually select the tenant's contractor.

The landlord generally requests detailed plans and specifications covering those tenant-proposed alterations which the landlord is entitled to approve.

Mechanic's Liens

Mechanic's liens are intended to ensure the payment of mechanics, laborers, and suppliers for the improvements they make to the real estate. Most shopping center leases contain a provision prohibiting the tenant from permitting a lien to be filed against the shopping center as a result of the tenant's failure to pay its contractor. The lease permits the landlord to pay to discharge this lien and to recover its costs and interest if the tenant fails to do so. The tenant usually asks for a reasonable time within which to remove the lien and the right to post collateral in the form of a bond. The removal of the lien is imperative to the landlord because the lien encumbers the landlord's title to the property.

Surrender

Surrender occurs either upon the early termination of the lease or upon the redelivery of the premises at the end of the term. Often a form of lease termination is used, in which the parties agree to perform their obligations up to the termination date. The rights of any subtenant must also be extinguished by the termination agreement; otherwise the subtenant may assert some rights to possession.

At the end of the term, tenants are usually obligated to remove their alterations, additions, and improvements and to restore the premises to the original condition. In premises in which minimal construction has been performed, this may not be a significant issue for the tenant; however, in instances in which the tenant's improvements have been substantial, the costs of removal can be burdensome on the tenant. Consider the example of a bank or a restaurant installation and the potentially enormous expense for the tenant to remove safes or restaurant equipment. The parties need to take account of these costs when negotiating the shopping center lease.

The tenant is invariably required to remove fixtures and personal property upon the expiration of the term. These are items that are not permanently affixed to the premise such as the cash wrap, tables, rounders for hanging garments, and the like.

Damage and Destruction

Damage to a shopping center diminishes the landlord's asset, interrupts cash flow, and threatens the performance of its mortgage obligations. For the tenant, its business is interrupted and its employees are jobless. When damage occurs, the landlord wants to rebuild the shopping center, preserve its income, and satisfy its lenders.

The key issues in shopping center leases relating to damage and destruction are whether the problem affects a stated percentage area of the project and of the premises, whether the cost of repair exceeds a stated cost or percentage of the value of the premises or the shopping center, and how long a period of time will be needed for the repair. Often the lease gives the landlord cancellation rights when the damage is extensive or costly or will take an extended period of time to repair.

The prudent tenant seeks to prevent the landlord from treating it differently from other tenants similarly situated within the shopping center. The tenant does not want the landlord to use a casualty as an excuse to terminate the lease and replace the tenant with another one it considers more desirable. The tenant also seeks to abate the payment of rent and additional rent during the period when it is not open as a result of the casualty. Abatement is usually based on the share of the premises that are rendered untenantable.

The landlord and tenant must also determine whether the premises will be rebuilt. Usually, if the landlord obtains sufficient funds from its insurance proceeds, it will agree to rebuild the shopping center and deliver the premises to the condition they were originally delivered to the tenant. Tenants often ask that their leases be extended for the period of interruption and that they be able to terminate if only a relatively short time remains on the lease. A tenant may not want to incur the expense of rebuilding if only two years remain on the lease.

Condemnation

Condemnation refers to a taking of private property for public use. When the property is taken, just compensation must be paid. The shopping center lease details the effect of the condemnation on the lease and the allocation of compensation between the landlord and the tenant.

Condemnation of shopping centers is extremely rare. When it does occur, it may be total, partial, or temporary. It may affect the premises or the common areas, or both. If the taking occurs at all, it most commonly affects the parking areas. The parties typically want to provide for their respective rights in the event parking is reduced below the ratio prescribed in the lease.

If a taking occurs, the lease may allow the tenant to cancel the lease if any vital parts of the shopping center are taken. Sometimes a compromise can be reached on a rent abatement, rather than outright cancellation. The key question in determining the abatement is the effect of the taking on the tenant's business. Most leases provide for lease cancellation if the entire premises are taken; temporary abatement during restoration, in the event of a partial taking of the premises; permanent abatement in proportion to the reduced floor area of the premises; cancellation upon taking of areas vital to the tenant; and cancellation if a specified portion of the common areas or parking has been taken. As with casualty, the tenant usually refuses the landlord's request to terminate unless the landlord terminates the leases of all other tenants similarly situated.

With regard to the allocation of the condemnation award, the parties usually agree that in the limited instances in which the landlord may permit the tenant to file a claim for its leasehold improvements, such claim may not reduce the landlord's award.

Subordination

Shopping center leases contain a provision rearranging the relative priorities of the lease and the loan encumbering the premises by subordinating the rights of the tenant to the rights of the landlord's lender. The landlord's lender usually requires that the tenant's rights that may be superior to the lender's rights (because a lease was entered into first) be made inferior or subordinated. As a result of subordination, the subordinate tenant will lose its lease in the event the lender forecloses on its mortgage. This is why tenants request a subordination, non-disturbance, and attornment (SNDA) agreement. Without an SNDA, the lender may use the foreclosure as a means to substitute another tenant, and the existing tenant will lose its investment. Attornment is the means by which the tenant agrees to remain after foreclosure and to treat the lender as the landlord. The landlord has no direct interest in subordination. It seeks only to satisfy the requirements of its lender. The form of SNDA is usually prescribed by the landlord's lender.

During uncertain economic times, it is extremely important for the tenant to secure an SNDA or else it risks losing its investment in the premises. Often the landlord agrees that it will "attempt" to secure an SNDA or will use "reasonable" or "best efforts" to do so. The prudent tenant demands the "best efforts" standard, because the consequences to the tenant can be dire.

Landlord's Access

The landlord expressly reserves the right to enter the premises. The tenant should insist on advance notice of entry (except in emergencies), request that it occur during business hours, demand that the landlord repair any damage that it may cause, and make certain that in its entry the landlord causes as little inconvenience as possible to the conduct of the tenant's business.

Indemnification

In a shopping center lease, the cost of property loss is spread among the tenants. The landlord insures the building with money from tenants, the tenant insures its property in its premises, and the landlord and tenant look to their insurers in the event of a loss. The liability risk arises out of the landlord's retained control of the common areas. Usually the tenant is responsible for claims arising in its premises and the landlord is responsible for claims arising in the common areas, or the tenant (or landlord) is responsible for claims arising from its conduct regardless of where the claim arises.

With an indemnification, the indemnitor (the party giving the indemnity) assumes responsibility for claims for personal injury or property damage asserted by third parties against the indemnitee (the party to which the indemnity is given).

Security for the Tenant's Performance

Security for the tenant's performance takes two forms: security deposits and guarantors. A landlord often insists on financial strength in the tenant, or ensures a ready source of payments in the event the tenant defaults.

Security deposits can be given in the form of cash or a letter of credit. They are usually measured by the amount of the landlord's risk and may cover not only minimum rent and additional rent but also the amount of time it might take the landlord to re-lease the space, the inducement the landlord might have to give to the replacement tenant, the amount of tenant allowance the landlord might have to give, and the amount of legal fees and brokerage commissions that the landlord might have to pay.

The security deposit is not intended as liquidated damages, but rather it ensures the payment of rent and the performance of the tenant's other obligations. The security deposit must be kept segregated from the landlord's own funds. State statutes usually determine whether it must bear interest and, if so, to whom the interest belongs.

Sometimes the tenant may request a reduction in the security deposit after it has demonstrated either an agreed-on creditworthiness or a history of performance during the term of the lease.

Guarantors, although not parties to the lease, are important from the outset because the landlord often has a concern that the tenant may not be able to perform its lease obligation. A guarantor agrees to pay a debt or other obligations in the event that the tenant defaults. Landlords usually look for a responsible guarantor—one that maintains a stated net worth. The landlord should make certain that the guarantor acknowledges any modifications to the lease document, including an extension of the lease term, or else the guarantor may not be bound. The guarantor will want a notice of the tenant's default and an opportunity to cure it in order to reduce its losses.

Quiet Enjoyment

A quiet enjoyment provision promises the tenant that its possession of the premises will not be disturbed by the landlord or anyone claiming by, through, or under the landlord, or by anyone else having an interest in the premises. This provision is particularly important as it relates to the landlord's failure to maintain the premises. The covenant is not breached unless there is an actual disturbance of the tenant's use and enjoyment of the premises.

Default

Shopping center leases are typically written to emphasize tenant defaults rather than landlord defaults. This is because the landlord's lender wants to have uninterrupted cash flow, and therefore the tenant is not granted any rights of offset, reduction, or withholding of rent; even though the tenant may want its costs and lost profits minimized. The shopping center landlord will usually not permit a tenant to make any repairs to the roof, structure, or systems serving the premises.

A tenant's defaults may not be intentional, and some may not involve either inconvenience or risk to the landlord. Some defaults may be susceptible to easy cure by the landlord, with the costs being charged to the tenant. The tenant usually will demand that those costs be reasonable, although the landlord's position is that the costs will be what they are and the tenant could have avoided them by not being in default in the first place. The landlord wants to make sure it has the right, but not the obligation, to cure the default. The tenant will insist on notice and the opportunity to cure its defaults.

The lease should specify the events of default as well as the landlord's remedies in the event a default occurs. The tenant usually asks for a grace period to cure the default. Grace periods for monetary provisions are usually shorter than for nonmonetary provisions, because the landlord's lenders do not usually give the landlord grace periods for mortgage payments.

Events of default typically include the following:

- Failure to pay rent or additional rent
- The tenant vacating or abandoning the premises
- Tenant insolvency or bankruptcy
- The taking of the premises by process of law
- The premises being subject to attachment
- The tenant failing to take possession or to remain open and operating
- The tenant's breach of any other agreement, term, covenant, or condition required by the lease.

The landlord's remedies may include monetary damages as well as lease termination. It may also permit the landlord to maintain the lease and sue for damages, as well as to sue for rent as it comes due. The lease may also permit the landlord to reenter and re-lease the premises, and the right to collect rent for the balance of the term of the lease in one lump sum. This last remedy is called rent acceleration. Often the tenant will request the accelerated rent so collected should be discounted to its present value.

The Bankruptcy Code may affect the landlord's rights, because many lease provisions are unenforceable against a tenant when it is in bankruptcy.

Many states will impose upon the landlord the duty to mitigate the tenant's damages in the event of a default. The prudent landlord will quickly advertise the premises for lease and take all actions to lease the premises. An interesting question arises when there are other available spaces in the shopping center. Which space does the landlord offer to a prospective tenant? Obviously the landlord will be faced with the duty to mitigate damages on all of the available spaces on which defaults have occurred (as compared to a location that is vacant because the lease term has simply expired).

Brokers

Most shopping center leases contain a provision by which the landlord seeks to protect itself from the claims of brokers that it has not employed. The prudent tenant asks to make this provision mutual and to add language stating that the party that retained the broker is responsible for the payment of its fee. In instances in which there is an identifiable broker, the landlord and tenant should specifically name that broker and the lease should clearly state who is to pay the fee of that broker.

Memorandum of Lease

Most shopping center leases prohibit the recording of leases, because the parties are reluctant to disclose the relevant business terms of the lease to the general public, other tenants, or the tax assessor. In some states, the recording of a lease can also result in the payment of a substantial recording tax. Because of these factors, the landlord and tenant may choose to record a "short-form lease," a "notice of lease," or a "memorandum of lease." This document typically contains only the essential lease terms but excludes details about rent.

Recording a memorandum of lease serves to give notice of the tenant's rights to possession even if the tenant is not then in actual possession of the premises (for example, the shopping center may not yet be built), and it also tends to strengthen the tenant's exclusive rights that may have been granted under the lease.

Holding Over

Holding over describes the conduct of a tenant that remains in possession of the premises after its term has ended. In the event of a holdover, the landlord can either evict the tenant or bind the tenant to another term. The shopping center lease will set forth the consequences of a holdover. Usually the lease provides for greater rent during the holdover period. It also often provides for the tenant to be liable to the landlord for any damages that the landlord has sustained because the landlord may have leased the premises to a replacement tenant to whom it is unable to deliver the premises on a timely basis. If the landlord and tenant are in negotiation to extend the lease, the tenant should try to negotiate an amount of time in which holdover rent will not apply.

Force Majeure

This provision takes account of the fact that one of the parties may not be able to meet its obligations in a timely manner because of a supervening cause beyond its control, and therefore that party's failure of timely performance is excused. However, force majeure never excuses the payment of money. The force majeure provision usually requires the delayed party to give notice of the delay and to use reasonable efforts to minimize it. Most shopping center leases contain force majeure clauses drafted solely in favor of the landlord. The tenant should demand that the protections be made mutual.

Financing Modifications and Approvals

In order to avoid the loss of financing because of an unacceptable lease, many shopping center leases reserve to the landlord and the landlord's lender the right to change the completed lease. Obviously such a provision deprives the tenant of the benefit of all of the modifications the tenant has negotiated. The prudent tenant insists that the lease may not be modified in a way that would increase the tenant's costs, diminish its rights, or increase its obligations, or the tenant should seek to require that the landlord's lender preapprove the lease.

Estoppel Certificates

Estoppel certificates are status reports on the lease that confirm its effectiveness and terms, as well as the absence of claims. Although usually requested by landlords for their prospective lenders or purchasers, they may also be needed by tenants for the benefit of their prospective transferees or purchasers. The typical shopping center lease reserves to the landlord the right to execute an estoppel certificate on behalf of the tenant if the tenant fails to do so within a prescribed period of time.

Notices

Shopping center leases usually specify the way in which notices must be given. Hand delivery is often allowed but is usually useless without a receipt. Tenants often resist delivery of notices to the premises if the premises are part of a multistore chain, because the person receiving the notice is usually not a person who is authorized to act on behalf of the tenant and may not even be reliable. The usual practice is for the parties to agree to delivery by mail, return receipt requested, or by courier service or telecopier. Often the parties add an attorney to the notice provision, because that acts as a backup and alerts the attorney to any possible problem. Finally, the lease usually specifies when a notice is deemed to be given—"when mailed" is the common language; "when received or refused" is preferable because of the vagaries of delivery.

Attorney Fees

The lease usually provides that the prevailing party will be entitled to recover its fees and costs in the event it is required to engage counsel on its behalf as a result of litigation, including all trials and appeals. Sometimes leases provide for attorney's fees even when the actions of one of the parties necessitates the other party to engage an attorney to enforce its rights regardless of whether litigation actually follows.

Waiver of Jury Trial

Shopping center leases typically provide for the tenant to voluntarily waive its rights to a jury trial. The reason the landlord gives for the inclusion of this provision is so as to avoid the legal expense and delay of getting a jury trial.

Conclusion

The shopping center lease is a complex legal document. All shopping center professionals should have a working knowledge of the various provisions of the lease. The different sections of the lease must be examined and understood by the parties involved, to make certain: first, that they are not inconsistent with any other sections of the lease; second, that they are approvable by each of the parties to the lease (and their lenders); third, that they accurately reflect the intentions of the parties; and fourth, that they establish a business framework within which each of the parties can adequately meet its business and strategic goals.

Andrew Shedlin, SCSM/CLS, is President of The Andrew Shedlin Companies, Inc., Highland Park, Illinois.

8 | UNDERSTANDING AND NEGOTIATING LEASES

Alan A. Alexander, SCSM/CPM

The variety of rents and terms involved in retail leasing often seems overwhelming, especially for someone new to shopping center leasing. In any given center, for instance, one tenant may pay $30 per square foot per year with a net lease and percentage rent clause, while another tenant pays only $16 per square foot per year with limits on the net items and a much lower percentage rent rate. Rents and incomes become even more confusing when one tenant pays a low rent rate and has better terms than the tenant next door. Over time, however, the newcomer to leasing develops an understanding of the importance of the different rents in relation to a center's merchandise mix.

In the initial stages of prospecting, generating interest, and lease negotiating, the leasing agent is the prospect's interpreter of the project and its ownership. Therefore, the leasing agent should establish strong credibility with all prospects. Retail leasing frequently necessitates working with a tenant in making more than one deal at more than one location. The relationship established through the signing of a lease becomes a long-term relationship. An unsure start can mitigate against a solid business relationship over the long term. The leasing agent should keep informed about the rents and terms of deals made in the center and be knowledgeable about how the center is to be merchandised and operated. The leasing agent should always offer honest and accurate answers to all questions, unless the questions do not relate to the deal under discussion or information is not available at the time for public release. The integrity of the leasing program should be at the forefront of every move made in the leasing of retail space.

Leasing Responsibilities

The purpose of any leasing effort is to fill space in a shopping center with qualified tenants that enhance the merchandise mix of the center and, at the same time, pay the optimum rent for the space in question. As a rule, the goal of the center owner is to obtain the maximum rent possible; however, there are circumstances when a landlord will accept less than the maximum rent in order to secure the best tenant for the overall success of the center. The primary role of the leasing staff is to make the best deals for all parties concerned and then get the leases signed.

The leasing agent sets out to fill space in a center with a strong file of suggested categories of retailers and often specific prospective tenants for each vacant space. The center owners, however, make the final decisions. It is not unusual for the ownership to reject a prospect that the leasing agent brings in, as not representing the best use for the space. However, a landlord may hold out for an ideal tenant and end up losing a first-class prospect in the process. Although the potential for disagreement about any given tenant is substantial, the astute leasing agent does not give up without providing the reasons that the current prospect is the best one. On the other hand, while most leasing agents value their reputations and their relationships with clients, landlords should be cautious with the occasional leasing agent who pushes a deal because it is easy. In the end, the better the communication between the owners and the leasing agents, the less likely there will be misunderstandings concerning which tenants are good for the center and which are not.

Setting Rents

The market sets the final rental rates for any given shopping center space. A center can argue that it needs a given level of rent to meet its pro forma, but the marketplace really does not care. Developers need to be competitive with rent and terms or the leasing program will suffer. If a center's rents are at market rates but its common area or bill-back expenses are well above those of the competition, again, the leasing program will suffer. It is not unusual for a developer to charge above-market rents and still fill spaces, especially in a strong market, but usually the end result is a series of failed tenants and a large turnover. If this situation persists, the entire project may fail within a few years of opening. Certainly, if a center considers itself to be the best in town, it can charge the highest rental rates; however, any other center is unlikely to bring in the rates that the largest and best one in town is charging.

In a new shopping center, the developers prepare a pro forma based on what the center will cost and on the rate of return envisioned for the project. Based on these two figures, the overall rental rates for the entire center are set (see Exhibit A: Pro Forma/Neighborhood Shopping Center). The overall pro forma does not set rents for individual spaces, but it does indicate the overall rents needed to support the project. For example, if a center is going to cost $10 million and the developers want a 12 percent return on their money, the rents will have to be $1.2 million over and above the operating expenses to be paid by ownership, including vacancy factors, leasing commissions, management fees, tenant improvements, marketing fund contributions, and any landlord portion of the common area expenses. If a center is 1 million square feet in size and the annual operating expenses are $300,000 net, the developers will need an overall rental of $1.5 million, or $15 per square foot on a net rental basis, in order to make the deal work.

However, if the rental market in the area shows that competitive space is currently renting for $13 per square foot, the developers should consider whether they are really going to be able to command the extra two dollars just because theirs is the newest center in that area. In addition, anchor tenants are not likely to pay $15 per square foot. Their rent will have to be computed separately, and then the developers will have to determine what they need from the smaller shops in order to satisfy the pro forma rents.

Impact of Financing

It is quite possible that the pro forma will work out, but this may not initially be the case once the available financing is factored in.

Although developers usually prefer to finance an entire project, that is becoming increasingly difficult. If, however, the developer is trying for maximum loans and the interest is calculated on the high side, it is very possible that the project's net operating income (NOI) will not be sufficient to service the debt. Most lenders plan a ratio of at least $1.10 of NOI for each dollar of debt; some ask for a much higher safety ratio. In the past, developers were allowed to operate on a negative cash-flow basis, but in today's more enlightened markets, lenders are not likely to allow such an approach. Because of this, it is important to be assured that the project is properly financed and that the owner has the ability to provide the required equity position.

Once satisfied with the overall pro forma figures, the developers look at each space in the center to set the proper rent for that space. Larger spaces usually rent for less per square foot. Spaces with odd shapes—such as an L shape, a pie-wedge shape with smaller frontage, back corner shops with little sign exposure, stores facing away from the main traffic, second-floor spaces, and spaces hidden behind a pad site—command less rent per square foot than the average.

Spaces at the front entrance or prominent corners, spaces next to the entrances of the anchor tenants, spaces with strong frontage, and spaces located in high traffic areas usually command higher rates per square foot than the average. Ultimately, the best spaces command the best rents. Pad sites often carry a higher rental premium, because of the excellent visibility and access. Premiums such as these vary from 20 percent above the highest rent in the center to as much as double the in-line space rentals.

The final test of a center's pro forma and its asking rents is acceptance in the marketplace. If leasing is slow in a good market, the leasing team should look at lowering the rents. On the other hand, if space is being committed to at a rapid pace, possibly the rents are too low and need adjustment.

The Lease Document

The leasing agent has little to do with the actual lease document when working for sophisticated owners and usually has little impact on the lease itself. Nevertheless, the leasing agent should become knowledgeable about the lease and bring to the attention of the owner any provisions inconsistent with the existing market. Suppose, for example, a lease calls for an administrative fee on common area maintenance and a bill-back of the center management fee in a very difficult leasing market. Bringing this to the attention of the owners will most likely result in the removal of the administrative fee and will help considerably with the lease-up of a center.

Rents and Value

One attraction in developing a shopping center is the value that can be created through a strong leasing effort. The goal is to create value over and above the cost of the project, thereby creating wealth. The value is established by the rents through a process called capitalization. Capitalization establishes value based on the income of the project. Explained in simpler terms, capitalization is the rate of return established in the marketplace for types of income-producing properties. During a steady market period, a shopping center with relatively few problems and a strong tenant mix may sell at a capitalization rate of 9 percent; the buyer considers the income of the center and accepts a 9 percent return on an investment, with the hope that it will grow over the years. In the case of a troubled property with high vacancy, high turnover, considerable deferred maintenance, or a short term remaining for anchor tenants, the buyer usually settles on a higher rate of return in order to accept that risk. It is likely such a center will sell at an 11 percent cap rate and therefore at a much lower price. The higher the cap rate, the lower the price.

Assuming a cap rate of 10 percent, it is easy to realize points relative to rents and value. Given that cap rate, every dollar of NOI is worth $10 in value; one dollar divided by .10 equals $10. If the cap rate is lowered to 8 percent, the value goes up: $1 of NOI divided by .08 delivers a value of $12.50. Using a hypothetical NOI of $285,000, the following table illustrates how increasing the capitalization rate actually decreases the value:

NOI	CAP RATE	INDICATED VALUE
$285,000	.08	$3,562,500
$285,000	.09	$3,166,667
$285,000	.10	$2,850,000

The highest possible rents usually are desirable in order to establish the highest possible value. The lending community has become very educated with the assessment of retailers since the setback of the 1980s. Creditworthy tenants are critical; otherwise the value of that income stream is less. Weak tenants paying a fairly high rental rate often erode a center's value. The investment community interprets such a center as weak and will apply a higher cap rate to its income stream.

CASH FLOW VERSUS VALUE

Although the major goal of shopping centers is long-term capital appreciation, most centers are also aware of the cash-flow requirements of a property. It is not unusual for a tenant prospect to offer a lower-than-asking rent and, when turned down, respond by saying the center is better off with a lower rent than with no rent at all. If cash flow is necessary for a center to remain financially solvent, it makes sense to accept a lower rent on a short-term lease and wait for better times. However, in a strong market most owners prefer waiting for the higher rent than accepting the lower cash flow.

For example, consider a space of 5,000 square feet with a market asking price of $30 per square foot, full net. The minimum rent totals $150,000 per year, and a capitalization rate of 9 percent represents a value of approximately $1,666,667. In such a situation, suppose a tenant with a strong financial statement and a good negotiator offers the landlord $27 per square foot for five years. The reduced rent is $135,000, and the capitalized value at 9 percent is $1.5 million. By rejecting that offer, the landlord risks losing the entire $150,000 rental; however, if the landlord accepts the lower rent, it is locked out of the value difference of $166,667 for the entire five-year period. Stated another way, the landlord has a full year to find a tenant at the market or asking rent before risking any monies. Assuming a strong market, it is not likely that such a space will remain vacant for an entire year. In this case, the landlord is probably better off waiting for the proper rent. If, on the other hand, the tenant in this example is the best possible tenant for the space and another equal or better prospect is not likely, the landlord should make a decision beyond the straight economics of the deal and consider the merchandising of the center. It is also possible for the landlord to agree to start the lease at the $27 figure but increase it each year, to satisfy both parties.

VALUATION BASED ON CASH FLOW

Another method of valuing a shopping center is to capitalize the cash flow and add that figure to the existing loan balance. Assuming the loan can be taken over by the buyer, this establishes the value to the seller of the property. It is quite possible that the value determined in this manner will be different from market value. For example, assume that the mortgage balance on a center is $1,250,000, the annual cash flow after expenses and debt service is $83,000, and the center owner wants to value the cash flow at a 9 percent return. In this example, the value to the owner is as follows:

Mortgage balance	$1,250,000
Net cash flow	83,000
Rate of return	.09
Value of equity ($83,000 divided by .09)	922,222
Value of shopping center ($1,250,000 + $922,222)	$2,172,222

If the ownership is financing the property, it has the opportunity to affect value by changing the terms of owner financing.

Space Measurement

With rare exception, retail space is leased on the basis of the square footage of the store space multiplied by the asking rental rate per square foot. All of the bill-back items are usually based on square-footage figures. As a result, it is important that the square footage of the stores be accurate. It is not the responsibility of the leasing agent to measure all of the spaces leased, but the agent should be aware of any apparent discrepancies and inform the owners.

As a general rule, retail space is measured to the outside of all outside walls and to the center line of any demising walls. Although there are no deductions for roof-support columns, any electrical cabinet protruding into the space is deducted. The leasing agent should always explain the method of measurement to less sophisticated tenants. Such tenants often interpret the square footage of the space according to what they can see and will likely use. This kind of interpretation often does not include walls or portions of walls. Most often the lease document addresses the methodology and indicates that both the landlord and tenant agree that the footage as stated is approximate. Courts offer landlords some leniency in space measurement but are not tolerant of a serious measurement error, especially if such an error is in the landlord's favor.

Concessions for Higher Rents

In the case of a new center opening in an established market, it is not unusual for such a center to ask for higher rents than those of its competition. In negotiating these higher rents, owners often make some concessions to secure the best tenants. For example, suppose a center asks for rents of $25 per square foot on a net basis, but the market is at $23. In this case, the center must find a way to attract the tenant and still meet the needs of the center. The following options are applicable: The center may choose to lower the rent to $23, but lowering the rent will drop the center's value. The center may also lease 1,000 square feet for three years, set the value at the $25 rate with a 10 percent cap rate, and go from $250,000 down to $230,000, for a loss of $20,000. Finally, the center may suggest a $25 figure to the tenant, but offer a construction allowance of $2,000 or free rent of $2,000. In this option, the tenant is down to the market rate while the center maintains the higher value. A similar adjustment can be offered using a moving allowance or an advertising allowance as a possible concession.

Types of Rent

Because other chapters in this book explain the different types of rent in greater detail, the following is only a summary of rent types as they apply to an understanding of how rents and income are determined.

MINIMUM RENT

Minimum rent is perhaps the most important type in that it is used to establish value. The minimum rent is usually determined by multiplying the desired rate by the square footage. The minimum rent is stated either as dollars per square foot per month or as dollars per square foot per year. In either case, the final numbers must agree. Most landlords agree that any rounding off of small amounts should be made in favor of the tenant, to avoid any tenant perception that the landlord is taking advantage. For instance, an annual rental of $35 per square foot does not come to a total in even dollars on a monthly basis. As a point of reference, the West Coast of the United States usually quotes rents on a monthly basis and the East Coast usually quotes rents on an annual basis.

INFLATION PROTECTION

If a center's leases are for more than one year and the center keeps its minimum rents the same for the entire lease term, center management should be concerned about the inflationary erosion of the dollar. In the case of smaller tenants, centers either negotiate an annual increase (5 percent per year is not unusual) or use the Consumer Price Index (CPI) to adjust rents on an annual basis. When the CPI is in the range of 2 percent per year, calculations do not create problems for centers. A CPI of 16 percent, however, once caused some severe problems for landlords and tenants alike. During that time, tenants asked for a cap or upper limit on the percentage a landlord used to raise the rents. If a landlord agrees to an upper limit, it most often will ask for a minimum increase.

Both anchor tenants and national tenants generally do not become involved in a CPI increase, but often they will negotiate rent increases during the lease term. Some large national chains allow for a 10 percent increase every five years, while other chains will negotiate an increase every five or ten years. Still others feel that a percentage rental provision provides the necessary inflation protection, so they do not allow for any inflation-related increase during the lease term. There are those that feel that annual increases are not necessary if you have a strong minimum rent to begin with and have a net lease, but those two facts have nothing to do with protecting against the ravages of inflation.

PERCENTAGE RENT

Percentage rents are unique to retail tenants. The theory behind percentage rents is straightforward. The landlord creates a strong retail environment by bringing together an effective mix of retail and services. Such a mix creates a synergy that generally results in more sales than if each merchant in the mix were standing alone in various parts of town. The landlord should therefore participate in the higher sales, through percentage rents. Typically, the tenant pays a monthly minimum rent; it is then subject to an additional rental as sales figures escalate beyond a set level. Regular sales reports provide the necessary information.

The appropriate percentages are available in several places, including *Dollars and Cents of Shopping Centers,* published by the Urban Land Institute. The appropriate percentages are a function of profit margins in the different types of businesses involved. Supermarkets typically have the lowest percentage, because they have the lowest profit margins. Generally, a supermarket pays a percentage rent rate of only 1 to 2 percent of gross. Drugstores, department stores, and hardware stores carry around 3 to 4 percent; stores selling merchandise such as clothing, shoes, and accessories carry 5 to 6 percent, and services are higher, in the area of 7 to 10 percent. These figures are negotiable, but they generally fall within these ranges. Because minimum rents are fairly high at the time of this writing and sales have not gone up dramatically in the past several years, it is unlikely that the typical tenant in a small center will actually pay any percentage rents.

Percentage rents usually do not add value to the center on the same basis as minimum rent, because percentage rent fluctuates from one month to the next and from one year to the next. Converting percentage rent to minimum rent is a wise option. As a rule, the cap rate for percentage rent is two to three points above the cap rate used to value the minimum rent and/or fixed charges. If the history of percentage rents is weak, the cap rate is as much as twice the amount; in extreme cases, the buyer does not attribute any value to percentage rents.

Natural Breakpoint

The point at which the tenant actually owes the landlord additional rent is called the breakpoint. Typically, the landlord and tenant negotiate the minimum rent and the percentage rental rate. The breakpoint is established by these two figures rather than by specific negotiation. For example, if an agreement calls for a minimum monthly rental of $1,000 and a percentage rental rate of 5 percent, the natural breakpoint is $20,000: $1,000 divided by .05 equals $20,000. In other words, the $1,000 minimum rent accounts for the first $20,000 in sales. For any total above that figure, the tenant owes 5 percent of all sales in excess of the $20,000 breakpoint. For example, if a tenant's sales are $22,500, the additional rental is as follows:

$22,500 sales − $20,000 breakpoint = $2,500 sales subject to percentage rents × .05 percentage rental rate = $125 additional rent due

Negotiated Breakpoint

Some tenants do not accept the natural breakpoint as the starting point for percentage rent payments. These tenants negotiate a different breakpoint. Various other situations also suggest a change in the breakpoint as a way to offset other considerations. Examples of negotiated breakpoint include split-level percentage, declining percentage rental rate, negotiated break in the landlord's favor, negotiated break in the tenant's favor, and deductions from percentage rents.

SPLIT-LEVEL PERCENTAGE

In a negotiation situation in which the landlord wants a 6 percent rental provision and the tenant is working hard to hold it to 5 percent, the compromise could be 6 percent to the breakpoint and 5 percent thereafter. This moves the landlord to the breakpoint faster, while the tenant pays only 5 percent on the sales above the breakpoint. Another compromise would set the provision entirely at 5.5 percent.

DECLINING PERCENTAGE RENTAL RATE

Supermarkets and other very high-volume tenants often indicate they are willing to pay the going percentage rental rate; however, once their sales reach a very high level, they feel they should pay a lesser rate on the high volume. A typical supermarket lease may have a rental rate of 1.5 percent to the breakpoint and/or the first $10 million in sales. The rate may then be negotiated down to 1 percent on the next $5 million in sales, with a further reduction to 0.75 percent on all sales above $15 million. These types of tenants are willing to share in their success with the landlord, but reason that their sales reach very high levels as a result of their own business practices at least as much as the developer's or owner's effective management.

NEGOTIATED BREAK IN THE LANDLORD'S FAVOR

A strong national tenant may indicate strong interest in a shop space within a center but be unwilling to accept the minimum rental level that the landlord suggests. If it is desirable to secure that tenant, the landlord may offer to accept a lower minimum rental but also ask that the breakpoint be set at a lower level than would be reached by the natural break. Under this arrangement, the landlord has the opportunity to recover some of the monies if the tenant does well.

Quite often a tenant asks that the center make certain improvements to the space and adds the return for those improvements to the rent. If the tenant is strong and the landlord has the means, this arrangement can result in a lease agreement. The breakpoint for percentage rent, however, should be based on the minimum rental portion of the negotiation rather than on the rental reached by adding in the improvements. For example, assume a monthly rental is agreed upon at $3,000 with a percentage rental rate of 6 percent. The tenant decides to have the landlord make improvements of $25,000 and then adds a percentage of the improvement amount to the monthly rental over the five years of the lease at an interest rate of 12 percent. This arrangement adds $556 to the monthly rental. If the figure of $3,556 is used, the natural breakpoint is $59,267, but using the actual minimum rental, the breakpoint is $50,000. If the tenant produces the sales, the landlord pays for the improvements out of the potential percentage rents.

NEGOTIATED BREAK IN THE TENANT'S FAVOR

Assume that a space for lease in a center is in bad condition, but the landlord does not have the funds to make the necessary improvements. A good tenant shows interest in the space and wants the improvements made as part of the lease agreement, but the landlord cannot comply because of limited funds. Under one possible compromise, the tenant could agree to pay the asking rent and make the improvements to the space. The tenant then would request that the percentage rental breakpoint be raised to give the tenant the opportunity to recapture the funds spent to improve the space.

Certain discount department stores will negotiate an artificial breakpoint because of their internal profitability levels. Generally, these tenants will reject the natural breakpoint and instead show the landlord where the store breaks into reasonable profit levels. The negotiation results in an agreed-upon breakpoint.

DEDUCTIONS FROM PERCENTAGE RENTS
While not a common approach, some supermarkets, drugstores, and department stores negotiate the right to deduct some or most of any extra charges from percentage rents. The most common of these charges is real estate taxes. For example, a large national tenant not only asks to deduct taxes from percentage rents, but wishes to deduct them on a cumulative basis. This means that any taxes paid from the commencement of the lease are deductible from percentage rents at any time during the lease term, but the landlord may never collect percentage rent even if the store does well.

Other Percentage Rent Considerations

REPORTING SALES
The health of a center depends on an accurate reporting of sales. Landlords prefer a monthly reporting of sales and a payment on percentage rent, with an annual adjustment. Most national and anchor tenants are prepared to provide an audited monthly report so the center can effectively track all sales. However, some large national and anchor tenants report and pay only on an annual basis. Because their fiscal year is different from the calendar year, these tenants typically negotiate for an annual reporting to coincide with their own internal fiscal accountability.

EXCLUSIONS FROM PERCENTAGE RENTS
The landlord should always negotiate any exclusions up front so there is no room for abuse, as well as to offer assurance that the

exclusion is in the best interest of the relationship between the center and the tenant. Some allowable exclusions include:

- Sales taxes excluded from the sales reported on percentage rents
- Returns and allowances
- Sales to employees
- Wholesale sales
- Mail-order sales.

Internet sales represent an increasingly significant issue in this regard.

AUDIT PROVISIONS

The landlord must always reserve the right to audit percentage rent sales reports. In the case of small tenants, audits are allowed within three years of the report. If an error of more than 3 percent is found, the tenant pays any rents involved and also pays for the reasonable cost of the audit. Anchor and national tenants frequently allow for audits with more conditions, many of which apply to home office locations.

Additional Monetary Considerations

One of the most contentious elements of the landlord-tenant relationship is common area costs, including common area maintenance (CAM), insurance, taxes, repairs and replacements, and the marketing fund. These are referred to as the operating costs of the center.

COMMON AREA MAINTENANCE

The common area maintenance clause is critical for the landlord. While the goal of CAM is to recapture the actual operating expenses, every dollar that the landlord does not recapture reduces the value of the center by approximately $10. Tenants often develop the impression that the landlord does not really care about keeping these costs under control, because they can be passed along to the tenant. However, that is not the case. Most landlords, in fact, realize that the sophisticated tenant looks at occupancy costs with great care. If a center's common area costs are not competitive, the occupancy costs of the center will be higher than those of the competition. This in turn makes leasing more difficult.

The lease language should state clearly what charges are included and how those charges are handled. It is crucial that the leasing agent fully understand the common area costs and how they are handled in an existing center or will be handled in a new center. The leasing agent should maintain copies of the current budgets as well as a history of the common area operations. Many landlords commence negotiations with the statement that the common area portion of the lease cannot be changed, and therefore both parties should look to other areas for any rental concession.

In addition to operating costs, the second most important area of common area maintenance is the administrative or supervision fee versus the center management fee. Because it is almost impossible to know how much it costs the landlord to oversee the entire common area effort, starting with the planning and ending up with final accounting to the tenants, most centers factor in an administrative or supervision fee. Such a fee typically represents 5 to 10 percent for anchor tenants and 10 to 15 percent for most other tenants. Anchors usually exclude some items from the administrative fee, such as insurance premiums, real estate taxes, and, quite often, utilities. The reasoning behind this approach is that little supervision or administration is actually involved in such matters. Although this is not the case, the anchors are more often in a stronger position in negotiations than the landlord.

An alternative to the administration or supervision fee is a billing arrangement with the tenants to cover the actual management fee of the center. Most national and anchor tenants will not accept this practice, but small tenants generally do not have the bargaining power to change it. In some instances the center will try to negotiate both an administrative fee and a bill-back center management fee. This approach, however, results in very high occupancy costs for the tenant.

REAL ESTATE TAXES
Real estate taxes are a major expense in most shopping centers. Typically, these taxes are passed on to the tenants on the basis of a pro rata square footage and are paid based on a monthly estimate. Any land that is not on the center site but is included as taxable must be clear. In the case of parcels held for future development, the tenant has the right to know if that land is included in the tax bills. If some parcels are excluded because tenants pay their taxes

directly or separately, the tenants have the right to know that as well. Prior to paying the landlord, anchor and national tenants usually insist on a copy of the tax bill as well as a receipt for the current payment.

INSURANCE

Tenants receive two billings for insurance, one for liability insurance and one for fire and extended coverage for the shop tenants. Liability insurance on the common area is charged to all tenants and is easily identifiable. More sophisticated tenants may want to know how much liability is carried and may even request that their participation be limited to a premium on a more limited basis. As part of the documentation for their payment, anchor or major tenants request a copy of the actual premium notice from the carrier. Fire and extended coverage for the shop tenants is established through the landlord and billed to the tenants for their pro rata share of the premium. The premium is sometimes difficult to sort out, as part of the agreement with the landlord includes a loss of rents for the landlord. In addition, the policy may carry a high deductible, which makes sense to the landlord but may not be seen as a benefit by the tenant. Negotiating the details is a challenge for both parties, but beneficial over the long term.

MARKETING FUND

The marketing fund presents its own negotiating problems. Most merchants are willing to join and pay, but only if all of the center merchants do so. Some large national tenants and anchors resist joining, because their companies have policies against participating in such a fund. In addition, large tenants already advertise and promote heavily on their own, so they do not stand to gain as much by the affiliation. Small tenants, on the other hand, will benefit from participating in the marketing fund and should understand how such a fund is administered.

Any provisions that relate to common area maintenance, insurance, taxes, repairs and replacements, and the marketing fund are important to understand. The sophisticated tenant will spend some time negotiating them and understanding how they are administered. The smaller tenant, however, may not even know what questions to ask and therefore may accept the provisions without the proper understanding. The leasing agent should make a point of knowing all aspects of any bill-back items and take the time to explain them to the tenant. The tenant should be aware of the current costs of these items and also be aware of the possibility that there will be unexpected increases periodically.

Educating the prospective tenant during the leasing process will save considerable time and effort in the future for management and thus strengthen the overall relationship between landlord and tenant. Most tenants adapt to situations as long as they know what to expect and are kept in the communication loop. For the inexperienced tenant prospect, the idea of open-ended common area billing is almost too much to anticipate. A well-planned and informative discussion up front, explaining why it is necessary and how it compares to that of the competition, should help to set the proper foundation for a good landlord-tenant relationship. It is also very helpful if the leasing agent has seen the competition and knows what each is charging for similar items, to demonstrate to the tenant prospect how it is benefiting from the charges it will become obliged to pay.

Negotiating Rents

Negotiating the lease is a complicated and time-consuming process. Whether the tenant is sophisticated or smaller and less knowledgeable, the leasing agent must fully understand the business reasons behind each lease provision and be prepared to sit down and discuss with the tenant the reasoning behind, and the impact of, each provision.

The first step in negotiating the lease is to fully understand the prospective tenant. Does the center need it more than it needs the center, or is it just the reverse? What is the tenant's position in the marketplace? Will the tenant help the center attract other tenants and create traffic for the center? Is the tenant strong financially, possessing good credit? Does the tenant fill a specific niche in the center merchandise mix that would be hard to fill with any other tenant? Is the tenant a rare find for the center?

There are six basic areas that the leasing agent considers when setting the final rent in a given space for a given tenant. These areas are category, location, amount of frontage, allowance, size, and situation.

CATEGORY

The category of merchandise will make an appreciable difference in the rent and terms offered to a prospective tenant. Fashion generally drives larger shopping centers. A large center will go out of its way to attract and secure a strong fashion store. Gifts, jewelry, accessories, shoes, and restaurants are all considered integral to a center's mix; consequently, a center is likely to give more consideration to these prospective tenants than to many other categories of uses. In the case of a hair salon, nail salon, pizza parlor, or another fast-food operator, a center is more likely to take a tougher stance, because of the easy availability of such tenants. The more a center needs a specific category of merchandise, the more likely it is to be willing to make necessary concessions.

LOCATION

As mentioned previously, the location of the space for rent has a direct impact on its rent. Pad site tenants will pay more, as will prominent corners, stores at the entrances to the anchor or major tenants, and those with substantial frontage. Spaces with visibility problems, difficult shapes, or inordinate depths will go for lower rents.

AMOUNT OF FRONTAGE

A typical retail store should have approximately one foot of frontage to every three to four feet of store depth. Corner shops and stores with a better ratio of frontage to depth command a higher rental.

ALLOWANCE

Rents are established with the intent of delivering the space to the tenant in an as-is condition or, in the case of a large and new center, in a raw-shell condition. If a center gives allowances to attract tenants, serious consideration must be given to how to recoup such allowances. The necessary allowances frequently are built into the original pro forma, but it is not unusual to find that allowances must be granted in excess of this in order to attract the desired tenants.

SIZE

On a square-foot basis, it is usually less expensive to build a large store than to build a small one. Therefore, on a square-foot basis, the rent for a larger space in a shopping center is, as a rule, lower than the rent for a smaller unit. Likewise, the rent on an anchor store is lower, because of its supposed traffic draw. Restaurants are the obvious exception. A 400-square-foot store costs appreciably more per square foot, as it has all of the amenities of the larger stores; those amenities, however, represent a much higher percentage of the overall cost to build.

SITUATION

Finally, the specific situation could have a dramatic impact on the final rent offered. If a given store is the last one available in a center, the landlord will be in a stronger bargaining position and therefore will ask for a higher rent. If a center has several vacancies and space is moving slowly, the rent is likely to be lower.

DURING THE NEGOTIATION

The six areas just covered are factors that go into the initial rental structure and are then negotiated from there. Concerning the initial quoted rental, some people believe in setting an amount that is proper and fair, and then holding firm to that amount. This may be more honest and efficient, but it also can give the impression that the owners are inflexible in general. The more common school of thought is always to quote a higher rent initially than is needed to make the deal, in order to give the tenant some room to negotiate downward.

Before a negotiation turns serious, there are often many discussions, which can cover numerous alternatives. Once negotiations begin in earnest, there should be a meeting of minds as to the starting point. For this reason, it is important for the landlord to make a statement concerning the deal on the table. Such a statement should address the following:

- Term
- Rent
- Bill-back items
- Allowances
- Free-rent periods
- Fit-up allowance time.

The tenant should not be allowed simply to pick any one item and focus on it without putting it in the context of the entire deal. For example, the landlord may propose a five-year lease, at $35 per square foot per year, with a percentage rent provision of 6 percent, a $2-per-square-foot allowance, and no options. In this situation, it is not unusual for the tenant to ask the landlord to consider some free rent up front. This particular question should not be answered until there is some agreement on the general terms. The situation can be approached by asking whether all of the other terms are agreeable, before discussing the free rent. The leasing agent may discover that the tenant wants to challenge all aspects of the offer, but it hopes to do so one point at a time and thereby gain concessions that individually do not seem all that critical.

It is important to summarize the negotiations as they proceed. This strategy reduces the chance of misunderstandings when the final lease is drawn up. Much of the negotiating process is actually conducted on a verbal basis, and it is easy for misunderstandings to develop if there is no continual update on the positions of both parties.

Alternatives for Negotiating Agreement on Rents

It is not at all unusual for the landlord and the tenant prospect to be at odds over the proper rents for any given space. Differences may exist between the landlord's effective rent and the tenant's effective rent, and these differences must be recognized. The landlord typically deducts commissions, concessions, and improvement allowances to arrive at an effective rent. The tenant adds the costs of improvements as well as common area costs and minimum rent to arrive at an effective rent. Each party should be mindful of the position of the other, especially if there is a strong desire to make the deal.

New retail and service shops need time for the business to mature to the point of breaking even and then making a profit. For this reason, the tenant is likely to attempt to keep the rent low, especially in the initial months, but will often ask for lower rent without the stipulation that this is most important in the early months. On the other hand, the landlord may be attempting to finance the shopping center or sell it and therefore wants to keep the rents as high as possible. A common solution in the past has been to grant the tenant a few months of free rent at the start of the lease, providing that the balance of the lease is at the market rent asked by the landlord. This approach gives the tenant some relief, yet still keeps the contract rent at the higher level, which in turn maintains the highest value of the shopping center.

Another negotiating approach is called stair-stepped rent, which gives the tenant some relief at the start of the lease but in turn gives the landlord the needed rents over the lease term. For example, on a three-year lease the quoted rent may be $30 per square foot per year with annual cost-of-living increases, but the tenant may indicates the need to start the rent at $25 per foot. Assuming a cost of living in the area of 2 percent per year, the landlord expects to average slightly over $30 per foot per year over the term of the lease. The landlord may offer to start the lease at $25 per foot per year, then go to $31, moving in the last year to $36 per foot per year, which works out to be a little higher than the original proposal. Each of the parties benefits from this approach. If the landlord is not going to sell or finance during the first year of the lease, there is little negative impact, except for a slight reduction in cash flow for that year. The offset to that is the higher value created by having a rental of $36 in the third year. This approach also makes the renewal negotiations easier for the landlord, as the existing rent will be $36 rather than the $31 that would have been the case with the starting position.

A similar effect can be accomplished by giving the tenant a construction or improvement allowance in an amount that equals the difference in the two positions. The main downside of this approach is that it requires money out of pocket at a time when many developers are short on funds.

Letter of Intent

Most professionals in the business agree that a letter of intent has little or no legal standing. However, once the discussions and negotiations have reached an advanced stage, but prior to the drawing up of the lease, a letter of intent serves a real purpose by summarizing the deal and giving both parties the assurance that they are serious. The letter of intent also serves as an entrée document toward the preparation of the lease. In addition, letters of intent are helpful documents when a shopping center is in the planning stages and not yet ready for leases to be drawn up. The letter of intent usually contains all of the pertinent economic terms that have been agreed upon, as well as any other lease provisions important enough to have been discussed up to that point. A letter of intent signed by both parties once indicated that a completed lease was all but assured; however, such assumptions are no longer the case. With so many items in the lease requiring discussion, the letter of intent is now just a serious show of interest in the location.

Compromise in Negotiations

Although compromise is good in theory, there are times when it is not reasonable, and certainly not necessary. When landlords set rent and terms at market levels and are satisfied with the level of positive activity, there is no obligation to compromise. If, on the other hand, a landlord is convinced that a prospective tenant will be good for the center by attracting other desirable tenants, bringing needed customer traffic to the center, or both, then compromise may be necessary to secure the deal.

Before making any compromise, the leasing agent must know what issues are on the table and the nature of the changes that the tenant is seeking. Whatever compromises are made during the negotiations, they should be made in the spirit of completing the deal and not granted with remarks that can sour the relationship. As leasing professionals often say, if you cannot compromise with grace, you probably should not make the deal.

The Leasing Cycle

Leasing is a numbers game. It can take up to 100 prospects for a leasing agent to find the one tenant that will sign the lease. In the process of working toward a lease, the leasing agent goes through several steps. The steps in the leasing cycle are prospecting, creating interest, negotiating the deal, getting the lease signed, and then starting all over again.

PROSPECTING
Prospecting is one of the most difficult steps in the leasing cycle, as there is no assurance that someone out there will have an interest

in what an agent is selling. Because prospecting is addressed in chapter 5, this paragraph only lists some of the proven techniques, among them cold canvass, telephone canvass, mass mailing, networking at trade meetings, advertising in trade journals, and networking with other leasing agents and/or tenants. An effective leasing agent should talk with almost anyone who may have interest or who may know someone with potential interest.

CREATING INTEREST

At this step, the leasing agent has talked with or corresponded with prospects that have shown more than a passing interest. It is now time to start to sell the project. The leasing agent should be armed with a nice but not necessarily expensive brochure, plot plans of the center, elevations if it is a center either under construction or still to be built, demographics of the area, information on the competitive centers in the area, aerial views, and traffic counts. The discussions at this point are fairly general, as the leasing agent is sizing up the prospect—and the prospect is sizing up the agent and the center. By this time, the leasing agent should have visited the prospect's existing store location in order to better evaluate whether this type of tenant will add to the center's merchandise mix.

NEGOTIATING THE DEAL

Creating interest and negotiating the deal are fairly intensive phases of the leasing program. Negotiating is the step in which the parties get serious and discuss the potential lease terms in detail. Phone calls, meetings, and documents move back and forth at a rapid pace. It is the job of the leasing agent to keep the negotiations on track and not allow the prospect's attention to be diverted. Remember that other leasing agents are likely working on this same prospect, so the goal is to keep all parties focused.

GETTING THE LEASE SIGNED

Once there is agreement on the terms, every effort should be made to prepare the lease, seek approval of the lease by proper counsel, and send the lease to the tenant. With rare exception, the tenant is expected to sign the lease first, followed by the landlord. There are exceptions to this procedure; for example, the landlord may be trying to convince the tenant that the offer is sincere; the landlord also generally signs first in the case of an anchor or major tenant. In any case, it is imperative that the tenant receive the lease as soon as possible and is then encouraged to work through lease comments and finalization as quickly as possible, with reasonable consideration for internal administrative channels. Once the tenant has signed the lease and returned it for the landlord's signature, the lease should be processed, signed, and returned to the tenant at the earliest possible time. Commercial tenants may experience buyer's remorse as easily as a home buyer, and a deal may be lost if the waiting period takes too long.

STARTING OVER AGAIN

The leasing agent has little time to celebrate the signing of a lease in the shopping center business. There are other spaces to lease and other deals to be made. Therefore, the leasing agent cannot spend too much time reflecting on the glory of the deal just done, but must get back out and start the process over again. When the leasing agent has no active prospects, time is spent out in the field looking for prospects. This is a full-time activity. However, once a prospect shows an interest, the leasing agent then will spend less time prospecting and more time working on creating interest and signing the deal. This reduces the number of prospects in the process at any one time and ends up sending the agent out again to find new prospects even sooner. The leasing agent is almost always balancing time between the need to find new people and the need to complete arrangements with those who have shown interest. It is not an easy job, and it often frustrates the new leasing professional.

Lease Term

The term of the lease is always a critical issue. It is often said that short-term leases make for good tenants. Quite often the lending agency will insist that a given number of leases be for long-term and credit tenants. Even in the case of local mom-and-pop tenants, the lender may well seek five-year leases. Large national tenants, major tenants, and anchor tenants are likely to insist on long-term leases of 10 to 15 years in the initial term, with up to ten additional five-year options in order to renew. These options to renew should be at the then market rents, but this is often difficult to accomplish with an anchor tenant that is badly needed for the success of the center.

Some tenants need a long-term lease in order to amortize their loans for the initial fit-up and purchase of store equipment. Tenants such as barber shops, beauty shops, ice cream stores, and restaurants have a heavy initial investment in the equipment necessary to run their businesses. As long as their credit is good, they can ask for an initial term of at least seven to ten years to cover the term of their fit-up loan. Landlords must be aware of the needs of the tenants and what is considered normal practice when setting the lease terms.

Typically, landlords will seek longer-term leases in situations in which they want to lock in better terms in anticipation of a difficult market. If it appears that the market is going to be strong in the immediate future, the landlord will seek short-term leases. It is not the intent of the landlord to throw out existing tenants and find new ones, but the landlord wants to control the space in the shopping center rather than let the tenants control it. Granting an option creates a one-way advantage for the tenant. For instance, if a tenant is doing poorly but knows that the center may want its space for expansion or rehabilitation, that tenant can exercise an option to get paid to leave the center. Options take away the flexibility that the landlord must have in order to guide the property to its maximum potential.

The granting of long-term leases, especially with multiple options, is usually not in the best interest of the landlord, except when necessary in order to secure a certain type of tenant. For small mom-and-pop tenants, a lease of three years without options is best for the landlord. If necessary, a local tenant may be granted a five-year lease—but seldom longer than that, except as indicated above.

If options must be granted, and generally this is a function of the local market or the specific needs of an important tenant prospect, then the landlord needs protections. For example, the option to renew is for the initial tenant only, not assignees or sublet tenants; a 180-day advance written notice is required; the tenant is not in default at the time the option is exercised; and sales have reached a minimum level in order to exercise the option. The rent for the option period should be at market level and not at some predetermined figure that is not fair to either the landlord or the tenant. If options are granted, the term of any option should never be for a period of time in excess of the initial lease term. The leasing team should not grant a three-year initial term and a five-year option;

rather, it should be for, say, a three-year initial term with a three-year option, or a five-year initial term and a three-year option.

Category of Tenant

The leasing approach to national tenants and to mom-and-pop tenants is substantially different. In both cases the leasing agent needs to know the property, the competition, the deal-making process, the market, and something about the tenant's business. However, the national or major tenant is generally very sophisticated in its approach and fully understands the making of lease deals; on the other hand, it often does not understand the center's market and may not be fully aware of the particular competitive situation. Unless the center already has an existing relationship with a large national tenant, or the owners have reason to believe that their site may be important to the prospect, it may be difficult to obtain an opportunity to make a full presentation. In such cases, it is helpful to send a package that is brief but tells the story, and then follow up with a phone call. National tenant representatives are very busy and receive more submissions than they can possibly handle. Most often they will not bother to send out a letter indicating a lack of interest. Even when they do have some interest, it is often hard for them to follow up on each possibility. For these reasons it is a good idea for the leasing agent to follow up with a phone call to see if answers to any questions can be provided.

 If possible, the leasing agent should talk with other leasing agents to see what type of deals a specific national tenant usually makes. Many of the national tenants have unusual lease requirements and will not make leases without them. Unless a leasing agent already knows this, it is very possible that this position will be interpreted as a tenant simply being difficult, and the deal will be much harder to consummate.

 The mom-and-pop store, on the other hand, is often unsophisticated and needs as much help as the leasing agent can provide. It is generally important to meet the prospect face-to-face. Likewise, it is a good idea to see the prospect's current operation. In the case of a start-up operation, the leasing agent should ask such prospects whom they plan to emulate in their business, and then discuss how they will do the same things and what they will change. Each prospect should be asked to fill out a qualification package that includes a two-year pro forma, information on its experience in the business it is proposing, general business experience, how it will run the business, what it sees as start-up expenses, a financial statement and permission to run a credit check, a proposed sales estimate, verification of cash, and references. With this information, the leasing agent will be in a good position to work with the prospect in putting together a realistic business plan. Conversely, it is possible that gathering and discussing this information may lead the prospect to realize that its plan is not practical. In such cases, although a deal is not realized, both parties have been protected from what could have resulted in a nonproductive venture.

Build-to-Suit Negotiations

The build-to-suit negotiation can be one of the easiest and least risky deals in the industry—or it can be among the most difficult. Build-to-suit should be offered only to tenants with a good credit record; otherwise, the center is not adequately protected. It is very possible that the tenant in this type of negotiation may hold up construction or make changes that cause the landlord additional expenses and/or delay the opening of the store and therefore the commencement of rent and charges.

Typically, the landlord sets the rent based on the value of the land and the cost of the improvements, multiplied by the desired rate of return. For example, assume the land is worth $200,000, the building estimate is placed at $600,000, and the landlord wants a 12 percent return on the investment. In this case, the annual rental will be $96,000, on a net basis. There are two basic ways to handle such a transaction. The most common is for the lease to call for these terms and then to indicate that the rent will start on a specific date, whether or not the construction is completed. In addition, the lease should indicate that any cost overruns will be at the tenant's expense, and it should spell out how this is administered. The best scenario is for the tenant to sign a work order at the time of the change and to fund the cost at that point in time.

Alternatively, if the funds are available, the landlord should agree that any costs over and above the initial estimate will increase the rental by 13 percent—or any other agreed-upon number—times the actual cost of the overrun. Even this approach should have a maximum overrun number; otherwise, the rent could reach a point beyond which the tenant is no longer profitable at that level, even though the tenant has in fact caused the overruns.

Another option is to have the tenant build its desired building, with plans and the construction contractor approved by the landlord. Upon receipt of the certificate of occupancy and the commencement of the lease, the landlord reimburses the tenant for the agreed-upon value of the building, regardless of any additional costs, overruns, and the like. Under these circumstances, the tenant must construct the building on the landlord's site for cash or unsecured loans and not allow any liens on the property. This approach works well with a sophisticated tenant that has experience in building its own buildings. It is not advisable to build to suit in the case of an inexperienced merchant or service provider. This is especially true for the restaurant business, as this represents one of the most volatile businesses for shopping centers.

Conclusion

Leasing is an art, not a science. Shopping center leasing is all about creating a merchandising concept in tandem with income. This challenge is what makes shopping center leasing one of the most complex forms of leasing in the real estate field. The role of the leasing agent is equally complex. It is imperative that the leasing agent understand both the relationship of the income to the value and the concept of the retail mix. The better informed the leasing agent, the more likely the opportunities for success. Although the leasing agent brings in the prospective tenants, the agent is seldom responsible for the final decision on which tenant to accept or what terms are acceptable. In reality, this is an advantage. The agent is the negotiator and link between tenant and landlord. Often the interchange between owner and agent results in the best possible situation for the property. The challenge for the agent is the delicate balance between securing the right tenant, maximizing the rents, increasing the value of the center, and maintaining a sense of professional integrity.

Alan A. Alexander, SCSM/CPM, is Senior Vice President at Woodmont Management, Inc., Scottsdale, Arizona.

Exhibit A:

Sample Pro Forma/Neighborhood Shopping Center

SIZE	RENT SQ. FT.	ANNUAL RENT	COST SQ. FT.	TOTAL COST
45,000	10.00	450,000.00	42.00	1,890,000.00
17,000	10.00	170,000.00	40.00	680,000.00
52,000	16.00	832,000.00	60.00	3,120,000.00
114,000				5,690,000.00

OPERATING EXPENSES:
MANAGEMENT – 5%	72,000.00
CAPITAL RESERVES .20 CENTS	22,000.00
VACANCY – SMALL SHOPS 5%	41,600.00
TOTAL EXPENSES:	136,200.00
NET OPERATING INCOME:	1,315,800.00
VALUE AT 10% CAP RATE	13,158,000.00

PROJECT COSTS:

LAND – 10 ACRES	2,200,000.00
BUILDING COSTS	5,690,000.00
LANDSCAPING	200,000.00
SITE WORK	1,100,000.00
ARCHITECT & ENGINEERING	400,000.00
LEASING @ 3.00 SQ. FT.	340,000.00
PROFESSIONAL FEES	200,000.00
TITLE AND CLOSING	150,000.00
INTEREST EXPENSE	750,000.00
MISCELLANEOUS	200,000.00
TAXES AND INSURANCE	150,000.00
CONTINGENCY	500,000.00
DEVELOPMENT FEE	400,000.00
TOTAL COSTS:	12,280,000.00

MORTGAGE:

NOI CAPITALIZED AT 10%	13,158,000.00
LOAN – 75% – 25 YRS @ 10%	9,868,500.00
EQUITY	2,411,500.00
ANNUAL DEBT SERVICE	1,076,100.00
CASH FLOW	228,200.00
RETURN ON EQUITY	9.46

Exhibit B:

Sample Lease Analysis/New Tenants
Uptown Square Office Building

YEAR: _____

						PER SQUARE FOOT PER YEAR OF LEASE			
TENANT	YEARS	SQUARE FOOTAGE	COMMISSIONS	TI'S	FREE RENT	COMM.	TI'S	FREE RENT	TOTAL
SERVICE	3	916	2,473	916	0	0.90	0.33	0	1.23
IMPORTER	5	428	1,926	1,284	1,284	0.90	0.60	0.60	2.10
INSURANCE	3	1,002	2,705	5,010	4,509	0.90	1.67	1.50	4.07
FINANCE	3	440	1,221	880	0	0.93	0.67	0	1.60
IMPORTER	5	1,288	5,957	2,576	3,971	0.93	0.40	0.62	1.95
SERVICE	3	896	2,554	2,688	2,837	0.95	1.00	1.06	3.01
CPA	4	1,244	4,976	6,220	4,146	1.00	1.25	0.83	3.08
ATTORNEY	5	1,568	7,840	7,840	0	1.00	1.00	0.00	2.00
FINANCE	3	922	2,559	0	2,842	0.93	0	1.03	1.96
COMPUTER	3	784	2,469	4,704	0	1.05	2.00	0	3.05
SERVICE	3	1,468	3,963	2,936	6,606	0.90	0.67	1.50	3.07
RETAIL	5	1,200	6,000	0	4,000	1.00	0.00	0.67	1.67
RETAIL	7	988	7,261	1,976	5,187	1.05	0.29	0.75	2.09

AVERAGE COST PER SQUARE FOOT PER YEAR FOR NEW LEASES: 2.38

9 | Managing the Design and Construction Process

Thomas W. Taylor and Paul J. Mackie

Every design and construction project, from the Great Wall of China to the improvements for your next tenant, has just three objectives: schedule, budget, and quality. The purpose of this chapter is to help you manage your projects with these objectives in mind. To manage a project means to plan, organize, direct, and control it so that all three objectives are optimized. Note that these objectives are not mutually exclusive; rather, they are interdependent. If you accelerate your schedule, for example, it will probably have an impact on your budget; if you reduce your budget, it will probably have an impact on quality.

This chapter is organized into three sections, on planning, organizing, and directing and controlling. The planning section discusses the construction exhibit, an attachment to the lease, and budget and schedule questions during this phase of the project. The organizing section summarizes project delivery methods and team assembly. Finally, the directing and controlling section outlines some of the more important ways to ensure that a project is successful.

Planning

One of the most important areas is planning, because it sets the stage for the entire leasing pro forma. A mistake here can cost either the tenant or the landlord a tremendous amount of money, and possibly lost deals in the future. So it is extremely important that the project manager plans properly. The planning stage involves several steps.

SITE INSPECTION

The project manager must make a visit to the space to determine its exact condition and what is needed to get it into leasable condition. This can be anything from a white box (meaning that the space is ready for the tenant to install its finishes, fixtures, and merchandise) to simple replacement of a few ceiling tiles. If at all possible, the project manager should walk through the space with the tenant coordinator or construction coordinator; if there is no construction or development department, the project manager should invite a contractor. It is important to have someone involved who has a construction background so that the project manager can receive accurate information to pass on to the leasing agent(s) during negotiations. The project manager should know what is in the space and the impact on costs if alterations are made.

While at the space, the project manager should not only verify the condition of the space but also know what utilities are in and outside it. Here, utilities are defined as electrical, water, gas, plumbing, and mechanical. Typically, "mechanical" is a system that requires utilities to operate, but for this discussion on site inspections, it is included under utilities.

Electrical System One of the first utilities to look at is the electrical system, required by all stores. A common mistake is to look at the electrical panel and add the numbers on the circuit breakers. If this is done it will give you an incorrect capacity size, because circuit breakers can be oversized or undersized. Another common mistake is to read the decal on the electrical panel. Although this is probably more accurate, it still leaves room for error. The correct way to find out the size of the electrical service (generally just called service) is to have an electrician verify it. Another way is to call the local utility company, but this requires that you know the precise address of the tenant space, and this process can take some time.

Typical service sizes are either 100 or 200 amps for retail use. Restaurants, computer stores, supermarkets, and the like have the potential for even more power—anywhere from 400 to 1,200 amps. The original shopping center's electrical requirements were designed for a certain number of retail and other high-end electrical users. An electrical engineer has calculated the electrical requirements space by space, and the local power company has reviewed and approved all of that work, which has taken into consideration not only the standard retailers but also any tenants with high demand, such as restaurants. Keep in mind that if the shopping center has been designed for a specific number of restaurants and the project manager is adding more, additional electric power may be needed for the center, which in turn could cost the landlord or tenant additional money. For example, if the lease exhibit is written so that the landlord supplies power to the space and it turns out that ample power is not available at the center, it will cost the landlord a tremendous amount of money to provide this. And if additional power is not figured into the pro forma, this deal might not make any business sense.

Voltage is the other factor the project manager should consider. This is either high voltage, 277/480 volts, or regular voltage, 120/208 volts. High voltage can reduce the number of amps required to operate the tenant space, but it does require the expense of a transformer. Many restaurants use high voltage, while typical retail uses regular voltage. So while amp requirements are important, you also must know what the tenant requires, and what is available, in terms of voltage.

Water The next utility to look for is water. Typically, all spaces have water provided to them in the original design of the shopping center, but it is still important to note if water exists and where it is located in the space. If the space is changing to a high-volume water user, such as a restaurant or hair salon, make sure you know the extent of the new tenant's water requirements to ensure that it can be provided. Considerable money will be spent if a new water line has to be brought to the space and it was not anticipated in the pro forma.

Gas Not all shopping centers have gas. If gas is not used, the size of the electrical system must be increased, because the heating, ventilating, and air conditioning (HVAC) must then be totally run electrically. It also means that the restaurants will need to be all electric instead of gas, which is what most restaurants use. Again, this has the potential to increase the size of the electrical systems. It should be noted here that a possible way to reduce the electrical load for a restaurant is to install gas for kitchen equipment, thereby removing some of the electrical requirements.

Mechanical System Mechanical systems can be divided into regular, split, and plenum systems. All of these work off the same principle, supplying either warm or cool air to the space; air is then removed from the space and either returned to the unit or dispersed into the air. Systems generally must be designed to keep the space under equal pressure—the same amount of air must be pushed out of a space as is pushed into that space. However, restaurants like to have positive pressure in their space, putting more air into it than they are removing, which pushes the cooking aromas into the center and entices people to come in and eat. It is a good idea to make restaurants have negative pressure, which means they are receiving more air from the space than they are pushing out.

> Regular system: This is the most inexpensive system to install and the most widely used. It consists of a rooftop unit with ductwork penetrating the roof and then running throughout the tenant space. Generally there is one duct that runs down the center of the space, with smaller ducts extending toward the sides of the store. These smaller ducts then bend down into the ceiling, and a grill is put over this duct.
>
> Split system: This is used when an obstruction exists between the unit and the tenant space. Obstructions include anything from another tenant space above to simply a lack of room to put ductwork through the ceiling. The split system requires only some small piping between the roof unit and the rest of the system in the tenant space. Although it does require space in the tenant's store, installation can be done on the ceiling of the rest room. This system has ductwork and controls similar to those of the regular system.
>
> Plenum system: This is a variation of the regular system. Both systems are designed the same in that ductwork supplies air to the space. But instead of having ductwork return the air to the unit or outside, the plenum system uses the ceiling as the return air duct. In other words, the ceiling space is used as a huge duct. This can present some problems. A major one is that the demising partition will not go all the way to the structure above. This could have an impact on a jewelry store, for example, because insurance companies require that its space be totally enclosed. In addition, light fixtures have to be tented and require a ceiling system

around them. Another drawback to this system is that nothing—such as telephone lines—can be run through the ceiling.

Inspections Once all utilities have been verified, special features that could present problems for future tenants in the space should be inspected. Some special features to look for are:

- Column location
- Ceiling space. Check to see what is there. If this is a renovated space, the previous ceiling may not have been removed.
- Floor penetrations. Is there anything penetrating the floor that could be a problem to a future tenant?
- Service corridors. Open the rear door and look into the service corridor or the rear of the building. Can the tenant receive its goods?

Two other areas that need to be mentioned as part of site investigation are environmental and zoning issues. Although the project manager typically cannot do the checking for environmental issues, you should know what exists in the space, because any problems that arise could have an impact on your pro forma. Zoning is the other area you do not have any control of, but you do need to know that the use you are putting into the center is approved for the shopping center and that you can provide parking for this use. You should be familiar with what uses will affect your parking requirements. If you are fortunate enough to have a development department, it can usually provide these answers. If you do not, call a local civil engineer or architect who can answer these types of questions.

SPACE LAYOUT

After completing the site inspection, you need to have a drawing made showing the vacant tenant space. An architect or other professional who is familiar with store construction should do this drawing. It should show perimeter demising walls, rest room locations, electrical panel location, floor to underside of structure above dimension, and any other special features the tenant should know about. It is also important to note that the tenant needs to come and do field verification.

COST ESTIMATE

To start to prepare your pro forma, you need to develop a cost estimate or preliminary budget of what it will take to put the space in a leasable condition. Methods of developing a cost estimate include:

Construction estimating publications. The most common publication on estimating throughout the shopping center industry is *Means*. The disadvantage of using this type of source estimating is that you generally have to know how all of the systems go together. You cannot just add or delete a rest room; you have to know about drywall, metal studs, toilet fixtures, painting, and so on.

Construction estimating software. There are many on the market today, and this is a very good way to obtain a budget. This method also assumes that a person has knowledge of how all systems go together.

Construction department. This can be either construction or tenant coordination. This method is probably the best way to get budget numbers for the vacant tenant space, because your people know the center and also have local pricing knowledge. They can also work with the project manager to get the price and scope of work that will work best for the shopping center.

Local general contractor. This also is a very good source to get a preliminary budget number. The general contractor knows the market and local code compliance and can generally give accurate numbers. It should be noted that an accurate scope of work needs to be provided. For providing you with this service, the general contractor should be included on the final list of bidders.

Additionally, design costs, permit fees, and contingency fees should be included in the budget numbers to obtain a complete cost for the project.

PRELIMINARY SCHEDULE

The final part of the planning stage is a preliminary schedule. This pertains only to a vacant tenant space that is being brought to a leasable condition and is not intended for any specific tenant. When a tenant is found, this schedule would be modified. The preliminary schedule consists of:

Cost estimate. This is based on one of the estimating procedures mentioned above.

Schedule of time. This must be based on drawing time, permitting time, and construction time. It can be a simple bar chart, but however it is done, it will determine when the tenant space can be delivered to the tenant. If time becomes a factor, a couple of ways to decrease the construction time are to start work before the lease is executed or to work double shifts. It is very important to know what the schedule is, because it has a dramatic impact on when rent is collected. Tenant work typically takes no more than six to eight weeks, so schedules should be updated weekly.

Organizing

After lease negotiations have occurred and preliminary terms and conditions have been developed, it is time to determine what delivery method you will use to complete the project. Any changes to the preliminary terms and conditions may have an impact on both the schedule and the budget, and so they must be addressed as quickly as possible.

DELIVERY METHODS
Delivery methods include the following:

- Traditional
- Negotiated
- Design/build.

During the course of design and construction, the various entities involved will be submitting applications for payment, or invoices. You or your representative must ensure that the applications are in order. If you are using an architect or owner's representative, that person should certify that each application is in order and recommend payment in whatever amount is deemed appropriate. Items that should be reviewed include that the percentages of payment being applied for equal the amount of work and materials used or on site by the date of the application. You or your representative should also check the lien waivers to make sure they match either the amount currently requested or the amounts previously requested and paid. You also need to check the retention amount. Retention is the portion you hold in reserve should there be any performance problems with your general contractor or subcontractors. Percentages vary, but owners most typically retain 10 percent until all the punch list items are complete and the owner has all waivers in hand. In most cases, owners require contractors to submit applications for payment on any standard forms used by the contractor, architect, or developer. One such form is the AIA Form G722.

TEAM ASSEMBLY

After you have decided which delivery method you are going to use, you need to begin to assemble the team. This section assumes that the traditional approach is being used, for two reasons. First, it is the method most often used; second, it is the most involved, requiring all the disciplines, and therefore best demonstrates the team assembly process. This process involves the following steps:

1. Select an architect/engineer to develop your project's plans and specifications. Many different contract forms can be used, ranging from those of the AIA to ones developed by the architect/engineer. The fees should be expressed as a stipulated sum for a specified scope of work. Developers often use letters of intent to start a consultant's work prior to the contract being fully executed, to expedite the completion of the work.

2. After the architect/engineer has completed the project's plans and specifications, the work is put out for bids. It is recommended that you solicit bids from at least three contractors who have extensive retail construction experience, preferably including work on the center where the project is being constructed. Typically, for simple white box work you should allow the contractors three weeks to prepare and return their bids. The solicitation process typically is in the form of a request for proposal (RFP). The RFP should include at a minimum the following:

- Bid form, prepared by the architect
- Black contract form
- Qualification statement—standard AIA form
- Statement from the contractor stipulating the number of calendar days after the permit is issued—you need to include information

in the RFP explaining when you think the permit will be issued—until the work is completed
- Copy of the certificate of insurance.

3. Concurrent with the bidding process, the plans and specifications should be submitted to the local municipality for permit review and approval. You need to familiarize yourself with the permit process in the community in which your center is located. You should be aware of such items as fees, duration of the review process, and special requirements (for example, new storefront plans often have to be reviewed and approved by the community's design review committee or historical preservation review board, if applicable, before the building department can issue a permit). Further, you need to be aware of these permit requirements so that you can inform your future tenants about what they will have to provide in order to get their permits.

Directing and Controlling

After the bids have been received, you and your architect should review them and select the apparent low bidder.

ACCEPTING A BID

The two of you should then qualify the selected contractor's bid to ensure that it has the full scope of work covered and the resources to complete the work in the time frame as detailed by your RFP. Look for such things as significant differences in the bid form line items. This often indicates that the contractor or the bidding subcontractor misunderstood the bid documents and does not have the full scope of the work covered in the bid.

After you have qualified the apparent low bidder, you need to issue a contract for execution. You should not make any payments until the contract is fully executed and all insurance forms are in place.

If the low bid is above your budget, you need to meet with the entire team and use value engineering to get the job within its budget limits. Value engineering involves evaluating all of the construction disciplines to see what less expensive alternatives might be used or to reduce the scope of work. This must be in accordance with the terms and conditions of the lease. In other words, if your lease stipulates new two-by-four lay-in lights, you should not substitute the reuse of existing lights.

BEGINNING THE WORK

During this time your contractor should pick up the project's permit and commence the work. The initial phases typically include laying the space out. This is nothing more than marking the floor plan on the slab with chalk lines. You may also allow the contractor to proceed with roughing in some of the work prior to completing all of your value engineering. The key is not to go so far that you eliminate your ability to reduce costs because some work has already been done.

Once you have gotten your project costs in line with your budget, you can release your contractor to complete the full scope of the revised plans and specifications. By this time you should have a full list of any subcontractors and suppliers from you contractor.

CONTRACT ADMINISTRATION

Now the next phase of the project begins. This is typically called contract administration. This is simply a means for the owner to ensure the quality of your project. There are many different ways for you to perform quality control on your project. You can have your architect include regular site visits in the scope of his or her work. These site visits should include reviewing the work to date to confirm that it is being performed in accordance with the project's plans and specification; answering any questions the contractor may have; and evaluating the progress of the work to confirm compliance with the project's schedule.

The advantage of this approach is a single point of contact to manage your project. The disadvantages include the potential for conflict of interest. If the architect is inspecting the work and there is an error in the plans or specifications, he or she might choose to ignore the problem or arrange with the contractor to change the work at the owner's expense. In addition, if the architect is from out of town, the costs for these site visits could be significant.

Another method is to hire an independent third-party firm to act as your representative. These entities are known as owner's representatives. The advantages of this approach are that it reduces costs if the architect is from out of town, and it eliminates the potential for conflicts of interest. The disadvantage is that you now have three contracts and vendors to manage instead of two. Making your owner's representative responsible for managing all contracts and applications for payment can alleviate this disadvantage.

If all you need is inspection of the work from a technical point of view, you may want to hire an inspecting architect. This means that you will need to manage the project's schedule by making regular site visits to ensure that the contractor is on schedule. The advantage to this approach is that it may save you money. The disadvantage is that it will require more of your time.

Finally, if you have the time and the technical expertise to entirely manage your project yourself, you can use this approach. To do this you must be able to read and understand construction plans and specifications in detail. You will also need to make regular site visits to ensure quality and adherence to your schedule by the general contractor. The key disadvantage is that this method will require even more of your time than any of the other alternatives. If your primary responsibility is leasing, for example, this may be a very poor use of your time.

CLOSEOUT PHASE

The final phase of a project is typically called the closeout phase. The first step in this phase is often the issuance of a certificate of substantial completion by your architect. This document is a statement attesting to the fact that the architect has inspected the space and it can be used for its intended purpose. You may also be prepared at this point to request a certificate of occupancy from the municipality in which your project is located. This is certification from the local government that the space is now ready for occupancy. You should note that it is possible to achieve substantial completion without being able to get a certificate of occupancy yet. For example, say you have constructed a new building for a big box, or large, single-use store, to suit the tenant's specific needs, and now all of your work is done. The municipal building department may not be willing to issue a certificate of occupancy until the tenant has completed the fixturing and merchandising of the store. Typically, the building department is worried about whether exit lights will still be visible or aisles still open after all of the tenant's fixtures and merchandise are in place.

Frequently, a joint or punch list inspection of the space is conducted as part of the substantial completion inspection and delivery of possession to the tenant. The parties attending this joint inspection should include a representative of the architect (if you are using your architect for contract administration), at least one representative of the landlord, a representative of the general contractor, and a representative of the tenant. Preferably there should be two representatives from the landlord at this inspection to deal with the transition between the development function and the property management function.

From this joint inspection the architect or owner's representative prepares a single list, called a punch list, of items that need to be corrected or completed. A copy of this list should be given to each member of the inspecting team. The general contractor uses this list to inform the subcontractors of the items they need to take care of before they will receive final payment.

The owner or landlord uses this list as documentation of the condition the space is in before the tenant assumes occupancy. For example, after the joint inspection has occurred and the tenant has occupied the space, a hole in the wall that is not on the punch list is discovered. The burden of proof in this situation is typically the tenant's, not the landlord's, and therefore the cost of repair is up to the tenant if another cause is not proved. You should also use this list to determine if you should pay the contractor's final application and release the retention. If all the work on the list is done, you can consider making final payment. The word *consider* is used because there are other matters to take under advisement. Has the contractor submitted final waivers for all contractors and subcontractors? Are the waivers signed and sealed, or have all state or province requirements been met from a legal point of view? Further, has the contractor supplied you with all warranties, as builts, and manuals for the work?

If the joint inspection is in fact the milestone event for delivery of possession of the space to the tenant, it is recommended that you send your new tenant a registered letter announcing that the terms and conditions of the landlord's work have been met and rent will commence per the terms of the lease. Because it is a legal document, your legal counsel should review this letter.

Completion

Your project is now complete. Your customer, whether it is the tenant that you are turning the space over to or the store manager who is ready to fixture his or her new store, will probably give you an opinion about the job you've done. This can often be quite a subjective process, based more on perception than fact, such as, "I thought you should have given me access to the space two weeks ago, so I could open the day you complete your work." For you to determine objectively how successful your project was, you must examine it from the points of view of schedule, budget, and quality.

Thomas W. Taylor is Principal at AT Associates, Inc., Park Ridge, Illinois. Paul J. Mackie is Vice President, Tenant Coordination at Combined Properties, Washington, D.C.

10 Lease Management and Administration

Karl D. Ehrlich

Shopping center professionals spend more time than ever managing and administering lease agreements. Although this effort encompasses a wide range of duties and is performed by a team of professionals, the industry simply refers to the entire function as lease administration. The term has become synonymous with lease enforcement, but, in fact, negotiation is more important than enforcement, management, or administration.

This chapter explores the roles played by everyone involved in lease administration, especially the leasing representative. The first section provides some historical perspective and describes how the leasing representative is involved. The next section explores the primary goals and objectives of the lease administration team and the obstacles they must overcome when tenants choose not to honor every commitment in the lease. This is followed by a look at the job each leasing team member plays from a how-to perspective: Who is involved? What role does each play? How does the team anticipate and deal with special problems? What tools does the job require? The next section examines the obligations of the tenant and the landlord and describes how the use of ingenuity and negotiating are essential tools, particularly when dealing with a tenant in default. Following that is a look at the root cause of common disputes from the landlord's and tenant's perspectives. The final section suggests some budget implications that are sometimes overlooked.

Overview

All shopping center professionals need to focus on financial aspects of the shopping center business, but the ones who add the most value to their properties understand that they are also partners with their tenants in the retail business.

HISTORICAL PERSPECTIVE

Like most industries that are affected by the health of the economy, the shopping center industry has experienced some periods of sustained growth and others of rapid contraction in its history. When the economy expands, customers spend more and retailers open more stores. In response, investors purchase properties, intending to enhance their value, improve tenant mix, gain market share, and raise rents. In down markets, when sales remain flat or decline, retailers curtail their expansion plans or even close stores. Then the supply of retail space tends to exceed retailers' demand for space, so investors conserve property value by maintaining occupancy levels and preserving the existing rent roll. Retail sales have generally been a good barometer of the economy, but during the 1990s, two forces whipsawed the industry and made it much less predictable. These two forces—global deflation in commodity prices and the development of new retail formats—have squeezed retail margins for many chain stores. As a result, amid this strong economy, some retailers have found new opportunities for expansion while others have had to close stores or file for bankruptcy protection. Retail chains that have adapted to the new forces have prospered.

Some people attribute the changes to the natural evolution or life cycle of the industry. They believe that some types of centers are past their prime, or "post peak," in common terminology. The expansion of the industry, starting in the 1950s and accelerating with suburban development in the 1970s and 1980s, resulted in saturation of some types of centers from the mid-1980s into the 1990s. During the 1990s, some centers closed, and fewer were built. With more than 20 square feet of retail space available for each man, woman, and child in the United States, up significantly from about 15 square feet, per capita in 1985, sometimes it seems as though there are just not enough retail tenants to fill all of the available space. Yet many similar properties prosper and gain market share, and retailers continue to expand in new and existing formats.

Everyone agrees that the pace of change in the industry has accelerated, but few agree on what the future holds.

What is generally agreed is that the increased competition and uncertainty have taken their toll on the relationship between retailers and landlords. Retailers have become more critical of landlords' role in their success, because in many cases rent and charges have increased faster than retail sales. Today, landlords and tenants both demand that they get the most out of every lease.

ROLE OF THE LEASING REPRESENTATIVE

It is no secret that most leasing agents describe their role in lease administration as a chore, not a pleasure. Certainly, the task is not as glamorous or as much fun as, say, earning a fat commission, negotiating a high rent, or finding a desirable new tenant to fill a vacant space. However, when disputes arise leasing agents must take an active role in the process for one simple reason: The leasing agent negotiates the business deal that creates the general terms and conditions in the lease contract. The agent has firsthand knowledge of the deal. Many others, who are called on later to administer the lease, do not. Also, when confronted with lower occupancy levels, leasing agents recognize that it is easier to retain an existing tenant than to find a new one. One of the leasing representative's primary jobs is to help retain tenants when called upon by management.

When a leasing agent reaches an agreement with a tenant on the lease's basic economic provisions—which are sometimes listed on the first page of the lease form for easy reference, and are often called "Fundamental Lease Provisions"—the agent instructs those drafting the lease as to what should be included in the document. Even with excellent lease drafting, however, disagreements may arise later.

When disagreements about the lease become disputes between the landlord and tenant, these invariably fall into one or more of three areas: 1) the specific language in the document; 2) the intent of the parties to the agreement; and 3) how implementation of the document differs from what is common practice in the industry. Take a situation in which a tenant disputes the provision in the lease regarding monetary terms—rent, percentage rent, or additional rent. If the tenant questions the amount billed for common area charges, the landlord must explain the expense or calculation before the tenant agrees to pay the bill. To research the amount, the tenant and lease administrator first have to check the written record (that is, the language in the lease, lease proposals, and correspondence). Then they will each talk to the dealmakers to understand the intent behind the agreement. If they still cannot agree, they will each cite examples of how charges are billed at other properties by other landlords. If either party does not believe that the dispute will be settled quickly, they should immediately consult their attorney, and avoid putting statements in writing that could be used against them in a court of law.

In addition to rental disputes, disagreements may arise over nonmonetary obligations such as hours of operation, employee parking requirements, advertising, and refurbishment. For example, in an enclosed mall, a lease may require the tenant to advertise, to carry specified amounts of insurance, and to refurbish the premises periodically to keep them in first-class condition. In a strip center, a food tenant may be required to clean its grease trap periodically, to maintain its sprinkler system, and to contract with a pest control service.

Although these responsibilities may not be classified as monetary obligations per se, they represent a real cost to the tenant. If the tenant fails to perform or pay for these obligations, the landlord will have to bear the cost or risk, directly or indirectly. The cost may not be obvious at first, but eventually, it is safe to say, any obligation that the tenant avoids will affect the property's bottom line in one or more of the following ways: It will lower the property's image, increase other tenants' common area expenses (thereby reducing their ability to pay rent), or pass directly to the landlord for payment. All provisions of the lease have financial implications. The entire lease must be enforced or the landlord's return on investment will suffer. Monetary and nonmonetary obligations alike are verified first by reading the documents, second by understanding the intent of the parties, and finally by reviewing common industry practice.

In a nutshell, lease administration enforces the terms of the lease because unpaid rent or a receivable account is not income; and unmet tenant obligations that a landlord must enforce and possibly perform for the tenant cost the landlord money which it may not recover from a weak or insolvent tenant.

Goals of Lease Administration

The establishment of primary goals of the lease administration team determines a focus for the team's efforts around three overall areas:

financial results, communicating priorities, and interpretation and negotiation.

FINANCIAL RESULTS
On a day-to-day basis, lease administration focuses primarily on financial results. The job is to collect rent, to monitor annual rental increases, to bill operating expenses, to track operating escalations, to monitor tenant sales and determine if percentage rent is owed, and to enforce audit provisions. From a larger perspective, though, the scope of the job is to interpret the lease agreement accurately and to enforce it aggressively, in order to allocate fairly the risks and obligations contained in the documents and any side agreements. Lease administration ensures that the landlord and tenant receive the benefit of the bargain each has struck. When leasing agents become involved, it is because, like all other shopping center professionals, they are in the rent business.

COMMUNICATING PRIORITIES
To ensure compliance with the most important provisions of the lease, management routinely communicates the landlord's expectations in various ways so that they are clear to the tenant. The landlord's dialogue with the tenant alerts the tenant about which lease obligations are a priority. Management may print a list of rules and regulations, distribute a newsletter, conduct merchants' meetings, or write a letter to enforce a lease provision. On the other hand, if the landlord chooses not to enforce certain provisions, management's inaction can create the impression that the owner does not care so much about those obligations. In extreme circumstances, if the tenant continually violates a clause but the landlord chooses to look the other way, the landlord may give up the right to enforce that obligation in the future. The legal term for giving up rights through inaction is *laches* (pronounced "latches"). The landlord is said to have waived the right or to be "estopped" from asserting the right.

INTERPRETATION AND NEGOTIATION
During the modern shopping center's four- or five-decade history, lease forms have become longer and more precise as attorneys have crafted language to deal with their experience. Leases in the 1960s

often were fewer than 10 pages long. Today, many regional mall leases run to more than 50 pages, single-spaced on legal-sized paper, without exhibits. Strip center leases are typically 15 to 25 pages or even longer. But no matter how many pages attorneys add to the boilerplate to deal with their what-if scenarios about unlikely events, or how successfully they craft language to document the understandings of the parties, it is not possible for them to anticipate every issue, or to document every expectation. For this reason, lease agreements are never fully precise.

Lease administration requires more than the administration of the documents and interpretation of the landlord's and tenant's understandings; effective lease administration tempers aggressive enforcement of the lease document with an appreciation of how retail sales may be stimulated by landlord and tenant. Lease administration tries to build a bond between tenant and landlord that resembles a partnership (though it is not one legally, since the parties do not own an interest in each other's companies; they are only obligated to perform certain actions under the contract). This synergistic relationship requires that the landlord understand and apply common industry practices, while continually negotiating rights and responsibilities to deal with unforeseen events. (For example, a dispute over what may be included in common area expenses may be settled using the standard of common retail practice. If the landlord were to include the cost of a central office employee as an operating expense, the tenant may dispute the item if common industry practice limits management expenses to on-site personnel only.) Because leases leave substantial room for interpretation, the boilerplate often contains a clause that requires the parties to be reasonable in their actions.

The Practice of Lease Administration

The practice of lease management and administration involves three main components: the team, record keeping, and policies and procedures.

THE TEAM

Unlike families, and most corporate organizations that are organized in a vertical hierarchy, lease administration departments generally are organized horizontally, in teams of professionals. The team usually includes the leasing representative, the property manager (including management and accounting), and a lease administrator. Others may participate from time to time, including tax and insurance consultants, lenders, attorneys, architects, and engineers. No team member is expected to be an expert in all aspects of the lease. The complexities of the lease require that the combined talents of role players perform the administration. When dealing with a problem outside the particular area of expertise, each participant needs to have access to the knowledge and experience of other team members. Sharing information is critical to successful lease administration.

Leasing Representative During lease negotiations, and sometimes throughout the lease term, the leasing representative plays a central role as a liaison between the landlord and tenant. This requires the representative to have a thorough understanding of both the landlord's and the tenant's businesses. The leasing representative negotiates the deal for the landlord. Then, as its agent, the leasing representative gives instruction to those drafting the document on what goes into the lease. The leasing agent also should communicate the tenant's concerns to the management team and, particularly for local tenants, explain the conditions of the lease to the tenant. Because the leasing agent must understand the document from both the landlord's and the tenant's perspectives, the leasing agent needs a thorough understanding of how the shopping center operates, what the tenant needs from the shopping center to be successful, and what the lease document provides.

The landlord's standard lease form contains many provisions that are intended to be applied uniformly among all of the center's tenants. These are often referred to as boilerplate provisions. When the leasing agent communicates a different understanding to the tenant about language in the standard lease, the agent's representation may create an obligation. This is true whether or not the final document is actually changed to reflect the new understanding. Unwritten representations are sometimes referred to as verbal contracts, side agreements, or simply understandings. Most leases have an integration clause which says that the document controls and that no other representations and the like are included.

Leasing agents should try to avoid misrepresentations and when in doubt, they should review their statements with their counsel. Many times, leasing agents inadvertently misrepresent what the lease says because they themselves do not understand all the language in the document, or how a particular shopping center works. For example, a leasing representative may lease multiple centers. One property may have a central heating, ventilating and air conditioning (HVAC) system that requires the tenant to pay a monthly charge. Another may require the tenant to install, or recondition, a rooftop unit. In the lease proposal, these types of charges should be highlighted. Failure to identify the charge for the HVAC system could create problems for the landlord and tenant later. It is important that the leasing representative understand the financial and legal terms in the lease so that no misrepresentations are made. When in doubt, the leasing representative needs to rely on other team members.

One of the leasing representative's primary jobs is to retain good tenants by facilitating their successful operation. After the lease is executed, the lease administration team may direct the leasing agent to communicate with the tenant again to reinforce the terms of the lease or to clarify what was intended. If a tenant questions or disputes a lease provision, or if it runs into a financial problem during the term of the lease, the tenant may contact the leasing representative before talking to other management personnel. At this point, the leasing representative may need to be reminded that the role he or she plays is as part of a team. If the leasing representative responds to the tenant that the problem is not the agent's responsibility, this message will be perceived as nonresponsive. As a team member, a more appropriate reply would be, "Let me review this with the management team, and one of us will get back to you promptly." From that point forward, the policies and procedures of the lease administration team will dictate who responds, and how the response will be formulated.

When the tenant asks the leasing representative to help solve problems with its business, the leasing representative naturally will feel torn between a duty as the landlord's agent and an obligation to ensure the tenant's successful operation. In these situations, the tenant may ask the leasing representative for some form of financial assistance or to renegotiate the terms of the lease. Before taking any action, the leasing representative must consider what role to play—tenant advocate, conduit, or management enforcer. One of the keys to walking this tightrope successfully is full disclosure. The tenant must always understand that the leasing representative's agency relationship is with the landlord, but what may be in the mutual best interest of the landlord and tenant is to find a solution to the problem that works for both parties.

Management Management's job is to operate the shopping center in a consistent manner, to create an environment that helps each tenant maximize its sales potential. When a leasing agent negotiates terms that significantly amend the boilerplate language, this complicates management's ability to operate the center in a nondiscriminatory manner. The more consistently rules and responsibilities are applied, the fairer the terms appear, and the more acceptance they will receive from most tenants.

Management is concerned with every portion of the lease, but it must pay particular attention to how it controls the tenant's impact on other tenants and on the center's common areas. Within the parameters of the lease agreement and the standards set for the center by its ownership, management tries to maximize each tenant's business without negatively impacting the businesses of other retailers. It is in the owner's best interest to help tenants stimulate sales, because strong sales lead to higher rent, and higher rent translates into higher property value. The landlord's ability to control the common areas is outlined in the boilerplate language, which may be supplemented with a lease exhibit called "Rules and Regulations." The landlord controls the tenant's hours of operation, sets standards for signage inside and outside the storefront, and limits the level of noise and odors that may emanate from the premises. In its effort to control the common areas, management faces some critical operational issues when a tenant's actions negatively affect the standards set for the center.

In addition to monitoring tenant operations and enforcing control over the common areas, management also provides an early warning if problems arise with the tenant's business. Some of the indications that a tenant has difficulties include:

- Slow payment of rent
- Slow reporting of sales
- Low merchandise levels in the store
- Merchandise perpetually on sale
- Low sales volume
- Lack of responsiveness to contact
- High cost of occupancy analysis.

When tenants experience financial problems, they are often unwilling to discuss the specifics. Management must confront the tenant to learn what is causing the tenant's problems.

Frequent, straightforward communication between management

and the tenant serves many purposes. Through its regular dialogue with tenants, management communicates the landlord's expectations and defines acceptable limits to the store and to the tenant's home office. This informal process is preferable to having to confront contrary behavior after the fact. When tenants know the limits beforehand, they actually gain a sense of security. The tenant knows what is important to the landlord and what actions or reactions to expect if it violates the rules. Maintaining an informal dialogue with retailers is especially important for store personnel. At the store level, this may be the only way they know what the landlord expects, since few store employees are allowed to read the lease. These interchanges reinforce the sense of partnership, keep expectations realistic, and help avoid unnecessary confrontations, ultimatum, and idle threats.

Accounting Rent and sales reports are among the accounting department's most important responsibilities in lease administration. Side agreements and other unrecorded negotiations between the tenant and landlord representatives can affect accounting's ability to perform these functions. Accounting personnel must be aware of all agreements, not just those contained in the document file.

The accounting department helps management identify tenant problems by tracking and analyzing sales and payment data. From experience, accountants know that two areas most likely to indicate that a tenant is experiencing difficulty are the tenant's accounts receivable balance (sometimes called "aging") and declining or low sales. Tenants that consistently run an aging balance of more than 60 days exhibit signs of cash flow problems. Tenants whose rent-to-sales ratio exceeds industry standards generally do not operate profitably.

Lease Administrators Lease administrators are management or operations personnel who deal directly with tenants to enforce the terms of the lease. In many organizations, the lease administrator's role is the key function in managing and administering the lease. Sometimes, people fail to distinguish between the role that an individual lease administrator plays and the function of lease administration, which is performed by a team. They may refer to the "lease administrator" as having taken some action, when in fact the lease administrator was actually the manager, acting on behalf of the lease administration team. In this way, lease administration is like the real estate committee; the lease administrator, or anyone else on the team, may speak to the tenant for the committee, but the team, not the individual, formulates policy.

One of the lease administrator's responsibilities is to analyze information gathered from the tenant, from the tenant's file, and from other team members, and to recommend action. The lease administrator must take into account changes in the relationship between the landlord and tenant and the long-term, and short-term, goals of each. Over time, the expectations and relative positions in the landlord/tenant relationship change. Even if the document prescribes a specific course of action, the lease administrator may recommend a different solution to maintain a positive relationship. Lease administrators feel a natural tension between strictly enforcing the lease document and retaining tenants. Although these goals are not always mutually exclusive, it is much more difficult to find a new tenant than to retain an existing one. When in doubt, lease administrators usually choose to work out their differences with tenants and help them solve their problems.

Management personnel, accountants, and lease administrators must coordinate their efforts to monitor notice dates for lease cancellation, termination, and renewal. Most lease administrators remind themselves of critical dates with a so-called bring-up list or tickler system that tracks such future events as the submission of remodeling plans, return of estoppel agreements, or delivery of annual certificates of insurance. The tickler system should track:

- Real estate tax payments and insurance policy renewals
- Tenant insurance certificates to ensure lease conformance
- Preventive and recurring maintenance programs to ensure that all monthly, quarterly, annual, or other routine maintenance and life safety inspections are conducted
- Options, such as volume-out, kick-out, expansion, and first-right-of-refusal provisions
- Renewals of letters of credit.

Legal Department The legal department, or outside lawyer hired by management, provides guidance on legal interpretation and enforcement of lease provisions. Most landlords use legal departments reluctantly, as the final step in a lengthy negotiation process. Not only is the use of a lawyer expensive, but also tenants know that lawyers are most often used to enforce leases only after negotiations have failed. So when lawyers provide official notice to tenants, both sides usually become less flexible.

Although industry-wide practice and understandings between the leasing representative and the tenant shape their expectations, the language in the lease takes precedence in most cases. The lease's boilerplate language tries to eliminate any confusion about prior understandings or expectations through a provision inserted in the agreement that voids everything that came before the executed lease. This exculpatory clause (also known as an integration clause) says something to the effect that the written lease document contains all of the agreements of the parties. Any verbal agreement, side agreement, or understanding that may have existed between the leasing agent and tenant prior to the drafting of the lease is no longer valid unless it has been included in this lease document. Such a clause is intended to put both the tenant and the tenant's attorney on notice that the lease document will be the entire agreement. To be valid, any other agreements or understandings not included in the current lease draft must be incorporated before the lease is executed. When the initial lease draft is prepared, the landlord's attorney forwards a preliminary copy to the tenant and the tenant's attorney for review and comment. The lease comment stage of negotiation, as it is called, results in a documented contract, generally referred to as the executed lease. Whatever came before is no longer relevant unless it has been incorporated into the executed lease.

After the lease is executed, the landlord's attorney uses the exculpatory language as a defense to limit the scope of discussion only to the language in the lease document. Tenants often try to bring into the record examples of intent and side agreements. Under some circumstances, courts permit the tenant to assert that the lease was amended by verbal agreements, representations, and the actions (or inaction) of the parties before and after the execution of the lease. Frequently, the reason to look beyond the lease is due to fraud, misrepresentation, ambiguous lease language, or simply a failure of the lease to deal with the issue at hand. For this reason, lawyers need access to all of the team's records, starting with the leasing representative's first contact with the tenant. If a tenant charges that language in the lease conflicts with common industry practice, or alleges that the leasing agent's misrepresentation or other action amended the lease, management may decide that a negotiated settlement is preferable to litigation. At such times, everyone is reminded how imprecise lease language can be, and how important are complete records.

Other Team Players Management may retain the services of tax and insurance consultants, lenders, auditors, architects, and engineers for guidance on lease provisions. Team members should use an additional level of control when outside parties are used, because with their narrow focus, specialists often lack knowledge or appreciation of the tenant's business.

RECORD KEEPING

Maintaining an accurate record of all dealings between management and potential tenants, new tenants, and ongoing tenants, as well as between various team members and management, is essential to effective lease administration.

The Lease Abstract To administer the lease, team members must have access to complete and accurate records, but they are not expected to maintain all files personally. For convenience, management prepares and distributes a lease synopsis that condenses the important elements of the lease agreement to one or two pages in length. The lease synopsis is sometimes called an abstract, a lease brief, or a lease summary. Management prepares the abstract when the lease is executed, and updates it whenever the terms of the lease are modified.

Team members use the information in the abstract for different purposes. For the accounting department, the abstract contains all of the terms and pay dates for the tenant's financial obligations—rent, percentage rent, common area charges, marketing fund dues, and so on. For management, the abstract lists operational responsibilities such as the tenant's insurance requirement, operating hours, and restrictions on use or radius of operation. For the marketing manager, the abstract lists the frequency with which the tenant is required to advertise, and its share of promotional dues. With so many team members relying on the accuracy of the information, it is not surprising that, in practice, they mistakenly treat the abstract as an official document, which it is not. Actually, abstracts are often incomplete or out-of-date, and they should not be relied upon as primary sources of information. Abstracts are more like a piece of internal correspondence that needs further verification.

Although the abstract is not a legal document, many people use it for quick reference:

- Leasing representatives check the economic terms after the leasing deal is completed
- Real estate professionals transfer the fundamental lease provisions to their reports when they perform due diligence for the purchase or sale of a shopping center
- Lenders gather financial data when they finance a mortgage
- Managers refer to dates and timing to monitor renewal periods, options, and special provisions.

Each time the user reads the abstract, he or she should ask when the abstract was updated last. Lease agreements are frequently amended or assigned. If the abstract has not been updated to reflect these changes, then the team may end up by acting on inaccurate information.

Estoppel Agreements Even at the time the lease is signed and abstract is created, the abstract may not be accurate, because a few terms are unknown. For example, in the case of a new shopping center, management cannot specify the commencement date of the lease's term (and consequently, the termination date at the term's end), because the completion date of the center is conditioned on the timing of the center's construction. Another piece of information often unavailable, or subject to revision, is the certified area covered by the lease. To ensure accuracy in items left vague in the lease document, these terms should be agreed on as soon as they are known, so as to avoid problems in the future. It is good practice for both parties to sign a certificate or an estoppel letter for their files that acknowledges the exact area and the term's commencement date. As with any new document, the certificate or estoppel agreement should be routed to whoever updates the lease abstracts so that there is no confusion later on.

Another time that estoppel agreements are requested is during the sale or refinancing of the property. To verify the landlord's rent roll and to flush out any unresolved disputes, buyers and lenders commonly request that tenants return an estoppel agreement that restates the economic terms of the lease, stating whether payments are current and listing any disputes. Estoppel agreements that do not agree with the primary documents will not amend the lease, but they do provide an anecdotal record of agreements and disagreements. More importantly, a party signing an estoppel agreement may be "stopped" in court from taking a position contrary to that set out in the letter. A party may sign an estoppel asserting the other side is "not in default" of the lease. That party may later be precluded from raising the default in court.

Permanent Records One set of the tenant's complete file should be kept in a centralized location in a fireproof file cabinet. At least one other complete set should be kept elsewhere. For many companies, one set is located at the property.

The entire tenant file is composed of four or five parts: correspondence, documents, financial data, construction documents, and sometimes a litigation file. Each file is organized chronologically, to create a historical perspective of issues raised. The historical record creates a contextual explanation for how and why decisions were made by the landlord and tenant. Well-maintained files are essential, especially in cases of litigation, though more often the files are used to settle disputes before they reach a courtroom. When disputes arise, the complete record is helpful in refreshing memories, and the chronology of events reflects a pattern of behavior. In a dispute, one of the strongest arguments that one of the parties can make is that it relied on a pattern of past practice by the other party.

Computer networks link information that is located at the property with records that are held at the home office and in the field by all members of the lease administration team. Computers can store and instantly transmit the entire tenant file, so that it is accessible for every member of the team at all times. In the future, even more information will be available on-line, such as the tenant's as-built drawings and live interactions between personnel at the center and in the field. Despite the great benefits of computer technology, though, widespread access to sensitive information raises issues of confidentiality and accuracy that require policy guidelines.

The Correspondence File. The correspondence file is often a catchall file. It contains anything that is not an official document, a financial record, or a construction document. Items typically found within correspondence files include:

- Written correspondence (for example, letters, memos, proposals, copies of e-mail)
- News articles relating to the tenant's business
- Logs from the leasing agent's conversations with the tenant, proposals and counterproposals, and other chronological negotiations
- Copies of printed material prepared by the tenant or tenant's broker (for example, store photographs, public relations literature, advertisements)
- Management reports about incidents involving the tenant (insurance claims, late opening reports)

- Default notices and other official notices (changes of address and minor defaults, such as an improperly parked car, late opening, broken neon light, use clause violation).

The Document File. The document file contains every contractual agreement or side agreement. When a dispute arises, this is the first place management checks to find the controlling agreements. Documents include:

- The current and any prior lease agreements
- Guarantee of lease
- Letters of credit
- Tenant's financial statement at the time the lease was signed, and perhaps an independent financial report
- Storage leases
- Lease amendments
- Lease assignments or subletting agreements
- Opening and/or closing certificates
- Estoppel agreements
- Proof of insurance
- Copy of security deposit check.

The Financial/Accounting File. The accounting department maintains the financial and accounting data. These files include:

- Sales and billing records
- List of security deposits
- Description of the pro rata calculation method for charges (for example, common area maintenance, taxes, and insurance). Several companies sell mainframe-based and PC-based software and computer systems that make these records available to team members on-line.

The Construction Documents File. The tenant's permanent record should contain its design and construction plans, regardless of whether outside consultants or the landlord's in-house architect reviewed them. These plans can be bulky, so the landlord may choose to keep one set of computer-aided design drawings (CADD) on a computer disk. The insurance company will want access to construction documents in case of a casualty, and the landlord and future tenants need them to verify as-built conditions. The construction file should contain:

- As-built drawing, signed by an architect and/or engineers
- Progress, conceptual, and/or design drawings
- Landlord's correspondence, such as plans "approved as noted"
- Punch list of construction items to be corrected
- Certificate of Occupancy (COO) from local jurisdiction
- Copies of contractor's (materialman's) bonds
- Notice of liens and lien releases
- Photographs and other details of materials and design
- Contact list of contractors/engineers
- Permits
- Proof of insurance
- Reports and record of compliance with regulations regarding hazardous materials.

The Litigation File (optional). Management should maintain a special litigation file in situations in which the landlord or tenant has initiated legal action. Once established, confidential items that are properly labeled "protected by attorney/client privilege" may not be assessed (or "discovered") by the opposing side. Landlord and tenant representatives should discuss the scope of the privilege with their attorneys as there are definitive requirements that a document must meet to be considered privileged, confidential information. Note that the comments above are not meant as legal advice. If a litigation file needs to be established, an attorney should direct the effort.

Leasing Representative Logs Many organizations require that leasing representatives prepare logs of their contacts with tenants (see Exhibit A: Lease Logs). Logs not only inform team members about the current status of negotiations, but also provide a historical perspective for future use. In fact, the leasing representative's logs provide one of the most valuable, if underutilized, permanent records of the party's intent from the time negotiations begin until the final agreement is executed.

In journal entries, the leasing representatives should record the negotiation's essential aspects, whether they were communicated by the tenant or provided by the real estate committee, and whether written or verbal. Sometimes the log records only the agent's thoughts or analysis at that moment. An entry might be as simple as the notation, "4/26: Traded calls," or as detailed as a description of all of the merchandise found in one of the tenant's stores that the agent reviewed on a certain date. The entire log journal, when reviewed later, provides a historically accurate perspective of the negotiating and decision-making process. Many leasing agents keep such logs on their computers in a journal software program. These programs allow the logs to be shared among other team members over the company's Intranet system. Other leasing representatives create their logs in a word-processing program and e-mail the files to other team members periodically. Logs can also be noted on paper, with copies routed to team members.

POLICIES AND PROCEDURES
Management ensures that leases are administered in a fair and consistent manner by establishing written policies and procedures to deal with conflicts. The uniform application of policies and procedures helps to safeguard the management company from the perception of discriminatory practices, and it provides management personnel with a road map to deal with common problems. As mentioned earlier, when management applies policies consistently, tenants can anticipate and accept management's actions more easily. Some common policies and procedures used by large landlords are:

- Late rent: Invoice on the 25th day of the prior month, call on the 5th of the month, send a letter on the 10th if late, send late notice with late fee on the 15th, default the tenant on the 25th.
- Request for rent deferment or reduction: Limit the period to no more than six months, and require a unilateral landlord option to terminate the lease (see Exhibit B: Tenant Workouts).
- Tenant promise to cure default: Require that written judgment be recorded, which will accelerate rent in case of further default.
- Audits of tenant's sales reports: Audit at least 10 percent of the tenants annually, including all tenants that report sales within 10 percent of the breakpoint, and that therefore might be required to pay overage rent. (Some landlords audit every tenant annually or biannually.)
- Request by tenant to audit landlord CAM: Either provide a copy of the annual independent audit or require tenants to accept the audit report of the largest tenant that has already audited the landlord's books.
- Consistent pattern of late payment or sales report: First late payment or report annually, send a reminder letter; the second,

send a warning of late charge and/or interest; third time and each time thereafter within a 12-month period, apply late charge and/or interest.
- Tenant completes construction before lease is signed: Tenant may not open until the lease is signed and mailed, and the landlord receives a facsimile copy of the signature page of the lease with the tenant's signature.
- Holdover after lease terminates: At least 30 days prior to the termination date, the landlord forwards an official notice of the new amount for rent and charges, usually at least 125 percent of the prior rent.
- Requirement for tenant to supply certified sales: Only the year-end statement needs a signature from the tenant, or tenant's certified public accountant, certifying that the sales are accurate.
- Proof of insurance: Require that certificates of insurance be supplied annually; however, insurance may be provided in an umbrella policy.
- Timing of renewal discussions: Management to forward an official letter to notify the tenant that the lease expires in six months. If the landlord is interested in renewal, the management suggests whom the tenant should contact. If no new lease will be offered, then discuss either terms or procedure for closing.

Obligations of Owner and Tenant

The industry commonly assumes that the lease administration process commences upon the execution of the lease contract. However, for the tenant and leasing representative, the obligations and liability start much earlier, while both parties are negotiating the business terms of the lease.

DUTY OF CARE
The tenant forms its first relationship with the shopping center through the leasing representative, who remains the tenant's primary liaison at least until the lease is signed. During the negotiation process, while the tenant is learning from the leasing representative what contractual obligations it must accept in exchange for the right to occupy a space in the center—in other words, the terms of the lease—the leasing representative must be careful and conscientious about being accurate and truthful. The words *conscientious, accurate,*

and *truthful* may take on legal implications if the tenant later claims that the agent misrepresented the situation or withheld material information. Like all contracts, the lease contract is defined as "a promise for a promise," or "quid pro quo." In this contract, the parties promise to honor all of the terms of the agreement, not selective terms. All of the obligations for one side are balanced by all of the obligations of the other party. Contracts are complicated, formal documents that require accuracy and honesty by all parties. If a court determined that one party misled the other party in negotiations, some or all of the obligations that resulted might be voided.

Under the law, an agent (in this case, a leasing representative) negotiating for a principal (the owner or management company) must use a "duty of care" to reveal all material facts, and not to misrepresent the opportunity. In some jurisdictions, the term *duty of care* is referred to as "honest and fair dealing." These terms mean that the leasing representative must provide accurate, truthful, specific information to the tenant when discussing a lease, and must not knowingly misrepresent the terms of the lease or withhold material facts. There can be a fine line between misrepresentation and trying to promote a shopping center to the tenant. The leasing representative must speak carefully when "selling" the center. It may be a breach of the agent's duty of care, for instance, not to tell the prospective tenant that a directly competitive center has received a permit to build across the street. If there is relevant information about which the tenant might not think to ask, the leasing representative must offer it.

Tenants base their decision to rent in a shopping center in part on the information that they receive from the leasing representative. Less sophisticated tenants rely more heavily on what the leasing agent tells them, and they conduct less independent research to verify what they hear. Unsophisticated tenants do not have much experience in shopping centers, nor do they have access to the body of information that is available to the national chain stores. To level the playing field, the leasing representative must take into account the tenant's level of sophistication when presenting information about the shopping center and the lease. Leasing representatives may need to write longer proposal letters and include more detail so that the tenant does not overlook any of the important terms in the lease. In addition, the leasing representative should always advise the tenant to consult a lawyer before signing a lease. This policy protects both the tenant and the leasing representative.

Sometimes leasing agents cannot give a definitive answer to the tenant, and so they qualify their statements about certain terms. For example, tenants frequently inquire about the amount they will pay for common area charges. The leasing representative may not know the exact charge, since these charges are billed based on estimates each year, and the amount may vary from year to year. For the agent, these charges are often difficult or impossible to determine in advance, especially in the case of a new center. If the leasing agent quotes a certain figure for these charges but the actual charges are higher, the shopping center might be held liable. In practice, experienced leasing representatives frequently use qualifiers and caveats when they provide information to the tenant. In lease proposal letters, for instance, the offer usually ends with a paragraph saying that the proposal is not a reservation to lease space, and that the offer does not bind the landlord or tenant to enter into a lease. (The qualifier in a tenant proposal might read, "The above proposal is subject to the approval of Landlord's Financial Committee and final execution by both parties of a lease, with supporting exhibits.") The tenant may read the agent's disclaimer and conclude that the proposal is not worth the paper it is written on. In a sense, the tenant is correct. A conditional proposal is not valid unless all of the conditions are met. Unsophisticated tenants are often shocked when they respond favorably to a conditional proposal, only to have it rejected by the real estate committee. Acceptance of a conditional lease proposal generally is not a deal in the United States. Either party may terminate negotiations right up until full execution of the lease. This protects both sides from being forced into an agreement by the other side based on a "proposal" letter. In Canada, however, a signed lease proposal may be legally binding in some instances.

COLLECTION

Tenants and landlords often have a different view of what it means to make prompt payments of rent and other charges. Tenants deal with merchandise vendors constantly, and they often receive discounted terms for paying promptly. If a tenant delays paying a vendor, it is rarely penalized. This behavior is common and generally permissible. Payments within 60 days, or even much longer, are generally considered timely. Landlords, on the other hand, tend to get upset when tenants do not pay rent by the tenth of the month. Slow rental payment is one of the most common areas of friction between tenants and landlords, and in some cases the delay becomes a game between the tenant and landlord: The tenant delays payment; the landlord bills the tenant a late charge; the tenant delays longer; the landlord defaults the tenant; the tenant pays the rent, but not the late charge; the landlord chooses not to sue to recover the late fee. The next month, the tenant delays payment again. This common series of events can result in hard feelings on both sides. Landlords must remember that when tenants pay rent late, it is not necessarily a sign of a financial problem or disrespect for the landlord. Rather than becoming personally involved, management should rely on their policies and procedures and remember the saying that "bills travel through the mail at twice the speed of checks."

Leases generally have two kinds of charges: recurring and nonrecurring. Recurring charges are due regularly, and the amount is generally known in advance. For instance, rent is a recurring charge because it is known ahead of time and due on a certain day (usually the first) of the month. Rent is usually late if not received by a certain day (usually the tenth of the month). Common area maintenance (CAM) and property taxes are also classified as recurring charges generally, though not always. These charges are estimated at the beginning of the year and due when rent is paid. The tenant is notified of the estimated amount to be paid every month, and this amount does not usually change until the second half of the year, when the charge is increased or decreased according to experience. The industry commonly calls this revision "actualizing the expenses." Recurring charges are known in advance, so the landlord often does not even bill them monthly. Nonrecurring charges, on the other hand, are not generally known in advance. They may be based on usage, such as electrical or HVAC bills, or reflect a contracted service from the landlord, such as replacement of light ballasts. The landlord bills the tenant for nonrecurring charges and provides a longer time to pay them, perhaps 15 to 30 days.

Because the amount of the recurring charge is generally known in advance, tenants do not typically ask for an explanation or backup detail. Some recurring charges that are estimated, however, such as CAM and taxes, may require backup detail when first estimated or when the actual expenses become known. Tenants eventually expect the landlord to provide backup information, so management should foresee their request. In the initial CAM billing, as well as when the account is actualized, management should include an explanation of the charges and method of calculations along with the invoice. Sometimes the explanation will raise more questions and spur additional requests for backup data. It is easy to see how a tenant that is determined to avoid payment could delay paying the bill indefinitely, simply by asking for more and more information. For this reason, landlords commonly demand that if the tenant disputes the amount of a recurring charge, the tenant must pay the entire amount due under protest, or at least pay the amount not in dispute pending receipt of a satisfactory explanation for the charge.

DISPUTE RESOLUTION
When a dispute leads to a tenant default, the parties may resolve the conflict through negotiation, arbitration, or a lawsuit, depending on the seriousness of the conflict and the strengths of their relative positions. As most attorneys can attest, disputes are almost always measured in shades of gray, not black and white. Therefore, negotiation is usually the preferred solution.

Nonmaterial Defaults Tenants often do not act strictly in accordance with the terms of their lease, but not every transgression is considered a material default. Examples of nonmaterial defaults include:

- Displaying merchandise or a lollipop sign beyond the lease line
- Playing loud music that can be experienced outside the store premises
- Not being open during all the hours specified in the lease
- Selling an incidental or seasonal item that is not included in the use clause (but does not infringe on other tenants' rights).

Defaults that are not material require management's ingenuity or leverage to control the tenant's behavior. Some national landlords prefer to use their power to force the tenant to comply. They use the leverage they gain over the tenant from managing other properties, or they threaten to take away special rights that they have conditionally granted to the tenant. Most landlords, though, choose to negotiate a reasonable solution that meets the changing needs of the landlord and tenant.

With more power today, tenants are more likely to receive special rights in their lease, such as an option to expand the premises or to extend the lease term. These rights generally require that the tenant remain in good standing and not be in default. If the tenant defaults, the landlord may take away the special rights. Sometimes special rights are understood, but not recorded in the lease. Favors are often granted to the tenant from time to time, depending on the strength of the landlord/tenant relationship. For instance, the tenant may ask management for a temporary storage space during the holidays, or a special location for its advertisement in the center's catalog. When a tenant defaults, it may get a cold reception from the landlord; where before it had enjoyed a friendly partnership, it may find an adversarial relationship.

Material Defaults The major differences between material and nonmaterial defaults are the seriousness of the infraction and the remedies available. Generally, the remedy should fit the offense. After all, not every material default warrants eviction. On the other hand, repeated nonmaterial defaults may be more serious than a single material default. Since nonenforcement can lead to a loss of rights through the concept of laches (described earlier in this chapter), landlords must respond to each and every material and nonmaterial default.

In the case of a material default, the lease's section on defaults allows one or more remedies from a potential list. In most jurisdictions, though, the courts have been reluctant to offer the remedy of eviction, except in extreme cases. In Canada, a tenant may be evicted through a self-help remedy, whereas in the United States, the individual state courts control eviction, and few states permit self-help. In the United States the judicial eviction process is often lengthy and expensive. This tends to protect the tenant from abuse by landlords, and it also has the effect of limiting the frequency with which landlords choose to evict. Because of the time and expense involved, landlords and tenants often prefer to negotiate a termination agreement, rather than seek remedy through the courts.

The judicial eviction process is generally called an unlawful detainer action. When the landlord brings such an action, the court's role is twofold: to uphold the contractual obligations under the lease, and to protect the parties from abuse. Experience has shown that powerful landlords in the past have used the pretext of a minor tenant default to regain possession of a space so that they could relet the space at a higher rent. Most states do not accept the use of eviction as a remedy for minor infractions so that the landlord can increase the rent.

Other Remedies for Defaults The landlord may seek other ways to force the tenant to comply with the terms of the lease, short of penalizing the tenant monetarily or through eviction. If negotiations fail to convince the tenant to comply, the landlord may seek an injunction, which is a court order that requires the tenant to perform an action (such as observe the open hours in the lease) or refrain from performing an action (such as opening a store within the prohibited radius). If the tenant breaches the injunction, that is considered contempt of court. Injunctions are speedier and less expensive than civil suits that assess damages, but injunctions are usually difficult to obtain.

When the nature of the default concerns a disagreement over the meaning of the language in a document, either party may request that a court interpret the language in what is called a declaratory relief action. Courts do not have any magical or divine powers when it comes to defining or interpreting vague or ambiguous contract language; however, through the use of a declaratory relief action, the parties can sometimes obtain a ruling, short of a lawsuit, that resolves a misunderstanding. In a declaratory relief action, the court states how it would interpret the document if it were later called upon to rule on the merits of a dispute.

Root Causes of Common Problems

A majority of the root causes of common disputes from both the landlord's and the tenant's perspectives relate to issues involving the commencement date, common area maintenance, real estate taxes and insurance, the lease term, and certain areas of finance.

COMMENCEMENT DATE

The first problem that landlords and tenants often encounter after the lease is signed is determining the meaning of the term *commencement date*. The specific definition within the document may differ from common usage. The commencement date may be defined as 1) the day rent is first due, 2) the day the tenant opens for business, or 3) the day the landlord delivers the premises to the tenant. These three dates may not be the same, and the term's vagueness causes confusion. Assuming that the parties understand the meaning of the term, they also have to decide what to do if the tenant must open late for a legitimate reason, such as:

- The landlord's work caused the space to be delivered late, delaying the tenant
- The tenant experienced what is called force majeure delays, beyond the tenant's control, such as contractor's strike*
- The previous tenant moved out late, delaying the tenant's possession.

Tenants may open later for any number of unacceptable reasons too, such as:

- The tenant's architect did not complete its construction plans in a timely fashion.
- The contractor did not complete the job on time.
- A franchisor failed to obtain a franchisee.

When the tenant must delay its opening date for legitimate reasons, the landlord may forgive some or all of the tenant's delay, and the lease may be amended to reflect the change. In such cases, the lease administrator should send the tenant a letter stating the official date that the lease commenced, and reciting the termination date as well, whether or not the termination date has changed. This will eliminate future misunderstandings about whether the termination date would float with the delay in commencement date. At the bottom of the letter agreement, the form should require that the tenant acknowledge the change(s) and sign, signifying acceptance of the new terms. Alternatively, the landlord may request that the tenant complete and forward an estoppel agreement with this information. Many leases automatically require the tenant to complete an estoppel agreement shortly after the lease commences.

Sometimes the tenant does not agree to the new dates. The tenant may dispute exactly when the landlord delivered the premises, for instance. In cases of force majeure, or other day-for-day periods of delay, management must then review the letters, logs, and/or other anecdotal records. These records help to clarify differences of opinion, such as when a space was to be considered available for posses-

---

*The term *force majeure*, meaning problems beyond anyone's control, may refer to "acts of God." Force majeure is a mitigating factor in determining when the tenant must complete work on time. Leases commonly permit a rent-free, day-for-day delay in opening. Not every situation beyond the tenant's control is a force majeure. Loss of electrical power may be; delays in plan approval may or may not be, depending upon whether the delay was avoidable. If the city caused the delay because it was short-staffed, then the parties may agree that the delay was unavoidable; if the tenant's plans were inadequately drawn and returned by the city for more work, the delay was avoidable.

sion by the tenant or when delivery by the landlord occurred. Because memories fade, management should send written confirmation to the tenant at the time these events occur. Later, the notice letters may include copies of these written notices as evidence.

Many disputes, such as problems of delivery date, are resolved first by looking at the written records, second by determining the intent of the parties, and third by agreeing on a reasonable solution. In the case of establishing a commencement date, the landlord may not be very sympathetic to the tenant's delaying its opening if it is for reasons within the tenant's control. After all, what the landlord is selling is simply time to use a particular space, and the tenant should not waste time. The landlord wants the tenant to take the space as soon as possible so that rent can start as soon as possible. But it is only reasonable that the landlord should deliver the space to the tenant in writing before starting the clock. Without proper notice of delivery, the tenant may be correct in asserting that the landlord did not deliver possession in a timely fashion. Sometimes tenants claim not to have taken possession, when in fact the center's security staff has recorded activity in the space. Again, a security record that the tenant already is in the space is evidence of when the space was delivered (or accepted).

COMMON AREA MAINTENANCE (CAM)
Many aspects of common area maintenance can spark significant discussions, and perhaps even disputes, between landlords and tenants.

Escalation Costs If tenants were polled, their number one complaint against landlords most likely would be the escalating cost of operating expenses. As operating expenses have increased as a percentage of tenant's sales, the tenant profits have declined. Before management adopts a strategy to deal with tenant complaints about CAM, it is necessary to understand all of the causes for the increase. Some factors that have caused CAM rates to increase as a percentage of sales cannot be controlled by the landlord:

- Tenant sales increased slowly due to global deflationary pressure on goods
- Commercial property tax rates increased more rapidly than residential property tax rates, and faster than the consumer price index

- Many shopping centers have entered the phase in their life cycle when they require more repair and replacement as a result of deferred maintenance.

The landlord can control some of the other costs that have increased tenant's CAM billings:

- Many landlords have chosen to charge tenants for a portion of capital improvements, such as repair and replacement of roofs, parking lots, food court equipment, and HVAC systems
- Many landlords want tenants to pay for the addition of new parking structures
- Center occupancy levels may cause each tenant's pro rata share to increase, depending upon the definition of "pro rata share" in the lease
- Department stores and other major tenants have reduced their contributions to CAM.

During the 1990s, as operating expenses grew as a percentage of the tenant's total cost of occupancy, tenants reacted in predictable ways:

- They hired outside experts, who asked for more and more detail in the CAM billing and demanded justification to explain the increased costs
- They asked to audit landlord's records, hoping to uncover unjustified expenses
- They refused to pay for certain expenses, such as capital items, food court costs, and interest expenses
- They demanded fixed charges or limits on future increases
- Some tenants filed class action lawsuits to reign in landlord excesses.

For their part, most landlords are sensitive to the tenants' concerns. They have tried to defuse the issue by fixing the amount that the landlord will charge for CAM, putting floors on occupancy levels to protect each tenant's pro rata expense, and capping the annual increases for CAM in some leases. Landlords have been reluctant, however, to protect tenants against charges that are out of their control, such as insurance premiums and property taxes. The landlord's efforts to cap the amount of CAM charged to tenants does not solve the basic problems:

- Many shopping center costs are beyond anyone's control
- Sales often do not keep pace with rents because too much retail space is on the market or too many goods are chasing too few customers.

Determining the Pro Rata Fraction Most shopping center leases are negotiated based on the tenant paying a share of operating expenses, taxes, and property insurance. All costs to operate the common areas are paid by the tenants, even though they do not control how much money is spent to do the job. Tenants assume that whatever the common charges are, they will be shared equally, in the ratio of each tenant's square footage to the area of all tenants. The ratio is commonly referred to as a proportionate share of expenses, or a pro rata share. The term *pro rata* is defined in the lease, but the definition can cause misunderstandings between the landlord and tenant.

In practice, management does not bill all tenants for the same items or on the same basis—far from it. Tenants think management pools all of the expenses for the common areas and then divides up the cost among all of the tenants on the basis of their square footage. In fact, management creates a number of different expense pools, sending bills to each tenant that pays a proportionate share of exactly the same items on the same basis. A regional mall lease may have more than 30 different CAM pools to deal with different lease forms, exclusions for certain tenants for specific items, different amounts tenants have negotiated to cover the landlord's cost to administer the common areas, and so on. The term *pool* means the total amount of expenses that may be billed to a particular group of tenants. Leasing representatives inadvertently create new CAM pools when they agree to exclude from the tenant's share certain expenses paid by other tenants. This not only complicates accounting's job; it also means the landlord must pay for the tenant's share.

Here is an example of how the pool works for tenants that are permitted in their lease to exclude capital improvements from their share of expenses: Management creates a list of all operating expenses (security, property taxes, cleaning maintenance, and so on) other than capital improvements. The tenant's share is then determined by dividing the tenant's leased area by the area of all of the other tenant leases in the center. That fraction is then multiplied by the costs in the CAM pool. Another CAM pool might cover all expenses, including an amortized amount for capital items, except for the interest expense necessary to finance capital improvements. In the first CAM pool, the landlord would pick up the cost of capital improvements for those tenants with the exclusion. In the second example, the landlord would pay for the unrecovered amount of the interest costs on capital items.

Major User and Anchor Tenants In theory, major users (as defined in the lease, such as theaters, junior department stores, big box tenants, or oversized specialty tenants with strong followings) and anchor tenants (such as department stores, supermarkets, or pharmacies) pay a smaller pro rata share of operating expenses than specialty tenants, because the large tenants typically generate most of the center's customer traffic. The economic terms of these leases reflect their importance to the center. Landlords subsidize anchor tenants, by offering lower rent and expenses, to entice them to occupy space in the shopping center. Without the subsidies, these tenants might not be able to afford to lease space in the shopping centers at all. Anchor stores generally spend a higher percentage of their sales on advertising to draw customers, and therefore they can afford less for rent. An anchor store, for instance, might budget 3 to 5 percent of its sales to advertising, but only 1 to 3 percent of sales for rent. In contrast, a specialty store merchant typically spends less than 1 percent on advertising but 8 to 10 percent or more for rent and charges. In general, the anchor relies on drawing its own customers to the store through advertising, while the specialty tenant relies on the center and the anchor tenants to provide the traffic to support its sales.

Because anchor tenants are essential to the center's success, landlords generally discount their share of common area expenses. Anchor tenants and major users tend to make only a modest contribution toward the cost of operating the common areas. Whatever contribution the anchor tenant makes reduces the total expense pool. The landlord then excludes the area occupied by these tenants from the leasable area of the center. Exclusion of the major tenant's area from the leasable area means that other tenants—not the landlord—pay the anchor's share of expenses.

Subsidizing anchor stores and major users is common and accepted practice. In the past, specialty stores generally did not object to the subsidy if they could see the tangible benefit they received from customer traffic created by the anchor, and if they could afford their share of expenses. Today, with expenses commonly increasing faster than sales, tenants are more likely to question whether the benefit they receive from anchors and major users warrants the amount of the subsidy.

The definition of an anchor tenant or major user varies. Some national landlords define a major user as any tenant that occupies more than 10,000 square feet, regardless of how much it advertises or how much traffic it generates. Others require that the user occupy a space of at least 50,000 square feet. Some leases specify certain uses that are anchor stores by definition—theaters, department stores, groceries, and drugstores. Large tenants and category killers are highly motivated to be designated major users. Even strong national chain stores, which typically occupy multiple storefronts in the same property and comprise, in total, more than 35,000 square feet, have demanded that they receive this designation. They, too, want to receive lower occupancy costs. They claim that other specialty tenants benefit from their national advertising programs and strong brand appeal. A tenant that receives the major user designation can reduce its share of operating expenses by more than half.

Leased Versus Leasable The lease language determines who pays common area expenses for vacant space in the shopping center. The decision boils down to which terms—*leased area, occupied area,* or *leasable area*—is used in the document, and how the term is defined. Sometimes these terms are abbreviated as GLOA (gross leased and occupied area) and GLA (gross leasable area). The tenant's pro rata share is the tenant's area divided by either the occupied area or the entire leasable area. Gross leasable area is defined as all specialty store space, but it may exclude some or all of the following areas:

- Anchor tenant area
- Major tenant area, such as theaters, junior department stores, groceries
- Outparcels, pad sites, and other areas not defined as being within the definition of "shopping center area"
- Nonretail space, such as office space, civic uses, community rooms
- Storage areas
- Retail space that has only an outside entrance and does not front on the mall

- Space occupied by carts and kiosks
- Common areas, including some interior stairwells within stores.

Tenants do not want to pay the expenses for unleased shop space. They argue that the landlord controls whether space is left vacant. Landlords, though, commonly calculate the tenant's pro rata share only as a fraction of occupied area (GLOA). If the tenant asks, they may agree to place a limit how low the occupancy level can go. A current standard is that the tenant's pro rata share will not go below an 80 percent occupancy level. If the center's occupancy falls below that, the landlord will pay the pro rata share for that space. The industry calls this practice putting a floor on the occupancy level.

Tenants come and go from shopping centers, creating temporary vacancies. Occupied area is calculated periodically by taking an average of the area leased throughout the year. Even when a center appears to be fully leased, its occupancy rate is rarely 100 percent, because space is considered vacant while a new tenant refurbishes the premises and is not obligated to pay rent. (Most of the top real estate investment trusts, or REITs, have an average occupancy rate of 80 to 85 percent.)

If occupancy levels decrease, landlords sometimes fill vacant space with short-term leases while they seek permanent replacements. Temporary tenants, sometimes called incubator tenants, provide extra income for space that would otherwise be vacant, and they keep a light on where a space would otherwise be dark. This gives the impression that the shopping center is more fully leased, which is a benefit to both the landlord and other tenants. Because they do not receive a long-term commitment from the landlord, temporary tenants in previously occupied space may or may not be charged as much rent as permanent tenants, and sometimes they are not expected to pay a full pro rata share of expenses. They are not considered permanent tenants, so the space they occupy may be exlcuded in the calculation of gross leased and occupied area if permitted under the lease. To be fair, most landlords deduct from the expense pool whatever contribution to CAM the temporary tenants make, in the same way that an anchor's contribution is deducted.

Tenant auditors often dispute the landlord's definition of leasable area and the calculation of occupied area. If management excludes temporary tenants from the leased area, tenants expect the landlord to deduct from the CAM pool whatever contribution these tenants make. Landlords may try to define all the income paid by temporary tenants as rent, rather than to apply some or all to expenses. They can do this by charging temporary tenants a gross amount for rent (including charges). Even if the landlord receives a gross amount for rent and charges, most will arbitrarily apply a portion toward common area charges, reducing the CAM expense pool accordingly.

Sometimes long-term tenants pay a gross rent, but unlike temporary tenants, the space they occupy usually is included in the leased area. In such cases, the fact that they pay their rent on a gross basis does not affect other tenants' shares. However, if the landlord excludes the area occupied by a long-term tenant, then other tenants' pro rata shares will increase unless the landlord allocates a full pro rata share of their rent toward expenses.

Interior Versus Exterior The lease form for some enclosed malls divides CAM into two separate pools, one for expenses relating to the interior areas and another dealing with exterior expenses. Management separates the common areas so that it may account separately for the expenses of anchor stores and stores fronting only onto the exterior of the center. Anchor stores, pad tenants, and mall stores that face only the exterior of the property may contribute only to the upkeep of the exterior common areas. Therefore, more tenants share in the expense of the exterior than of the interior.

When landlords create separate CAM and tax pools for the center's interior and exterior portions, they must allocate some charges between the two, such as security and maintenance expenses. The method of allocation may increase the share for tenants whose stores front onto the enclosed mall or may inflate the expenses of exterior tenants. Fairness is in the details. A consistent, reasonable policy is required to allocate charges between accounts. It is also vital to comply with the lease provisions to avoid problems with the tenant's auditor and their lawyer.

Controversial Items Included The language in the lease determines what items may be included in CAM; however, the landlord's boilerplate language is deliberately vague to permit some flexibility. When controversies arise, they generally fit into one of three categories: 1) The charge appears to overlap or duplicate another expense; 2) the charge could also be categorized elsewhere; or 3) the charge is generally paid by the landlord.

An example of duplication is including in administration expenses a portion of the manager's salary and/or the cost of an independent CAM audit, while also charging an administration fee of 10 to 15 percent on the total CAM bill. The landlord might claim that these charges are on-site supervisory expenses required to manage personnel who maintain the common areas. The tenant may well ask, What does the fixed administration fee cover, if not supervision?

In the second category—categorization of expense—landlords commonly classify as operating expenses items that may also be charged to the promotional fund. Examples of promotional expenses that might cause controversy include the amortized amount for the purchase of Christmas decorations, the cost to provide customer service, an information booth, or seasonal gift-wrapping services. Tenants might argue that by redirecting these expenses to an operating-expense account, the marketing and promotion budgets are increased.

The third type of charge that creates controversy is one that the tenant expects the landlord to absorb as a cost of doing business. The landlord pays for many capital items. These including constructing the building, roof, common areas, parking lots, and air-conditioning. After the center is constructed, tenants primarily pay to maintain these improvements. In addition, landlords charge tenants to repair or replace capital items, including the costliest portions of the physical plant: the parking lot and roof.

Food Court CAM Food court merchants pay a separate fee for the operation of the food court common areas (such as the dining area, dish room, and cleaning stations), in addition to a pro rata share of the shopping center's common areas. Landlords separate the charges for operating the food court common areas and charge these only to the food court tenants, because they are the direct beneficiaries. Also, food vendors build out only their kitchens and serving counters, so they require the use of a dining area in common with the other food tenants. If they had built an entire restaurant space, it would have included a seating area. In new centers, landlords frequently charge tenants an additional capital construction charge to pay for the installation of furniture, fixtures, and equipment in the common seating area.

The lease for food court tenants generally addresses the expense and operation of the common areas in a separate exhibit. Expenses may be charged in a manner similar to other center expenses, as a pro rata share based on area—the area of the tenant's booth divided by the area of all booths, either GLOA or GLA. Another method for determining each tenant's share is as a percentage of sales achieved. A tenant that produces $500,000 in business theoretically uses more supplies and services than a tenant with sales of only $350,000. Some food court exhibits use a combination of shares based on sales and shares based on area. To administer the food court operation, management often hires a food court manager, who becomes a member of the lease administration team.

All tenants in the center must be aware of what charges are paid only by the food court merchants, and which expenses may be added to all tenants' common area expenses. Any expense that solely benefits the food court merchants should be billed exclusively to the food court tenants, not added to the general common area expense budget. But the beneficiary is sometimes difficult to determine. Expenses that are generally included only in the food court budget include:

- Personnel, serving only the food court, who clear dishes and wipe tables
- Cost of grease trap cleaning
- Manager to administer the operation of the food court
- Cost of trays and cleaning supplies used only for food court areas
- Plumbing repair for pipes serving only restaurants
- Floor sealer in the seating area to prevent leaks to the lower level.

Some food court items, or a portion of them, may be billed to another operating account:

- Tabletop advertisements supplied by the marketing director
- Furniture repair or replacement in the seating area used by people other than food court patrons
- HVAC and electrical charges not separately metered
- Security charges
- Roof repair over the seating area.

Food court patrons are not the only ones who use the dining areas. Shoppers often choose to meet and relax at the tables before continuing their shopping. Knowing this, management sometimes applies a portion of the food court operations cost to all tenants. As with many issues in the lease, allocating food court expenses has no right or wrong solution.

REAL ESTATE TAXES AND INSURANCE

Real estate taxes and insurance may be billed separately or may be included partially or entirely within common area expenses. Many lease forms divide the property tax bill into two portions, one covering the tenant's premises and the other covering the center's common areas. When landlords include the common area taxes in the common area billing, they can charge an administrative fee for those taxes. In lease negotiation, many tenants try to exclude the common area taxes from the CAM bill to avoid the administrative fee.

In some states, property taxes are reassessed whenever the property is sold. This can significantly increase a tenant's occupancy cost, so some tenants try to negotiate some protection over a sudden increase in taxes based on a sale. They argue that the landlord has some control over when the center is sold. Landlords generally argue that the amount of taxes is out of their control. If the lease contains no language to the contrary, however, any tax increase is the tenant's responsibility.

Insurance rates are generally much lower than tax rates, but insurance premiums still generate disputes. For one thing, properties in some states, among them California and Florida, maintain riders to protect the landlord's buildings from such natural disasters as earthquakes and hurricanes. Some tenants object to the portion of the insurance bill that covers these events, because they think these risks should be part of the landlord's cost of doing business. The amount of taxes and insurance is estimated at the beginning of the year, paid on a monthly basis, and actualized at the end of the year, like CAM.

LEASE TERM RENEWAL OPTIONS

Before they sign the lease, the landlord and tenant agree on what date the lease will terminate, but they often have different expectations of what will occur after the termination date. Once a tenant has occupied a space for a period of time, the tenant develops a sense of ownership of the space. From the tenant's perspective, the space almost becomes synonymous with the business. The stationery, phone numbers, and advertising are tied to the location, and the tenant becomes rooted in the location by investing physical and emotional capital in the premises.

To illustrate the point, consider how the press publicizes the event when a popular tenant puts up a "Lost Our Lease" sign in the window. The press and public usually view this event as a tragedy for the merchant and the community, not as an opportunity for it to obtain a new store that will do more business. This is true even if the tenant can reopen for business across the street. From the landlord's perspective, the tenant whose lease is not renewed contracted only for the right to conduct business in the location for a specific amount of time, after which the landlord expects to be able to change the use of the space or to increase the rent to the most it could obtain from a new tenant. These two perspectives cause the parties to approach the renewal and relocation process differently.

Administering tenant options depends largely on the language in the document. Some renewal options state when the option needs to be exercised, and when it is no longer valid if the option has not been exercised in writing. Few options become automatic through inaction. If a tenant is obligated to exercise an option by a certain date, but forgets, the landlord should notify the tenant that the opportunity to exercise the option has passed. This may not end the tenant's right, however, because many courts have reinstated tenants' options if they inadvertently missed a notice date. In this way, courts favor the tenant's right to occupancy over the landlord's ownership right to the real estate. From the tenant's standpoint, its lease administration team should closely monitor the option dates to avoid missing a notice date and losing the location on favorable rent.

LEASE TERM TERMINATION OPTIONS

To maintain control of the merchandise mix, landlords prefer not to give renewal options. They also try to keep lease terms short to retain the flexibility to change the use or to select a stronger tenant with the same use. One way landlords keep control is to negotiate a termination right if the tenant does not achieve a certain level of sales. Termination options may be unilateral, to the benefit of either the landlord or tenant, or mutual. When either the landlord or tenant may terminate, there may be a different standard set for the landlord to terminate the tenant's lease than for the tenant to terminate. During negotiations, the landlord may expect the tenant to achieve a certain level of sales, and if the tenant does not reach this level during a certain year, or any consecutive 12-month period, then the landlord has the option to terminate the lease. If the landlord exercises its right to terminate, sometimes it will pay the tenant a termination fee to compensate the tenant for its unamortized investment in leasehold improvements. Sometimes the lease will provide that the landlord not only can regain possession, but also can charge the tenant for the unamortized portion of any tenant allowance it has provided to the tenant.

Administering termination options appears to be straightforward, but when the landlord exercises its option to terminate a tenant for nonperformance, the tenant may find many extenuating circumstances that prevented it from reaching the necessary sales level. Tenants sometimes claim that they did not understand the clause, or were hindered by some landlord action from achieving the necessary sales. Sometimes the tenant wants to stay in the center so badly that it is willing to renegotiate the terms of its lease. Courts consider termination of a tenant's lease to be a severe consequence, so it is important that the landlord follow appropriate notice procedure and start the process early—at least six months in advance. A tenant requires substantial lead time to accept the idea that the lease will terminate, and adequate time to find a new location.

SECURITY DEPOSITS

Landlords are less likely to require a security deposit today than in the past. Many chain stores successfully argue that the size of their financial statement is an adequate guarantee of performance and security in case of default. Experience has shown, however, that even the largest tenants sometimes seek bankruptcy protection, leaving the landlord without the ability to apply the security deposit against unpaid rent while the landlord seeks a replacement tenant.

The first lesson in managing security deposits is to keep good records. Not only is it good policy to update the landlord's financial statements with the location and amounts of security deposits, interest, letters of credit, and lease guarantees, but also management should keep a copy of the check or letters of credit in the tenant's document file. Some security deposits require that the money be invested on behalf of the tenant, with the interest accruing for the tenant. The language in most leases, however, permits the landlord to hold the money, without interest. At the end of the term, or after the period specified in the lease, the landlord must be prepared to return the tenant's money immediately. Many states have strict laws penalizing landlords that do not return the money promptly.

If the tenant defaults during the term, the landlord has a right, under the default clause, to apply a portion of the security deposit against the receivable. This must be done in writing. Once the landlord reduces the amount it holds as a security for the tenant, the tenant is required to replenish the security account.

Letters of credit from a bank, offered in lieu of a lease guarantee or security deposit, must be renewed annually. Management often employs a computerized reminder file, sometimes called a bring up or tickler, to track when the letter of credit must be renewed and when to send reminder letters to tenants. The tenant's failure to renew a letter of credit may be a breach of the lease, or may require the tenant to substitute a cash security deposit.

ASSIGNMENTS

The boilerplate language details the procedure for tenants to request an assignment or sale of the lease. Regardless of the language, state laws often prescribe the parties' rights and responsibilities. In some states such as California, tenants have an absolute right, within certain limits, to transfer their interest in the lease, even if the language in the landlord's lease prohibits transfer. When in doubt, management should consult with an attorney regarding landlord and tenant rights for a lease assignment. Many leases permit the landlord to charge a fee for the review of the information that the existing tenant (the assignor) and the new tenant (the assignee) submit. This fee helps the landlord offset its expenses, including the use of an attorney, to analyze the assignee's and assignor's businesses. Many companies require the tenant to pay this fee before they will consider the application. This is a good policy for the landlord. Many assignments initiated by tenants are not consummated, but the landlord has already gone through the time and expense of analyzing the data. If the sale or assignment does not go through, the tenant is not entitled to a refund.

The appropriate standard for accepting or denying a request for an assignment is whether the landlord will be in at least as good a position after the assignment as it would be if the assignment had not occurred. The landlord generally does not have to accept an assignment of lease if it requires any amendment to the terms, such as a change of use or rent. Unless the lease says otherwise, the landlord also does not have to release the prior tenant from liability for the new tenant's financial performance. In analyzing whether the landlord will be no worse off, some of the landlord's considerations should be:

- Does the new tenant have the equal or greater net worth?
- Does the new tenant have adequate experience operating the same kind of business?
- Does the new operator intend to operate in the same manner as the current tenant? (For instance, if the prior operator sold shoes at retail, is the new tenant a discounter?)
- Has the previous operator had any problems with law enforcement?
- Is the new company a foreign entity that the landlord will have trouble suing in a foreign court if it defaults?

No two tenants are exactly alike, and it is often difficult to judge how a new tenant will perform prior to taking occupancy. Once a tenant finds a potential assignee, it is eager to finalize the deal. Once the employees find out that the store will be sold, they are more likely to jump ship. Despite pressure by the tenant to make a quick decision, management must be as thorough in its analysis of a new tenant as it would be before it signs any new lease.

BANKRUPTCY

A tenant bankruptcy can be one of the most complicated and frustrating tasks for the lease administration team to manage. It can no longer negotiate directly with the tenant, rely on all of the terms in lease document, or follow the landlord's policies and procedures to enforce the lease. Instead, the tenant's creditors and the court manage the lease. The lease administration team must develop a relationship with new role players who represent the court and creditors. The court appoints a bankruptcy trustee to manage the lease as an asset. The tenant hires a law firm to protect its interests, and sometimes the tenant also hires an outside real estate company to market the lease. The landlord assigns an attorney to act on behalf of the lease administration team. Although the tenant and management may continue to talk throughout the bankruptcy process, power rests with the tenant's court-appointed trustee.

When a tenant seeks bankruptcy protection, after the federal court takes jurisdiction from the state court it may temporarily set aside parts of the lease agreement that are not in the best interest of the tenant's creditors. By law, the bankruptcy court must decide whether to accept or reject the lease within 60 days; however, extensions are common and the process can often drag on for months or even years. The court requires the tenant to make full payment of rent and charges under bankruptcy protection, but any receivable amounts remain unpaid until the creditor's committee deals with all of the tenant's assets and liabilities. The disposition of the lease is just one of many assets that the trustee must consider, so lease administration often feels as if the shopping center's needs are not important to the court.

To administer a lease during bankruptcy protection requires patience and planning. Management must predict whether the lease will be terminated, and how the court might try to amend the lease so that it can be sold to another tenant. The landlord may or may not want to accept a replacement tenant proposed by the court, and may want to purchase the lease itself. Most landlords discuss these issues with any other landlords of the bankrupt tenant, and often several landlords may agree to share the cost of an attorney to represent them before the court.

Budget Implications

The process of lease administration is ingrained into the everyday management of a shopping center, not found in a separate section or line item of the budget. The one area missing from most shopping center budgets, that should be attributed to lease administration is an amount set aside for tenant retention. Office tower leases always dedicate an amount to this account. In the shopping center budgets, however, the function of tenant retention is often relegated to the marketing or promotions manager. As has been pointed out above, tenant retention is the job of every team member in lease administration.

Conclusion

The task of lease management and administration involves the efforts of a team of shopping center professionals, whose job is to negotiate and accommodate the changing needs of the tenant and landlord while enforcing the terms of the lease document. Team members must respect the tenant's perspectives while interpreting and administering the contract, and they must remain focused on two goals: increasing retail sales and retaining good tenants. Even though the lease is written in black and white, the issues are generally colored in shades of gray; lease administration is the art of continual negotiation, balancing the landlord's short-term goal of rent against the long-term goals of higher sales and higher property value. Leasing representatives play an active role in the process because they initiate the contract negotiations and have firsthand knowledge of the terms of the lease. They also must maintain a relationship with the tenant to improve the chances of retaining good tenants.

Karl D. Ehrlich is Principal at Retail Leasing Solutions, San Mateo, California.

EXHIBIT A: LEASE LOGS

Timepieces, Etc.
[A fictitious store]

Category:	Jewelry Specialty		
Contact:	Corporate Leasing Representative	(phone) 999-555-1234	
		(fax) 999-555-4321	
Contact 2:	Owner's name	(phone) 800-555-1234	
Store name:	Timepieces, Etc.	(E-mail) timepieces@_ _ _.com	
Company:	Division of Nat'l Jewelry Marts, Inc.	Number of stores: 9 (1998)	
Address:	Spring Road	Number planned: 25 (99); 25 (00); 25 (01)	
	Anytown, OH 12345	Average sales per store: $500 per square foot	

5/7/98 Met with broker who introduced new watch concept store for National Jewelry Marts. Stores require 800 square feet in A and B malls. Will consider regional malls, lifestyle centers, specialty centers, downtowns with high tourist counts, or Mills-type properties. Plan to roll out 25 stores per year for next three to five years. Competition from Watch Station and Watch Works. Requested financial statement and vendor list. Broker to send merchandise list by 6/1. Put on bring up list.

7/24 Never received vendor list from broker. Reviewed store in XYZ Mall. Location was about the 25-yard line, in a portion of the mall with many junior apparel tenants. Noticed they carried the following lines. Price points between $50 and $150 primarily, but maybe higher in some cases. Incidental sale of batteries. Repair service?

7/28 Traded calls with broker.

7/30 Broker called to say that company now represented by in-house leasing agent. Left call for her at the corporate office.

8/1 Had pleasant conversation with new real estate rep for Timepieces, Etc. They are not ready to commit to deals throughout the U.S., but rather want to concentrate on locations in Chicago and St. Louis first. We discussed a location in Great Mall of Indiana for 2000. No specific locations. Will forward a lease package.

9/1 Discussed lease package, general demographics, and psychographics for Great Mall. The profile fits with what Timepieces likes. Parent Company, National Jewelry Marts, already has a location in the mall that does $1 million, so they know the property. Identified two potential opportunities for 2000, including Spaces D-135 and F-248. Timepieces, Etc. is not ready to commit.

9/30 Discussed the mall again and the expansion of Timepieces. They now operate nine stores in Illinois and Missouri. Two are not doing as well as expected, while the three in the A malls are doing great. Leasing agent would not give me exact figures, but stores project about $500 to $600 psf for 800 sf.

10/28 In preparation for meeting in New York, we discussed locations in two centers, Great Mall and the Midwest Plaza. Both opportunities seem appropriate. Will forward locations.

11/4 Locations accepted. I will forward proposals with the following terms:

Midwest Plaza

Space/Area   #2116 / 852 sf, irregular

Rent   3 years @ $45 psf vs. 8% over natural breakpoint
4 years @ $50 psf vs. 8% over natural breakpoint
3 years @ $55 psf vs. 8% over natural breakpoint

Commencement August 1, 2000

Great Mall

Space/Area   D-135 / 789 sf, irregular

Rent   3 years @ $42,000 ($53.23 psf) vs. 8% over natural breakpoint
4 years @ $45,000 ($57.03 psf) vs. 8% over natural breakpoint
3 years @ $48,000 ($60.84 psf) vs. 8% over natural breakpoint

Commencement July 1, 2000

11/11 Tenant received proposals and will take them to its board for approval.

11/18 Left word.

11/20 Tenant has a problem with rent at Great Mall and Midwest Plaza. Tenant asked to cap CAM and add a recapture from overage rental, and it needs 90 days to construct. Told her probably no, but will ask. Is there any allowance available? If the tenant opens early, can it open with percentage rent only? What about a first right of refusal or exclusive? Tenant will not agree to radius clause, they say.

11/23 Talked to management about above issues. No allowance or recapture for this use. We never give exclusives. We will waive radius for this use, but not for jewelry use in our National Jewelry Mart deals. We will substantially conform both leases to the Nat'l Jewelry Mart deal at Great Mall, if they want.

11/30 Hope to close deals in NYC at fall deal making.

12/1 At meeting in NYC: Agreed to $40/$42.50/$45 psf at Midwest Mall. For Great Mall, $40,000/$42,500/$45,000. Some open issues remain, which we will have to deal with in lease comments. Sent confirming proposal letter for each deal. Asked for signature on the proposal letters so that I could attach a copy of the approved proposal to the lease requisition.

Exhibit B: TENANT WORKOUTS

Tenant workouts are generally unique as to the specific situation. The following questions need to be answered when considering bad debt workouts.

- Will the tenant fail anyway?
- Is tenant's occupancy imperative to the property?
- Will the loss of the tenant have an affect on the property?
- Was tenant's rent too high in the first place?
- Is rent relief the answer?
- Can rent be deferred rather than forgiven?
- What is the cause of the receivable problems? Is it a company-wide problem, local economy, inventory, or overexpansion, etc?
- Is the tenant a franchise, and if so, what is the franchisor doing to help?
- Do we have an investment in the tenant?
- What is the likelihood of reletting the space?
- Do we have a personal or corporate guarantee?
- What steps is the tenant taking to help the problem?
- Can we tie the rent reduction to an advertising expenditure by the tenant?
- Do we have the tenant elsewhere?
- Has the tenant done everything possible to restructure its business?

Other options for tenant workouts include:

- Negotiation of a termination fee or a note payable in the future.
- A use clause change to better suit the market.
- With reduced rent, can the percentage or breakpoint be improved in order to participate in increased sales?

It is recommended that all rent relief require a landlord's right to terminate during the relief period.

This exhibit is supplied courtesy of Lend Lease.

11 | Remerchandising Centers in Redevelopment

Mark N. London, SCSM/SCMD

Both the fundamental nature of shopping centers—as they serve consumers and merchants—and the *business of shopping centers*—relating to ownership, operation, and financing/capital markets access—have been evolving continuously since they first appeared in great numbers, following the Second World War. Shopping centers have been changing and evolving along with the lifestyles of their consumers. Change is a relentless and unstoppable force, inherent to the most fundamental nature of shopping centers.

This chapter focuses upon the process of leasing in the context of the redevelopment or the significant remerchandising of a center. This process has grown increasingly more important and far more common than ever before. This author's view is that throughout the next few decades the ability to successfully re-lease or remerchandise centers will be as important as new center merchandising, if not more so.

The reasons that redevelopment has assumed a more prominent role are summarized in Table 1: The Growth of Redevelopment's Importance.

Planning Is the Core Element

Thomas Edison reportedly said, "Genius is one percent inspiration and 99 percent perspiration." If so, then the corresponding analogy in remerchandising an existing center may be 50 percent planning,

TABLE 1

The Growth of Redevelopment's Importance

KEY FACTORS	CONTEXT, EXPLANATION, AND COMMENTS
Environmental Sensitivity	Commercial sprawl has become a widespread topic across the U.S. and in many municipalities. Citizens and towns are beginning to focus on ways to reduce the invasion of new shopping center parking lots. Redeveloping existing properties, rather than creating new ones, will become increasingly important as the real estate already devoted to existing centers evolves to being viewed as a scarce resource by twenty-first-century shoppers/citizens.
Investor and Lender Emphasis Upon Redevelopment	Commercial lenders and real estate investment trust (REIT) investors have not forgotten the overindulgence in real estate development in the 1980s. Redevelopment will maintain a preferential cachet in comparison with new development for the community that financially underwrites the shopping center industry.
Clicks and Mortar	Recent holiday seasons significantly verified that "brick and mortar" shops were not going to be made obsolete by the Internet. However, e-retailing, when viewed as another viable distribution channel, underscores the historical need for change, updating, and refreshment that has always been central to the nature of shopping centers.
Maturation of the Business	If one considers the timeline of the shopping center business, its "mature" nature stands out. With so many centers having already been developed, it makes logical business sense that many are going to require "rethinking" as retail formats and businesses evolve and as markets and populations at local levels change.

40 percent execution, and 10 percent innovation. For most redevelopments, it is usually accurate to predict that the stronger the planning and preparation—prior to any physical work—the higher the success rate of the final product.

The following are fundamental concepts that apply to most redevelopment and remerchandising projects. To ignore them usually leads to the increased risk of failing to meet a project's goals:

- Start any contemplated redevelopment with the "big picture" plan for the center. Figure out what you expect to accomplish overall in regard to the center when any prospective program is completed.
- In creating any plan, be aware that what is left out of the process is almost always left out of the product. Incorporate as many members on your team as possible who are appropriately representative of key disciplines.
- The remerchandising plan is always subordinate to and supportive of a center's overall redevelopment program.
- Diligence counts. Recall the Thomas Edison comment, and remember that it is usually far easier to underplan than overplan most aspects of a redevelopment. Although no one has time to waste, underplanning for the sake of saving time is usually a poor practice.

Leasing Is the Key Planning Element

It is easy to argue that the leasing team has the most critical role in a redevelopment. Leasing has to convince the owners that it can do the leasing required by a redevelopment plan. Leasing must also convince the targeted merchants to join a project, at the rates specified by the plan. In short, leasing has to generally produce the improvement in income that will drive or justify a redevelopment, producing the return on investment (ROI) desired by the owners and the lenders or investors.

It is critical to note that virtually every remerchandising program requires a leasing story—a narrative, sometimes written but more often spoken, that tells the story of what the center is trying to do in regard to a redevelopment. The story has to take a merchant representative from the center's existing position to where you are trying to go, with believable logic and sound reasoning.

Thus, each redevelopment team will need to work out a center's story, based upon the overall plan. The team must buy into it first. No merchant will ever be convinced if those who are leasing space are not. Fine-tune, hone, refine the critical story.

COMMON BUSINESS PLANNING ELEMENTS
Most redevelopments contain the following component elements:

Element	*Nature of Element*
1. Determine the Need	Why redevelop? What is the basis for considering a plan to redevelop a center?
2. What Are the Plan Options?	What are the various scenarios under which a center could be redeveloped?
3. What Are the Economic Implications?	How would the costs and new income produce an ROI in each scenario?
4. What Are the Risk Implications?	What are the factors determining the risk of succeeding or failing in each scenario?
5. Soliciting Ownership and/or Lender Support	What do they think? Do the ROI and final product support the risk/reward in proceeding?

This chapter is concerned with remerchandising or leasing a redevelopment. Leasing plays an important role in every one of the five steps listed above. In steps one through four, leasing is the key determinant for each process; in the fifth area, ownership's and/or a lender's perspective on the ability to lease and perform as planned will determine the assessment.

When one considers the most frequently encountered types of redevelopment leasing challenges, they can be sorted as shown in Table 2: Redevelopment/Leasing Situations.

Key Planning Focus Areas for Redevelopment Leasing

RESEARCH
Typically, research will be needed to serve several different audiences in a prospective redevelopment program. The landlord will usually conduct research in order to (a) figure out how to reposition

TABLE 2
Redevelopment/Leasing Situations

Redevelopment Goal	*Leasing Challenge*	*Special Leasing Priorities*
To make a strong center even stronger	This usually means going upscale—capturing those specialty stores. What story does leasing need?	Will the center's role seem logical to key merchants? Which three are most critical to consider before all others?
To make a moderate performer into a top center	This usually will be a bigger leasing challenge than the one above. In smaller markets, this strategy may involve adding big boxes or power center-type anchors.	Getting merchants to rethink their impressions of your center. Do you have the support for this type of leasing, or do you need special help?
To drastically change the nature of a center	This could involve "de-malling" or unenclosing an enclosed mall, changing the format, price points, and/or other basic aspects of a center.	You must be sure that your new target audience for leasing believes in what you are trying to create. You must be sure that you have both merchant and consumer credibility.

a center—assessing what consumers want and need based upon the existing competitive situation—or (b) substantiate the plan that has been created. Such research is usually quantitative, involving either shopper intercept or telephone surveys, or both. Intercepts tend to address a center's existing consumers, while telephone surveys are thought to address both a center's current shoppers and its potential shoppers. Certain situations may dictate the need for qualitative research, focus groups being the best example. If qualitative research is used, it is usually in conjunction with, rather than in place of, the quantitative studies.

The other audiences for research are usually (a) retailers to whom you will be trying to lease space, (b) anchors or larger stores that a landlord may hope to include in the redevelopment, and/or (c) lenders/investors for the project. While a basic core of research may serve all of the foregoing audiences, there certainly will be situations that may dictate the need for a specific research approach to underwrite a special need.

Key research considerations include the following:

- Research, while critical, may not yield all of the answers. When hatching a redevelopment, the project team's assessment of issues such as how consumers will shop or react in the future may not be derived fully from research. Redevelopment is neither a completely quantitative nor completely qualitative exercise, but rather part art, part science, in popular terms. Thus, research should be very helpful in most cases, but do not expect it to provide every answer.
- There are some exciting technological improvements in research that can be very helpful in redevelopments. As noted above, once a redevelopment has gotten under way, you will often need further and ongoing research (a) in order to determine whether a center is performing as planned, and/or (b) to further substantiate your selling platform to certain merchants—particularly if some merchants are taking a wait-and-see approach as to whether to join the center.
- Be receptive to new avenues of input and sources for them. Following is an example of the type of lifestyle-related informational challenges that are already being faced today; they will only become more complicated in the future.
- Is there a Web site to be utilized to collect data?
- Are there e-mail-related opportunities for you to communicate with certain consumer groups?
- Does a retailer with whom you work have any consumer data that are relevant?

CONSIDER ALL IMPORTANT VARIABLES

When the time finally arrives to create the merchandise plan, try to benefit from the nature of today's actual and tomorrow's probable realities of consumer and retail evolution.

The following is a list of issues important to most redevelopment teams:

A Redevelopment Example

You are part of the redevelopment team for a middle market regional shopping center, the only enclosed one for a radius of 45 miles. Although it dominates the college-town market of 250,000 households, the best stores are still in the suburban large-market centers in the large city about 65 miles away. The team believes that the center should add a largely upscale wing of stores. The market perception of many of the upscale merchants is that they would probably like to have a store in the market at some point. Currently, however, they tend to believe that there are much higher priority markets elsewhere.

The team believes that the center should not rest on its past glory, but rather should preempt any competitive specialty or lifestyle center concept from future development.

The team needs research in order to help shape the direction of its plan and to help raise the prevailing merchant perceptions regarding the importance level of the project—or their sales projections, to be precise. The team needs to communicate with the segment of existing center shoppers that travels to the city on two or three trips per year for major purchases.

Will the team members use the industry standard in nonshopper research, the telephone survey, targeting both shoppers and nonshoppers? Or will they use a different means? If a telephone survey requires the participant to spend 15 to 25 minutes on the telephone, does that create a prejudice in the survey group that undermines the effort? Could the Internet be used to reach the key shopper segments? What other information sources exist today?

Critical questions might include these topics:

- Should the new section resemble the existing center or be different?
- Which stores are the most critical to have?
- Should there be easy direct access to the new area?

Such questions are almost limitless. You may receive considerable input but few direct answers. Thus, extrapolating the implications for the project is partly subjective as well as objective.

- Competition: In many cases, retail formats are competing for both a consumer's time and dollars. Thus, redevelopers must at least consider the addition of box retailers. At the same time, those engaged in the redevelopment of unenclosed centers must consider the increasing variety of merchants that were once only in enclosed malls.
- Hybridize: Increasingly, both landlords and retailers are having success via the creation of hybrid center formats, such as incorporating big boxes—bookstores, for example—or what were once only enclosed mall merchandise mixes into unenclosed centers. Many of the best merchants are increasingly considering new types of locations.
- Time is currency: Don't waste the consumer's time. Relentlessly pursue conditions that will reinforce to consumers the fact that your center respects their time.
- A symphony, not a free-for-all: The center's merchandise mix, format, amenities and other key attributes should work together to produce a product that consumers can understand and interpret. Moreover, it should fulfill an opportunistic niche, relative to the other retail selections open to its consumers.
- Think ahead, not backward: Consider a merchandise mix that will be effective when one considers future retailing and consumer issues. Do not base your strategy on trends that are already changing or have passed.
- Try to incorporate flexibility into your plan: It is rare that every detail in an original plan comes to fruition. Anticipate change to the best degree possible.
- Disclosure: The need to work through several aspects of a comprehensive project with many parties dictates that details for a planned major expansion or renovation not be disclosed until the appropriate time. For example, consider the 25,000-square-foot local merchant, with two years remaining in the lease term, whose store is in the path of an important expansion of a very successful national chain store. It is going to be much easier to gain the merchant's cooperation if he or she does not know about having significant leverage. Therefore, resist the temptation to broadcast pending plans until all such situations have been resolved.

RETURN ON INVESTMENT

How much of a return on investment is enough? Such decisions will usually be made at the most senior levels of the majority of landlord companies. Most companies will seek returns that are in the 12 to 15 percent range for existing stable property redevelopments. Riskier properties will command higher return rates, often 15 to 25 percent. All of the foregoing return percentages are on a simple return basis, not factoring in the time value of money (compound interest, for example). Your company will usually determine the return threshold, based upon an asset's situation.

Developing the Core Strategy

As stated previously, thorough planning is the most critical step of the successful remerchandising of any redevelopment project.

EVERY REDEVELOPMENT NEEDS A COHERENT OVERALL STRATEGY

Every redevelopment demands that an overall primary strategy for the project exist and serve as a consistent guide for all major aspects of the program. The primary strategy and any supporting merchandising plan should have a mutually supportive and seamless relationship.

Test your prospective redevelopment by using the concepts in Table 3: Overall Objective and Remerchandising Planning Tool for Proposal Projects.

FOCUS ON THE OVERALL STRATEGY

Although Table 3 exhibits basic logic, it is easy to overlook even simple reasoning in the priority to improve a center. Without exception, each prospective redevelopment must have a comprehensive strategy or objective that is in turn supported by each of the project's major component disciplines:

- Leasing
- Center operations
- Marketing to consumers
- Marketing to merchants
- Physical renovation: Design and architecture
- Public relations/media

TABLE 3
Overall Objective and Remerchandising Planning Tool for Proposal Projects

1. What is the objective of the redevelopment? (This should define the new retail niche of the center.)	Every redevelopment must have a guiding strategy. What is the expected overall result? If there is no clear purpose, usually there should be no project. Do not mistake the challenge in clarifying a project's overall purpose, or its supporting merchandising plan, into actionable terms for the absence of a definable objective.
2. How can a revised merchandise mix best support the primary strategy for the center after the redevelopment is completed? (Can the deals identified be made, as your plan dictates?)	Any revisions to the center's merchandise mix must support the primary strategy for the center's revised position. Set priorities and develop a backup list of the 7 to 15 most critical deals. Prioritize the 3 most important deals in the above list. Which are the most important to make before the others, relative to overall merchant perception and total allowance costs?

3. Is the new merchandising strategy sound relative to each of its critical audiences in key areas of performance?

Key Audiences and Performance Areas	
Financial	Will it meet financial and ROI criteria?
Retailers	Will it be viewed as a key opportunity and stimulate leasing demand?
Consumers	Will consumers support it through visitation and buying?

Often the physical aspects of a property's renovation are more straightforward and easily interpreted than its remerchandising possibilities. This sometimes facilitates the consideration of a center's renovation and remerchandising plans in separate contexts. It is usually far more prudent to consider the relationships of all major components within the unifying context of the comprehensive objective.

THE NATURE OF THE CORE STRATEGY

Is your overall program defensive or offensive—and for what purpose? See Table 4: Core Strategy.

TABLE 4		
Core Strategy		
Strategy/Target	*Objectives/Reasoning*	*Situation*
Defensive **1. Competition**	Center has upcoming new or redevelopment competition.	Competition is likely to steal the center's former market share.
Offensive **2. Market Share**	Center can reposition itself and gain market share.	Pursue an existing weakness/opportunity in the existing retail alignment in the market.
3. "Fix and Sell"	Owner plans to market the center to prospective buyers.	Buyer is likely to be a REIT but may not be. Market situations may vary.

Remerchandising Plan Strategies

Creating the ultimate revised merchandise mix plan is usually a labor that requires diligence in both planning and creative problem solving (see Table 5: Remerchandising Strategies):

- Planning: One must study and review the market's existing and pending retail alignment, consumer demographic and psychographic data, local vehicular traffic conditions and many details regarding the existing merchants.

TABLE 5
Remerchandising Strategies

Project Goal	Remerchandising	Action Plan
Defensive: Competition	Create a revised merchandise mix that will effectively compete with a mall, lifestyle, specialty or unenclosed center.	Incorporate big box stores, such as bookstores or a specialized clothing store, into an enclosed center. Offer a village or lifestyle center merchandise mix as an alternative to a mall. Move upscale from the competition with higher price point specialty stores.
Offensive: Market Share Gain	Create a revised merchandise mix that will facilitate the center's growth in market share, consumer visits, sales productivity.	Action plan options are often very similar to those above. Find a strategic opportunity based upon the retail and/or consumer conditions in the market. Devise a leasing strategy to support the opportunity-based revised niche.
Offensive: "Fix and Sell"	Create a revised merchandise mix that will support the owner's ability to market and sell the center. The owner's goals in regard to the eventual type of buyer and approximate pricing will usually help to define the key parameters of the remerchandising plan.	How far to go in regard to the merchandise mix, allowance costs, types of merchants, etc., will usually be defined by the ownership's economic perspectives regarding its existing investment costs and ROI plus its selling price for the center. What is possible?

- Creative problem solving: One must also review which new merchants could potentially enter the market and the most current criteria for their store size, format, deal economics—all relevant critical parameters.

Evaluation Criteria

Prior to finalizing the overall redevelopment plan and remerchandising plan, the following issues should receive your thorough consideration. Their actual importance to any specific project situation will depend on the exact nature of the plans.

START WITH THE EXISTING MERCHANTS
One of the most challenging components of many redevelopment projects is the need to make critical decisions regarding a center's existing merchants, particularly local and independent operators. As you consider a center's future merchandising options, one of the realities is often the fact that there simply is not enough space for every shop that desires to be in the center. In addition, some existing stores that have been successful to date may be unable or unwilling to meet the revised leasing rates for your project. The problem can often be very challenging.

For example, a dominant and important national merchant wants to expand and needs more space. Adjacent, there is a solid local merchant with an expiring lease. Do you keep the local merchant? Do you offer the local merchant another location at the center? Such issues are part of almost every remerchandising effort. One of the main reasons for having all of the key disciplines represented on your team is to make sure that the right associate addresses the local merchant's importance.

Refer to Table 6: Remerchandising Analysis/Existing Merchants. This table is an example of the type of analysis required by most projects. It is not intended to be comprehensive, but rather representative.

ANALYSIS TOOL
Create a chart or spreadsheet that lists every merchant on the y axis (or left-hand side of the page) and the specific focal areas across the x axis (or top of the page), Please note that by using a program like

SHOPPING CENTER LEASING

TABLE 6
Remerchandising Analysis—Existing Merchants

(The table below is an example of the type of analysis that most projects require. It is not intended to be comprehensive, but rather a representative sample; the dollar amounts are for example only.)

Space No.	Merchants	Basic Data: Lease Expires	Size-SF Current	Size-SF Ideal	Sales 1998 Full Year	Sales Co. Use Avg.	Current & Market Rents: Current Effective PSF	Market Rent Same Use	Market Rent New Use	New Use Type	Store Renovation: Last Effort	Lease Trigger	Relocation: May Need	Landlord Right	Contact: Our Best	In-House	Comments
104	National Chain	Apr-00	4,500	8,000	$2,250,000	$2,250,000	$24.00	$28.00	$30.00	R-T-W	1995	No	Yes	No	Rep.		Can we upsize, by moving them slightly?
106	National Chain	Jan-01	12,000	6,000	$1,500,000	$2,000,000	$17.00	$22.00	$22.00	Various	1990	No	No	No	Rep.		Can we recapture significant space?
108	Regional Chain	Jan-01	4,000	4,000	$1,000,000	$1,000,000	$28.00	$28.00	N/A	N/A	1990	Yes	Yes	Yes	Gen. Mgr.		Relocate for important National Chain expansion.
110	National Chain	Jan-05	2,500	3,000	$750,000	$750,000	$29.00	$29.00	$35.00	Various	1995	No	Yes	No	Gen. Mgr.		Can we get them to add luggage à la new stores?
112	National Chain	Jan-05	4,000	4,000	$1,600,000	$1,200,000	$35.00	$35.00	N/A	N/A	1995	No	Yes	No	Rep.		Can we renew and expand them—early—and add children's?
114	Regional Chain	Jan-02	3,500	N/A	$700,000	$700,000	$19.00	N/A	$32.00	Various	1991	No	No	No	Gen. Mgr.		Replace ASAP with stronger merchant; merchant wants to leave.
116	National Chain	Jan-05	1,500	1,100	$500,000	$400,000	$28.00	$30.00	N/A	N/A	1994	Yes	No	Yes	Rep.		Can we recapture 350 to 400 SF for new space/store?
New 116A	Target: Local	N/A		400			$28.00	N/A	$70.00	Accessories	N/A	N/A	N/A	N/A	Gen. Mgr.		Local team has interested merchant, was temporary.
118	Local Merchant	Jan-05	2,000	N/A	$1,000,000		$37.50	$37.50	$40.00	R-T-W	1994	Yes	Maybe	No	Gen. Mgr.		Relocate for XYZ merchant—will take only this location.
120	National Chain	Apr-01	3,300	3,300	$1,000,000	$1,000,000	$24.00	$28.00	$35.00	Various	1990	No	No	No	Rep.		Do we want to retain this use in the center?
122	National Chain	Jan-01	5,000	Varies	$1,750,000	$1,750,000	$20.00	$24.00	$28.00	Various	1990	No	No	No	Rep.		Should they convert this to their Home format?
124	National Chain	Jan-05	2,500	2,500	$1,000,000	$1,000,000	$33.00	$35.00	N/A	N/A	1994	No	No	Yes	Rep.		Are there any issues to consider?
126	Local Merchant	Jan-05	1,500	N/A	$500,000	N/A	$25.00	$30.00	$33.00	Various	1994	Yes	No	No	Gen. Mgr.		Need to monitor remodel carefully.

FURTHER ISSUES TO CONSIDER
Has a merchant asked to terminate the lease early?
Does the landlord have any termination rights?
What are the merchant occupancy costs?

Microsoft Excel, you can sort the data according to the specific needs of the situation, representative of the type of information that should be included. While you can include almost any type or level of detail, the following is a list of the most common existing merchant issues:

- *Lease expirations,* looking forward three to five years
- Current *store size* versus the merchant's current working standard
- Current *sales productivity* versus the merchant's current chain average or the center's average for the category, or overall for nonchain stores
- Current *effective (minimum plus percentage rent) rent* versus the merchant's current working standard and the market-next value of the space to another merchant in a similar category
- Date and scope of the *merchant's last store renovation*
- Any *automatic store renovation clauses* triggered by the landlord's pending work
- *Relocation spaces within the center*—what space is left available if center merchants need to be moved in order to execute the new merchandising strategy.

Special Remerchandising Situations and Considerations

The following pivotal questions and situations should be addressed prior to developing a remerchandising strategy.

SHOULD BIG BOXES BE INCLUDED IN CENTER PROJECTS?

During the past decade, there has been more diversification and growth in the big box—large stores often devoted to a single-use concept, at least 10,000 square feet and up to 100,000 square feet or larger—than in the mall specialty store sectors. This has been an evolutionary trend, in concert with the consumer's shrinking free time, and is designed to capture both greater time spent and greater purchasing by visiting shoppers. The large bookstores and office supply stores are representative of this genre.

By incorporating big boxes, the landlord will usually sacrifice greater specialty store rents for stronger, destination-oriented, higher-volume stores. It is not unusual for a 20,000- to 30,000-square-foot big box store to outperform some of the national traditional department store chain units that are four to five times larger.

By including a big box, you may enhance consumer visitations to your site. In most cases, it is the big boxes that compete with malls for the consumer's time, dollars and attention. A landlord may also preempt some of the peripheral competition that usually develops around an established and successful mall. Thus, a landlord can ensure strong traffic, sales and customer visitation—hopefully making up for any big box income sacrifices in other areas of the ROI.

There are also negative ramifications to consider. Many big boxes may require an exterior entrance, thereby diluting interior mall traffic. Many traditional department stores will allow the big bookstores into a mall but will oppose the home store operators, on competitive grounds.

The primary issues for most landlords often tend to be: (1) How much do they want to service their consumers' needs and convenience? (2) How much will their own need for ROI affect their decisions? (3) What flexibility do they have in regard to anchor store rights?

The following issues will usually require focus with a big box effort:

- What site control rights do the department stores have?
- Most big boxes are accustomed to being the primary anchors in unenclosed centers. Joining an existing mall will usually require strong levels of trust between the merchant and you, as the landlord, because in many cases you will need to go back to the existing department stores in order to secure their permission on key issues like signage and site/building adjustments.
- Adding a big box will require that you review common area maintenance (CAM) and REIT calculations to determine the impact of the big box; most boxes will pay full REIT but only a contribution toward CAM, not the whole per-square-foot small shop billing rate.

SHOULD YOU RECONFIGURE A BLOCK OF DEEP SPACE?

At one time it was not unusual to have mall shop space that was 150 to 200 feet in depth. Today, mall shop space is most commonly 60 to 80 feet in depth. One of the benefits of remerchandising may be to better utilize such deep space. In many cases, shops or larger stores and boxes may be added on the exterior of the mall, utilizing 50 percent to 75 percent of the total available depth. The remainder of the space can then be used as interior mall shop square footage. Often, in a productive center, eliminating excess mall shop space raises the value of the remaining space.

DOES YOUR PLAN MEET LIFESTYLE AND COMMON-SENSE CRITERIA?
It is usually not enough to simply add a multiscreen cinema complex to an empty pad or failed department store pad, if the goal is to create a viable entertainment component. One has to fully consider how all of the entertainment components will work together within the framework of a consumer's typical visit:

- How do the quick-service and sit-down restaurant locations relate to both parking and the cinemas?
- Forcing customers to take illogical or extraordinary steps to meet their needs is usually unwise. Ideally, it should be easy for customers to locate an accessible parking space, get to their entertainment venues—food and movies—and to shop, before or after, conveniently.
- With the advent of "lifestyle shopping centers," often based around entertainment components, the consumer quite often has the option of a different or better "mousetrap."

If you are making the effort to renovate a center, try to fully consider exactly how the consumers will navigate their trips. Make it easy and logical for them.

STRUCTURE THE AMENITIES PLAN TO SUPPORT YOUR LEASING AND MERCHANDISING
This topic sounds more complicated than it really is. For example, experience has shown that construction and placement of a children's play area in a shopping center during a renovation not only can perform within the specific goals established for the amenity, but also can:

- Increase traffic and sales to nearby impulse food merchants, in most cases by more than 35 percent.
- Raise the market rent level of the surrounding mall shop spaces by $4 to $6 per square foot, within 6–18 months.
- Generally increase traffic in the entire wing or corridor.

Thus, a children's play area not only provides a center with a differentiating amenity, but it can help to create an ROI on its cost, enlivening what were previously inactive, secondary court areas. The lesson is to plan on all these things from the outset. Create a merchandising plan that best suits such an amenity. Establish rents that preconceive the benefits.

Remember to plan some impulse food—such as cookies or pretzels or a juice bar—near a play area, where adults will often be sitting for up to 30 minutes.

INCLUDE THE DEPARTMENT STORES IN THE PLANNING STAGE

When planning a renovation, it is easy to overlook one of the most important missions in many centers—the traditional department stores. Do not expect each of the existing department stores to evaluate its own physical plant or merchandising thrust. For example, if you are planning to bring in more upscale merchants, is the existing traditional department store planning to carry the appropriate price points and brands to support your overall plan?

It is normally wise to generate a comprehensive package, outlining your project goals and reasoning and incorporating research. This should be conveyed to the department store chains. Although you may have to work through the traditional real estate departments, it can be very advantageous to create a meeting that incorporates their regional operating and marketing associates. Getting to explain your goals directly to those overseeing the operation of the store is usually better than working through a real estate department.

MOTIVATE THE EXISTING MERCHANTS TO SUPPORT THE PLAN BY RENOVATING THEIR STORES

Although this is certainly easier said than done, many landlords already have boilerplate lease language supporting a major center redevelopment. However, you may find that you need to be creative and persistent in finding a way to motivate most of the merchants to renovate their stores. Early renewals are the historical solution, but creativity often pays dividends.

EVALUATE AND ESTABLISH CRITICAL STORE OPENING (AND REOPENING) DATES FOR ALL DEALS

One of the most important areas is the effective management of not only merchant design criteria, but also exactly when the new stores will be open, or an existing one reopened. It is imperative that the entire project team—including leasing, tenant coordination, development and the local/on-site team—focus on this issue. It must be an important component of every merchant discussion and negotiation. In most cases, leasing will initiate such discussions.

Executing the Plan

REPORTING RESULTS
When you have fully considered as many of the preceding concepts as appropriate, it is finally time to execute. By the point of execution, the project team should have established a regular and effective means of communication—usually not less frequently than monthly. Depending on the nature and scope of the project, most teams choose to meet weekly, biweekly or monthly. For the leasing or remerchandising responsibility, there should be a report that is distributed in conjunction with the team's chosen meeting frequency. Typically, the project's developer and the senior leasing representative will have agreed on the format, content and frequency of such a report. The leasing associates often tend to minimize the importance of such reports, but both lenders and public companies are usually very focused on these updates. Thus, it is incumbent on the leasing team to do a good-quality job of not only leasing, but also reporting on its activities.

MARKETING TOOLS
A great variety of effective marketing tools can be utilized to facilitate the leasing activity for a redevelopment. Refer to Table 7, Marketing Tools, for several actions and tools to consider.

INCOME DYNAMICS
It is critical to maintain up-to-date tracking, deal by deal, regarding rental income, allowance costs and anticipated landlord space preparation costs—all based on lease-up progress. It is just as important to make the most important deals first; typically, such deals will lower subsequent allowance costs for the next tier of deals. You will also want to have an understanding of the implications of rent-based allowance overruns. If, for example, the developer agrees, it may be possible to use more allowance dollars than specified in the pro forma in making deals by offsetting this with additional income.

TABLE 7

Marketing Tools

Marketing Need	Tools—Options
Does the center need to create a new image with retailers?	If you are changing the existing direction of the center, you will usually need to focus first on altering retailer perceptions. Use a high-impact brochure or a teaser—a mailer campaign—in order to generate top-of-mind awareness and get your message across.
Is your plan heavily dependent upon several key retailers?	Consider creating a specialized effort—focused solely on these key merchants. Focus your efforts in a way that will get the immediate attention of the key decision makers. While the effort may use almost any means to capture attention, be sure that you can back up your claims. Be prepared to be able to forward more solid supporting data whenever needed.
For most projects, consider the creation of an on-site marketing center or closing room.	Virtually every retailer will insist on a site visit before making a decision. In many cases, the center product that merchant representatives—often including real estate and operations—will experience is not the final product. In order to best promote the project in every case, create a room with the appropriate renderings and support materials so that a visitor who is unfamiliar with the center and market can easily perceive what you are trying to do. The cost is usually nominal as compared with the leasing budget and project cost. In most cases, this room is created in a space that will eventually be leased, is 500 to 1,250 square feet in size, and has costs that depend on the condition of the area. Essentially, it is an exclusive conference room—with your project materials dominating the space.
Make sure the local team is prepared for action—on little notice.	Because merchants will be visiting the project throughout its duration, the on-site team—often the general manager and marketing manager—must be prepared to conceptually walk such visitors through the project. Increasingly, merchant representatives from operations do not want to be accompanied by the landlord's real estate representatives, so it is a good idea to have a watch system in order to be on the lookout for such visitors.

For example, if the project pro forma is $35 per square foot in rent and $30 per square foot for allowance, it may be possible to proceed with a $40 per square foot allowance deal if there is $2 per square foot more, or $37 per square foot in total rent. This would create a simple return of 20 percent on the additional allowance, beyond pro forma parameters. However, project capital may be very limited, so it is important to have an exact understanding early on.

THE INTERNET
The Internet is a good place to focus your ongoing effort in regard to updating all of your audience regarding the project's progress. It covers consumers, merchants and a host of other peripheral audiences. Although it will not be easy to maintain an updated Web site regarding your project, it will most likely be easier and less costly than trying to completely individualize your communication by audience.

Conclusion

Coming full circle to where we started at the beginning of the chapter, planning is the core component of all redevelopment. The stronger the planning and preparation prior to any physical work, the higher the success rate of the final product. Part of effective planning is the creation of an overall strategy for the project that will serve as a consistent guide for all major aspects of the redevelopment program.

Mark N. London, SCSM/SCMD, is President of Mark London & Associates, LLC, Lake Bluff, Illinois.

12 Retailing

Shannon Alter, CPM

Leasing managers must contend with a variety of issues on a daily basis, dealing with the different demands of owners, tenants, and property managers. To some shopping center leasing managers, the very idea of learning about retailing seems a burdensome chore. After all, it is just one more thing to add to an already full plate. Nevertheless, learning more about retailers and their businesses can help the astute manager contribute to enhancing the value of both the center and the landlord/tenant relationship.

Understanding retailing must begin with understanding the unique nature of shopping centers and of retailers as tenants. Within reason, it does not matter if a tenant in an office is an accountant or gives computer classes, or if an office or industrial tenant's business increases, as long as the tenant continues to pay the rent and follow the rules. But shopping center tenants are different from tenants in other types of property. Retailers expect landlords to provide the right tenant mix in a comfortable atmosphere that will encourage customers to shop. The primary reason a merchant is in a shopping center rather than in another type of property is because that merchant wants to derive the benefits that come from being near compatible merchants—in other words, from the synergy of a shopping center. In turn, landlords anticipate that merchants will draw upon one another to achieve overall success for their stores and the entire shopping center. Landlords also often share in a merchant's success via percentage rent. Even if a merchant does not pay percentage rent, it is important to collect sales reports. Sales matter because they offer an important barometer of how individual tenants, as well as the entire center, are faring.

When it comes to promoting a center, how can a leasing manager strike the delicate balance necessary to meet an owner's goals and desires and still satisfy the merchants? To realize increased revenue in the long run, managers must learn that while their goal is to maximize revenue to the center owner, a retailer's goal is to strengthen and enhance the value of their business through increased sales. Landlord and tenant must essentially work as partners to achieve their goal and increase sales.

This chapter looks at how the leasing manager can be more successful by understanding the following components of retailing:

- The Relationship Factor
- What to Look For
- Demographics and Psychographics
- Retailer's Business Strategies
- Understanding Key Retailing Processes
- Qualifying Prospective Tenants
- Signs of Trouble.

The Relationship Factor

Essentially, shopping center leasing is a relationship business. But what does that mean? As an example, consider a leasing manager—call her Joan Smith—who has a large portfolio of shopping centers with several demanding owners. She is in a new job and anxious to prove herself, but she is also mired in leasing reports and additional paperwork. Consequently, she rarely has an opportunity to visit with merchants, either in her center or in the local area, and she depends on an assistant to handle most initial leasing requests. She just does not have the time. After all, she does not see any need to talk with tenants until negotiations really start.

Does this scenario sound familiar? The sheer volume of matters that a leasing manager must deal with can be overwhelming. So what can a busy leasing manager do? The fact is, no matter how busy leasing managers become, they should never overlook the importance of developing a long-term relationship with merchants through friendly, personal, consistent contact. After all, property managers and the marketing manager have to live with the tenants that leasing managers choose. Before our leasing manager can begin to learn anything about the retailers and their businesses, she must first establish a relationship with them.

Most people enjoy talking about themselves and their interests. What interests retailers the most is retailing, the business they live and breathe. Establishing consistent communication can be sometimes difficult due to turnover in store managers, particularly those of chain tenants. Still, leasing managers can learn more about their merchants' businesses and encourage them to talk by paying them regular visits; similarly, they should visit with other tenants they wish to target. At the same time, it is important to remember not to ignore the store managers of major or chain tenants, or to assume that a personal visit is unnecessary because the property manager has already visited the retailer. Store managers are often a wonderful source of information, both about their own stores and about the center. A leasing manager's good relationship with a store's manager or company real estate department can be invaluable, especially if there are difficulties in another area of the retailer's operations.

It is important to ask how sales are going. Sometimes major tenants, for example, are not required to provide sales figures other than at specified times, and managers are reluctant to ask for sales information in between. It is still important to ask. Even if the store is not required to provide proprietary information, a good relationship with a store or district manager may yield beneficial information, such as how this store is performing chain-wide, whether sales as a whole have been up or down, and so on. It is extremely important for both retailer and landlord to be able to track sales and create overall reporting that can be shared with the merchants.

But how significant is such information if the leasing manager does not know how to use it? Knowledgeable managers, for example, become familiar with expected sales per square foot by merchandise category, such as jewelry, women's ready-to-wear, restaurants, or supermarkets. The first comparison to make is with sales at other centers within the manager's portfolio. Merchandise categories may be broken down further into general merchandise, apparel, furniture/home furnishings and other (GAFO) types of similar merchandise and non-GAFO categories, such as fast food and regular restaurants, supermarkets, and drugstores. These industry statistics can be found in many places, including *Monthly Mall Merchandise,* published by the International Council of Shopping Centers (ICSC).

The Store Visit: What to Look For

Our leasing manager has worked hard to develop a relationship with the retailers in her center. What does she need to understand first about the retailing business? Inexperienced leasing managers will still learn much about a store upon visiting it, so the first thing our manager does is shop the store. She does not need to go shopping with an intent to purchase, but she should view the store from the customer's perspective. Here are some elements of retailing leasing managers should look for when shopping the retailers in their centers or neighborhood:

- What is the ambience—the feel—of the store? Is it comfortable and pleasant?
- Is the customer greeted by a store employee and offered assistance, or is the clerk unavailable?
- What image does the store project? Is the retailer's merchandise focus easily understood? Is merchandise displayed well, with prices clearly marked? Are price reductions clear and well marked?
- Is the store well stocked? Has the retailer taken every opportunity to display its merchandise effectively?
- Is the store's signage and advertising effective? Are signs professional and informative?
- Does the staff have a working knowledge of the products or services offered?

Following the store visits, talk informally with the center's retailers and summarize observations from the store visits. This type of conversation with retailers requires careful preparation. It is important that the merchants do not interpret the conversation as an inquiry. Rather, start the conversation referring to your observations concerning the store's image and merchandise focus. The retailer should clearly understand the target customers and the trade area from which the store draws its primary customers.

The Demographics and Psychographics

In short, the retailer must have a demographic profile of the store's customers to be sure that the type of customer in the area is the right type for that retailer.

It is also important that the merchant understand the center's psychographics, which provide lifestyle data about potential shoppers in the merchant's trade area. Psychographics point to why customers shop in a certain store, when they shop, and what type of quality or price attracts them. By understanding who the retailer's target customers are, leasing managers can better evaluate a prospective tenant and the likelihood of its compatibility with other tenants in the center. Following are some pertinent questions typically addressed in psychographic data:

- Who are the store's core customers, from which the retailer generally realizes 20 to 30 percent of its business? An example is a store targeted toward surf and beach wear for young women under age 25.
- What are the lifestyles and activities of those core customers? In this example, the customers enjoy casual clothes and an outdoor lifestyle, are mostly single, and have some discretionary income.
- What are their shopping habits? For example, the typical surfwear customer may be going to school and available to shop during the day, taking a bus or borrowing a car to get to the center.
- Is the core customer value-oriented versus quality-conscious? The customer in this example may not require top-of-the-line clothing, but she still wants fashion at a reasonable price.
- Which stores represent major competition? Does the retailer keep up with trends? Does he or she regularly shop the competition?

The Retailer's Business Strategies

Have you ever had the unsettling experience of walking into a shop where you were not quite sure what the retailer was selling, not much of it was on the shelves, and no one was available to assist you?

You almost certainly ventured into a store where the retailer did not have a strategy, a plan for how to get and keep target customers.

Now that our fictitious leasing manager has assured herself that her retailers understand their target customers, she will want to review the strategies that these retailers use to distinguish themselves from others and draw those target customers into the store. A retailer's strategies should include areas such as merchandising and assortment, price points, growth, ambience, creativity, service, and advertising. The following pages focus specifically on merchandising and assortment, ambience, service, and advertising. Price points are discussed later in the chapter.

MERCHANDISING AND ASSORTMENT

As discussed previously, the store's direction, image, and focus should be very clear and immediately identifiable. There should be no mixed messages; neither customers nor staff should be confused. Perhaps the most important point to remember is that a customer's impression of a store is molded as soon as he or she steps in the door.

When leasing managers visit retailers, either prospective or existing ones, they should consider several additional points concerning effective merchandising:

- Is the store a high-end, cutting-edge-of-fashion store or low-end and value-oriented?
- What assortment of items is offered? Although it is important for a store to have depth and uniqueness, no retailer can offer everything. The range of merchandise must be narrow enough for a particular retailer to gain advantage over the competition in the area. Typically, several related categories are offered to round out the assortment.
- What is the store's lifestyle appeal? Does it have a special branded image?
- Does the store offer gift wrapping? Are customers reminded of gift-giving opportunities in the form of gift certificates, packaging, and the like?

Although it is important for a retailer to round out the assortment offered, or to carry items related to the primary products, it is also necessary for the leasing manager to determine whether the merchandise offered is in fact clearly focused and defined. The retailer must always offer the basic products, recognizing this is why customers come to that store. And the retailer must offer enough of them. Nothing can shortcut a retailer's sales faster than making the mistake of not carrying the basics or distracting customers from the primary products. For example, a leasing manager might be considering a coffee tenant who also wants to sell pastries and related gift items such as coffee mugs, coasters, books, and compact discs. The tenant's primary goal is to sell coffee, so if sales of other, incidental items are permitted, the items should only be ones that will both enhance sales and not detract from the retailer's main focus. Here, the leasing agent may want to restrict sales of compact discs and books to a certain percentage or type to ensure that customers get what they primarily came for: coffee.

AMBIENCE
The store's look or vision should be evident at a glance. The physical store itself should provide the shopper with a pleasant shopping experience and should support all of the information pertaining to it, such as promotions, signage, displays. For example, has merchandise been categorized by color, product, or use to draw attention to the items for sale? Some stores provide certain items for demonstration, so that customers can try them out. Coffee bars or bakeries often provide samples of certain items.

SERVICE
Everyone has had the unfortunate experience of being the recipient of poor service. The clerk was rude, the special order never arrived, a return could not be made, because "it isn't store policy." Are customers likely to return to a store with such poor service? With the quality of service declining in many areas of this time-pressured world, customers often refuse to shop again at stores where they received inferior service. They simply do not have the time, particularly when they have errands that can just as easily be done elsewhere, in a more welcome atmosphere.

Many times, customers will not take the time to complain about inferior service; they just do not come back. But they do tell their friends. Service is truly an intangible but essential part of a retailer's "inventory," and substandard service can have a considerable negative impact. On the other hand, outstanding service distinguishes a retailer from its competition and is clearly a way the retailer can add value. Retailers must recognize this strategy to gain advantage and market share over competitors. Focusing on service is an excellent way to do precisely that.

Just as the retailer must understand its target customer, it must also comprehend what that customer expects once he or she arrives in the store. For example, studies show that people today theoretically have more leisure time than ever as a result of the many time-saving devices available. In reality, they are also busier than ever and have increasing demands on their time. Consequently, a grocery store customer, for example, might expect other convenient services, such as banking and dry cleaning, to be available in the grocery store. The customer might expect delivery service, or the ability to order specific products. The customer expects to save time. All of these services can add value to the shopper's experience.

What, then, does the category of service include? What do a retailer's customers expect? What is the customer's perception of service? Consider the following guidelines:

- Friendly, empathetic, responsive, well-trained staff
- High-quality merchandise
- Convenient hours
- Easy store layout
- Satisfaction guarantee
- Availability of desired merchandise
- Outstanding knowledge of products or services
- Ability to place special orders
- Creativity, such as special gift wrapping
- Owner or store manager on site (for independents)
- Personal phone calls or newsletters regarding sales or special promotions.

Service, it is said, begins and ends with the employees. Everyone knows how frustrating it is to encounter an apathetic, inconsiderate, or impolite attitude toward service. Think of stores with a reputation for excellent service. Customers are very likely to return to them, because those stores make things easier and more pleasant for shoppers. Customer-friendly employees can be an invaluable asset for a retailer.

Likewise, the personal involvement of an on-site owner makes a difference in service and attention at the level of a small shop. Outstanding service is a precious commodity that can definitely distinguish the retailer from its competition. It is clearly a means by which the retailer can add value.

Leasing managers can often be a valuable source of industry information for merchants, particularly smaller ones. There are also many excellent trade magazines that print articles relating to retailing. Merchants often do not see these, and it is helpful to provide them with copies of pertinent articles. ICSC, for example, publishes *The Retail Challenge* each quarter. This publication provides tips and information helpful to retailers on selling, merchandising, and customer service strategies.

ADVERTISING

As with merchandising, a retailer's chosen advertising must be very specific. Typically, a retailer will spend between 2 and 5 percent of annual sales on advertising. Retailers sometimes view advertising only as an added expense, when it is really an investment in the future. Not just anything will do; it must be focused and consistent, and it must appear at the right time and in the right place. The leasing manager should find out what forms of media the retailer plans to use. For example, is the store part of a chain that has regular direct mailings? Although a center marketing or promotional program is a good starting point, most merchants cannot live by center advertising alone and must have their own program.

The primary objective for the retailer is to build its image and awareness and create sales. First, a retailer must clearly understand why customers shop at that store and then determine how to best penetrate the right market. The retailer then must tie in advertising concepts to support the store's merchandise and appeal to its target customers. The retailer must then develop a plan and create a calendar. Only then will the retailer be able to turn visits into sales and first-time customers into loyal clients.

The Key Retailing Processes

Leasing managers next should focus on some of the retailer's key business processes and understand how they relate to the deal at hand. Retailers handle some similar activities as real estate managers: supervising and training staff, developing and managing budgets, planning advertising. In addition, they must know how to effectively buy, display, and manage merchandise. Armed with knowledge about a retailer's key business processes, leasing managers can better qualify tenants by understanding the combination of factors that point to a merchant's success or lack thereof.

When calculating many of these key ratios, a merchant's net sales figures are used. Net sales are gross sales less refunds to the customer.

OCCUPANCY COST

Aside from visiting merchants, another strategy to gauge how each tenant is performing is to check with the property manager to find out the tenant's occupancy cost. Leasing managers will typically know the extent to which the center's common area maintenance (CAM) expenses affect marketing the available space, but understanding occupancy cost can also prove to be an effective tool. To a retailer, all costs are important, because the store's sales volumes must support its costs. Therefore, rent, CAM, taxes, insurance, and percentage rent are typically all included in occupancy cost, even though the numerator is often labeled just "rent." The ratio is calculated as follows:

$$\frac{\text{Annual Rent}}{\text{Annual Sales}} = \text{Occupancy Cost (as a \%)}$$

For example, say a retailer with 1,500 square feet is doing $225 per square foot (psf) in annual sales, with a rent of $1.50 and CAM of $.40 per square foot per month, including taxes and insurance. Let us say the retailer does not yet pay any percentage rent. The occupancy cost is then calculated as follows:

Rent: $1.50 per month × 12 = $18.00 psf × 1,500 sf = $27,000 annual rent

CAM: $.40 per month × 12 = $4.80 psf × 1,500 sf = $7,200 annual CAM

Total: $1.90 per month × 12 = $22.80 psf × 1,500 sf = $34,200 annual costs

Total Annual Sales: 1,500 sf × $225 psf per year = $337,500

$$\frac{\$34{,}200 \text{ (Annual Rent)}}{\$337{,}500 \text{ (Annual Sales)}} = \text{approximately } 10\% \text{ Occupancy Cost}$$

As a general rule of thumb, the merchant's occupancy cost percentage should not be more than double the rate of percentage rent. Suppose that the prospective tenant has negotiated not to have a percentage rent requirement in the lease. The lease manager can still check what percentage rate normally would be, by investigating industry sources such as *Dollars and Cents of Shopping Centers*, published by the Urban Land Institute. This annual publication lists typical percentage rent rates for various types of retailers, as well as other expense- and rent-related information for different types of shopping centers.

An excellent strategy in estimating likely rates of percentage rent is to take a look at similar retailers in similar locations, if within the lease manager's portfolio. Another strategy is to check with the property manager and with other leasing managers. Associations such as the International Council of Shopping Centers and other industry-related groups offer networking opportunities, which may give a leasing manager the chance to compare notes with other managers.

Suppose the sample merchant's occupancy cost turned out to be 18 percent rather than 10 percent? When a merchant's occupancy cost is higher than desired, it is a sign that the store's sales cannot support the costs and the retailer is likely headed for trouble. Just as this ratio can be used as a measure of the viability of a store location, merchants too must be aware of and analyze their success. It is easy to see, then, why increasing store sales volumes must be the retailer's primary focus.

INVENTORY TURNOVER

Another ratio that is critical for a retailer is the inventory, or stock, turnover. This ratio describes the rate at which the retailer's average inventory has been turned over, or sold. Determing this turnover first requires determining average inventory: This represents the sum of the retail inventories that are done at the end of each month, added to the initial opening period, and then divided by thirteen.

Average inventory is calculated on either the beginning of the month (BOM) stock or end of the month (EOM) stock, as shown below:

$$\frac{\text{Total Inventory}}{\text{Number of Inventories}} = \text{Average Inventory}$$

A retailer's goal is to stock the items people want and to stock very little of what people do not want. Unsold merchandise represents a financial investment that is tied up, and it occupies valuable shelf space that could be used for newer, faster-moving items. Consequently, a higher turnover rate is desirable because it generally is indicative of greater productivity and higher profit. Inventory control is critical because it is a measure of how efficient a retailer is at buying, selling, and managing inventory. The merchant also is likely to have a better chance of gaining repeat business through greater merchandise exposure. Inventory turnover is calculated as follows:

$$\frac{\text{Net Sales}}{\text{Average Inventory}} = \text{Inventory Turnover}$$

As an example, compare the inventory turnover for two stores:

	Store #1	Store #2
Sales	$1,200,000	$900,000
Average Inventory	300,000	300,000
Number of turns	4	3

Store number 1 has a more desirable turnover rate. Typically, stores such as supermarkets will have high turnover rates, while stores selling higher-end items, such as jewelry stores, will have lower turnover rates. Turnover rates for different types of retailers can be found in *Dollars and Cents of Shopping Centers* (Urban Land Institute) and similar industry publications.

MARKUP

In order for a retailer to manage inventory well, the retailer must know how to price the merchandise so that it will sell well once it gets into the store. Merchants know their prices must be in line with those of their competition, yet they must also manage to make a profit. When retailers buy goods, they mark up or mark on to create a planned profit over the initial cost of the goods and all related costs such as transportation and preparation.

The terms *markup* and *mark-on*, which are synonymous, show us the difference between the cost of an item and the selling price. Markup is always expressed in terms of the marking relative to the retail price, not the cost, either in dollars or as a percentage. The retail sales price results from a combination of the cost of goods and the initial markup. Knowing the retail price and the cost of the merchandise item makes it possible to calculate the markup percentage, as follows:

$$\frac{\text{Retail Price} - \text{Cost}}{\text{Retail Price}} = \text{Markup \%}$$

As an example, if the cost of an item is $9 and the retail price is $16, the markup is about 44 percent:

$$\frac{\$16 - \$9}{\$16} = 44\%$$

Retailers may also use a specific markup to establish the sales price. The ingredients of the formula remain the same, using the cost complement (reciprocal percentage):

$$\frac{\text{Cost}}{100\% - \text{Markup \%}} = \text{Retail Price or } \frac{\$9}{100\% - 44\%} = \$16.00$$
$$\text{(specific markup)}$$

Another method of markup is called keystone markup, which exactly doubles the cost of an item—the markup is 50 percent. For example, a dress that cost the retailer $75 will be priced at $150. The only potential problem with this method is that it does not focus on the demand for the item. If the item is in great demand, such as the year's most popular toy, or unique to a particular store, then the item should be marked up accordingly.

MARKDOWN

Of course, a retailer hopes that all merchandise will be sold at the original retail price, but some may have to be marked down in order to move it. Markdowns are reductions in the original price of an item with the express purpose of getting it to sell. The inability to sell merchandise at the previously determined sale price may be due to poor buying (for example, still carrying peak stock too late in the season), incorrect pricing, or simply a change in the seasons. Markdowns reflect depreciation in the cost value of the merchandise; therefore, it is important for retailers to analyze which vendor's merchandise sells.

Markdowns are important to a retailer because they affect the ability to turn over goods and add new merchandise for the new season. For example, retailers may choose to carry lower stock levels in January, when business is typically slower; hence, there are post-holiday sales. Additionally, retailers want to make space available for new merchandise to spark customers' interest and bring in new sales. Usually a retailer will take repeated markdowns until the item is finally sold.

Qualifying Prospective Tenants

Once the leasing manager is familiar with what should happen inside a retailer's store, he or she should look at other important factors in qualifying a prospective tenant. First, it is important to obtain a business résumé from the tenant, describing his or her background and experience in the chosen area of retailing (see Exhibit A: Prospective Tenant Qualification Information Form). Typically, a leasing agent wants to find out information that will help him or her better determine if the prospective tenant is the best one for the space. This may include:

- Nature of experience and number of years in the business
- Number and location of current stores (plan to visit a representative location)
- Photographs or brochures
- How retailer will fund either acquisition (if taking over a lease) or new improvements or equipment (if a new lease)

- Who will work in the store (will the owner be on site?)
- What income will be available to the retailer (is the store the only source of income, or will funds be available from another job?)
- Expansion plans
- Business plans.

This information is important because it will show whether the retailer has a great idea but is operating on a shoestring, or truly has both a well-thought-out plan and the funds to support that plan. Smaller retailers may balk at preparing this type of information, particularly the business plan, because they may not have had to provide it before. It is the leasing agent's job to convince prospective retailers that it is actually in their own best interest to carefully work their way through a solid plan to better ensure success.

At the very minimum, the leasing agent should request a retailer's financial information, particularly the current balance sheet and income statement for the business. If the retailer is a start-up tenant and does not have prior information, it can be projected using the form shown in Exhibit B, Pro Forma Operating Statement. Sometimes a small retailer who is asked about prospective sales per square foot will throw out a random number; this indicates that the retailer has not thought through the process. On this form, the retailer must list projected revenues and expenses—not only a good personal exercise, but also very telling for the leasing agent. For example, the leasing agent can review sales projections to gauge whether they are within expectations, both for the center and for the industry.

The leasing agent also will be able to see what the retailer's intended start-up costs are (initial inventory, fixtures and equipment, and store buildout) and what the retailer will use for start-up funds (personal funds, borrowed funds, and so on). See Exhibit C, Pro Forma Statement of Cash Flow. For example, certain tenants, such as dentists, doctors, and restaurants, generally lease considerable equipment, which can be very expensive. The leasing agent will want to know how the tenant plans to pay for this—will the monthly cash flow cover such costs as well as the rent and other lease charges? Many times, small tenants with new stores underestimate the amount of capital they will need until the store gets off the ground.

Recognizing Signs of Trouble

Say our hypothetical leasing manager has recently taken over leasing for a community shopping center and has visited the center's gift store for the first time. The owner is an independent who is out at the time of our leasing manager's visit. There is one employee in the store, who is friendly and offers assistance. The leasing manager notices that the store seems to have a little bit of this and that, but things appear to be difficult to find; there does not appear to be much selection, and some shelves look rather empty. On the other hand, the display case at the front counter is cluttered.

This retailer is likely headed for trouble and clearly has some challenges related to merchandising. Our leasing manager cannot be entirely clear at this point that the retailer is not salvageable, as she does not have enough information. Prior to visiting this merchant, there are several things both the leasing manager and the property manager can address:

- Monthly sales figures: Have there been any changes, and if so, why? Check with the property manager for any changes in store ownership. How does this merchant compare to others in a similar category in the center or in the landlord's other centers and in the trade area? Have the sales reports been correctly computed according to the lease?
- Payment history: Is the merchant paying the monthly promotional dues assessments on time? Find out from the property manager whether the retailer is making other payments in a timely manner or has objected to a rent increase or requested a rent reduction.
- Occupancy cost: As noted earlier, a retailer's occupancy cost includes all costs: rent, common area, promotions, and so on. The store's sales must support its occupancy costs. Remember that a store's occupancy cost should not be more than double its percentage rent rate. Therefore, a store with an occupancy cost of 20 percent and a percentage rent rate of 6 percent is likely treading in troubled waters.
- Outside influences: Are there other extenuating circumstances in the center that may have influenced this retailer? For example, did the grocery store right next to the gift shop move out six

months ago? Is the main city street bordering the center undergoing prolonged construction?

Generally, even less experienced leasing managers who take the time to visit merchants regularly and communicate with their property managers can discern when a store is showing signs of trouble. If a leasing manager is looking at a prospective tenant, it is important to find out as much as possible about these factors as they relate to the tenant's existing location.

Here are some tactics to recognize signs of trouble:

- The merchant is paying slowly or is always late
- Merchandise is too scattered and lacks focus
- Visual presentation of merchandise is poor and does not confirm the store's image
- Stock is low or shelves are empty. Just like a full buffet table, full shelves induce confidence
- There's always a sale, complete with hand-lettered signs
- The store and windows are dirty
- Inventory is old and stale—no changes are made in the merchandise when changes should occur
- The retailer has stopped advertising saying it is too expensive.
- Employees are apathetic, unfriendly, or unknowledgeable
- The merchant does not attend center marketing meetings or participate in promotional programs because he or she is "too busy."

How the Leasing Manager Can Help

As mentioned earlier, offering guidance to a retailer can be a challenge for a variety of reasons. Most common are (a) the retailer might not recognize he or she needs guidance; (b) the leasing manager may not have the knowledge or resources necessary to offer guidance; or (c) the merchant may not be inclined to listen because he or she does not have a good relationship with the property manager. Whatever the reason, evaluating and assisting a retailer with the right kind of guidance can take finesse on the leasing manager's part.

Following are some suggestions a leasing manager can use to assist merchants:

Continually monitor and stay on top of merchant sales reports. Even though a space has already been leased, the job is not yet done. Resourceful leasing managers stay in tune with their current tenants in the event there are new vacancies or other changes in the center or in the market. Talk with merchants about any material change in sales. Know how sales are going for similar merchants at other centers.

Be a resource. Provide information to merchants such as results of surveys or focus groups, industry statistics, pertinent articles, and so on. It may be helpful, for example, to provide tenants with sales-per-square-foot figures by category for the center or over the manager's portfolio so they can see how they measure up.

Assist the marketing manager in scheduling a presentation by an in-house expert or an outside consultant on things such as better storefront displays, effective visual merchandising, and productive advertising. Merchants may need help in these areas, but it is often difficult to get those merchants who particularly need help to attend. Once again, the relationship is crucial.

Pay for an outside consultant to help a tenant merchandise, making sure that the most important issues are the ones addressed and that recommended solutions are in fact feasible.

Keep a running list of troubled stores, or of those on the edge. Assist the property manager in developing an action plan with the landlord for working with these merchants.

Taking the time to learn more about retailers' businesses can truly benefit the shopping center leasing manager's relationship with merchants and enhance the long-term value of the center. Leasing managers can contribute to the success of the merchants by first understanding the key business strategies that retailers use and then knowing how to monitor them and assist when needed.

Shannon Alter, CPM, is Owner of Retail Management Services, Tustin, California.

Exhibit A

Prospective Tenant Qualification Information Example Form

Business Information
Owner Name: _____
Business Name: _____
(If same corporation as other stores, attach financial statement of parent corporation)
Number of Stores: _____
Nearest Location Comparable to New Location: _____
_____
Manager of New Location: _____
Leasehold improvements and equipment at new location will be: ❏ New   ❏ Used
Do you plan to open additional stores in the future? ❏ Yes   ❏ No
If yes, how many total? _____
How many per year? _____

New Business Owner Information
Do you plan to continue working at your current job? ❏ Yes   ❏ No
What is the nature of your experience in the proposed business?
_____
_____
How many years' experience in this type of business? _____
Is lease to be personally guaranteed? ❏ Yes   ❏ No (If yes, attach personal financial statement.)

Start-Up Funding
Funds available	$ _____
Personal	$ _____
Borrowed	$ _____
Other	$ _____
Total funds available	$ _____

Start-Up costs
Initial inventory	$ _____
Fixtures and equipment	$ _____
Store buildout	$ _____
Other	$ _____
Total start-up costs	$ _____
Working capital	$ _____

NOTE: Working capital = funds available – start-up costs.
*For borrowed funds indicate source and repayment schedule:

NOTES AND COMMENTS: _____
_____
_____
_____

©IREM 970701—MKL404LES5 SG

Exhibit B

Pro Forma Operating Statement Example Form

Store Name: _____ Preparation Date: _____

PROJECTIONS	Year 1	%	Year 2	%	Year 3	%
Sales revenue						
Starting inventory						
Merchandise purchases (add)						
Ending inventory (subtract)						
Cost of goods sold						
Gross profit						
Stock turnover						

OPERATING EXPENSES
Payroll
  Owner/manager salary
  Sales personnel
  Other personnel
  Payroll taxes
  Employee benefits
    Total wages/related costs

Advertising

Occupancy Costs
  Rent
  Utilities
  Telephone
  Real estate tax
  Personal property tax
  Property insurance
  Liability insurance
  Repairs and maintenance
  Lease expense
  Depreciation
    Total occupancy costs

Store/office supplies
Accounting/legal services
Shipping/delivery
Travel
Debt service (financed eqpt)
Interest expense (__%____yrs)
Other nonspecific costs

Total Operating Expense

Net Operating Profit

©IREM 970701—MKL404LES5 SG

Exhibit C

Example of a Pro Forma Statement of Cash Flow

Store Name: _____ Preparation Date: _____

Initial Capitalization   Pre-Opening
    Cash (personal funds)   _____
    Borrowed capital   _____
    Other funds   _____
    Total funds available   _____
    Distribution of Capital   _____
    Opening inventory   _____
    Fixtures and equipment   _____
    Improvements to leased space   _____
    Other start-up costs   _____
                                      _____
                                      _____

    Total Development Costs   _____

Unused Initial Capital   _____

Cash Flow for Full Operating Years from Store Opening

	Year 1	Year 2	Year 3
Source of Cash			
Operating profits	_____	_____	_____
Depreciation (added)	_____	_____	_____
Other	_____	_____	_____
Total Cash from Operations	_____	_____	_____
Allocation of Cash			
Inventory increase	_____	_____	_____
Accounts receivable increase	_____	_____	_____
Income taxes (federal/state)	_____	_____	_____
Debt service (principal)	_____	_____	_____
Other	_____	_____	_____
Total Cash Allocated	_____	_____	_____
Increase in Cash	_____	_____	_____
Schedule of Change in Cash			
Starting cash balance	_____	_____	_____
Added cash	_____	_____	_____
Ending cash balance	_____	_____	_____

©IREM 970701—MKL404LES5 SG

13 Specialty Retail Leasing

Frederick J. Delibero, CLS

Specialty retail leasing has evolved from the mom-and-pop business it once was into a highly competitive segment of the shopping center industry, enriching retailers and property owners alike. Even in the early 1990s, many property owners were unaware of the extra income that specialty retail leasing is capable of generating. By contrast, nearly every major property owner now has a staff dedicated to creating, building, and maintaining a top-performing specialty retail leasing program. Today income from specialty leasing is no longer considered extra income. In fact, many property owners claim that specialty retail leasing may account for 10 percent or more of their total revenue. The success of specialty retail leasing has also spawned a multitude of national retail companies generating millions of dollars in newfound revenue each year from shopping centers.

For the property owner, a productive specialty retail leasing program can add revenue and create added value for the property. It can increase occupancy by generating excitement in-line and in the common area. Specialty retail leasing can also add variety to the merchandise mix, creating more of a unique and enjoyable shopping experience for the property's customers. Long term, some specialty retail tenants will evolve into valuable and permanent in-line retailers.

For the retailer, the barriers to entry into specialty retail leasing are fewer than those presented in opening a permanent in-line store. Specialty retail tenants enjoy more flexible economic terms than permanent merchants and have significantly less capital improvement investment. They are able to target specific selling seasons appropriate to their product. In addition, they often start their business with smaller inventories than permanent retailers.

For the specialty leasing representative, specialty retail leasing is unique because representatives are usually responsible for all aspects of their business segment. From marketing the program to negotiating the deal, and from working with the property staff to purchasing equipment, the specialty leasing representative's job is multifaceted and requires a broad set of skills.

One thing is certain: Specialty leasing and the specialty retailers it attracts are here to stay.

Specialty Retail Leasing Organizational Structures

Although there are no hard and fast rules, specialty retail leasing at many companies is organized as a function of either the leasing department or the property management department. Both approaches have their advantages and disadvantages. For example, a specialty leasing staff serving under the head of leasing may be more in tune with available space and the merchandising needs of the property, and it may have greater success incubating tenants from a short-term status into long-term tenants. On the other hand, a specialty leasing staff serving under the head of asset or property management may be more focused on cost control, more informed about center events, and more sensitive to the appearance of each individual specialty retailer. In some organizations, a head of specialty leasing may report directly to the president of the company.

At the property level, there are many different approaches to achieve the specialty leasing goals and strategies. While some property owners take an on-site approach, holding the property's general manager accountable for specialty leasing, others take a regional or national approach, holding field or corporate level employees accountable. Companies often use a combination of both approaches. There is no right or wrong way to organize the specialty retail leasing function; however, it is important that each company organize the department to best serve the company's goals and strategies.

Whether accountability lies with the property's general manager or a national specialty leasing representative, many property owners believe employing an on-site person to handle the day-to-day tasks of specialty retail leasing is crucial to increasing program revenue and enhancing the appearance of the program.

In structuring the specialty retail leasing function, it is important to initiate open communication between the on-site specialty leasing personnel and the general manager, marketing director, operations director, permanent leasing staff, property accountant/bookkeeper, and corporate office support staff. Open communication minimizes potential conflicts and maximizes potential revenues.

Working with Permanent Leasing Representatives

Building strong relationships and maintaining consistent open communication with the permanent leasing team are paramount to meeting revenue goals, identifying outposting opportunities, and incubating specialty retail tenants into permanent tenants. The specialty leasing representative must maintain an awareness of available space and permanent leasing activity, as well as understand the merchandising needs of the property. In addition, when incubating tenants from nonpermanent to permanent is a goal, the representative must work closely with the permanent leasing team to structure acceptable lease deals. The specialty leasing representative can improve the relationship with the permanent leasing team by following some simple recommendations.

> **Share information:** Discuss active prospects and details on established nonpermanent tenants performing well enough to be considered as permanent retailers.
>
> **Build relationships:** Meet with the permanent leasing representative on a regular basis and establish an open line of communication.
>
> **Share common goals:** Work on the business-planning process together with the permanent leasing team and set mutual goals relating to incubation and vacancy.
>
> **Ask questions:** Attend permanent leasing meetings and ask questions about potential deals. In addition, learn the "language of leasing."

Respect use clauses, exclusives, and restrictions: As in all non-permanent leases, permanent merchants have a use clause in their lease allowing them to sell specific categories of merchandise. In some cases, they may even have the exclusive right to sell a particular category of merchandise in the property. Specialty leasing representatives should work with permanent leasing so that either such restrictions are eliminated in leases or the loss of revenue to the landlord is made known to the permanent representative. Further, the leases of some in-line retailers may have a restriction against placing kiosks close to their storefront. The specialty leasing representative must be keenly aware of these use clauses, exclusives, and restrictions in order to avoid putting a competing use near a permanent merchant or violating an exclusive or restriction. In addition, the specialty leasing representative should avoid placing an oversized or poorly merchandised specialty retailer in front of an in-line store; this may be considered an eyesore or block visibility and sight lines, creating a conflict with the permanent tenant.

Common Area Space

The flexibility, design, and appearance of the common area unit has improved significantly from the simple pushcart with two large wagon wheels and very little merchandising space to a well-designed, larger, and more efficient unit offering ample room for merchandising and product storage. Different types of common area equipment include the following:

Pushcart: The traditional two-wheeled unit, usually 3 by 6 feet with little storage or merchandising space. This unit is typically no longer used.

Retail merchandising unit (RMU): The contemporary version of a pushcart, the retail merchandising unit utilizes state-of-the-art design and materials to create a durable and functional display on which to showcase the wares or services of the specialty retailer. The RMU is considerably larger than the traditional pushcart and may be square, rectangular, round, or even elliptical. Although the units are still mobile, rolling casters mounted underneath have replaced the large wagon wheels. Many designs incorporate large display areas, ample storage, high-intensity lighting, and state-of-the-art security features. The RMU, like the pushcart, is staffed from the outside.

Kiosk: The word *kiosk,* meaning "temporary structure," was derived from the original Eskimo language. The kiosk is the largest of the common area units and contains open, interior space to house a cash register and sales staff. The merchandise is "wrapped around" the center, usually on shelves or in display cases. While typical kiosk footprints range in size between 10 by 10 feet and 10 by 16 feet, larger and smaller sizes are available.

Wall unit: The wall unit presents an excellent opportunity for the property owner to profit from barricaded stores or otherwise unused wall space. Typically 3 to 4 feet wide by 7 or 8 feet high, wall units may be placed either in front of a wall or recessed into a Sheetrock wall for a cleaner appearance. Two or three of these units are frequently placed next to each other to create a selling area for one retailer. Often incorporating high-intensity lighting, movable shelving, and lockable security shutters, wall units are ideal for merchandising apparel or small gift items.

Custom units: Usually provided by the specialty retailer, custom units come in all shapes and sizes. For example, one apparel company merchandises its clothing in refurbished vans, complete with shelving and lighting. Careful consideration must be given to placement of these units in the center, as they may be more likely to block sight lines or interfere with traffic flow in a tight area.

Deciding what works best for a property is a matter of preference, often tied to budgetary constraints. RMUs and kiosks are available in several different shapes and sizes. They are constructed using a multitude of materials including various types of wood and metal, and each can cost as little as $5,000 or as much as $30,000. When preparing to purchase new equipment for a property, work with the architect to create a color and materials scheme that complements the property, and keep in mind that building a functional unit is as important as appearance.

A specialty leasing representative responsible for purchasing common area equipment may consider the following steps in the purchase process:

- Define needs and create specifications
- Work closely with local building departments in the design stage to secure any approvals
- Bid out the project to several reputable cart fabricators
- Contract with a fabricator to build the equipment
- Build a prototype if a highly customized unit is being contemplated
- Make payment arrangements
- Coordinate delivery, keeping in mind that fabricators frequently send along support staff with the delivery.

In-Line Space

The renting of temporary in-line space is another important element of a successful specialty retail leasing program. During periods when the permanent leasing team is unable to lease a vacancy, it is the specialty leasing representative's responsibility to rent the space to a merchant who complements the property's merchandise mix and adds an interesting element to the center. However, it is important to keep in mind that a specialty retail tenant is not expected to renovate a store as a permanent tenant renovates, because of the short-term nature of the rental deal. The property owner typically improves the space to a minimum standard of appearance and functionality. In doing so, a nonpermanent, in-line store is usually rented with the following finish work complete, at a minimum:

- **Storefront:** Framed glass with hinged glass doors or a grill gate for security
- **Flooring:** A low-grade commercial carpet with center tile to the lease line
- **Ceiling:** A 2-by-4-foot or 2-by-2-foot accoustical lay-in ceiling tile system
- **Lighting:** One 2-by-4-foot or two 2-by-2-foot fluorescent light fixtures with parabolic lenses per 100 square feet of store area, plus supplemental track lighting if needed
- **Columns:** All exposed columns in space wrapped in Sheetrock or other suitable material and finished
- **Walls:** Sheetrock installed, taped, sanded, and painted with vinyl base molding

- **Electricity:** Installation of 120-volt wall outlets every 10 feet along the side and back walls
- **Stockroom:** As space allows, a stockroom should be created with drywall and a hollow core door separating the sales area. Vinyl tile flooring, open ceiling, and fluorescent lighting are acceptable. Install a rear door if required by code.
- **Telephone lines:** Two lines provided to the space
- **Storefront signage:** Electricity should be provided to the storefront to service the future tenant's sign
- **Toilet room:** A rest room per code, compliant with the Americans with Disabilities Act (ADA)
- **Heating, ventilation, and air-conditioning (HVAC), sprinkler system, and exit signs:** As required by code.

In cases where a vacant store space is either unfinished or in too poor a condition to rent as a temporary in-line store, a bump back store may be constructed on the site, in the front portion of the space. In this case, a white box is usually created from the front of the space back 4 to 8 feet. The Sheetrock is painted and a grid ceiling system and lighting are installed, along with carpet and basic electric service. The finished bump back becomes a perfect "ministore" for a nonpermanent tenant.

In either case, every property owner must set individual guidelines and strategies for recovering the costs associated with making an in-line space ready for a nonpermanent tenant. As a general rule of thumb, many property owners require that these costs be recovered through rent in six to twelve months.

In addition, many property owners require nonpermanent in-line tenants to have a lighted sign. Working with an experienced designer, such tenants can create a suitable lighted sign and install it for a moderate amount.

Some nonpermanent tenants prefer in-line space because it gives them the extra room needed to display a large variety of merchandise, resulting in greater sales, and because it offers them on-site storage. The specialty leasing representative must ensure that nonpermanent in-line tenants are capable retailers possessing the merchandising skills, inventory buying power, and business savvy needed to compete next to the many other professional in-line merchants doing business in the center. With that in mind, specialty leasing representatives frequently choose to groom nonpermanent tenants in common area units before offering them the opportunity to move into in-line space with the eventual goal of signing a permanent lease. To help nonpermanent in-line merchants look their best, it is advisable to keep information on hand about local fixture suppliers and visual merchandisers. Collect good-quality used fixtures from stores that have closed.

Types of Specialty Retail Tenants

Specialty retailers fall into three basic categories:

- Those that sell *goods,* such as a jeweler or apparel retailer
- Those that offer a *service,* such as tax preparation or real estate advice
- Those *promoting or advertising* a good or service outside of the center, such as a movie studio, automobile manufacturer, or time share resort.

National, regional, and local prospects commonly seek temporary space in all three categories.

Understanding the Property and Market

Powerful marketing materials, effective promotions, and successful personal selling are the result of significant preparation and a keen understanding of the shopping center, its customers, and the surrounding market. When leasing a property, the specialty leasing representative starts by gathering as much information as possible about the trade area demographics, psychographics, and merchandise voids or weaknesses.

Demographics include vital statistics about the market area such as average income, age, sex, number of children, housing costs, education, and occupation. These statistics are quantifiable and readily obtained from many public and private sources.

Psychographics, on the other hand, are the motivating forces that influence shopping patterns and consumer behavior; in other words, they are the lifestyle choices people make. For example, although two families meet similar demographic profiles, their lifestyles may be completely different. While one family may have a retreat for camping and hiking each weekend, the other may prefer to stay at home gardening, enjoying movies, listening to music, and shopping in the neighborhood. In each case, the families have very different interests and very different shopping patterns. The first family may shop in the evenings during the week for sporting goods and outdoor apparel, while the second family might enjoy a regular trip to the local shopping center on the weekend to browse and purchase home decor items, compact discs, and gardening equipment. Because the psychographics of a trade area are frequently difficult to quantify, they are more challenging to pin down and require time spent in the market exploring residential neighborhoods, entertainment venues, and retail shopping destinations.

After researching the trade area, leasing representatives focus on trends within the center to assist in selling the property to prospective specialty retail tenants. Several factors should be taken into account, including the following:

Distinctive features or services, such as an ice-skating rink or valet parking, help to differentiate the property from its competition.

Marketing events can often tie in with a prospective tenant's product, creating cooperative marketing opportunities. For example, what local toy retailer would not want to be in the property at the same time that an event geared toward children is going on?

Anchor stores can influence a prospective specialty retailer's decision to set up shop in the property and affect its preference on location within the center once it is committed. The specialty retail representative usually makes a point of knowing department store rankings and sales when marketing a center. A specialty retailer selling upscale merchandise, for example, may be more comfortable near a fashion anchor than near a discount department store.

Merchandise mix influences decisions too. For instance, a teen apparel retailer might be interested to know that there are already several very successful stores catering to the same market in the property. In addition, consider the merchandise mix created when placing common area specialty retailers in the property. Avoid placing conflicting uses too close together. In some instances, leasing representatives decide to pass on a conflicting use altogether in an already oversaturated category.

Use clauses of permanent in-line tenants are important in helping to avoid direct product conflicts between permanent retailers and specialty retailers.

Center layout and traffic flow patterns are also important to skilled retailers. Expect questions about traffic flow at the entrance and anchors.

Know the *condition, availability, and value* of every in-line space in the property and be prepared to propose a specific space to prospective tenants based on the size requirements, merchandise category, and budget of each.

Marketing Materials

Prospective tenants should receive a comprehensive marketing package designed to inform them about the property and trade area, as well as to entice them to rent space. It should include some or all of the following:

- A personalized *introduction letter,* which mentions the points discussed during a personal meeting or telephone call, compliments the prospective tenant's business, and points out several key advantages to locating at the property being marketed. (This is a vital step in building the relationship between the specialty leasing representative and the prospective tenant.)
- A brief *demographic and shopper profile summary sheet,* highlighting important demographic information such as trade area population, age, and average household income, as well as area information that communicates the flavor of the community
- A *lease plan,* highlighting space that is available either in the common area or in-line
- A *"Top 10 Reasons to Open Your Business In XYZ Shopping Center"* sheet, which can be a fun and useful selling tool to help the prospective tenant understand and focus on the main selling points of the property
- *Testimonials,* which can be a useful selling tool to help prospec-

tive merchants relate to their peers who have already made the same decision they are contemplating
- *Photographs, line drawings,* and a *rendering* of the common area equipment available at the property
- *Recent news* about property marketing events and tenant success stories
- A *company brochure* listing all of the properties in the portfolio
- A *folder* with the name of the property or company name embossed on the front and a *business card* inside, which makes a nice presentation while serving as a useful place for a prospective tenant to keep information gathered during the research process.

In addition to creating a comprehensive marketing package, the specialty leasing representative should prepare specialty leasing brochures and posters to be used in promoting the specialty retail leasing program within the property and at other venues.

Prospecting for Tenants

One of the most important parts of a specialty leasing representative's job is prospecting for tenants. The continual flow of fresh leads is paramount to the accomplishment of program goals and objectives. While many specialty leasing representatives find a great number of leads come from interested prospects who stop by or call the management or leasing office, this alone is not a sufficient source of leads to accomplish the task of maximizing revenue while creating excitement through innovative and unique merchandising. With that in mind, the specialty leasing representative must canvass, or "hit the streets," in search of leads.

Canvassing is the process of targeting venues and physically visiting them in search of good merchants with desirable merchandise. During the visit, talk to and learn more about those tenants that would be an ideal addition to the property being leased, making sure to get their name, address, and telephone number for followup use after the visit. Some of the many places worth exploring are:

Regional shopping centers: Specialty retailers operate small businesses in almost every shopping center, and these tenants are already versed in nonpermanent leasing and specialty retail. One approach is to visit area shopping centers that have less foot traffic or generate lower sales volumes than the property you are leasing, in hopes of finding good-quality merchants looking to expand or improve their situation.

Power, community, and neighborhood centers: These centers, often referred to as strip centers, can be an excellent source of nonpermanent tenants. Specialty retailers here may be looking to move into the center, or open a second location during the holidays.

Downtowns: Many downtown areas or older business districts are excellent sources of entrepreneurs operating small but successful retail businesses. However, frequently their rents are low with no percentage rent clause, and they may not be used to working the longer hours demanded by a shopping center.

Festival marketplaces and entertainment centers: A variation of the traditional center, a festival marketplace or entertainment center usually lacks significant anchors but incorporates more entertainment and restaurants into a mix of unique specialty shops, often with a local flair.

Flea markets, craft and art shows: Many successful specialty retailers began in these popular venues. In addition, many specialty retailers that operate in shopping centers during the holidays move to these venues during the summer months.

Merchandise mart: The merchandise mart is an excellent place to network about product trends and learn from the wholesalers about specialty retailers in the area that are interested in expanding.

Tourist attractions: These high-traffic destinations often attract the best specialty retail operators. These retailers may be looking for additional locations or may be searching for a place to move their business during the winter months in colder climates.

The ideal outcome of a canvassing trip is the identification of a good specialty retailer selling a great product and interested in renting space. However, the specialty leasing representative should also be on the lookout for hot products in the marketplace that he or she can recommend to a strong retailer already doing business in the property.

In order to excel at the task of canvassing and renting space, specialty leasing representatives must be highly organized and able to keep track of and follow up with prospective tenants. Many accomplish this using computerized lead-tracking software. Recording the name, address, and telephone number of each prospect, along with important information about conversations, correspondence, and follow-up notes, is a vital tool used in closing more deals.

In the specialty leasing business, persistence has its rewards. Good lead-tracking software not only should act like a card file but also should alert its user when it is time to make a follow-up call or schedule a meeting, along with helping to merge contact information into letters and proposals.

In addition to canvassing, there are several strategies to capture the interest of prospective specialty retail tenants. These strategies include:

Advertisements in local newspapers: There are three basic types of newspaper advertising to consider. Run a classified advertisement in the business opportunity section of the paper, place a display ad in the business or money section of the local newspaper, or run an advertorial in the business section. An advertorial is an editorial-type article paid for by the property owner that may spotlight the property's specialty leasing program or a particular nonpermanent merchant. Of the three, an advertorial can be an especially effective vehicle for attracting prospective specialty retailers, because it allows the writer to tell a more complete story than a simple advertisement can, providing the reader with contact information at the end for those interested in opening a retail business.

Publicity/public relations: There is no less expensive form of advertising. The specialty leasing representative should send the local newspaper business editor a press release announcing each new tenant. In addition, periodically send out a release announcing special offers or highlighting the success of a particular specialty retailer. A good press release should include a newsworthy human-interest spin.

In-mall signage: Often overlooked, in-mall signage is an effective strategy to generate interest from shoppers already in the center who envision themselves running a successful business there. This medium usually results in many walk-in inquiries. Mall signage is also a great way to promote owner-operator programs offered through one of the many successful national specialty retailers.

Retail opportunity day: Creating and hosting a half-day seminar about the business of specialty retailing for people interested in operating their own business is often an effective means of generating leads. Invite the center management staff, a local banker, a representative from the Small Business Administration (SBA) and Service Core of Retired Executives (SCORE), as well as representatives from various national specialty retailers offering owner-operator programs. Arrange to have these representatives and experts speak to the audience about running a retail business, the realities of specialty leasing, financing, business planning, and marketing. Encourage attendance by creating a personalized mailer sent to area retailers and to those who have inquired about leasing space in the past, run display advertisements in the local newspapers weeks before, send out press releases announcing the event, and mail invitations to specific target households in the property's trade area.

Direct mail: Create and mail a package two to three times a year to prospective specialty retail tenants offering a special deal for renting space. For example, the special offer might include a free sign or free rent with a signed contract.

Phone book: The telephone book is an excellent resource for service business or promotional prospects. Using the yellow pages, identify strong prospects and contact them by telephone. Follow up with a marketing package or personal visit if interest is established.

Current tenants: Basic business principles dictate that it is easier to keep a current customer than it is to attract a new customer. Target strong tenants currently in the property being leased with the goal of helping them to expand into selling a new product from an additional RMU or store. When permanent in-line tenants rent temporary space it is often called "outposting." Also, offer current tenants a referral fee for bringing in new specialty retail tenants. For example, try offering two weeks' free rent for each referral that signs a new license agreement with a duration of three or more months.

Past tenants: Periodically communicate, either by mail or telephone, with past merchants. If they usually return during a certain time of the year, contact them early, giving them the opportunity to return again.

Networking: Specialty leasing representatives are salespeople and should network with other professionals in the community and in the specialty leasing industry with the objective of recruiting new merchants.

ICSC events: Attendance at regional and national ICSC events offers unique opportunities to specialty leasing representatives. These venues are occasions to network and meet prospective merchants and industry professionals.

Industry publications: Read industry publications often to learn about new retailers and product or equipment trends.

License Agreement

Although some property owners use a modified version of the traditional lease, the license agreement is the vehicle most often used to document a specialty leasing arrangement. In many states, a lease gives the licensor (or merchant) certain property rights that can make it difficult to move or evict them. On the other hand, a license agreement is simply a space rental agreement containing no real property rights and allowing for the quick relocation or removal of the licensor or merchant. Therefore, the license agreement provides the property owner with greater control over the common area. A word of caution, however: In many states, a license agreement with a duration greater than one year is considered a lease under the law.

Some important points to consider in negotiating and preparing a license agreement:

Term: The term may vary from one day to one year. In the case of a property with low traffic or sales, make every effort to lock the merchant into a one-year agreement if appropriate. On the other hand, if the property is a strong one with high traffic and sales, try to limit the merchant to a month-to-month agreement, providing the flexibility to improve both license fees and merchandise mix at a quicker pace.

Use clause: The use clause should detail the various product categories that the licensor will be allowed to sell from the space. It is important to be specific to avoid conflicts with permanent tenants or exclusives contained in other leases. An example of a poor use clause for a jewelry merchant is "the retail sales of jewelry, gift items, and related merchandise." Clearly this use clause is very open-ended, giving the merchant too much leeway to carry just about anything. After all, what does not qualify as a "gift item"? A better use clause is "the retail sales of 10-karat and 14k gold and silver rings, earrings, necklaces, bracelets, and pendants; gold by the inch; watches with a retail value not to exceed $100.00; the on-site repair of jewelry and the sale and replacement of watch batteries only." In this case, the boundaries are very clearly defined.

License fee: This is the base fee, not counting triple net charges (such as common area maintenance, or CAM, taxes, insurance, and marketing), expressed as a daily, weekly, monthly, or yearly figure. In the case of a percentage fee in lieu of a license fee only, this section defines the percentage of gross sales that the licensor will pay each month.

Percentage fee: This section details the agreed-on percent rate and the sales breakpoint at which the licensor begins paying a percentage of sales above and beyond the license fee. The breakpoint may be either natural, in which the breakpoint is calculated by dividing the license fee by the specified percentage, or unnatural, in which the breakpoint is set at an arbitrary figure.

Ancillary charges: Sometimes referred to as triple net or side charges, this section defines additional fees to offset CAM, real estate taxes, insurance, and marketing fund contribution. Ancillary charges may also include a charge for security, trash removal, or any other charge that the property owner chooses to pass on to the licensor. In the case of a temporary license agreement, some property owners choose to include ancillary charges in the license fee or list them as one charge, for the sake of simplicity, rather than break each one out separately.

Right to relocate or terminate: It is customary for a license agreement to provide the property owner, but not the licensor, with a right to relocate or terminate the licensor at any time with proper notice. In many cases, the notice period is 5 days; however; it can range from 24 hours to 60 days or longer. The right to relocate or terminate is an important tool to avoid potential common area conflicts with in-line merchants or to take back an in-line space quickly in the event it is leased to a permanent tenant.

Rules and regulations: This section spells out the rules and regulations that each licensor is expected to follow. It is important that the license agreement be clear and concise in detailing those issues vital to the safe and secure operation of the property.

Late fees and fines: This section details the charges and fees that the licensor will be assessed for late payment of a rent obligation and for a violation of the rules and regulations.

Default provisions: This section defines the consequences for a breach or default of one or more of the license terms.

The typical license agreement usually contains many more sections and a lot of legal language, all of which the specialty leasing representative should be expected to understand completely. It is advisable to sit down with legal counsel or an experienced specialty leasing professional to discuss each of the sections in greater detail. In addition, the specialty leasing representative should be aware that even the slightest alteration to the basic document that the attorneys have prepared might have a substantial impact in the event of a casualty, default, or lawsuit. Therefore, it is best to stick to one agreement that works and not change it. If a change must be made, get legal advice on any possible effects that the change may have.

Structuring the Economic Deal

Profit is the major motivating factor influencing a retailer's choice to open or expand a business. In structuring a rent package, focus on an economic arrangement that allows the merchant to make an acceptable profit based on projected sales while taking into account total occupancy costs. Occupancy costs are the total of all charges the tenant pays to the property owner.

The proper rent structure can make or break a deal. The creative specialty leasing person has many different options available to help structure the best deal for both the property owner and the merchant.

While it is typical to have a base rent with a fixed percentage of sales payable over a natural or unnatural breakpoint plus ancillary charges, this is not always attainable. Closing a deal may require a more creative approach. In closing the deal, consider these different types of rent structures:

Triple net deal: In a triple net deal, the tenant is required to pay a base minimum rent at specified intervals, along with ancillary charges such as CAM, real estate taxes, insurance, and marketing fund contribution. The tenant is often also required to pay a percentage of gross sales over a specified breakpoint.

Gross rent: In a gross rent deal, the tenant pays one rent payment, which includes all fixed and variable costs such as CAM, real estate taxes, insurance, and marketing fund. A gross deal may have a percentage rent factor with a natural or unnatural breakpoint, or may have no percentage rent due at all.

Modified gross rent: Very much like a gross rent deal, a modified gross rent deal requires the tenant to pay a portion of the ancillary, or variable, charges. In many cases the tenant does so by paying one fixed ancillary fee in addition to base minimum rent. This is a popular structure in use by property owners.

Percentage rent only: In this deal structure, the tenant pays no base rent. Instead, the tenant agrees to pay a fixed percentage of gross sales as rent. In many cases, the property owner may require a higher percentage of sales than they might if the tenant were paying a minimum rent plus percentage. For example, in a traditional triple net deal, the percentage factor for a temporary tenant might be 10 percent over a natural breakpoint. If the deal is a percentage rent only deal, the property owner may require the tenant to pay 15 percent of gross sales as rent. In that case, the property owner is rewarded for taking a chance on a tenant with no guarantee of minimum rent.

Stepped rent: In a stepped rent structure, the tenant starts with a lower base rent at the beginning of the term to help offset the costs of opening, and then the base rent climbs, or steps up, at various intervals in the lease. This is more common with in-line nonpermanent tenants in one-year agreements that have added costs for repairing, updating, or fixturing a store. For example, the tenant may start the term with a base rent of $1,000 per month for the first three months, after which the rent "steps up" to $2,000 per month for the remainder of the term.

Stepped-down percentage: In this economic arrangement, in addition to the base rent, the tenant pays a percentage of sales, which changes at specified sales volumes. For example, the tenant may pay the greater of $2,000 per month or 15 percent of the first $15,000 in sales per month, 12 percent of the next $10,000 in sales per month, and 10 percent of all sales above $25,000 per month. If the tenant's sales were $30,000, the total rent for the month would be $3,950.

In structuring the best economic deal for both parties, it is important to understand occupancy costs as they relate to the tenant's business. Occupancy costs, or the total of all charges the tenant pays to the property owner, must be set at a fair level to allow the retailer to purchase inventory, pay a sales staff, and make an acceptable profit at the end of the day. The higher the costs of goods and staffing, the lower the acceptable occupancy costs. For example, a clothing retailer with a 50 percent margin may be able to afford a 15 percent occupancy cost while a food service operator with a 75 percent margin may be able to afford a 25 percent occupancy cost. As a general rule, based on the strength of the center and the margins inherent in their product, nonpermanent tenants can usually afford a total occupancy cost of between 12 and 25 percent.

Closing the Deal

When negotiating and closing a deal, the specialty leasing representative should take a long-term approach, expecting to have a business relationship with the prospective tenant for years to come.

While the intent of this chapter focuses on overall specialty retail leasing rather than on negotiating or closing a deal, following are a few tips to jump-start the negotiations and help convince the prospective tenant to sign a license agreement.

First, learn the prospective tenants' business and motivations. A basic understanding of the business and what motivates the tenant is key to building a relationship in which each party respects and trust the other, which in turn is key to closing a deal.

Second, paint a picture. In other words, help the prospect envision himself or herself as a tenant in the property operating a profitable business. The prospect must want to be in the property before a deal can ever be closed.

Then, structure a deal. Discuss projected sales volumes, inventory costs, and profit expectations in order to arrive at an economic proposal. Briefly discuss the feasibility of the terms with the tenant and, after all objections have been overcome, follow up with a written proposal. A written proposal to a prospective tenant should always include a disclaimer that clearly states that it is a proposal only and that the deal is not binding until both parties have executed the required documents.

Next, follow up with the prospect and discuss the proposal. Get any final objections out in the open and resolve them before moving to final negotiation of the economic terms.

Finally, ask for the deal. Closing a deal requires asking for the deal. After all objections have been resolved and a price has been settled, close the deal by asking the prospect to affirm the agreed-to terms and conditions. One way to close the deal is to ask a question like "Shall I send you the license agreement for your signature or would you like to stop by my office to sign it?" This question assumes a deal exists, and it leads the prospect into closure.

When negotiating, in many instances it is better to throw something in rather than bargain down the rent. Some forms of incentive that work particularly well in temporary leasing include:

Free rent: As an incentive to sign a one-year agreement or open earlier than planned, offer the prospective tenant one month's free rent. It is ideal to tack this free month on to the end of the agreement rather than the beginning.

Tenant allowance: When renting an in-line space that requires some capital improvement, offer the tenant an allowance, preferably in the form of free rent, to help offset the cost of improvements. Another way to approach this is to offer to have the owner's contractor make the improvements on the tenant's behalf. Whenever offering a tenant allowance, make sure to recover it through minimum rent with an acceptable return on investment in accordance with the standards set by the property owner.

Reduced rent: In exchange for a longer-term agreement, offer the tenant a reduced rent during the slow periods in return for full rent during the busy holiday periods. Try getting a slightly higher percentage factor in return for the reduced rent. This incentive can work particularly well if the tenant ends up posting strong sales.

Free sign: When negotiating an in-line license agreement, try offering a free sign, or a sign credit of up to $500, as an incentive to enter into an agreement with a longer term, or in lieu of negotiating down the base rent.

Visual assistance: Offer three hours of free visual merchandising assistance from management's visual merchandiser to close the deal. It's an inexpensive bonus that the retailer will appreciate, and the property will benefit from getting a well-merchandised tenant.

Percentage only: To keep the common area program full after the Christmas holiday, offer tenants a percentage in lieu of minimum rent for January if they agree to stay through January at the time they sign their license agreement.

Administration

Administration of the specialty retail leasing program is another of the many responsibilities assumed by the specialty leasing representative. Some of the administrative items that must be addressed on a day-to-day basis may include, but are not limited to, the following:

- Budgeting and business planning
- Billing and collection of accounts receivable
- Preparing license agreements and license agreement summaries
- Monitoring retailers and enforcing program rules
- New tenant orientation
- Maintaining tenant insurance certificates
- Recording tenant sales weekly or monthly
- Preparing reports for distribution to management
- Interacting with staff at all levels.

Common Expectations

Once the temporary rental agreement is signed by both parties and the specialty retailer opens for business, the specialty leasing representative has the right to expect certain things from the tenant, including a high-quality operation, attractive visual merchandising, well-trained sales staff, adherence to the license agreement, and cooperation.

At the same time, the specialty retailer has every right to expect effective property management, effective marketing and sales promotion, a strong merchandise mix, a clean and well-maintained facility, and cooperation.

Identifying and Working with Problem Tenants

An important part of the specialty leasing person's job is to recognize problem tenants as early as possible. By doing so, the leasing representative can take action to save the tenant by helping to correct the problem. Some of the warning signs of a poorly performing nonpermanent merchant include:

- Inadequate or poorly trained staff
- Low sales volume or a high rent-to-sales ratio
- Delinquent rent payments
- Inadequate inventory levels or poor merchandise selection.

Incubation

In the early 1990s, many traditional in-line retailers consolidated or entered bankruptcy, leaving growing vacancies in shopping centers. At the same time, specialty retail leasing was evolving and growing at a rapid pace. Many people in the industry believed that the evolution of nonpermanent tenants into permanent ones was the answer to rising vacancy problems. Although specialty retail leasing did not turn out to be the answer to all in-line vacancy problems, the specialty retail leasing industry evolved into a multimillion-dollar part of nearly every property owner's business.

The reality is that the majority of specialty retail tenants are temporary. Many plan on operating just for a holiday season, while others sell products that have great impulse demand during one time of the year or another but could never prove profitable year-round in an in-line store. In addition, with minimal entry barriers such as low rent and inventory requirements, as well as a short-term commitment, specialty retail leasing does not always attract retailers skilled enough to become successful permanent tenants. Still, incubation, or the process of developing a specialty retail tenant into a permanent one, is often a worthwhile pursuit that can generate permanent in-line lease deals as long as expectations are reasonable. An attainable goal in many centers includes incubating one or two specialty retailers a year into permanent merchants.

With so many specialty retail tenants and so little time, it is important to focus efforts on only those candidates that truly display the traits of a successful retailer. Ideal candidates for permanent tenancy should be outgoing and dedicated to training their sales staff, skilled at purchasing merchandise that is in demand, constantly striving to re-create themselves, and displaying excellent visual merchandising skills. Finally, they must have sufficient capital to grow the business.

Candidates that possess all of these attributes should be considered for inclusion in an incubation program consisting of the following elements:

Goal assessment: In a personal meeting with the retailer, discuss and set a specific goal for sales volumes and target a specific time frame in which the transition from nonpermanent to permanent tenant will be made. Frequently, that time frame is between one and three years.

Rent escalation program: In order to make the transition from nonpermanent to permanent a smooth one financially, the tenant's rent should increase as sales increase, maintaining a total occupancy charge equivalent to that of any other retailer in the same category. In the first couple of months, it is a good idea to introduce the concept of side charges as well. For example, start charging 25 percent of the actual triple net charges at the outset of the program and gradually increase them by one-quarter every three months until the tenant is used to paying full side charges.

Marketing plan assistance: Each new specialty retail tenant should be given the opportunity to meet with the property's marketing director to review the tenant's individual marketing plan as well as opportunities to get involved with property-sponsored marketing programs. Tenants that are being targeted as an incubation candidate should receive quarterly marketing reviews in which the tenant's marketing strategy can be refined as its business grows. The inclusion of specialty retail tenants targeted for incubation into the center's regular marketing plan is key to their long-term success.

Visual merchandising assistance: Many properties today employ full-time visual merchandising personnel to assist specialty retail tenants in merchandising their store or common area unit. Proper direction on presentation, display, and the use of signage can set a tenant apart, paving the way toward retail success.

Business planning assistance: Almost every successful businessperson will admit that to be successful, an entrepreneur needs a good business plan that serves as the road map to reaching desired goals. The same holds true for a specialty retail tenant with aspirations of becoming a permanent merchant. Either the specialty leasing person or the marketing person should have training in preparing a basic business plan and should communicate that knowledge to those tenants that are candidates for incubation. Every incubation tenant should receive a package with sample business plans and outlines and be required to submit a business plan as a condition of its ongoing tenancy. The specialty leasing person should also take that opportunity to discuss the realities of becoming a permanent tenant, addressing such issues as rents, terms, use clauses, store design requirements, capital investment, and general lease language.

Conclusion

Specialty retail leasing is an exciting and challenging segment of the shopping center business. The specialty leasing representative is a vital member of the management and leasing team, making a positive contribution to the property's merchandise mix and income.

Frederick J. Delibero, CLS, is Senior Manager, Retail Leasing at Copaken, White & Blitt, Leawood, Kansas.

14 | Peripheral Land

Richard T. Parker

Will Rogers once said, "Making money in real estate is easy. All you have to do is find the piece of property you want and buy it; then, when the price goes up, you sell it. If the price doesn't go up, then don't buy it." Wouldn't it be nice if this were the way it worked.

Actually, the business of peripheral land does work almost exactly this way. Developers buy land, and when the price goes up, they realize the value through a sale or lease. The difference, of course, is that it is what the developer does (action that carries risk associated with it) that should cause the value to rise. It is precisely this opportunity, created mostly by a developer's project with its associated development activity, that is the subject of this chapter.

Creating value through peripheral land sales and leasing took on a sense of renewed, almost profound importance to developers during the late 1980s, when project financing was disappearing at the same time that raw land costs were appreciating to very high levels. Separate departments at many major development companies sprang up almost overnight; at the start of the new century, however, the bulk of peripheral responsibility is still handled by individual project leasing personnel.

This chapter will examine the different types of peripheral land and the range of deal structures most commonly used. A comprehensive section outlines the basic elements of the peripheral land business, along with a discussion of the most important skill necessary for success in the sale and leasing of peripheral land: balancing the needs of those competing interests inherent in all projects of substance—the developer, the project anchor tenant(s), the community, and, last but not least, the outparcel tenant. At the end of the chapter is a series of illustrations of these competing interests, which should make the nature of the differing perspectives on a peripheral parcel obvious. Be sure to read the notes accompanying each illustration carefully. You will be introduced, perhaps for the first time, to a few technical terms frequently used when performing activities related to peripheral land. An attempt has been made throughout the discussions to balance the perspectives of both the developer and the tenant.

Making land transactions happen is the way in which many people make their living. Therefore, the chapter deals with a variety of matters essential to ensuring timely completion of these transactions, such as understanding the scope of necessary information and the proper documentation of a deal. Additionally, there are deal summary forms for both a land lease and a land sale transaction. While not intended to be comprehensive, these might function as a checklist for your negotiations and deal processing. Finally, refer to the Glossary at the end of the book for definitions of all terms used in this chapter.

Note that the terms *developer, seller,* and *landlord* are used interchangeably, as are the terms *purchaser, tenant,* and *end user.* This chapter is not meant to provide precise definitive answers to all related questions but rather to be an informational guide to what the peripheral land business is all about. It is hoped that this will help to develop your passion for this business.

What Is Peripheral Land?

A great shopping center location will usually produce terrific opportunities for substantial peripheral land development. The nature and extent of these opportunities are a direct function of the size and type of development being contemplated. All shopping center developments have several land components, which generally break down as follows:

> **Shopping Center Parcel:** This includes the shopping center building area, its associated parking, and any anchor or anchor parcels included within the shopping center building area.

Non-Income Parcels: These include the project roads, landscape buffers, storm water retention areas, project wetlands, conservation easement areas, and any other non-income-generating land components of the overall project.

Peripheral Land: This component generally includes the following:

1. Pad Sites: This usually refers to the land area occupied by freestanding uses situated in the parking lots of either enclosed malls or other types of shopping centers. It sometimes includes the land for the parking area (and other needs) required by the freestanding use, but normally the parking and other needs for a pad site are accommodated through a reciprocal easement agreement (REA), which provides for the use of the shopping center parcel by the pad site user's customers.

2. Outparcel: This typically refers to the entire parcel required to support a freestanding use adjacent to the shopping center development. This includes the land area necessary for the building, parking, building setback area, landscape buffers, and in many cases the on-site storm water retention area.

3. Residual Land: As the name implies, this usually applies to the land that is left over and adjacent to the shopping center development. It is typically subdivided into what then becomes the outparcels for the center. It is common for developers on major projects to purchase other residual land parcels not immediately adjacent to their intended development for future development or sale.

With respect to the different components within the definition of peripheral land, this chapter will focus primarily on pad sites and outparcels, and the factors that affect their development, sale, and leasing.

Peripheral Sales and Leasing Objectives

There are numerous reasons developers and landlords include outparcels and pad sites within their developments. Some of these reasons are:

- To extract the value created by the overall shopping center development from the adjacent property
- To enhance the shopping center merchandising mix with tenants that typically would not locate inside the shopping center and that would also contribute to the needs of the center's customers
- To generate income to accomplish one or more of the following:
  1. The sale of outparcels might be used to generate funds necessary to advance the rest of the project, such as paying for the installation of utilities, road work, or other development-related costs.
  2. The sales or leasing commitments on outparcels might be included as part of the requirements for obtaining financing to develop the overall project.
  3. Funds from the sale of all outparcel or residual land may be used to meet other corporate or company expenses; for example, in small companies it is not uncommon to use real estate proceeds to pay employees.
  4. Outparcel value creation may also be used to reward ownership for the risks involved with undertaking the shopping center development.

Often the developer is striving to achieve one or more of the above objectives, and in some cases all of them. The good news is that a well-planned project with a focused marketing program has the potential to do just that.

Balancing Competing Interests

Those readers who have been in the shopping center leasing arena for any length of time know that landlords and tenants sometimes have different ideas and opinions about each other's capabilities and what the role of each should be. These can become crystal clear when you examine the needs of the developer and what the peripheral land user typically considers when locating and selecting an outparcel for its use. Many communities have stringent zoning design and development controls, which can also have an impact, and there are also the needs of anchor tenants—the main reason most shopping centers ever get developed.

Creating a successful balance in satisfying these competing interests can determine the success or failure of any peripheral land effort and the professionals responsible for it. The illustrations at the end of the chapter indicate the likely results if each of these interested parties could have it all its own way. Remember that unless the needs of each party are met, it is unlikely that a peripheral land transaction will ever occur.

Basic Elements of the Peripheral Land Business

Understanding these key elements is required to deal successfully with land sale and lease transactions for outparcels and pad sites:

- Peripheral land use categories
- Shopping center and development categories
- Predevelopment planning
- Market and competitor knowledge
- Location and trade area demographics
- Parcel and site characteristics
- Valuation and pricing
- Deal and transaction types
- Developer and end user financing considerations
- Budgets and costs
- The deal process.

It is important and necessary to be well versed in all of these factors affecting the transaction in order to achieve the desired results.

PERIPHERAL LAND USE CATEGORIES

There are an unlimited number of uses to consider for any given land inventory. However, they generally fall into one of the following categories, depending on the parcel and the trade area characteristics of the location:

1. Restaurant: fast food, casual theme, family restaurant, and so on
2. Automotive: full or self-serve gasoline, repair, retail parts, new and used car dealerships, rental cars, and so on
3. Financial: bank, drive-through, automated teller machines, credit unions

4. Freestanding retail: small, midsize, and big box retail
5. Health: fitness club, medical office, urgent care, assisted living, and so on
6. Entertainment: movie theaters, bowling, miniature golf, and so on
7. Strip shopping center: community through power centers
8. Lodging: economy, midprice, full service
9. Office: single, multilevel
10. Miscellaneous:
    - Government, such as library or fire station
    - Churches and other places of worship
    - Single-family and multifamily residential developments
    - Public utility uses, such as telephone switching stations.

When considering a pad site, outparcel, or residual land parcel for sale or lease, basic market research is necessary to determine which of the above is the highest and best use. Each use category has very specific requirements and opportunities in one or more of the following areas:

- Parcel size
- Parking space requirement
- Building height
- Competitive presence
- Sign sizes
- Visibility and access
- Economics and affordability
- Zoning requirements.

It is important to evaluate and understand how each of the above items relates to the use categories. This will improve the likelihood of concluding a deal at the optimum price with the most appropriate user. It is easy to invest a significant amount of time attempting to develop an outparcel or pad site for the use that you may desire rather than one that the market suggests is the appropriate use. Many developers attempt to practice what could be called land use by proclamation, and several are very successful at it; however, that is still the provenance of municipal governments, and it is a good idea instead to read the clear signals from the marketplace.

SHOPPING CENTER OR PROJECT DEVELOPMENT TYPES
The demand for outparcels and pad sites has a considerable amount to do with the specific type of shopping center development with

which they are associated. Large regional and super-regional centers are generally preferred by national chains of all types over smaller community centers. Outparcels with frontage on a main thoroughfare are generally chosen over those sites that face internal ring roads. In the final analysis, it is the physical quality of the site (access, visibility, parking, and so on) and the strength of the trade area and traffic flow that will influence the final location decision.

PREDEVELOPMENT PLANNING

If the shopping center is a new project, it is critical to be as involved in the predevelopment planning of the outparcel land area configuration and all other aspects of the peripheral program as your development organization permits. This will help ensure that those things affecting the developer, the outparcel user, the anchor tenant, and the municipality are all considered by each of the affected parties. In this way, the specific needs of each may be addressed early enough in the project to ensure a balance among all the factors. This will include very lively discussions (and, hopefully, productive planning decisions) about such items as the outparcel sale and leasing pro forma and schedule, building size and height objectives, permitted signage, proposed use restrictions, cross easement parking and/or access, outparcel design requirements, reciprocal easement agreement (REAs), the condition of the land parcels (utility extensions, grading, curving, sidewalks, fire hydrants, street lighting, project landscaping on peripheral land, project signs on peripheral land, and so on), recoveries for the developer's work, common area maintenance programs, and marketing funds. Addressing these issues in the beginning is almost always the most painful part of the process, but it will result in a top-quality peripheral program of parcels that are usable, valuable, and in demand.

MARKET AND COMPETITOR KNOWLEDGE

Leasing and selling outparcels and pad sites are similar to the process used for in-line space; however, there is a more limited supply of prospects, and the nature of the transaction behaves more like an anchor or major tenant deal. An outparcel sale typically requires a larger financial commitment, and it is certainly a more permanent transaction than a lease. In that regard, to be effective, a thorough analysis of the competition for the product is essential. You need to know as much about any available competitive sites as your own, to make a credible presentation to a potential end user possible. This includes a survey of all similarly situated projects, based on your shopping center type.

The physical survey of the trade areas surrounding the major shopping center developments in a given market will provide you with a comprehensive list of the national and regional outparcel users present in that market. The local brokerage community is an excellent source of information on items affecting the trade area where your peripheral land is located. If you are not located in the same market where your inventory is, a subscription to the local business press will help you stay informed. There is no substitute for knowing your competition for those potential users and the pricing patterns that are occurring in your market.

LOCATION AND TRADE AREA DEMOGRAPHICS

To market the site effectively, you need to have the following information readily available, complete, and updated on a regular basis:

- Trade area population, median household income, and education levels in the one-, three-, five-, and seven-mile radii surrounding the location
- Traffic counts on frontage streets and shopping center project roads, both existing and projected
- Total amount of office square footage in the trade area
- Total number of daytime employees in the trade area
- The major employers in the trade area and their economic status
- Sales productivity at the shopping center in dollars per square foot, and the trend in or projected productivity for new centers
- Annual customer counts at the center or projected counts for new centers
- Availability, cost, and time required to obtain alcoholic beverage permits.

In addition to pricing, timing, and the status of the shopping center development, these will be the major factors an outparcel user will review in making the location decision. Full awareness and understanding of all of these criteria are important to completing a land transaction.

PARCEL AND SITE CHARACTERISTICS

The physical condition of the property and development constraints will affect not only the value of a given parcel but also the lease or purchase decision and the timing of the completion of the transaction. Information should be readily available on all of the following:

- Parcel size and dimensions
- Grading (is the property level and has the soil been "compacted"?)
- Storm water management (on-site retention or off-site underground system discharge)
- Utilities (location of the nearest point of connection to electric, water, sanitary sewer, natural gas, telephone, cable, and any other available utilities)
- Access to public streets, to shopping center project roads and parking, and to adjacent outparcels
- Building and parking setbacks (front, rear, and side yard)
- Environmental condition (has a Phase I study been completed?)
- Soil condition (are soil-boring logs available?)
- Zoning classification and permitted uses
- Parking code requirements by use
- Surveys (boundary and topographical)
- Legal description
- Subdivision status (is a plan of subdivision available?)
- Signs: What signage is permitted or required; for example, are the outparcel's signs individual or shared, and are they to be pylon (pole mounted) or monument (ground mounted)? How many building signs are permitted, and what is the maximum size?
- Building height: Are there view corridor restrictions that control the placement of the building? Is there a conceptual site plan (plot plan) available that depicts the building area and/or view corridor restrictions?
- Recorded or proposed deed restrictions
- Easements affecting the use of the property, including, among others, access, utility, maintenance, signage, and conservation
- Design or development constraints or criteria by the landlord or seller
- Landscape requirements.

Thorough knowledge of the above information and complete disclosure at the appropriate time to the proposed purchaser or tenant will help ensure that the tenant's project will work on a parcel that has been proposed. All of these items go into both the feasibility and the evaluation analysis completed by the tenant or purchaser, and therefore they should be made available in a timely and orderly fashion.

VALUATION AND PRICING

Price and value often get confused in the peripheral land business. When it is time to determine a pricing structure, homework is the most important element. Professional appraisals, recent comparative land sale prices, awareness of market transactions, knowledge of what specific use occupancy cost factors are, and, of course, the required returns for the project are all factors to be considered. As simple as it sounds, good sites are better than bad sites and will price higher. Many buyers have repeated the mantra that they could surely pay too much for a good site but never too little for a bad one. Be very careful on pricing and you will help to ensure occupied land at optimum values.

DEAL AND TRANSACTION TYPES

Most peripheral transactions fall into one of four transaction types: land lease, land sale, build to suit lease, and contribution lease.

Land Lease Also referred to as a ground lease, this is a favorite structure of real estate investment trusts (REITs), due to the rental income potential versus the onetime gain of a sale. The tenant may lease a parcel to accommodate both its building and parking, or only its building. The latter case is generally known as a pad lease, and parking is normally provided for by cross-easement parking agreements. The tenant is generally responsible for maintenance, taxes, and insurance, and in many cases will contribute to shopping center exterior common area costs and marketing funds. Landlords will not normally pledge their ownership interest in the land to a tenant's construction lender, so most land leases are referred to as unsubordinated. The length of term varies but normally is equal to or greater than the term of the tenant's financing or franchise agreement, if applicable. Base rents are typically computed as a percentage of the value of the land. For example, a $1,000,000 parcel would command a $100,000 annual rent based upon a required annual return of 10 percent to the landlord.

The rent will reflect not only the value of the location but also the physical condition of the land (zoning, grading, utilities, and so on). The total length of any renewal or extension option terms generally will not exceed the amount of the primary term. Most landlords require increases in base rents during the term, usually based on the change in the consumer price index (CPI), and percentage rents based on annual sales. Land lease percentage rents are normally computed as a percentage of sales applied to annual sales in excess of all sales over the minimum base rent, divided by the percentage rent factor (the natural sales break point). For example, if the base rent is $100,000, and if the percentage rent factor is 3 percent of sales over the natural sales break point, then the natural sales break point equals $3,333,000 in annual sales ($100,000/.03). In the above example, the tenant would pay 3 percent of sales for all sales that occur beyond $3.333 million annually.

Land Sale In this case, the end user purchases a parcel suitable for its planned use, including required parking. In major developments, land use is highly controlled by sellers, and a peripheral land sale often operates very much like a land lease, in which the rent is paid once, in the beginning, at the closing on the purchase of the parcel. That is, through deed restrictions, sellers may highly control use, design, alterations, operating covenants, maintenance, access, resale, and other owners' rights. This level of control often ensures a high-quality development. The documents used to put into effect this control are recorded as encumbrances on title, and known under a variety of terms, such as:

- CC&Rs: conditions, covenants, and restrictions
- COREAs: construction, operation, and reciprocal easement agreements
- ECRs: easements, covenants, and restrictions
- REAs: reciprocal easement agreements
- Deed restrictions
- Declarations of restrictions
- Master declaration of easements, covenants, conditions, and restrictions.

You will see one or more of these terms on most projects, and certainly on any shopping center-based peripheral development parcel.

Build to Suit Lease In a BTS situation, the landlord prepares the land and builds the tenant's building according to plans that the tenant provides. The tenant is normally responsible for costs that exceed the budget used to compute the agreed-on rent. For example, retailer X signs a build to suit lease with developer Y that provides for a building construction cost of $400,000 at a rent of Z dollars. If the actual costs exceed this amount, the rent will be increased or the tenant will make a direct contribution to cover the difference. It is common for new retailers on major system rollouts, especially theme restaurants, mall anchor stores, and power center and community center anchor stores, to develop using this method.

Contribution Lease This is basically a hybrid of the land lease and the build to suit lease. In this case, the landlord agrees to provide both the land and a contribution toward the construction cost of the building and site improvements. The tenant is responsible to develop the improvements according to plans agreed to by each party and approved by the landlord. Funds are advanced by the landlord according to a construction milestone completion schedule, sometimes referred to as a draw schedule. Annual rent is computed based on the value of the land plus the contribution; for example, if the landlord requires a 12 percent return, the land is valued at $300,000, and the contribution for the building is $500,000, then the base annual rent required would be $96,000 (12% × $800,000 [$300,000 + $500,000]). This type of lease is often used when the retailer is better able to provide the construction function, such as with a highly specialized building. This is common in recent years with the development of stadium-seating megaplex theater projects.

DEVELOPER AND END USER FINANCING CONSIDERATIONS

Unlike the routine analysis and evaluation of a proposed tenant's financial condition and capability for in-line lease space, there are major financing factors facing buyers and tenants of outparcels, pad sites, and residual land parcels. These items require consideration when structuring any type of transaction.

For sellers and landlords, these items include:

- Lender's approval to sell or lease
- Mortgage release price of parcel to be sold
- Impact on the REIT status of a sale
- Tax consequences of the transaction type
- Source of any funds required to complete the transaction (for example, construction funds on both sides)

- Rights of buyer or tenant's lender if the buyer or tenant defaults on mortgage or lease.

For purchasers and tenants, these items include:

- Lender's acceptance of deed restrictions
- Timing of funds and ability to comply with the purchase or lease agreement terms
- Appraised value versus contract price or rents
- Lender's rights if the borrower defaults.

It is important to understand the concerns of the various lenders involved on either side of these transactions in order to ensure the ability to structure a deal that gets completed successfully.

BUDGETS AND COSTS

As with almost any project or sale opportunity, essential budget and cost considerations need first to be forecasted and then considered according to several cost factors.

Sale and Lease Forecasting How much and when? These two questions are what really matters to buyers and sellers in any typical peripheral land transaction. Budgeting land transactions to answer these questions is at best an educated guess. However, there are some helpful things to remember that generally hold true and will assist with a realistic forecast.

1. New project land will move sooner and at a higher value than existing inventory.
2. It will usually take anywhere from six months to a year to complete a transaction from the time an interested party is identified.
3. Budgeted prices are only targets and have limited impact on what may be the reality of the value of a site in the marketplace when a deal is negotiated, which might easily be much higher—or lower.
4. A thorough understanding of the location, its market, the competition, and the most likely highest and best use is important to produce reliable sales and leasing budgets.

Costs and Expenses A variety of cost factors, some that may apply to all types of land deals and others that are site or deal specific, need to be considered and included in the budget and financial analysis phase.

1. Site-Related Costs: First, look at a list of typical cost items that are related to the condition of the property. The question is, who is expected to pay? This will directly affect the net proceeds or investment factors in a given parcel.
- Utilities: cost to install or extend to meet user's needs
- Grading: How will the site be delivered? Will grading be required, and who will provide it?
- Project landscaping: Will it be provided by the landlord or will the tenant be required to provide it?
- Sidewalks, street lights, fire hydrants, curbing, and so on
- Zoning or rezoning costs
- Subdivision costs and process
- Environmental cleanup
- Demolition of any existing structures or removal of vegetation, trees, or other extraneous site preparation.
2. Seller/Landlord-Related Costs: Next, there are specific costs that by definition are the responsibility of the landlord or the seller:
- Seller's legal expenses for the transaction and development process
- Seller's broker fees
- Marketing materials
- Developer fees
- On-site marketing signs: Don't forget to put up on-site sale/lease signs early. Keep them simple, such as Land Sale/Lease, your number, your name. The number should be direct to you and in the largest print on the sign; these calls can get lost in large companies.
- Tenant's allowance on a BTS lease or contribution lease
- Miscellaneous architectural, engineering, and deal-processing expenses.
3. Purchaser-Related Costs: Certain items are cost factors normally borne by the purchaser or tenant:
- Tenant transaction and development legal expenses
- Feasibility testing, including Phase I environment costs
- Permit application and processing fees
- Architectural plans

- Buyer's broker's fees.
4. Transaction Expenses: The costs shown here are typically absorbed or shared by the buyer or seller, as negotiated in the deal.
- Title insurance
- Survey (boundary and topographical)
- Real estate property taxes
- Escrow fees
- Real estate transfer taxes
- Deed and/or mortgage recording fees (documentary stamps)
- Special assessments for roads, schools, and the like.

THE DEAL PROCESS

Land lease and sales transactions are for the most part complex business dealings that require the coordination of several professional disciplines to ensure a closing, or rent commencement in the case of a lease. You may be familiar and used to dealing with the attorneys and architects on each side of the transaction for a typical space lease. The similarities with land transactions pretty much end there. For your convenience, included at the end of the chapter is a land sale deal summary form and a land lease deal summary form. These will assist in obtaining key information, and they may serve as useful checklists for you in organizing a transaction.

Here is a typical critical path for a transaction involving a peripheral parcel:

1. Identify the user.
2. Prepare and provide a letter of intent.
3. Negotiate and sign the letter of intent.
4. Prepare the lease or purchase and sale agreement.
5. Negotiate and execute the lease or purchase and sale agreement.
6. Tenant or purchaser performs a feasibility study and inspection of the property.
7. Landlord or seller reviews and approves the tenant's building plans.
8. Tenant or purchaser applies for building permits.
9. Permits are issued by appropriate governmental authorities.
10. Purchaser closes on the property and commences construction, or the tenant commences construction and payment of ground rent.
11. User opens for business.

Although this is a straightforward process, there are several persons involved in completing it. Depending on how your organization is set up, it is possible that contact with all these persons will be necessary to get the job done. This is much more likely in a small organization. It is worthwhile to become aware of just what role each of these listed professionals plays, even if the responsibility usually rest with others. Most transactions at one time or another involve the following:

- Lender-purchaser
- Lender's attorney-seller
- Lender's attorney-purchaser
- Lender-seller
- Title officer
- Traffic engineer
- Seller's land planner
- Anchor tenant attorney
- Anchor tenant (if anchor consents required)
- Seller's attorney
- Purchaser's attorney
- Property manager
- Zoning attorney
- Civil engineer
- Environmental engineer
- Purchaser's architect.

All of these professionals are members of the team required to complete the processing, and each of them has a vested interest in making it happen.

Conclusion

It is easy to conclude that the business of peripheral land is a complex one that means different things to different interests. The success or failure of a given location can rise or fall with the fate of a sign, existence of or lack of a traffic signal, or any one of a number of other reasons. The ability to develop and market outparcels effectively revolves around information control, from preliminary project planning to market activity awareness.

Pad sites, outparcels, and residual land have provided opportunities for developers to realize substantial income through land sales or leases. This income is often what provides the overall economic return necessary to justify developing the shopping center, particularly in very densely populated areas with high land prices.

Success in an outparcel program means finding a prospective purchaser or tenant willing to pay the market price for a parcel on which a developer, municipality, and anchor tenant(s) will collectively direct what use will be permitted, where a building may be placed, how tall it might be, and what it might eventually look like. Balancing these interests is the most important responsibility of a peripheral land professional, because only when they are all in balance is it likely the transaction will happen.

Creating your land transaction from start to finish requires a good understanding of the basic elements of peripheral land development: peripheral land use categories, shopping center or project development types, predevelopment planing, market and competitor knowledge, location and trade area demographics, parcel and site characteristics, valuation and pricing, deal and transaction types, developer and user financing considerations, budgets and costs, and the deal process.

In the end, it is all about creating value by those developers with the investment risk in the project, and realizing that value through the efforts of skilled and knowledgeable land professionals. Information is essential—about your product, your competition, your customer, and your market—and the information is there for the taking.

Richard T. Parker is Principal at EIR Development Company, LLC, North Potomac, Maryland.

336 ■ SHOPPING CENTER LEASING

Exhibit A

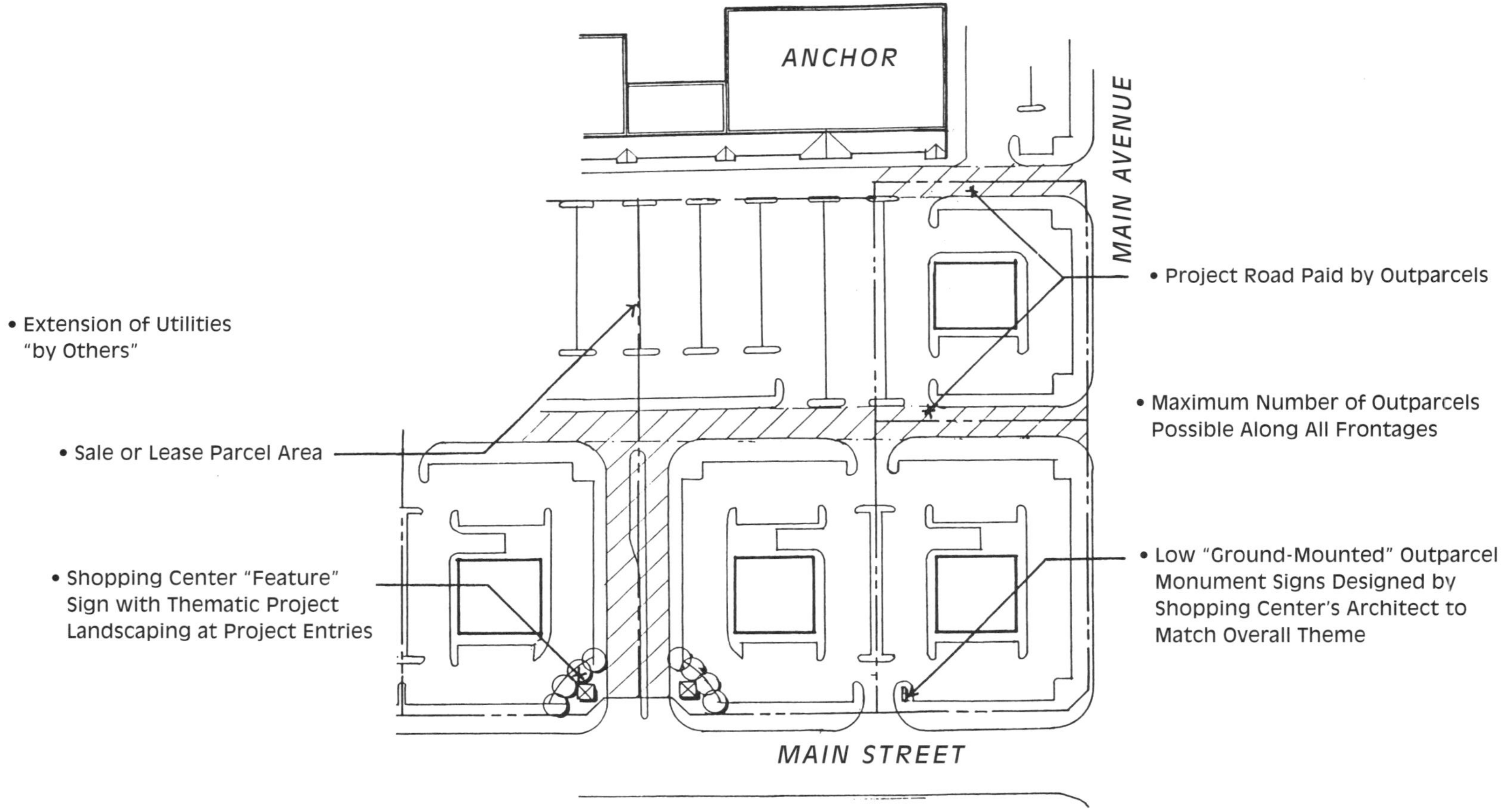

- Project Road Paid by Outparcels
- Maximum Number of Outparcels Possible Along All Frontages
- Low "Ground-Mounted" Outparcel Monument Signs Designed by Shopping Center's Architect to Match Overall Theme

MAIN AVENUE

MAIN STREET

ANCHOR

- Extension of Utilities "by Others"
- Sale or Lease Parcel Area
- Shopping Center "Feature" Sign with Thematic Project Landscaping at Project Entries

© 1999 Site Signatures, Inc.

PERIPHERAL DEVELOPMENT FROM THE DEVELOPER'S PERSPECTIVE

PERIPHERAL LAND ■ 337

Exhibit B

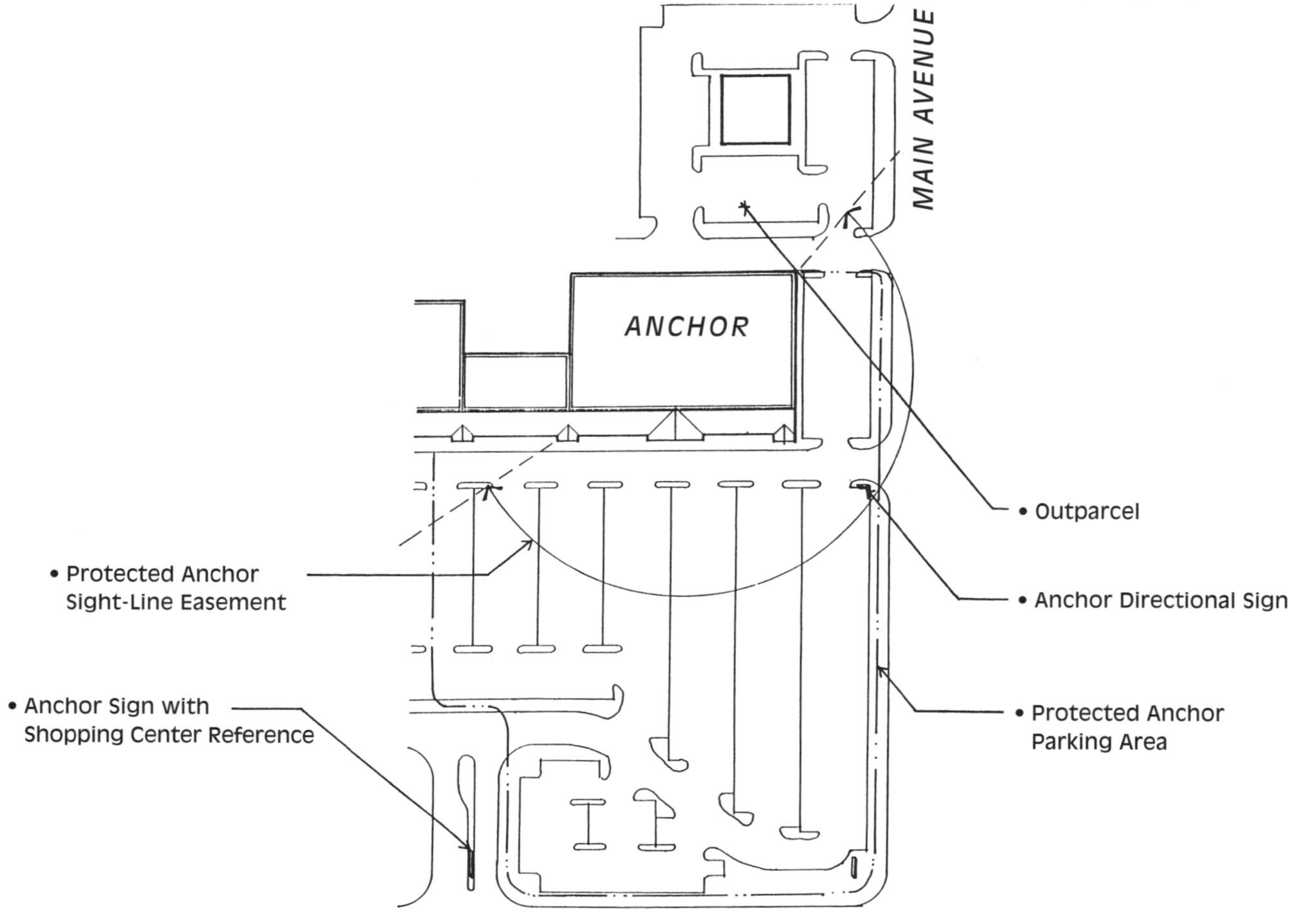

- Outparcel
- Anchor Directional Sign
- Protected Anchor Parking Area
- Protected Anchor Sight-Line Easement
- Anchor Sign with Shopping Center Reference

MAIN AVENUE

ANCHOR

MAIN STREET

© 1999 Site Signatures, Inc.

PERIPHERAL DEVELOPMENT FROM THE ANCHOR'S PERSPECTIVE

338 ■ SHOPPING CENTER LEASING

Exhibit C

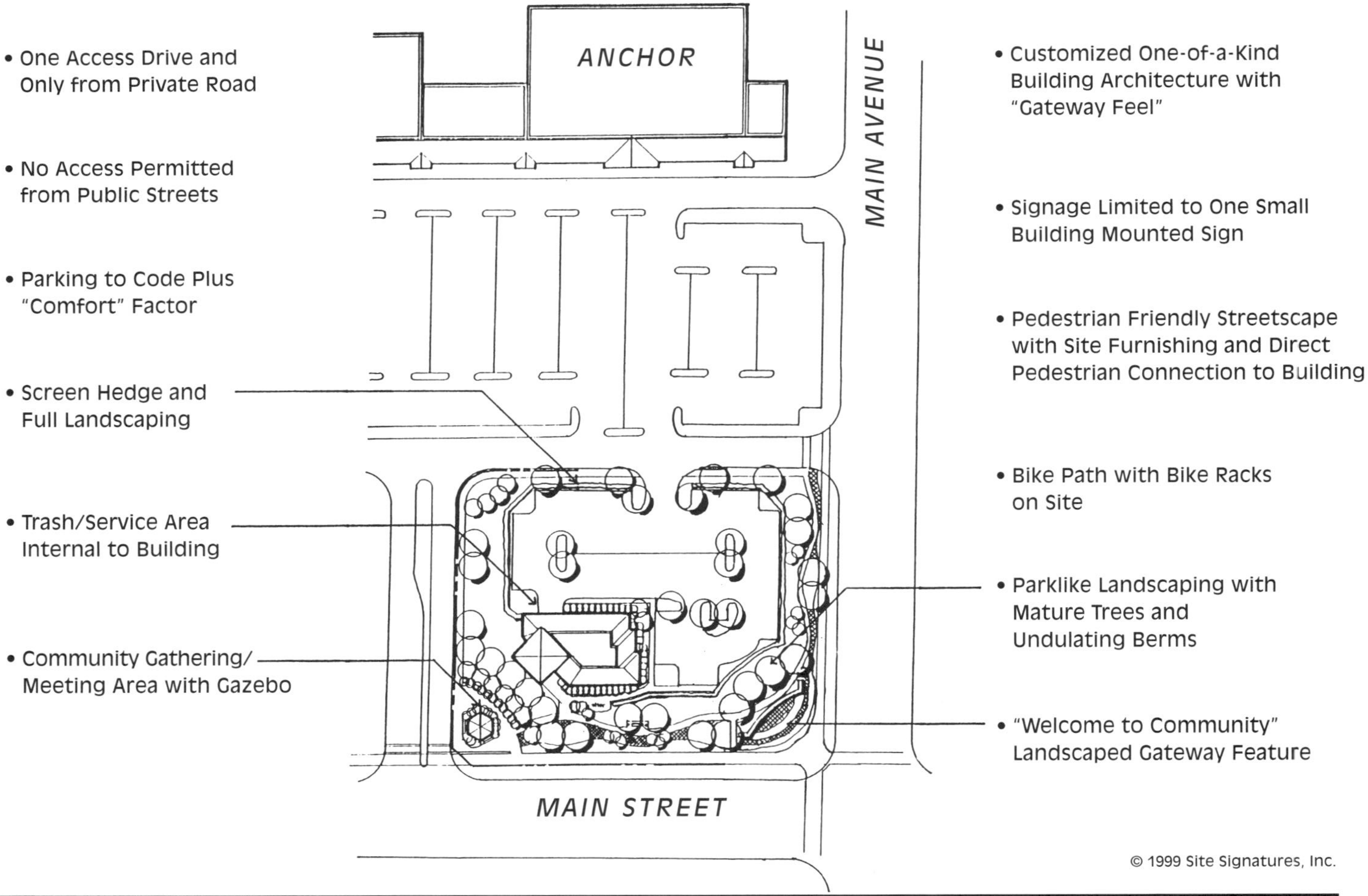

PERIPHERAL DEVELOPMENT FROM THE COMMUNITY PERSPECTIVE

- Customized One-of-a-Kind Building Architecture with "Gateway Feel"
- Signage Limited to One Small Building Mounted Sign
- Pedestrian Friendly Streetscape with Site Furnishing and Direct Pedestrian Connection to Building
- Bike Path with Bike Racks on Site
- Parklike Landscaping with Mature Trees and Undulating Berms
- "Welcome to Community" Landscaped Gateway Feature

- One Access Drive and Only from Private Road
- No Access Permitted from Public Streets
- Parking to Code Plus "Comfort" Factor
- Screen Hedge and Full Landscaping
- Trash/Service Area Internal to Building
- Community Gathering/Meeting Area with Gazebo

© 1999 Site Signatures, Inc.

Exhibit D

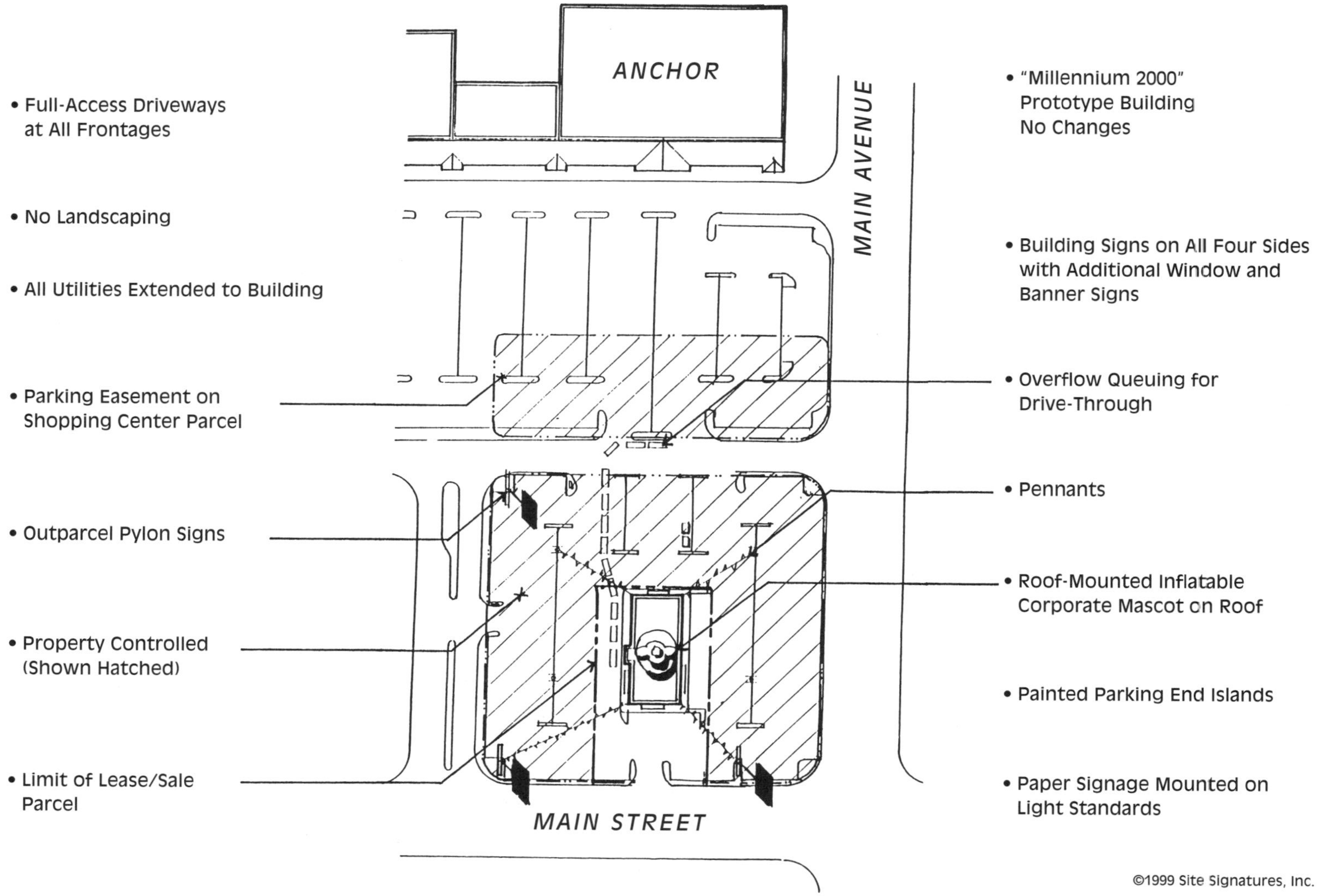

Peripheral Development from the User's Perspective

- Full-Access Driveways at All Frontages
- No Landscaping
- All Utilities Extended to Building
- Parking Easement on Shopping Center Parcel
- Outparcel Pylon Signs
- Property Controlled (Shown Hatched)
- Limit of Lease/Sale Parcel

- "Millennium 2000" Prototype Building No Changes
- Building Signs on All Four Sides with Additional Window and Banner Signs
- Overflow Queuing for Drive-Through
- Pennants
- Roof-Mounted Inflatable Corporate Mascot on Roof
- Painted Parking End Islands
- Paper Signage Mounted on Light Standards

MAIN AVENUE

MAIN STREET

ANCHOR

©1999 Site Signatures, Inc.

Exhibit E

DEAL SUMMARY
LAND SALE

Project: _____ Prepared by: _____

Site ID: _____ Parcel Size: _____ Date: _____

Building Size: _____ Height: _____ Parking: _____ Required: _____ Provided: _____

1. Purchaser: _____

2. Purchaser is Parent Company or Franchisee: _____

3. Price Total: _____ Per. Sq. Ft.: _____

4. Deposit: _____ Terms: _____

5. Broker Commission: _____

6. Study Period: _____

7. Proposed Use: _____ Trade Name: _____

8. Closing Contingencies: Subdivision ____; Zoning/Variance/Special Use Approvals ____;

    Grading ____; Sanitary Sewer ____; Electrical ____; Water ____; Gas ____; Curbs ____;

    Phones ____; Building Permits ____; Title ____; Other _____

9. Estimated Closing Date: _____

10. Use Restriction: On Buyer – _____

                      On Seller – _____

11. Operating Covenant: _____

12. CAM Contributions: _____

13. Promotion Contributions: _____

14. Anchor Consents Required: _____

15. Prelim. Site Layout Reviewed: _____

16. Planned Opening Date: _____

17. First Right of Refusal on Sale: _____

18. Right to Repurchase for No Build: _____

19. Miscellaneous: _____

Exhibit F

DEAL SUMMARY
LAND LEASE

Project: _____ Prepared by: _____

Site ID: _____ Parcel Size: _____ Date: _____

Building Size: _____ Height: _____ Parking: _____ Required: _____ Provided: _____

1. Tenant: _____ Guarantor: _____

2. Tenant is Parent Company or Franchisee: _____

3. Primary Term: _____ Option Term(s): _____

4. Deal Type: __ Land Lease; __ Build to Suit; __ Contribution Lease Amount: $ _____

5. Rent Base: _____ Increases: % Rent: _____

6. Rent Commencement: _____ Inspection Period: _____

7. Permitted Use: _____ Trade Name: _____

8. Lease Contingencies: Subdivision _____; Zoning/Variance/Special Use Approvals _____;

   Grading ___; Sanitary Sewer ___; Electrical ___; Water ___; Gas ___; Curbs ___;

   Phones ___; Building Permits ___; Title ___; Other _____

9. Use Restriction: _____

10. Radius Restriction: On Landlord – _____

    On Tenant – _____

11. Operating Covenant: _____

12. CAM Contribution: _____ Taxes: _____

13. Promotion Contribution: _____ Insurance: _____

14. Anchor Consents Required: _____

15. Prelim. Site Layout Reviewed: _____

16. Planned Opening Date: _____

17. Right to Assign or Sublet: _____

18. Right to Terminate for No Build: _____ Broker Commission: _____

19. Miscellaneous: _____

Glossary

abatement period A period of time during which the landlord defers or reduces rent or other payments, as an incentive to a tenant to open at the earliest possible time.

acceleration clause *See* rent acceleration.

actualizing expenses Recalculating the tenant's share of expenses based on actual expenses and occupancy levels, after having billed based on estimates.

additional rent An amount beyond minimum rent, including reimbursements to the landlord for repairs and attorneys' fees.

ADT *See* average daily traffic.

advertorial An editorial-type article about an individual or business, which is paid for by the person or business inserting it in a newspaper or magazine.

aging report An accounting report that categorizes late payments by month.

allowance Landlord contribution to tenant improvements. *See also* tenant allowance.

amortization Gradual paying off of a debt by periodic installments, generally in equal payments at regular intervals over a specific period of time.

anchor pad A parcel of land occupied by a shopping center anchor store (a major store, usually part of a chain). The land area usually consists of just that property underneath the building. It may be controlled by the anchor through either a ground lease or a land purchase.

anchor parcel A parcel of land occupied by a shopping center anchor store (a major store, usually part of a chain), including the building area and associated parking areas. It may be occupied pursuant to a ground lease or may be owned by the anchor store.

ancillary charges Commonly known as triple net or side charges, these may cover all or a portion of the pro rata operating expenses of the shopping center, including common area maintenance (CAM), real estate taxes, and insurance. A marketing fund contribution is sometimes lumped into the ancillary charges. The charges, paid by the tenant, may be expressed as either a pro rata share or a set fee.

assignment The transfer of a tenant's rights and interest in a premises, but not its liabilities, to another party.

attornment Part of an agreement by which the tenant agrees to remain after a foreclosure and treat the lender as the landlord. *See also* subordination, non-disturbance, and attornment agreement.

average daily traffic (ADT) A count of traffic on a 24-hour basis along a frontage street of an outparcel.

average inventory An average of the stock on hand at representative dates throughout the year or season.

base rent *See* minimum rent.

big box A single-use store, anywhere from 10,000 to 100,000 square feet or more, such as a large bookstore or office-supply store.

blackout period A period of time when a tenant is able to delay an opening because it is too close to a holiday period and therefore too costly for that tenant to open; also called a dark period.

blanket coverage One insurance policy rather than multiple policies.

boilerplate language Standard clauses in the lease meant to be applied uniformly.

boundary survey *See* metes and bounds.

breakpoint The point at which the level of sales triggers percentage rent.

buffer zone An area of land that provides a transition from one use type to another; for example, a landscape buffer zone might separate an outparcel parking area from a project road or street.

buildable area That portion of a parcel that is usable for a building and its associated parking requirements. It will typically exclude wetlands, storm-water retention areas, tree preserves or other easement areas, and the like. Most outparcel users consider the buildable area when determining the price they are willing to pay.

bump back store A white box, or temporary store space, built about four to eight feet back from the front of a vacant store space.

business interruption insurance Rent insurance purchased by the tenant if the lease does not provide for abatement of rent after a casualty.

canvassing The process of identifying specific shopping centers or other venues to visit personally in search of prospective tenants or trendy product lines.

capitalization rate The rate of return that a potential buyer of a property is willing to accept on the investment.

certificate of occupancy Permit issued by the governing authority indicating that a building has met the requirements for occupancy and allows the tenant to open for business.

closeout An offer by a manufacturer or retailer to clear away the inventory. The savings are often passed along to the consumer as a closeout sale, used to generate increased store traffic.

closing The transfer of title to a parcel of real estate, in accordance with a purchase and sale agreement.

common area maintenance (CAM) The amount of money charged to tenants for their share of maintaining a center's common areas.

common area units Several types of stand-alone displays occupying the common area of a center. *See also* kiosk; retail merchandising unit (RMU).

common areas Those portions of a shopping center that are used jointly by all tenants in the center. In connection with outparcels, exterior common areas typically include project roads, landscape buffers, project entry features, storm-water management systems, project landscaping, and the like.

conceptual site plan A site plan that depicts, on a specific subdivided parcel of land, the location of a building, parking, ingress and egress, and other elements of a development, to determine the usability of the parcel; also called a plot plan.

concession The privilege of maintaining a subsidiary business within a premises.

condemnation A taking of private property for public use, for which just compensation must be paid.

continuous operation The requirement that a tenant remain open during prescribed business hours.

cost complement The average relationship existing between the cost of merchandise and the retail value of the items handled during an accounting period. The dollar value of the inventory.

coterminous Lease terms that are the same.

custom units Various types of common area units, usually provided by the specialty retailer.

dark period *See* blackout period.

debt service coverage ratio The relationship between projected net operating income and expected debt service, expressed as NOI divided by debt service. A ratio of 1.0 (NOI equals debt service) means there is no margin of error; any drop in NOI will leave insufficient cash to pay the debt service. The higher the ratio, the higher the margin of error, and the greater the chance that the loan will be repaid.

dedication The transfer to a public entity of the title to a property, for public use; for example, project roads or retention facilities or utilities are often dedicated to the appropriate municipal authorities to ensure proper maintenance.

deductions The amount by which gross sales are reduced; for example, sales taxes.

deed restriction A provision written into a deed that governs the use of the land covered; for example, a parcel may be deed-restricted specifically for use as a restaurant.

demising Generally used to determine the separation of tenant spaces. Walls that separate tenant space.

demographics Vital statistics about the market area, such as average income, age, number of children, cost of homes, education, and ethnic factors.

discount rate An interest rate commensurate with perceived risk; used to convert future payments or receipts to present value.

draw The payment of funds from a construction lender to a developer at an agreed-on interval.

due diligence Proper examination of necessary information, to satisfy oneself as to its accuracy.

duty of care The leasing representative's responsibility to use information conscientiously when dealing with tenants.

easement The right of one party in the land of another; for example, an outparcel owner may require an access easement to that parcel from the shopping center parking area to ensure access to all traffic.

encumbrance Any claim, lien, charge, or liability that affects or limits the title to a property.

escalations Cost-of-living adjustments, percentage rent, and other negotiated increases in payments.

estoppel agreement A legal theory under which a person is barred from denying facts that the person previously acknowledged were true and others accepted on good faith.

estoppel certificate A status report that confirms a lease's effectiveness and terms, as well as the absence of claims against it.

exclusions Amounts that should never be included in gross sales, because they are never part of a sale; for example, returns to shippers.

exclusive A provision limiting the number or square footage of other tenants with substantially similar uses of their premises to those of the tenant covered by the lease.

exculpation A limit on a landlord's potential liability to the tenant.

exculpatory clause A provision that invalidates all previous agreements other than those contained in the lease documents.

executed lease A lease that has been signed by all parties and delivered.

exhibits Attachments, usually at the end of a lease, specifying location, legal description, and tenant's construction specifications.

floor area ratio (FAR) The relationship between the building area and the land area on any given parcel; for example, a 10,000-square-foot building on a 40,000-square-foot parcel of land has a .25 FAR.

force majeure A major unavoidable event or act of God or people—anything beyond the control of the people under a contractual obligation—that prevents an action from progressing as required. Such a provision can favor both parties, but it often favors just the landlord.

funds from operations (FFO) A measurement favored by real estate investment trusts (REITs) that approximates the cash-generating power of a company; analogous to net operating income, it consists of net income, excluding gains (or losses) from debt restructuring and sales of property, plus depreciation and amortization after adjustments for unconsolidated partnerships and joint ventures.

GAFO An acronym for General merchandise, Apparel, home Furnishings, and Other types of similar merchandise normally sold in regional shopping centers.

geographic information systems (GIS) Market research from a GIS program that supports demographic information.

grantee The person who receives the title to a property in a purchase and sale transaction.

grantor The person who gives the title to the grantee in a purchase and sale transaction.

gross building area (GBA) The total area contained within a building, normally measured from its outside walls. Most outparcel transactions use GBA in computing the floor area ratio, or making pro rata calculations for various payments.

gross leaseable area (GLA) The total area in a shopping center on which tenants pay rent, including storage and miscellaneous space as well as selling space; the total area in a center that produces income.

gross lease A lease in which the landlord is responsible for paying most of the expenses, such as common area maintenance (CAM), real estate taxes, and insurance; the tenant pays a gross amount of fixed rent.

ground lease A lease only for the land; also called a land lease.

guarantor A third party in the landlord/tenant relationship whose credit standing is used to guarantee the tenant's performance or lease obligations.

highest and best use A term, typically used by appraisers, that generally means the use that is legally permitted and most likely to produce the greatest return on the value of the land and/or building.

holding period The time frame anticipated by the property owner to hold on to a given shopping center.

holdover When a tenant remains in possession of the premises after its term has ended; the landlord can evict the tenant or bind it to another term.

HVAC Heating, ventilation, and air-conditioning, handled by fairly large machines.

incubation The process of assisting a nonpermanent tenant in developing into a permanent one over a period of time.

incubator tenants Specialty leasing tenants (also known as temporary tenants) often need incubation before they are financially strong enough or experienced enough to have a long-term lease.

indemnification The assumption of responsibility by one party (the indemnitor) for claims of personal injury or property damage against another party (the indemnitee) by a third party.

indemnity contracts Property and liability insurance to preserve the position of the insured as it would have been if a loss had not occurred.

inflow market The geographic market located outside the primary and secondary markets from which a center obtains shoppers or sales.

internal rate of return (IRR) A discount rate at which the present value of projected cash flow exactly equals the initial investment.

inventory turnover A ratio measuring the adequacy and efficiency of the inventory balance, calculated by dividing the cost of goods sold by the amount of the average inventory; also called stock turnover.

keystone markup A 100 percent markup or a markup recommended by a manufacturer.

kickout The right of early termination based on the failure of a tenant to achieve specified sales volume during a specified period.

kiosk The largest of the common area merchandising units, containing an open interior space to house the cash register and sales staff. The merchandise is "wrapped around" the center, usually on shelves or in display cases.

laches Delay or negligence in asserting one's legal rights.

land lease *See* ground lease.

lease A contract transferring the right to the possession and enjoyment of property for a defined period of time; the signed agreement between landlord and tenant that establishes responsibility, sets standards, and states what is recoverable from tenants for the maintenance process.

lease abstract A synopsis or abbreviated form of a lease used as a management tool; also called a lease brief.

lease administration The function of administering, managing, and enforcing the provisions in a lease.

lease comments The response to a preliminary lease that seeks changes and/or explanation.

lease plan A detailed plan showing the size and configuration of each space located within the shopping center. Each space is typically numbered for quick identification.

leasehold mortgage The right of the lender to the interest of a tenant in real estate; generally referred to as a lien.

leasing summary A form used by owners and managers to summarize or briefly state the most important lease terms.

letter of intent A document expressing a serious show of interest in a location; often issued during an advanced stage of negotiations but before the completion of a formal lease, it states all of the pertinent economic terms that have been agreed upon, and any other lease provisions important enough to be discussed up to that point. It has little or no legal standing but can serve to assure both parties about the progress of an impending deal.

license A right to do some particular act or series of acts on land without possessing any estate or interest therein, and is, ordinarily revocable at the will of the person granting the license, and is not assignable. It is a privilege to go upon land to perform some act without any interest or estate in the property.

license agreement A short-term space rental contract between the licensor (property owner) and the licensee (retailer) that defines the location, term, charges, and responsibilities of each party to the other. Perhaps the most important and defining aspects of the license agreement are that it transforms no estate or interest in the property and is ordinarily revocable at the will of the person granting the license, and is not assignable.

licensee The person granted the license, which may be by express invitation (to transact business with the owner of the land or to transact business for the benefit of the owner and/or the licensee) or by permission (to enter onto property for the convenience, curiosity or entertainment). In the case of specialty retail leasing, the licensor is a person who has been granted a license to use space on the property for a fee.

licensor: A person who grants a license. In the case of specialty retail leasing, a licensor is typically the property owner who grants a license to another person to use space on the property for a fee.

lien An encumbrance against specific property, i.e. using the property as security for a mortgage or other obligation. Permitted liens, such as a mechanic's lien, may be filed as a claim on the title and therefore become a matter of public record.

line drawing A scale drawing detailing the exact dimensions of a store or common area unit.

lis pendens This Latin term means there is a lawsuit pending and that a notice of the suit has been recorded as a matter of title to a certain piece of real property. A dispute in a purchase and sale transaction that does not get resolved may result in the buyer filing a lis pendens action.

markdown Retail price reduction caused by the inability to sell goods at the original or subsequently determined retail price.

market research Studies, such as surveys of customers, required to make marketing decisions.

markup (or mark-on) The difference between the retail selling price of the merchandise and the cost of the merchandise to the retailer.

mechanic's lien A lien granted by law on a building or other improvement on land, and on the land itself, as security for payment for labor done and/or materials furnished for improvement.

memorandum of lease A document with only essential lease terms, not details about the rent; an alternative to the recording of a lease, which many shopping centers prohibit.

merchandise mix The variety and categories of merchandise offered by the tenants in a particular shopping center.

merchandising plan An overall plan locating merchandise mix throughout the lease plan.

metes and bounds A way to describe a portion of land that indicates the boundaries, including where they start and the angles formed by where they join; generally referred to as a boundary survey.

minimum rent A fixed amount of rent, paid by the tenant to the property owner, that is not based on the tenant's sales; also known as base rent.

monument sign Typically a ground-mounted parcel sign identifying the occupant of a building on an outparcel.

net lease A term used to describe a lease in which the tenant pays a gross amount of fixed rent plus taxes, utilities, and other assessments associated with the land and/or building so that the rent paid to the landlord is net of all expenses.

net operating income (NOI) The income received by the property owner after vacancy expenses, operating expenses, management fees, and nonreimbursable costs have been subtracted from gross revenue.

net sales Gross sales less returns and allowances, freight-out, and often cash discounts allowed; often simply the net amount finally received from the customer.

net-net lease A net lease in which the tenant also pays for required repairs and maintenance.

occupancy cost The sum of a tenant's fixed minimum rent, percentage rent, and ancillary or triple net charges; also called the total rent.

off-site costs In the land-development process, costs related to expenditures for construction items, and the like, not directly on the parcel of land being developed; for example, the cost of bringing sanitary sewers to a project from a distant point.

operating budget An outline of how much income a shopping center has and how that income will be spent; includes all income other than sales of capital assets, offset by all items of expense other than depreciation and interest on debt and payments on debt principal or added investment.

operating covenant The promise of the tenant to open and operate its business in the leased premises for a specified period of time.

outparcel Typically, a parcel of land at the boundary of a shopping center, including the building and parking and other areas necessary for the development and construction of a freestanding use.

outposting When an in-line permanent tenant rents short-term space in the common area of a shopping center in addition to its in-line space, in order to promote its store, test-market a new line of products, or focus on selling a particularly popular product line.

pad site This normally refers to the land area occupied by a freestanding building within the parking area of a shopping center or enclosed mall. Parking for a pad site use is generally provided through cross-easement access and parking arrangements with the shopping center owner.

parcel A piece of land or property under single ownership; for example, a lot in a subdivision.

parcel map Typically, this refers to the location of a subdivided parcel within a larger development; for example, an enclosed mall project. A parcel map is often attached to a ground lease or a purchase and sale agreement to identify clearly the location of the specific land in question.

pass-throughs Common area maintenance (CAM), real estate taxes, and utilities, as well as any other expenses that the tenant has agreed to pay.

percentage rent An amount of rent paid annually, in addition to the tenant's minimum or base rent, based on a percentage of gross sales; the rate is defined in the lease.

permanent tenant A tenant that has signed a lease with a term longer than one year.

Phase I environmental study The preliminary study typically performed by outparcel users or residual parcel purchasers. This is the first level of investigation to determine whether there are any potential environmental hazards associated with the property. Most construction lenders require the outparcel user to provide the results of a Phase I study.

plat A drawing or map of a specified land area; for example, a plot of land within a subdivision, sometimes called a plat of survey.

plot plan *See* conceptual site plan.

preliminary lease The first draft of a lease.

present value A calculation that relies on the discount rate to determine what the present value of a known future amount of money should be.

price point The price tag on a specific product.

pro forma A developer's estimates of all costs of planning, developing, building, and operating a shopping center; estimates of revenues and expenses allow the developer to compute anticipated net income and projected value.

pro rata share A proportional share of payments.

psychographics The motivating forces that influence shopping patterns and consumer behavior, determined by studies.

pylon sign Typically, a sign mounted on a pole and used to identify the occupant of a freestanding building on a shopping center outparcel. Most municipalities and shopping center developments now discourage pole-mounted pylon signs and prefer ground-mounted monument signs.

radius restriction A provision prohibiting a tenant from conducting the same or substantially similar business within a specified distance from the shopping center.

real estate investment trust (REIT) A trust established by a group of investors that owns real estate such as a shopping center; allowed under income-tax laws to avoid corporate income tax. A REIT must meet several conditions, and if it distributes 95 percent of its income, it is not taxed on that income.

recapture out of percentage rent A right, usually held by major tenants, to deduct such items as common area maintenance (CAM) or insurance paid from percentage rents that may be owing.

reciprocal easement agreement (REA) An agreement between the owners of two or more parcels of property granting one another reciprocal rights to the use of their respective parcels for such things as parking, access, signage, and the like. In most shopping centers, the anchor stores have significant input and control over the rights and obligations granted or restricted under an REA, which could include items ranging from the use of land to development and design controls, such as permitted parking ratios. Any REA in place generally will be recorded in the public land records.

recurring charge A repeating charge for which the timing and amount are known in advance.

REIT See real estate investment trust.

relocation clause A provision, often heavily contested by the tenant, permitting the landlord to move the tenant to another location.

rent acceleration The right of the landlord to collect rent for the balance of the term of the lease in one lump sum in case of default.

rental income insurance This is purchased by the landlord if the lease abates rent after a casualty.

rental value insurance This is purchased by both the landlord and the tenant to insure against the loss of value of an occupancy.

retail merchandising unit (RMU) A state-of-the-art updating of the traditional pushcart, using modern design and materials to create a durable and functional display on which to showcase a specialty tenant's wares or services. The RMU, staffed from the outside like the pushcart, is considerably larger and may be square, rectangular, round, or even elliptical. It is also mobile, although rolling casters mounted underneath have replaced the pushcart's large wagon wheels. Many designs incorporate large display areas, ample storage, high-intensity lighting, and modern security features.

retail visual restrictors (RVRs) This term generally relates to large landscape or architectural features imposed on the entryways or boundaries of major developments by overzealous architects, municipal planners, or developers in creating a project. When these features block the visibility of outparcels, that can reduce the value of those outparcels.

return on investment (ROI) The amount that goes to the owner beyond the return of the investment's capital; calculated by dividing net operating income by the cost of the project.

right of first negotiation An option giving a tenant the right to negotiate for a time before the landlord can offer the space to another tenant.

right of first offer A provision requiring the landlord to offer vacant space to the tenant before offering it for lease to anyone else.

right of first refusal A provision requiring the landlord to give the tenant the option of leasing a space on terms negotiated with another prospective tenant.

riparian rights The rights of a property owner whose land is near a river, lake, or other body of water, pertaining to the use of the water.

risk premium The difference between a discount rate and a risk-free, or safe, rate of return such as that of a U.S. Treasury note; this factor compensates the investor for inherent market risks, business risks, portfolio management, and loss of liquidity.

run with the land This term refers to the rights or restrictions that affect all owners, both present and future, in the chain of title to a parcel of land; for example, the use of a parcel that is written in as a deed restriction will run with the land to all future owners.

sales test The requirement that a tenant prove that gross sales have been negatively affected before a landlord must provide relief under a co-tenancy provision.

security deposit Cash or a letter of credit to ensure payment of rent and a tenant's other obligations.

shopping center site plan An overall map of a given shopping center development which indicates the placement of all buildings, streets, parking, storm water management features, and other aspects of the shopping center development. It will normally indicate the major or anchor tenants, but it is not typically intended to depict the entire tenant mix.

special assessment Fees (taxes) levied against a property that pay for a particular public improvement. Normally these improvements directly benefit the property but not in all cases, such as those used to pay for new schools as opposed to utility extensions.

specialty retail leasing The process of increasing shopping center net operating income (NOI) by licensing for a fee, usually for one year or less, space within the shopping center.

stepped-up rent Escalations in minimum rent by fixed amounts, or percentages, at fixed intervals.

sublease A tenant's transfer of some of its rights to all or part of the leased premises; in effect, the tenant acts as landlord to the subtenant.

subordination A lease provision making the rights of the tenant inferior to those of the landlord's lender.

subordination, non-disturbance, and attornment agreement (SNDA) Protection for a tenant against a lender using foreclosure to substitute another tenant in that space.

tenant allowances Money distributed by landlord to assist tenants with tenant shop build out.

testimonial A positive letter or statement from a current or past customer detailing that person's experience in the shopping center.

title insurance Insurance purchased by the purchaser of property that protects them or their lender against any losses incurred due to any defects in the title.

title report A report that indicates the current status of the title, describing easements, restrictions, liens, covenants, or any defects in the title.

total rent *See* occupancy cost.

triple net charges *See* ancillary charges.

triple net lease A net-net lease, plus the tenant pays for some capital improvements.

unlawful detainer action A legal proceeding to regain possession of occupied premises.

unsubordinated land lease This term means that the owner's interest in the land is not going to be pledged as collateral for any financing that the tenant obtains to develop the leased parcel.

use clause A provision inserted into a retail lease agreement or temporary license agreement that restricts the category of merchandise or items a retailer is allowed to sell.

value A determination about a company, set in the marketplace, that is based on the income it produces year after year; it is calculated by dividing net operating income by the capitalization rate.

view corridor The area in a parcel that cannot be occupied by a building or anything else that obstructs the view of what exists beyond the outparcel. Most major shopping centers, and especially anchor tenants, require view corridors from the main highways to their building and signage so that they can be seen by the public.

wall unit A retail selling area placed against unused wall space or recessed into a gypsum wallboard; typically three or four feet wide by seven or eight feet high and incorporating high-intensity lighting, movable shelving, and lockable security shutters, it is ideal for merchandising apparel or small gift items.

white box A space partially completed by the landlord or licensor based on negotiations with the tenant, and usually including HVAC (heating, ventilation, and air-conditioning) systems, walls, floors, a stockroom wall and door, basic electrical and plumbing work, a rear door, and a storefront; also called a vanilla box.

List of Resources

Alexander, Alan M., CSM. *Shopping Center Lease Administration: A Manager's Guide to Improving Financial Record Keeping*. New York: International Council of Shopping Centers, 1986.

Alexander, Alan A., SCSM, and Richard F. Muhlebach, SCSM. *Operating Small Shopping Centers*. New York: International Council of Shopping Centers, 1997.

American Demographics. Stamford, CT: Intertec Publishing.

Chain Store Age. New York: Lebhar-Friedman Inc.

Crafting Lease Clauses: Meeting Shopping Center Landlord and Tenant Objectives, Volume 1. New York: International Council of Shopping Centers, 1994.

Crafting Lease Clauses: Meeting Shopping Center Landlord and Tenant Objectives, Volume 2, 1994–1998. New York: International Council of Shopping Centers, 1999.

The Dealmakers. Mercerville, NJ: TKO Real Estate Advisory Group.

The Dictionary of Real Estate Terms. Hauppauge, NY: Baron's Real Estate Guides.

Dollars and Cents of Shopping Centers. Washington, DC: Urban Land Institute.

ICSC Keys to Shopping Center Leasing Series. New York: International Council of Shopping Centers, 1995.

The ICSC Temporary Tenant Handbook. New York: International Council of Shopping Centers, 1994.

Industry Norms and Key Business Ratios. Murray Hill, NJ: Dun & Bradstreet Information Services.

Journal of Property Management. Chicago, IL: Institute of Real Estate Management.

Key Shopping Center Legal Issues: Understanding Current Laws Impacting Leasing and Management. New York: International Council of Shopping Centers, 1995.

Keys, John R., Esq. *The Antitrust Aspects of Restrictive Covenants in Shopping Center Leases.* New York: International Council of Shopping Centers, 1994.

Leasing Small Shopping Centers. New York: International Council of Shopping Centers, 1997.

Messinger, Stephen, and Barnett Ruttenbert. *Understanding Major Lease Clauses.* New York: International Council of Shopping Centers, 1991.

The Out of Home Entertainment Business News. Novato, CA: Ecklien Communications, Inc.

Shedlin, Andrew, Esq., and Roy Green, Esq. *Lease Negotiations* [Audiocassettes]. New York: International Council of Shopping Centers, 1988.

Shopping Center Study Lease. New York: International Council of Shopping Centers, 1994.

Specialty Retail Report. Norwell, MA: Specialty Retail Report.

The Theme Restaurant Report. Novato, CA: Ecklien Communications, Inc.

Urban Land. Washington, DC: Urban Land Institute.

Wolf, Irving., CSM/CMD, ed. *Essential Factors in Shopping Center Leasing.* New York: International Council of Shopping Centers, 1992.

Index

Abatement period, 126, 130, 152–53, 343
Abstract, 217–18, 350
Acceleration clause, 157, 355
Accounting file, 220
Accounting staff, 41–42, 214, 220
Actualizing expenses, 226, 343
Additional rent, 123, 129, 130, 152, 155, 170–71, 343
Administration. *See* Contract administration; Lease administration
Advertising, 85–86, 281, 307
Advertorial, 307, 343
Age groups, 21
  future trade areas and, 24–25
Aggregate household income, 24, 27
Aging report, 214, 343
AIA Form G722, 198
Allowances, 13, 174, 178, 269, 314–15
  construction, 90, 104, 113, 126, 135, 168
  improvement, 180, 181
  pro forma and, 76

Alterations, 150
Ambience, 279
Amenities plan, 170, 267–68
Americans With Disabilities Act (ADA) of 1990, 146
Amortization, 127–28, 343
Analysis, 39
  redevelopment and, 263–65
  rental feasibility, 74, 75–76
  sensitivity, 67–68
Anchor pad, 343–44
Anchor tenants, 303, 344
  CAM and, 135, 175, 234–35
  co-tenancy and, 143–44
  CPI increases and, 169
  delayed occupancy and, 125–26
  exclusives and, 142
  lead times, 90
Ancillary charges, 73, 310, 344
Application, for lease, 48, 51–54
Approval, 113–15, 158–59
  for landlord's agent, 113–14
  lease approval form, 48–49, 57–58
  for retail leasing representative, 114–15

Architect engineer, 198–99, 201–2
Area survey, sample, 23, 35
Art shows, 306
Asset managers, 61
Assignments, 105, 146–47, 243–44, 344
Assortment, 278–79
Attorney fees, 129, 159–60
Attornment, 153–54, 344
Attornment agreement, 153–54, 357
Audits, 222
  CAM, 136–37, 209, 222
  percentage rent and, 134–35, 173
Average daily traffic (ADT), 344
Average inventory, 283–84, 344

Bankruptcy, 157, 244–45
Base rent. See Minimum rent
Benchmark percentage, 27
Benchmark resources, market research and, 29–30
Best use, 324, 331, 349
Bids, 198–99
  accepting, 199–200
Big boxes, 265–66, 344
Blackout periods, 126–27, 344
Blanket coverage, 140, 344
Boilerplate language, 210, 211, 213, 216, 243, 344
Boundary survey. See Metes and bounds
Breakeven rents, 74
  rental feasibility analysis and, 74, 75–76
Breakpoint, 130, 134, 344
  natural, 130, 170–71
  negotiated, 171–73

Broadcast media, 87
Brokerage community, 84, 157, 326
Budget rents, 11
Budgets (budgeting). See also Operating budget
  construction, 113, 196, 199
  for lease administration, 245
  peripheral land and, 331–33
Buffer zone, 345
Buildable area, 345
Build to suit lease, 329–30
Build-to-suit negotiations, 187–88
Bump back store, 301, 345
Business interruption insurance, 139, 149–50, 345
Business planning assistance, 318
Business term, 111–12

Canvassing, 82–84, 305–7, 345
Capitalization rate, 40, 66, 70, 165, 345
Carts, 49, 236, 298
Cash flow, 12, 13
  pro forma statement of, 293
  valuation based on, 62, 167
  value versus, 166
Catalogs, 86
Center analysis, 39
Certificate of occupancy, 188, 201, 221, 345
Certificate of substantial completion, 201, 345
Chain retail tenants, selling to, 106–7
Charges
  ancillary, 73, 310, 344
  nonrecurring, 226
  recurring, 226–27, 355
  side, 73, 310, 344
  triple net, 73, 310, 344

Children's play area, 267–68
Circuit breakers, 192
Closeout phase, 201–2, 345
Closing the deal, 110, 117, 312, 313–15, 345
Collection, of payments, 225–27
Commencement date, 125–28, 218, 229–31
Comments, 111, 184, 350
Common area(s), 345–46
  configuration and standards, 148–49
  specialty retail and, 298–300
Common area maintenance (CAM), 135–37, 174–75, 231–40, 282–83, 345
  administrative fees, 175
  controversial items included, 237–38
  expenses excluded, 136, 233–34, 237
  food court, 238–40
  interior versus exterior, 237
  leased versus leasable, 235–37
  major user and anchor tenants, 135, 175, 234–35
  operating costs, 135–37, 174–75, 231–33
  pro rata share, 232, 233–34
Common area units, 298–300, 345. *See also* Kiosks; Retail merchandising unit
Community centers, 306
Competition, 24, 80–81, 258
  canvassing the, 82–84
Competition key, sample, 23, 34
Compliance, 145–46, 209
Compromise, in negotiations, 182
Conceptual site plan, 327, 346
Concessions, 13, 346
  for higher rents, 168
Condemnation, 152–53, 346
Configuration, 2–3
  of common area, 148–49
Construction, 191–203
  allowances, 90, 104, 113, 126, 135, 168
  budgets, 113, 196, 199
  directing and controlling, 199–202
  organizing, 197–99
  planning, 191–97
Construction documents file, 220–21
Consumer Price Index (CPI) rent increases, 169
Continuous operation, 143–44, 346
Contract administration, 200–201
Contribution lease, 330
Controlling, 199–202
Conventions, 85
Correspondence file, 219–20
Corridor restrictions, 327
Cost(s), 14, 120, 136, 200. *See also* Expenses
  CAM, 136–37, 174–75, 233–34
  development, 69, 71
  escalation, 129–30, 317, 347
  occupancy, 72–73, 282–83, 288, 313, 353
  off-site, 353
  peripheral land and, 331–33
Cost complement, 285, 346
Cost estimate, 196–97
Cost-of-living adjustment, 128, 129, 130, 181
Co-tenancy, 126, 143–44
Coterminous, 124, 346
Covenants
  operating, 16, 353
  restrictive, 16, 355

Craft shows, 306
Creativity, in negotiations, 112–13
Customer flow, 3–4, 5
Customer retention, 27
Customer service, 279–81
Custom units, 299, 346

Damage, 152
Dark periods, 126–27, 344
Date of lease, 121. *See also* Commencement date; Opening date
Dead zones, 5
Debt service coverage ratio, 68–69, 71, 346
Declining percentage rental rate, 171–72
Dedication, 346
Deductions, 346
　gross sales, 132–33
　percentage rent, 132–33, 173–74
Deed restriction, 327, 329, 346
Defaults, 156–57, 227–29, 242–43, 311
Deferment, request for rent, 222, 249
Delayed occupancy, 125–26
Delivery methods, 197–98
Demising, 14, 48, 347
Demographic radius studies, 27–28
Demographics, 6–7, 23–24, 29–30, 80, 81, 277, 302, 304, 326, 347
Department stores, 22–23, 173, 232, 266, 268
Deposits, security, 154–55, 242–43, 357
Depth of space, 2–3, 266–67
Design, 191–203
　directing and controlling, 199–202
　organizing, 197–99
　planning, 191–97
Design shows, 85
Destruction, 152
Development, 1–4. *See also* Redevelopment
　customer flow and, 3–4
　depth of space and, 2–3
　sight lines and, 3
　size and, 1–2
Development costs, 69, 71
Development economics, 70–72
Development Project Valuation Analysis, 71, 78
Directing, 199–202
Direct mail, 308
Discount rate, 64–65, 347
　IRR and, 69, 70, 350
Displays, 83
　temporary, 49–50
Dispute resolution, 227–29
Document coordinator, 42
Document file, 220
Dollars and Cents of Shopping Centers, 170, 283, 284
Down markets, 83, 206
Draw, 330, 347
Due diligence, 218, 347
Duration of lease, 125–28
Duty of care, 223–25, 347

Early occupancy, 126
Early termination, 127–28, 151
Easements, 327, 347
　REA, 16, 321, 325, 355
Electrical system, 192–93
Encumbrance, 347
End of lease, 125–28
Entertainment, 9, 46–47, 267, 306, 324

Environmental issues, 140, 195
Environmental study, 327, 354
Escalations, 129–30, 317, 347
Essential lease provisions, 120–24
Estoppel agreements, 215, 218, 347
Estoppel certificates, 159, 347
Evaluation
　development process, 1–4
　redevelopment process, 4–6
Eviction, 228, 229
Exclusions, 347
　gross sales, 132–33
　percentage rent, 132–33, 173–74
Exclusive uses, 141–43, 298, 347
Exculpation, 122, 347
Exculpatory clause, 216, 347
Executed lease, 70, 216, 348
Exhibits, 122, 148, 193, 210, 213, 348
Existing tenants, 5, 7
　negotiations with, 44–45
　redevelopment and, 263
　renovation of, 268
　as resource for market information, 22
Expenditure potential, 24
Expenses, 63
　actualizing, 226, 343
　operating, 129, 209, 231–32
　peripheral land and, 332–33
　reconfiguration, 14
Extended occupancy, 126–27
Extensions. *See* Renewals

Feasibility analysis, 74, 75–76
Fees, 198
　administrative, CAM and, 175
　attorney, 129, 159–60
　brokerage, 84
　late, 311
　management, 136, 149, 175
Festival marketplaces, 306
Field verification, 195
Financial/accounting file, 220
Financing, 330–31
　impact of, 163–64
First-time retail operators, selling to, 108–9
Fixed conditions review, 5–6
Fixture manufacturers shows, 85
Flea markets, 306
Floor area ratio (FAR), 348
Focus groups, 28, 39, 255
Food court CAM, 238–40
Footage. *See* Square footage
Force majeure, 158, 230–31, 348
Forecasting, 331
"For lease" signs, 86
Format for lease inquiry, sample, 96
Franchise shows, 85, 100
Free rent, 130, 135, 180–81, 314
Funds from operations (FFO), 63, 348
Future trade areas, 24–25

GAFO (general merchandise, apparel, furniture/home furnishings, and other types of similar merchandise), 26–29, 87–88, 348
Gas, 193
General lease provisions, 120–24
Geographic information systems (GIS), 23, 29–30, 348
GIS (Geographic Information Systems), 23, 29–30, 348

GLA (gross leasable area), 1, 2, 39, 67, 235–36, 348–49
GLOA (gross leased and occupied area), 235–36
Goal assessment, 317
Grantee, 348
Grantor, 348
Gross building area (GBA), 348
Gross leasable area (GLA), 1, 2, 39, 67, 235–36, 348–49
Gross leased and occupied area (GLOA), 235–36
Gross leases, 129, 349
Gross rent, 312
Gross sales, 131–35
  deductions and exclusions, 132–33
Ground lease, 328–29, 349
Guarantors, 145, 154–55, 349

Hazardous materials, 13, 145–46
Heating, ventilating, and air conditioning (HVAC), 193, 301, 349
Highest and best use, 324, 331, 349
Holding period, 62–64, 349
Holdover, 158, 223, 349
Household income, 24, 27
Housekeeping, 84, 147–48
HVAC (heating, ventilating, and air conditioning), 193, 301, 349

Improvement allowances, 180, 181
Income, 269, 270. *See also* Rent
  aggregate household, 24, 27
  net operating (NOI), 63–64, 66, 68–69, 71, 164, 165–66, 352–53
  specialty leasing, 295
Income projection, 62–64, 77, 349
Incubation, 49, 316–18, 349
Incubator tenants, 236, 349
Indemnification, 154, 349
Indemnity contracts, 139, 349
Inflation protection, 169
Inflow market, 19, 25, 349
In-line space, 49, 295–96, 298, 300–302
Inquiry form, leasing, 97
Inspections, 192–95
Insurance, 138–40, 176, 240
  business interruption, 139, 149–50, 345
  liability, 139, 176
  property, 139, 176
  rental income, 139, 355
  rental value, 139, 355
  title, 333, 357
Integration clause, 211, 216
Intercept surveys, 28, 89, 255
Internal rate of return (IRR), 69, 70, 350
International Council of Shopping Centers (ICSC), 101, 276, 281
  events, 90, 309
Internet, the, 271
  prospecting on, 86–87
Interpretation, 209–10
Introduction letters, 304
Inventory turnover, 283–84, 350

Judicial eviction, 228, 229

Keystone markup, 285, 350
Kickout, 127, 135, 350
Kiosks, 236, 298, 299, 350

Laches, 209, 228, 350
Land lease, 328–29, 341, 349
Landlord(s) (owners), 120–21
  access by, 154
  expectations of, 39–40
  negotiated break in favor of, 172
  obligations of tenants and, 223–29
Landlord's agents
  approval from, 113–14
  selling to, 109
Land sale, 329, 340
Language, of lease, 119–60
  alterations, 150
  assignment and sublease provisions, 146–47
  attorney fees, 159–60
  boilerplate, 210, 211, 213, 216, 243, 344
  brokers, 157
  common area configuration and standards, 148–49
  common area maintenance, 135–37
  compliance with laws, 145–46
  condemnation, 152–53
  damage and destruction, 152
  default, 156–57
  estoppel certificates, 159
  financing modifications and approvals, 158–59
  force majeure, 158
  general provisions, 120–24
  holding over, 158
  indemnification, 154
  insurance, 138–40
  landlord's access, 154
  leased versus leasable, 235–37
  mechanics liens, 151
  memorandum of lease, 157–58
  merchants' association, 148
  notices, 159
  quiet enjoyment provision, 155
  real estate taxes, 137–38
  rent, 129–35
  repairs and maintenance, 149–50
  rules and regulations, 148
  security for the tenant's performance, 154–55
  specialty retail, 309–11
  subordination, 153–54
  surrender, 151
  the term, 125–28
  use provisions, 140–45
  utilities, 138
  waiver of jury trial, 160
Late fees, 311
Late payment, 129, 222–23, 225–26
Leasable area, 235–37
Lease(s)
  administration of. *See* Lease administration
  build to suit, 329–30
  contribution, 330
  definition of, 350
  executed, 70, 216, 348
  forms, 48–49, 164–65
    interpretation of, 209–10
    sample, 51–58
  gross, 129, 349
  ground, 328–29, 349
  land, 328–29, 341, 349
  language of. *See* Language, of lease
  net, 129, 353
  net-net, 129, 353
  preliminary, 354
  sample, 55–56
    restaurant, 95

Lease(s) *(cont'd)*
  retail, 94
  termination of. *See* Termination
  terms of, 48, 125–28, 184–87, 309
  triple net, 129, 312, 358
  unsubordinated land, 328, 358
Lease abstract, 217–18, 350
Lease administration, 205–49, 350
  budget implications of, 245
  common problems and, 229–45
  contract, 200–201
  goals of, 208–10
  historical perspective on, 206–7
  obligations of owner and tenant and, 223–29
  overview of, 206–8
  practice of, 210–23
  specialty retail and, 315
Lease administrators, 214–15
Lease application, 48, 51–54
Lease approval form, 48–49, 57–58
Lease comments, 111, 184, 350
Lease forecasting, 331
Leasehold mortgage, 350
Lease plan, 88, 304, 350
  evaluation of, 1–6
Lease provisions, 120–24, 155. *See also* Use provisions
Leasing brochure, 88, 305
Leasing cycle, 182–84, 206
Leasing presentation tools, 27–29
Leasing representative logs, 221–22, 247–48
Leasing representatives, 61, 205, 211–12
  advertising and publicity and, 85–86
  approval from, 114–15
  market research and, 81–82

  role of, 207–8
  specialty retail, 297–98
Leasing strategies, 27, 37–59, 40–44
  negotiating tools and strategies, 44–45, 48–50
  prospecting and, 43–44
  team members and, 41–43
  tenant mix and, 38–40
Leasing summary, 11–12, 350
Leasing team, 40, 41–43, 205, 210–17
  redevelopment and, 253–54
  role of, 162
  specialty retail, 296–97
Leasing team member, 43–44
Legal department, 215–16
Legal term, 111–12
Letter of intent, 181–82, 198, 351
  sample, 94, 95
Leveraging, 68–69
  IRR and, 69
Liability insurance, 139, 176
License agreements, 351
  language of. *See* Language, of lease
  specialty retail, 309–11
Licensee, 351
Licensor, 351
Liens, 351
Lien waivers, 151, 197–98, 351
Lifestyle shopping centers, 267
Line drawing, 305, 351
Lis pendens, 351–52
Litigation file, 221
Local retailers, selling to, 107–8
Locator maps, sample, 23, 32

Maintenance, 149–50. *See also* Common area maintenance

Major users, CAM and, 234–35
Management, 205, 213–14. *See also* Lease administration
Management fees, 136, 149, 175
Markdown, 286, 352
Market analysis, 39
Marketing, 269, 270. *See also* Prospects
  specialty retail and, 304–5
Marketing fund, 176–77
Marketing manager, 41
Marketing plan assistance, 318
Market rents, 67, 72–74, 162–63
  rental feasibility analysis and, 74, 75–76
Market research, 19–35, 80–82, 352
  addressing center's competition, 24
  addressing the market, 23–24
  benchmark resources and, 29–30
  benefits of, 21–23
  future trade area and, 24–25
  GAFO and, 26–29
  goals for effective use of, 19–21
  knowing the retailers, 25–26
  peripheral land, 325–26
  redevelopment and, 254–56
  specialty retail and, 302–4
Market share, 26–29
Markup, 284–85, 352
Material defaults, 228
Measurement of space, 123, 167–68
Mechanical systems, 194–95
Mechanics liens, 151, 352
Media, 87
Memorandum of lease, 157–58, 352
Merchandise mart, 306

Merchandise mix, 8–10, 25, 303–4, 352
Merchandising, 278–79. *See also* Remerchandising
Merchandising document, 352
Merchandising plan, 10–11, 37, 39, 46–47, 82, 352
Merchants' association, 148
Metes and bounds, 327, 345, 352
Minimum rent, 129, 168–69, 310, 352
Modifications, 158–59
Modified gross rent, 312
Monument sign, 327, 352

National retail tenants, selling to, 106–7
Natural breakpoint, 130, 170–71
Negotiated breakpoint, 171–73
Negotiations, 44–45, 90–91, 109–17, 177–80, 183, 209–10
  alternatives in, 180–81
  approval and, 113–15
  build-to-suit, 187–88
  compromise in, 182
  creativity in, 112–13
  during the, 179–80
  with existing tenants, 44–45
  factors to consider in, 178–79
  lease discussions and, 110
  with new merchants, 45, 48–49
  opening date and, 110
  preparations for, 88–89
  proposal letter and, 90–91
  reviewing lease comments and, 111
  right of first, 124, 356
  time for, 110
  understanding business and legal terms and, 111–12

Neighborhood centers, 306
Net leases, 129, 352
Net-net leases, 129, 352
Net operating income (NOI), 63–64, 66, 68–69, 71, 164, 165–66, 352
Net present value (NPV), 41, 59, 65–66, 67
Net sales, 282, 284, 352
Networking, 84, 86, 309
New merchants
 negotiations with, 45, 48–49
 opening dates, 268–69
NOI (net operating income), 63–64, 66, 68–69, 71, 164, 165–66, 352
Non-income parcels, 321
Nonmaterial defaults, 227–28
Nonrecurring charges, 226, 352
Notices, 157, 159, 220, 231
NPV (net present value), 41, 59, 65–66, 67

Occupancy
 certificate of, 188, 201, 221, 345
 delayed, 125–26
 early, 126
 extended, 126–27
Occupancy costs, 72–73, 282–83, 288, 313, 352
Off-site costs, 352
On-property advertising, 86
Opening date, 110, 121, 268–69
Operating budget, 12–14, 352–53
 allowances and concessions and, 13
 other costs, 14
Operating center plan, 6–7
Operating covenants, 16, 353

Operating expenses, 129, 209, 231–32
Option to expand, 124
Option to extend or renew, 128
Organization (organizing), 197–99
 delivery methods, 197–98
 specialty retail, 296–97
 team assembly, 198–99
Outparcels, 321–22, 324–27, 334–35, 353
Outposting, 353
Overplanning, 115
Owner(s). *See* Landlord

Pad sites, 81, 164, 178, 321–22, 324–26, 353
Parcel map, 354
Parcels, 353
 non-income, 321
 outparcels, 321–22, 324–27, 334–35, 353
 size of, 1–2, 326–28
Parking, 81, 148, 149, 152, 195, 321, 328
Parties to the lease, 121–22
Pass-throughs, 129–30, 354
Payments, 133–34
 collection of, 225–27
 late, 129, 222–23, 225–26
Penetration study, 39
Percentage rent, 130–35, 169–74, 282–83, 310, 312, 354
 breakpoint and, 169–71
 components of, 131
 computation and payment periods, 133–34
 deductions and exclusions, 132–33, 173–74
 recapture out of, 13, 147–48, 355

record keeping, 134
verification, 134–35, 173
Peripheral land, 319–41
  balancing competing interests and, 322–23
  basic elements of business, 323–34
  definition of, 320–21
  sales and leasing objectives, 321–22
Peripheral land use categories, 323–24
Permanent tenant, 354
Phase I environmental study, 327, 354
Placement of tenants, 10–11
Plan(s)
  amenities, 170, 267–68
  lease, 88, 304, 350
    evaluation of, 1–6
  operating center, 6–7
  plot, 327, 346
  site, 88, 357
    conceptual, 327, 346
Planning, 191–97
  cost estimate and, 196
  peripheral land and, 325
  preliminary schedule, 196–97
  redevelopment and, 251, 253–54
  site inspection and, 192–95
  space layout and, 195
Plat, 354
Plenum mechanical systems, 194–95
Plot plan, 327, 346
Policies and procedures, 222–23
Population density maps, sample, 23, 29, 31
Potential expenditures, 24
Pre-leasing, 11, 15

Preliminary lease, 354
Preliminary schedule, 196–97
Premises, 120, 122–23, 141
Present value, 62, 69, 354
  net (NPV), 41, 59, 65–66, 67
Price point, 9, 20, 83, 101, 354
Print media, 87
Pro forma, 76, 163–64, 354
  statements, 189, 287, 292, 293
Project economics, 61–78
  breakeven rents, 74
  capitalization rates, 70
  economics of development, 70–72
  leveraging, 68–69
  market rent, 67, 72–74
  rental feasibility analysis, 75–76
  valuation process, 62–68
Project manager, 192, 195
Project size, 1–2, 326–28
Property insurance, 139, 176
Property taxes, 226, 231, 240
Proposal letters, 90–91, 116
  samples, 93, 94, 95
Proposal, request for (RFP), 198–99, 355
Proposed use restrictions, 325
Pro rata share, 232–36, 354
Proration, 104, 115
Prospects (prospecting), 79–90, 182–83
  defining, 102–4
  finding and identifying, 82–87
  leasing team members and, 43–44
  market analysis and, 19–20, 80–82
  negotiation preparations and, 88–89
  negotiation tools and strategies, 44–45, 48–50

Prospects *(cont'd)*
  qualifying, 286–87, 291
  separating the, 87–88
  specialty retail and, 305–9
Provisions of lease, 120–24, 155.
  See also Use provisions
Psychographics, 81, 277, 302–3, 354
Publications, 85
Publicity, 85–86, 307
Public relations, 307
Pushcarts, 49, 236, 298
Pylon sign, 123, 327, 355

Quiet enjoyment provision, 155

Radius demographics, 27–28
Radius restriction, 111, 145, 355
REA (reciprocal easement agreement), 16, 321, 325, 355
Real estate investment trust (REIT), 236, 252, 266, 328, 355
Real estate taxes (RET), 137–38, 175–76, 240
Reasonable wear and tear, 149–50
Recapture out of percentage rent, 14, 147–48, 355
Reciprocal easement agreements (REAs), 16, 321, 325, 355
Reciprocal percentage, 285, 346
Reconfiguration expenses, 14
Record keeping, 217–22
  percentage rent, 134
  permanent records, 219–21
Recurring charges, 226–27, 355
Redevelopment, 4–6, 251–71
  developing core strategy, 259–60, 261
  evaluation criteria, 263, 265
  example of, 257
  executing the plan, 269–71
  fixed conditions review, 5–6
  issues important to, 256, 258
  key audiences and performance areas, 260–61
  planning and, 251, 253–54
  reasons for, 251, 252
  research and, 254–56
Reduced rent, 126, 166, 315
Reduction, request for rent, 222, 249
Regular mechanical system, 194
Regulations, 148, 311
REIT (real estate investment trust), 236, 252, 266, 328, 355
Relationship factor, in retailing, 274–76
Relocation clause, 111, 124, 311, 355
Remerchandising, 261–63. *See also* Redevelopment
  special situations and considerations, 265–69
Renderings, 88, 89, 305
Renewals, 41, 44–45, 128, 240–41
Rent(s), 128–35
  acceleration, 157, 355
  additional, 123, 129, 130, 152, 155, 170–71, 343
  breakeven, 74
    rental feasibility analysis and, 74, 75–76
  budget, 11
  concessions. *See* Concessions
  free, 130, 135, 180–81, 314
  gross, 312
  market, 67, 72–74, 162–63
    rental feasibility analysis and, 74, 75–76

minimum, 129, 168–69, 310, 352
modified gross, 312
percentage. *See* Percentage rent
reduced, 126, 166, 315
request rent deferment or reduction, 222, 249
setting, 162–63
specialty retail and, 311–13
stepped-up, 130, 181, 312–13, 357
taxes, 129
total. *See* Occupancy costs
types of, 168–70
value and, 165–67
Rental factor, 106, 108, 355
Rental feasibility analysis, 74, 75–76
Rental income insurance, 139, 355
Rental value, 355
Rental value insurance, 139, 355
Rent escalation program, 317
Repairs, 149–50, 239
Representatives. *See* Leasing representatives
Request for proposal (RFP), 198–99, 355
Request for rent deferment or reduction, 222, 249
Research. *See* Market research
Residual(s), 64, 66, 68, 355
cap rates, 66, 70, 71
Residual land, 321, 322, 324, 334–35
Restaurant lease, sample, 95
Restrictions, 16, 298, 327
deed, 327, 329, 346
exclusive uses, 141–43, 298
radius, 111, 145, 355
Restrictive covenants, 16, 355

RET (real estate taxes), 137–38, 175–76, 240
Retailer(s)
business strategies of, 277–81
knowledge, 25–26, 39
selling to, 105–8
Retailing, 273–93
components of, 274–89
demographics and psychographics and, 277
key processes for, 281–86
qualifying prospective tenants, 286–87, 291
relationship factor in, 274–76
retailer's business strategies and, 277–81
signs of trouble, 288–89
specialty leasing. *See* Specialty retail leasing
store visit, 276
Retail lease, sample, 94
Retail leasing representatives. *See* Leasing representatives
Retail merchandising unit (RMU), 49, 298–99, 356
Retail opportunity day, 308
Retail sales price, 285
Retail visual restrictors (RVRs), 356
Retention, 198, 356
customer, 27
tenant, 63
Return on investment (ROI), 64, 259, 356
RFP (request for proposal), 198–99
Right of first negotiation, 124–25, 356
Right of first offer, 124–25, 356
Right of first refusal, 124–25, 356
Riparian rights, 356

Risk premium, 64–65, 356
ROI (return on investment), 64, 259, 356
Rules and regulations, 148, 311
Run with the land, 356

Sale forecasting, 331
Sales, 99–109, 115–17
 elements of the deal and, 104–5
 to first-time retail operators, 108–9
 gross, 131–35, 352
 groundwork for, 99–105
 land, 329, 340
 to a landlord's agents, 109
 to national and chain retail tenants, 106–7
 net, 282, 284, 352
 project and, 100–102
 prospects and, 102–4
 to retailers, 105–6, 107–8
 techniques for, 105–9
Sales test, 144, 356
Satellite tenants, 126, 135–36, 137, 357
Schedule of time, 197
Security deposits, 154–55, 242–43, 357
Security for the tenant's performance, 154–55
Sensitivity analysis, 67–68
Service, 279–81
Shopping center manager, 41
Shopping center parcel, 320
Side charges, 73, 310, 344
Signage, 213, 276, 301, 307–8, 315, 325, 327
Signing, the lease, 183–84
Single-purpose (shell) corporation, 122

Site inspections, 192–95
Site lines, 3, 81
Site plans, 88, 357
 conceptual, 327, 346
Space(s)
 common area, 298–300
 depth of, 2–3, 266–67
 in-line, 49, 295–96, 298, 300–302
 layout of, 195
 measurement of, 123, 167–68
Special assessment, 333, 357
Specialty retail leasing, 295–318, 357
 administration and, 315
 closing the deal, 313–15
 common area space and, 298–300
 common expectations and, 316
 incubation and, 316–18
 in-line space and, 300–302
 license agreements, 309–11
 marketing materials, 304–5
 organizational structures, 296–97
 permanent leasing representatives and, 297–98
 problem tenants and, 316
 property and market and, 302–4
 prospecting for tenants, 305–9
 structuring economic deal and, 311–13
 types of tenants, 302
Split-level percentage, 171
Split system, 194, 357
Square footage, 178–79
 measurement of, 123, 167–68
Stair-stepped rent, 130, 181, 312–13, 357
Stepped-down percentage, 313
Stepped-up rent, 130, 181, 312–13, 357

Storage space, 124
Strategies for leasing. *See* Leasing strategies
Subleases, 146–47, 357
Subordination, 153–54, 357
Subordination, non-disturbance, and attornment agreement (SNDA), 153–54, 357
Surrender, 151
Surveys
  area, sample, 23, 35
  boundary, 327, 345, 352
  intercept, 28, 89, 255

Taxes
  property, 226, 231, 240
  real estate, 137–38, 175–76, 240
  rent, 129
Team assembly, 198–99
Telephone book, 308
Temporary displays, 49–50
Temporary merchants, 49, 50
Tenant(s)
  anchor. *See* Anchor tenants
  existing. *See* Existing tenants
  incubator, 236, 349
  mix of. *See* Tenant mix
  negotiated break in favor of, 172–73
  obligations of, 223–29
  placement of, 10–11
  satellite, 126, 135–36, 137
  selling to, 105–9
Tenant category, 186–87
Tenant contacts, 90
Tenant coordinator, 42–43
Tenant defaults, 156–57
Tenant mix, 38–40, 81
  evaluating, 38–39
  leasing strategies, 40–44
  ownership expectations and, 39–40
Tenant retention, 63, 245
Tenant workouts, 222, 249
Termination, 49–50, 128, 151, 153, 223, 240–42, 311
  early, 127–28, 151
  options, 241–42
Term of the lease, 48, 125–28, 184–87, 309
Testimonials, 29, 304–5, 357
Timetable, 15
Title insurance, 333, 357
Title report, 358
Total rent. *See* Occupancy costs
Trade area by zip code, sample, 23, 33
Trade area market support factors, 81, 92
Trade area office worker survey, sample, 23, 35
Trade publications, 85
Trade shows, 85
Traffic counts, 28, 82
Traffic patterns, 81, 123, 304
Triple net charges, 73, 310, 344
Triple net leases, 129, 312, 358
Turnover, of inventory, 283–84, 350

Unlawful detainer action, 228, 358
Unsubordinated land lease, 328, 358
Urban Land Institute, 170, 283
Use clause, 104–5, 142, 298, 304, 310, 358
Use provisions, 140–45
  co-tenancy, 143–44
  exclusives, 141–43
  radius restriction, 145

Utilities, 138
    site inspection, 192–93, 195

Vacancies, 37, 49–50, 63, 179, 196, 236
Vacancy/loss reserve, 63, 358
Valuation, 62–68
    cash flow and, 167
    discount rate and, 64–65
    income projection and, 62–64
    net present value and, 65–66
    peripheral land and, 328
    sensitivity analysis and, 67–68
Value, 358
    cash flow versus, 166
    rents and, 165–67
Value engineering, 199–200, 358

Verification, of percentage rent, 134–35, 173
View corridor, 327, 358
Visual merchandising assistance, 318
Voltage, 193

Waiver of jury trial, 160
Walk-throughs, 4–5, 5
Wall units, 299, 358
Water, 193
Wear and tear, 149–50
White box, 192, 198, 301, 358
Written policies and procedures, 222–23

Zoning issues, 195